The City of Chicago In The Spirit of Du Sable

The City of Chicago In The Spirit of Du Sable

Haroon Rashid

The Pointe! Image Book Publishing
Boston Massachusetts

THE CITY OF CHICAGO
IN THE SPIRIT OF DU SABLE
Published by:
The Pointe! Image Book Publishing
Boston MA
dusable2001@yahoo.com

Haroon Rashid, Publisher / Editorial Director
Yvonne Rose/Quality Press.info, Book Packager
Cover & Back page photo image by Laurel Stradford

ALL RIGHTS RESERVED

No parts of this book may be reproduced or transmitted in any form or by any means electronic or mechanical, including photocopying, recording or any information storage and retrieved system without the written permission from the authors, except for the inclusion of brief quotations in review.

The publication is sold with the understanding that the Publisher is not engaged in rendering legal or other professional services. If legal advice or other expert assistance is required, the services of a competent professional person should be sought.

Copyright © 2018 by Haroon Rashid
ISBN # : 978-1-937269-78-4
Library of Congress Control Number: 2018932838

DEDICATION

I dedicate this book 'The City of Chicago, In the Spirit of Du Sable to my mentor in the spirit of Du Sable, Dr. Margaret T. Burroughs.

In the beginning of my mission to commemorate Chicago's founder, Jean Baptiste Pointe Du Sable, I established a not-for-profit corporation, now known as Friends of Du Sable.

Soon after, I had the honor to meet and receive guidance by a Chicago legend, Dr. Margaret T. Burroughs. She taught me what she knew and trusted me to deliver her knowledge in an honorable way.

At the very beginning of my mission I named my organization Serene Entitlement and Empowerment Association. Our mission was to tell the stories of people of African descent and to tell of their legacy and contributions in America. These are stories that might not be told otherwise.

It was Dr. Burroughs who suggested that, since I was attempting to talk about the founder of Chicago, I should narrow my agenda down to Jean Baptiste Pointe Du Sable and to refer to our Not For Profit Corporation moving forward, as Friends of Du Sable.

I agreed and we changed our name. I loved her like a mother and she treated me like a son or trusted student, so much so, that she gave to me a copy of her book with information about Jean Baptiste Pointe Du Sable called *'His Name Was Du Sable and He Was the First'*. She also suggested that I should help her promote her book, just before she passed away.

In this book, (The City of Chicago, In the Spirit of DuSable), I include some excerpts from Dr. Burroughs' book and I encourage you to purchase it.

I dedicate (The City of Chicago, In the Spirit of DuSable), to all the multicultural and ethnically diverse children of Chicago and across

America as a way to send a message to them that 'they can become leaders in their lifetime'.

I do this as a way to infuse in them the potential spirit of a remarkable Renaissance man who laid a foundation for multicultural diversity and leadership in America.

ACKNOWLEDGMENTS

I can never thank enough all of the dedicated, brilliant and talented people that contributed in any way to the completion and success of this book. If there is anyone or any enactments that I might have missed in this list of persons and organizations, I apologize and please let me know so that we can make the adjustments.

-Haroon Rashid, Founder and President of Friends of DuSable

Friends of DuSable Board members: Mrs. Mairea Jossey Owens, Board member co-founder of Friends of DuSable; Mr. Douglas Pendarvis, and Vice President of Friends of DuSable; also Mrs. Jada Goodlett Russell, who was a co-founder of Friends of DuSable; Mr. Pat Patterson, Board member and co-founder of Friends of DuSable; John Low, Board member; Acting President of Friends of DuSable; Mr. Russell Lewis, Friends of DuSable - Board Chair; Mrs. Peggy Montes; Mr. William Walley, Friends of DuSable Treasurer; Andrea Knowles, Friends of DuSable Board member; Mr. Arnold Romeo, Director, Commission of Human Relations Council on African Affairs and Board member, Friends of DuSable; Elsa Tullos, Friends of DuSable Board member; Ms. Hannah Bonecutter, Friends of DuSable Board member; Ms. Aki Antonia, Friends of DuSable Board member; Darrell Barnes, Friends of DuSable Board member.

Chicago Public Schools; First lady Michelle Obama, for her work and services with Friends of DuSable; My gratitude also goes out to: Cardinal Francis George, Chicago Archdioceses; Mark Garski, Director of the Catholic Archdioceses Schools; Mr. Fred Luster, CEO of Luster's Products Company; Mrs. Linda Rice Johnson of Ebony magazine and Fashion Fair Duke/Ebonie Products; many of the pictures in this book of the DuSable Bridge ceremony were taken by Mr. Fred Miller, a consultant for Soft Sheen & L'Oreal Products company; Mr. Reynard Allison, CEO, Enduser Media Productions, advisor and consultant for this book; Mayor of Chicago, Richard M. Daley and Mayor Rahm Emanuel; Ms. Erika Summers, Executive Assistant to Mayor Richard M. Daley; Chicago Commission on

Human Relations, Commissioner Clarence Woods; Mrs. Bessie L. Neal, President of The DuSable League; Mrs. Virginia Jullian, The DuSable League Historian; Mr. Lonnie Bunch, President Smithsonian African American History Museum; Mr. Lerone Bennett Jr., Laurent historian; Mr. Walter Burnett, Chicago Alderman - 27th. Ward; The Chicago Aldermanic Black Caucus 2010 -19 Members; Mr. Danny K. Davis, U.S. Congressman of Illinois; Imam Wallace D. Muhammad, CEO of The World Community of Islam; Minister Louis Farrakhan, Leader of Nation of Islam; Mr. Scott and Erica Muhammad, DuSable film documentarian; Mr. Kwame Raoul, Illinois State Senator; Mr. Dick Durbin, Illinois U.S. Senator; Mr. Lesley Conde', Consulate General d' Haiti; Mr. Richard Barbeyron, Consul General De France; Mr. Burton Natarus, Chicago Alderman - 42 Ward; Mr. Brendan Reilly, Chicago Alderman - 42 Ward; Mr. Joseph Podlasek, President, American Indian Center, Mrs. Janet Carl Smith, Chicago Dept. of Cultural Affairs; Mrs. Louis Weisberg, Chicago Commissioner of Cultural Affairs; Mr. Wayne D. Watson, Ph.D., President, Chicago State College; Mr. John Chikow, President & CEO, the Greater North Michigan Avenue Association; Mr. Tye Tabing, Executive Director, Chicago Loop Alliance; Mr. Michael Towns, President, the Chicago Commission on Human Relations Advisory Council of African Affairs; Dr. Serge Pierre Louis, President, DuSable Haitian Heritage Association; Ms. Antoinette Wright, CEO/President of the DuSable Museum; Proceeded by Dr. Carol Adams, CEO/ President of the DuSable Museum; Ms. Irma Tranter, President, Chicago Friends of the Parks; Ms. Eleanor Roemer, Legal Consultant for Chicago Friends of the Parks; Mr. Dana Starks, Commissioner, Chicago Commission on Human Relation Professor Dr. Thomas Morsch, Northwestern University Business School Director in Chicago; Ms. Paula Wells, Students Assistant at Northwestern University Business School in Chicago.

Dr. Margaret T. Burroughs - Founder, the Du Sable Museum - Chicago; The DuSable Memorial Society; The DuSable League - Bessie Neal, Virginia Julian; Friends of DuSable Board and members; Johnson Publishing Company; Ebony Magazine - Helen Hornbeck

Tanner; Chicago History Museum; The Library of Congress; The Bronzeville Children's Museum - Peggy Montes; Mitchell Museum of the American Indian; R. David Edmunds - Tecumseh leader of the Shawnee Native; Americans Medio Images/Getty Images Wikipedia; Bronzeville Arts Blog - Publisher/Editor - Aki Antonia; What the Traveler Saw - Founder - Laurel Stradford; Quality Press – Director – Yvonne Rose

CONTENTS

Dedication -- i

Acknowledgments -- iii

Contents --- vii

Preface -- ix

Introduction *His Name Was Du Sable and He Was the First!* ------- 1

Chapter One : Du Sable's Settlement Becomes Chicago ------------- 5

Chapter Two : The First Non-Native Permanent Setteler In Chicago -- 14

Chapter Three : The First Religious Parish In Chicago --------------- 45

Chapter Four : DuSable's Settlement Becomes A City -------------- 59

Chapter Five : Chicago Rebuilt Quickly ------------------------------- 72

Chapter Six : Chicago: The Home of America's First World Fair: Columbian Exposition ------------------------------------- 101

Chapter Seven : African American Entrepreneurs In Chicago ---- 118

Chapter Eight : The Richest African American Woman In America, In The Twenty First Century and Man in the 1980's -- 187

Chapter Nine : Chicago's First Dusable Commemoration-Collaborations --- 208

Chapter Ten : Social Activism with African American Leadership in Chicago --- 255

Chapter Eleven : The New Spirit of DuSable in Chicago, under the First Elected African American's Mayor's Leadership --354

Chapter Twelve : DuSable Legacy During the Leadership of Mayor Richard M. Daley in Collaboration with Friends of DuSable ------366

Chapter Thirteen : The First Elected: African American President, of the United States of America, was from Chicago ------435

Chapter Fourteen : The DuSable Bronze Bust Instalment and DuSable Bridge Naming ------455

Chapter Fifteen : President Obama Second Presidential Election: In The Spirit of "From DuSable to Obama" ------468

Chapter Sixteen : I am Haroon a. Rashid; In The Spirit Of DuSable ------479

About the Author ------485

PREFACE

WHY I WROTE THIS BOOK

After living in Chicago for many years I cannot tell you about the many times that I have asked myself and others about the social community lifestyle of citizens in the city of Chicago. It is safe to say that there have been many first and great people and preliminary enactments that have taken place in Chicago. The spirit to create something from nothing, or to achieve what others might think is impossible, has always been the characteristic of the city of Chicago and its citizens. There has always been a "Yes I can" do and an "I will" spirit among the residents of Chicago. When those slogans are carried out progressively, and or with vigor, it has been proven that there are absolutely no limits of expectations in Chicago.

In knowing what I know about the in creditable legacy of Jean Baptiste Pointe DuSable; the first non-native settler and founder of Chicago: it is clear to me and many others that the spirit of DuSable can and does define a lot of important decisions and leadership for all over America and the world. What makes the phenomenon so surreal is that the narrative of characteristics is being based on an American immigrant man of African descent. I wrote this book to be a historical reference to be used as a guide for excellent American citizenship behavior, especially for the so-called minority citizens "To Be like DuSable": in the city from which all his glorious roots have sprung, the city of Chicago.

I have previously mentioned in my book "My Cultural Birthrights and The Other Black Gold" that my life had always been one that I felt born to feel and know that I was a free sovereign man, and that I would stand on the side; and to identify with those that exercised those same rights. When I finally learned about the rich history and legacy of DuSable, he became a person in character that I wanted to be like and would identify with. I became immersed in his accomplishments and was shocked to witness how unbeknown to so many fellow Americans his legacy was to them. I became fascinated that all the information you would need to know was right within plain sight, it was available upon research. I have personally seen the value for myself and others, in particular people of the African Diaspora, develop a great American pride in diversity with a true sense of inclusion and entitlement once they discovered that the third largest city in America, Chicago, was founded by a person that looked like and was one of them. In the narrative that is now popular in Chicago, in which I was fortunate to begin leading the discussion that led to Chicago's WTTW-TV network using the brand name for the film documentary: From "DuSable to Obama".

There is a great message for the next generations of future leaders' visions of the compatibility of these two great men's valuable lifestyles. I believe that both of their glorious roots were destined to emerge in Chicago. That is why I included in my historical timeline, so thoroughly, the services of Du Sable which no history will show in part, all that I was instrumental in accomplishing in the city of Chicago, with pride, for full public discloser. I give this comprehensive information with the intent that if I don't tell it, it might not become transparent or it might become compromised. I repeat one of my mottos is that 'one might come to the conclusion at any given time that I have completely immersed myself into the character mode of DuSable in my senior years of social political service' and I must affirm that is absolutely true.

I truly believe that there will be a measure of encouragement for some that will read within the timeline of my services in Chicago, during which I proudly and deliberately promoted this very important character in my Chicago history of advocacy; and that is why I soon adopted the narrative that "I Am DuSable!" in a mission-orientated way. I contend that the Chicago spirit, in particular, is tainted and needs healing from a history of false legacy and negative reactions, as does America. So, we have designed a concept that we think can address some of these issues, we call it the "Spirit of DuSable Healing and Wellness".

We believe there is a first step to wellness, and that is healing. We believe a lack of the sense of personal entitlement or knowledge of self brings into play all the negative factors that destroy our natural growth. Many of us will abort our personal success or happiness, not to mention the rest of the African Americans, because we just cannot believe we deserve it. I believe that Chicago, more than any other major city in America, struggles with a psychosocial disparity, which spawns apathy, particularly to people of African Descent. Know for sure, this is no accident; oh no, this has been a deliberate action on the part of every immigrant cultural society that came to Chicago. The city of Chicago that was hosted by its First People Native Americans, and developed into an immigrant and migrant settlement for so many people, eventually became America's third largest city. Yes, it was a well-kept secret that a man of African descent, Jean Baptiste Pointe DuSable, founded the development of Chicago. Imagine if African Americans, nationally, and people of African descent, globally, would have known they too had an ancestor in American history that was credited and celebrated on the same level as Columbus, Lincoln, Jefferson, Pulaski and other great American pioneers; and unlike the stories that were told for centuries that the only accomplishments that the African American accomplished was centered around the experiences of slavery. Of course, we know that African Americans were not the only people that were brought to America as slaves and given freedom; the Irish, the Asians and other indentured slaves also came to America as property of others. But the deliberate manufacturing and institutionalizing of the Negro as was done to the so-called Negro on the Caribbean Island was recorded in the Willie Lynch papers.

This book is intended to tell the rich and glorious timeline history of Chicago's founder and how it affected leadership from the days of Jean Baptiste Pointe DuSable until the first African American President of the United States of America, Barrack Husain Obama - both of whom left their monumental marks in history from the city of Chicago.

There have been many attempts to tell different versions of this great man's valuable American history and legacy. I have included some of them as they were recorded, and you will see that some collaborate with others, and some will tell a slightly different version. However, they mostly contend that Jean Baptiste Pointe DuSable was the first permanent settler and founder of the city of Chicago.

From DuSable to Obama there has been a spirit of multicultual global diversity in the city of Chicago, that has always been the root and driving force for a "Can do" and "I will" spirit for success.

-- Haroon Rashid

INTRODUCTION

His Name Was Du Sable and He Was the First!

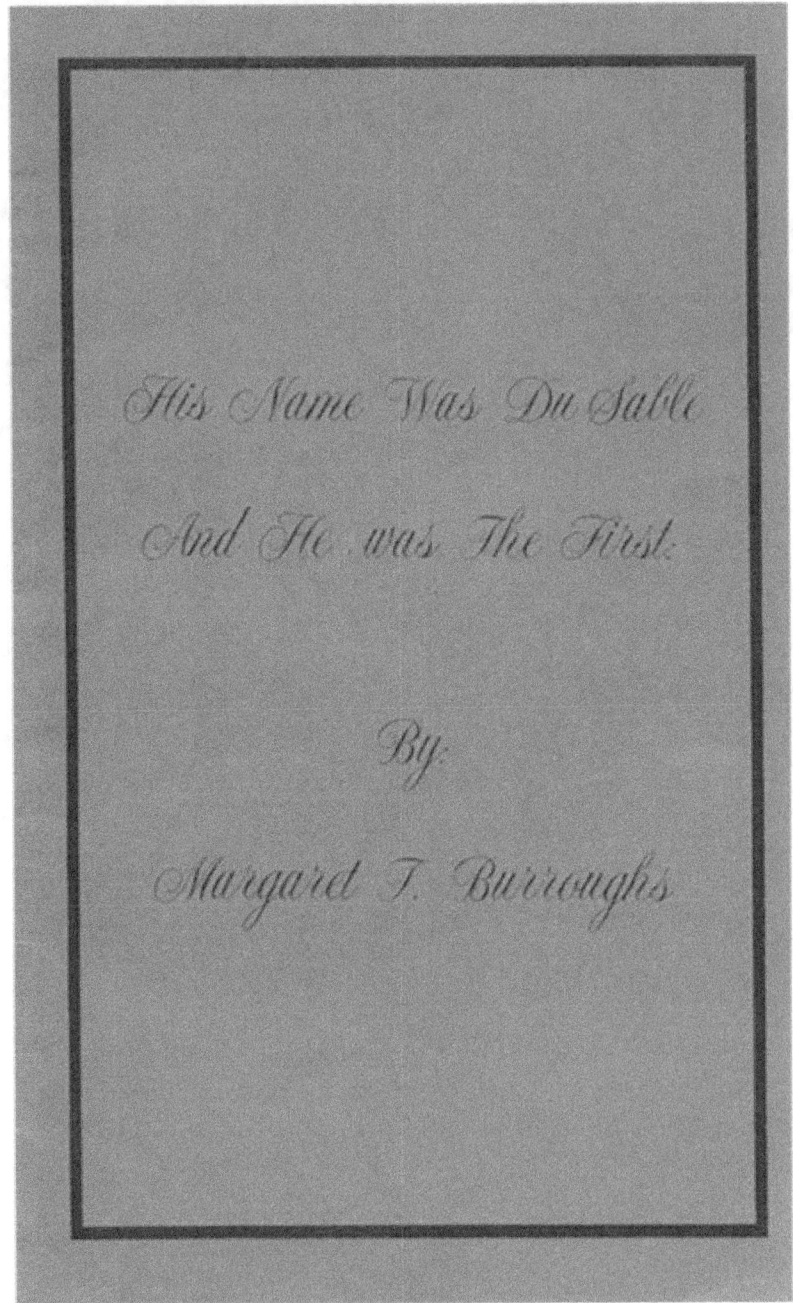

His Name Was Du Sable
And He was The First

By:

Margaret T. Burroughs

The city of Chicago In The Spirit of Du Sable

Jean Baptiste Pointe Du Sable
1745-1814

Despite the various assertions the title of "first Chicagoan" belongs to Jean Baptiste Pointe DuSable, a man whose name can be substantiated by at least three contemporary documents. He resided in Chicago for almost twenty years, reared two children there; and even in the last years of his residence, saw a grandchild born in almost the heart of the present-day city.

On the north branch of the Chicago River, somewhere between the Tribune Tower and the Merchandise Mart, DuSable built the first permanent home in Chicago.

In the 1800s Point Du Sable moved from Chicago to Peoria and thence to St. Charles, Missouri, where he died in 1818. For many years, his grave was unmarked; but in 1968, to mark the Illinois Sesquicentennial, a marble headstone was erected at the place, thought to be his grave, in St. Charles Borromeo Cemetery in St. Charles.

Of Du Sable, Monsignor Meehan in ending his Thesis says, "For more than twenty years his name was associated with Chicago and in such manner that the City needs no apology for him. Here was a frontiersman who lived an air of regality, and if the city which traces her permanency from him adopted at a later date, the motto, "I Will," she can be sure that the first Chicagoan had all the qualities that this slogan implied."

Now, will we wait another one hundred or two hundred years before a proper monument is mounted to Du Sable? A statue, an obelisk, an arch, a wall, an Expressway, a bridge, a fountain, a public square, a park, a main thoroughfare. We at Du Sable Museum are trying in our modest way to honor his contributions.

- Dr. Margret T. Burroughs

CHAPTER ONE

Du Sable's Settlement Becomes Chicago

TIME LINE: THE SEVENTEENTH TO THE TWENTY FIRST CENTURIES

We begin our historical tour in 1673, some seventy-two years before the birth of a man of African descent who became the founder of modern Chicago. This timeline continues into the twenty-first century. Chicago has a rich history of global leadership and it is the home base of many global businesses.

History shows that Jean Baptiste Pointe DuSable was the forbearer of that legacy since he was the first permanent settler of the many that followed in his footsteps. Du Sable's settlement was the model that later created the beginning of a new multi-cultural society that would come to be called Chicago. DuSable also was the first permanent immigrant, entrepreneur and non-native leader in the Chicago area.

Chicago is the city that boasts "I will Make No Small Plans":

Jean Baptiste Pointe DuSable was a famous frontier trader, fur trapper, farmer, international scout, businessman, and authenticated father of the nation's third largest city in America- Chicago. Historical records do not agree as to the origin of this great man. But I would like you to consider the theory that hypothetically speaking he was looked at in his time, as an African Moor; we will talk about the importance of that later. However, history insists that DuSable was born a free black, around 1745, in St. Marc, Saint Dominique (Haiti).

He was the son of a French mariner and an African-born slave mother. His father took him to France to be educated, and afterwards, he worked as a seaman on his father's ships.

It is written that he was a powerfully built man, well-educated and cultured. He had a love for European art and, at one time, owned twenty-three Old World art treasures. He spoke French, English, Spanish and several Indian dialects. At the age of twenty, DuSable was injured on a voyage to New Orleans. Upon reaching the shores of New Orleans, he learned that the Spanish government had taken over the territory. The French Jesuits, a Catholic order, protected Du Sable from being enslaved until he was well enough to make his way up the Mississippi River. He later settled in Peoria, Illinois.

In the early 1770's, DuSable built a cabin and eventually owned more than 800 acres of land in Peoria. He enjoyed a special relationship with Illinois territorial Indians. He took a Potawatomi Indian (Kittihawa), Catherine, as his common-law wife and fathered a daughter, Susanne, and a son, Jean. There is a parallel of the African American labor and the South African Colored people whereby many of the African American freed men and women and runaway slaves turned to the Native Americans for support, and mates; as did the Indonesian labors in South Africa, who turned to the Africans for the same. Some years later, he left Peoria and made his way north until he reached the Great Lakes area. The promise of greatness of the "Chicago" area, where DuSable decided to settle, had been passed over by others who arrived before him. None had the foresight to look beyond its barren, damp, marsh condition, nor did they have fortitude to make "nothing" into one of the greatest locations in the Western Hemisphere. In 1779, starting from scratch, DuSable built the first permanent home on the north bank of the Chicago River, where the present-day Tribune Tower stands. His land extended onto the present Wrigley Building site and beyond, on the Chicago River front. It was a well-constructed house consisting of five rooms and equipped with all the modern conveniences of the times. Later, despite the disadvantages, DuSable established a thriving trading post. In a short time, he became well-known as far away as Wisconsin, Detroit and Canada. The trading post consisted of a mill, bake house, dairy, smokehouse, workshop, poultry-house, horse stable, barn and several other smaller buildings. His post was the main supply station for white trappers, traders, woodsmen and the Indians.

The Chicago portage boomed. It became the key route for merchant trading, and DuSable sent wheat, breads, meats, and furs to trading posts in Detroit and Canada. DuSable became a man of considerable wealth and means. He also owned a substantial quantity of field and carpentry tools, which indicated that he must have hired men for fieldwork and building assignments. In addition, he owned an appreciable quantity of livestock, poultry, and hogs. In 1784 DuSable brought his wife and children to Chicago. And, as DuSable was a devout Catholic, he waited for the first Catholic priest to come in the area to marry him to his wife Catherine in a Catholic ceremony. In 1796, their granddaughter became the first born in the city of Chicago. On May 7, 1800, DuSable sold his entire wealth for a mere $1,200 and moved to Missouri, where he continued as a farmer and trader until his death. On August 28, 1818, DuSable died and he was buried in a Catholic cemetery in St. Charles, Missouri. In 1968, the State of Illinois recognized Jean Baptiste Pointe DuSable as being the founder of Chicago. Let's look back at the timeline of DuSable's legacy and the beginning of the immigration and migration of the city, now known as Chicago Illinois:

Jolliet and Marquette discovering Chicago

Jacques Marquette was born at Laon, France, on June 1, 1637 and joined the Society of Jesuits at age 17. After he worked and taught in France for several years, the Jesuits assigned him to New France in 1666 as a missionary to the indigenous peoples of the Americas. He showed great proficiency in learning the local languages, especially Huron. In 1668 Father Marquette was moved by his superiors to missions farther up the St. Lawrence River in the western Great Lakes region. He helped found missions at Sault Ste. Marie in present-day Michigan in 1668, St. Ignace in 1671, and at La Pointe, on Lake Superior near the present-day city of Ashland, Wisconsin. At La Pointe, he encountered members of the Illinois tribes, who told him about the important trading route of the Mississippi River. They invited him to teach their people, whose settlements were mostly further south. Because of wars between the Hurons at La Pointe and the neighboring Lakota people, Father Marquette left the mission and went to the Straits of Mackinac; he informed his superiors about the rumored river and requested permission to explore it.

Father Jacques Marquette

Leave was granted, and in 1673, Marquette joined the expedition of Louis Jolliet, a French-Canadian explorer. They departed from St. Ignace on May 17, with two canoes and five voyageurs of French-Indian ancestry (Métis). They followed Lake Michigan to Green Bay and up the Fox River, nearly to its headwaters. From there, they were told to portage their canoes a distance of slightly less than two miles through marsh and oak plains to the Wisconsin River. Many years later, at that point the town of Portage, Wisconsin was built, named for the ancient path between the two rivers. From the portage, they ventured forth, and on June 17, they entered the Mississippi near present-day Prairie du Chien, Wisconsin.

The Joliet-Marquette expedition traveled to within 435 miles (700 km) of the Gulf of Mexico, but turned back at the mouth of the Arkansas River. By this point, they had encountered several natives carrying European trinkets, and they feared an encounter with explorers or colonists from Spain. They followed the Mississippi back to the mouth of the Illinois River, which they learned from local natives provided a shorter route back to the Great Lakes. They reached Lake Michigan near the site of modern-day Chicago, by way of the Chicago Portage. In September, Marquette stopped at the mission of St. Francis Xavier, located in present-day Green Bay, Wisconsin, while Jolliet returned to Quebec to relate the news of their discoveries.

Marquette and his party returned to the Illinois Territory in late 1674, becoming the first Europeans to winter in what would become the city of Chicago. As welcomed guests of the Illinois Confederation, the explorers were feasted *en route* and fed ceremonial foods such as saga mite.

In the spring of 1675, Marquette traveled westward and celebrated a public mass at the Grand Village of the Illinois near Starved Rock. A bout of dysentery which he had contracted during the Mississippi expedition sapped his health. On the return trip to St. Ignace, he died at age 37 near the modern town of Ludington, Michigan.

A Michigan Historical Marker at this location reads:

Father Jacques Marquette, the great Jesuit missionary and explorer, died and was buried by two French companions somewhere along the Lake Michigan shore on May 18, 1675. He had been returning to his mission at St. Ignace which he had left in 1673 to go exploring in the Mississippi country. The exact location of his death has long been a subject of controversy. A spot close to the southeast slope of this hill, near the ancient outlet of the Pere Marquette River, corresponds with the death site, as located by early French accounts and maps and a constant tradition of the past. Marquette's remains were reburied at St. Ignore in 1677.

French Canadian Explorer Louis Jolliet

When Louis Jolliet was seven years old, his father died; but his mother remarried a successful merchant. Jolliet's stepfather owned land on the Ile d'Orleans, an island in the Saint Lawrence River in Quebec that was home to First Nations. Jolliet spent much time on Ile d'Orleans, so it was likely that he began speaking Aboriginal languages at a young age. During his childhood, Quebec was the center of the French fur trade. The Natives were part of day-to-day life in Quebec, and Joliet grew up knowing a lot about them. He entered a Jesuit school, as a child, and focused on philosophical and religious studies, aiming for priesthood. He also studied music, becoming a skilled harpsichordist and church organist. Yet, he decided to leave the seminary as an adult and pursued fur trading instead.

Jolliet attended a Jesuit school in Quebec and received minor orders in 1662, but abandoned his plans to become a priest in 1667. He spoke French, English, and Spanish.

Exploration of the upper Mississippi

Map of Marquette and Jolliet's 1673 expedition.

While Hernando de Soto was the first European to make official note of the Mississippi River by discovering its entrance in 1541, Jolliet and Marquette were the first to locate its upper reaches, and travel most of its length, about 130 years later. De Soto had named the river Rio del Espiritu Santo, but tribes along its length called it variations of "Mississippi".

On May 17, 1673, Jolliet and Marquette departed from St. Ignace Michigan with two canoes and five other voyageurs of French-Indian ancestry (today's Métis). The group followed Lake Michigan to the end of Green Bay.

They then paddled upstream (but southward) on the Fox River to the site now known as Portage, Wisconsin. There, they portaged (carried their canoes and gear) a distance of slightly less than two miles through marsh and oak forest to the Wisconsin River. Europeans eventually built a trading post at that shortest convenient portage between the Great Lakes and Mississippi River basins. On June 17, the canoeists ventured onto the Mississippi River near present-day Prairie du Chien.

The Jolliet-Marquette expedition traveled down the Mississippi to within 435 miles (700 km) of the Gulf of Mexico. They turned back north at the mouth of the Arkansas River. By this point, they had encountered natives carrying European goods, and worried about a possible hostile encounter with explorers or colonists from Spain. The voyageurs then followed the Mississippi back to the mouth of the Illinois River, which friendly natives told them was a shorter route back to the Great Lakes. Following the Illinois River upstream, they then turned up its tributary, the Des Plaines River, near modern-day Joliet, Illinois. They then continued up the Des Plaines River, and portaged their canoes and gear at the Chicago Portage. They then followed the Chicago River downstream until they reached Lake Michigan near the location of modern-day Chicago. Father Marquette stayed at the mission of St. Francis Xavier at the southern end of Green Bay, which they reached in August. Joliet returned to Quebec to relate the news of their discoveries.

Marquette returned to what later became the Illinois Country in late 1674. He became the first European to winter over in what would become the city of Chicago.

1673: It is commonly believed that because DuSable was the well-educated son of a French mariner from France, he was most likely privy to the tales of Louis Joliet and Father Jacques Marquette.

These two French Canadian men (one being an explorer and the other a Catholic priest) came to Chicago area under the commission of the French/ Canadian government and the Native Americans or 'First People' of the region greeted them warmly.

History says that Louis Joliet and Father Jacques Marquette, in their explorations, discovered the vast amount of beavers along the Chicago and Des Plaines River. Joliet and Marquette knew the area would be an excellent location to hunt for felts to market for the booming fur trade business on behalf of France and throughout Europe.

CHAPTER TWO

The First Non-Native Permanent Setteler In Chicago

Jean Baptiste Pointe DuSable

Jean Baptiste Point du Sable (or Point de Sable, Point au Sable, Point Sable, Pointe DuSable) (before 1750 – August 28, 1818) is regarded as the first permanent resident of what became **Chicago**, Illinois. The little that is known about his early life is that Jean Baptiste

Point Du Sable was born in San Marc, Haiti, in 1745. It is widely believed, that DuSable's mother was probably killed by the Spanish when he was around ten years old. It is further believed that in around the year 1764 Du Sable and his childhood friend Jacques Clemorgan sailed from Haiti to New Orleans. DuSable was eventually thankful for moving to New Orleans because it was there that he and his friend Clemorgan met their future partner of a trading post in New Orleans, and later in what would become Peoria, Illinois. The young man Du Sable and Clemorgan met was a Native American Indian named Choctaw, from the Great Lakes. At the time, Choctaw was working at a Catholic mission, soon after becoming friends, Du Sable, Clemorgan, and Choctaw later moved to an Indian River settlement in Peoria Illinois. Choctaw taught them things of value for their entire life. They learned how to set traps and where to find martens, small animals trapped for their fur. The three men started a trading post. Du Sable and Choctaw spent their time trapping in the woods, while Clemorgan devoted his time to hauling pelts downstream to New Orleans.

NATIVE AMERICANS LIVING IN ILLINOIS

Chief Pontiac

While trapping one spring day with Choctaw, Du Sable met Chief Pontiac, an important Native American leader. Little did they know that they would gain the respect of all the Indians of the Midwest in the weeks to come? Pontiac asked Du Sable and Clemorgan to arrange a peace treaty between the Ottawa, Miami, and Illinois tribes. Du Sable eagerly arranged the meeting in order to restore peace between the tribes. This enactment made DuSable the first negotiator among the "First People" which made him the most valuable person in the region and he received a great reputation as the "Great Negotiator".

Du Sable and Choctaw stayed a little longer than expected, but Du Sable was thankful, for it was during the stay that he met Kittihawa (Catherine), a Potawatomi. Kittihawa and Du Sable were later married. He was admired by the "First People" and was given a Native American name as "Climbing Bear" by the Chief of the Potawatomi Tribe because of his remarkable feats. They had two children and lived in a cabin built by Du Sable and Choctaw. This cabin was built on a waterway that is now called the Chicago River. But Du Sable called it Checagou, the name given to it by the Indians.

Du Sable became well-known for trading goods throughout the Midwest. He expanded his cabin to a trading post, which later became a small community with a church, school, and store. By 1776 Du Sable had commercial buildings, docks, a mansion house with fruit orchards, and livestock. Pleased with his partner's accomplishments, Clemorgan went to St. Louis, Missouri, to close his own trading post for fear of damage during the war between Spain and Britain.

Du Sable's trading post was very prosperous. Settlers came to Du Sable's post from Quebec because of difficulties with the English, who enforced strict rules regarding travel and free trade and heavily taxed them. Many wanted to buy land from Du Sable, but he refused to sell the land. Instead, he gave them some land.

Conditions, however, deteriorated in Du Sable's remote outpost. In 1778 British soldiers began to build a fort on Du Sable's land. They arrested Du Sable and about a week afterward the Indians ambushed more than half the troops at the fort and wounded many others. Thus, Indians became a colonial ally in the American Revolution.

In 1779 war was declared on the British because they would not give up the fort, nor would they leave the Great Lakes. It was then that Du Sable understood that he and his friends could not keep the red coats away from the Great Lakes, and that they would be there for years to come.

It was here that Du Sable lived prior to the 1770s. In 1779, he was living on the site of present-day Michigan City, Indiana, when he was arrested by the British military on suspicion of being an American sympathizer in the American Revolutionary War. In the early 1780s he worked for the British lieutenant-governor of Michilimackinac on an estate at what is now the city of St. Clair, Michigan, before moving to settle at the mouth of the Chicago River.

In 1800 after Du Sable's son and wife died, Jean sold his land to Jean Le Lime, an employee of his: Le Lime later sold the land to John Kinzie. Meanwhile, Du Sable moved with his daughter, Suzanne, to St. Louis. Later, Suzanne and her husband moved to Canada and Du Sable lived with his granddaughter. Du Sable bought a house on a farm that he deeded to his grandchildren, Eulalie and Michael. This was on condition that Eulalie care for him and promise to bury him with Catholic rites in a Catholic cemetery. For the next few years Du Sable lived quietly on his St. Charles farm in Missouri. On August 29, 1818, Jean Baptiste Point Du Sable at age seventy-three died quietly in his sleep. True to her word, Eulalie had a funeral mass held for her grandfather and buried him at the Catholic cemetery in St. Charles, Missouri.

Point du Sable has become known as the "Founder of Chicago". In Chicago, a school, museum, harbor, park and bridge have been named, or renamed, in his honor; and the place where he settled at the mouth of the Chicago River in the 1780s is recognized as a National Historic Landmark, now located in Pioneer Court.

1856 Juliette Kinzie memoir:

There is no known record of Point du Sable's life prior to the 1770s; his birth year, place of birth, and parents are unknown, though he is known from contemporary sources to have been of African descent. Juliette Kinzie, another early pioneer of Chicago, Illinois, never met Point du Sable; but stated in her 1856 memoir that he was "a native of St. Domingo" (the island of Hispaniola). This became generally accepted by scholars as his place of birth. Historian Milo Milton Quaife, however, regarded Kinzie's account of Point du Sable as "largely fictitious and wholly unauthenticated". Quaife later put forward a theory that he was of French-Canadian origin. A historical novel published in 1953 helped to popularize the commonly recited claim that he was born in 1745 in Saint-Marc in Saint-Domingue (now Haiti). Point du Sable married a Potawatomi woman named Kittihawa (Christianized to Catherine) on October 27, 1788 in a Catholic ceremony in Cahokia, an old French missionary town on the Mississippi River; though they were likely married earlier in the 1770s in the Native American tradition. They had a son named Jean and a daughter named Susanne.

In a footnote to a poem titled *Speech to the Western Indians*, Arent DePeyster, British commandant at Fort Michilimackinac from 1774 to 1779 (a former French fort in what was by then the British Quebec Territory), noted that "Baptist Point du Sable" was "handsome", "well educated", and "settled in Eschecagou". When he published this poem in 1813, DePeyster presented it as a speech that he had made at the Indian village of Abercroche (now Harbor Springs, Michigan) on July 4, 1779. This footnote has led many scholars to assume that Point du Sable had settled in Chicago by 1779; however letters written by traders in the late 1770s suggest that Point du Sable was, at this time, settled at the mouth of Trail Creek (*Rivière du Chemin*) at what is now Michigan City, Indiana. In August 1779, Point du Sable was arrested at Trail Creek by British troops and imprisoned briefly at Fort Michilimackinac. From the summer of 1780 until May 1784, Point du Sable managed the Pinery, a tract of woodlands claimed by British Lt. Patrick Sinclair on the St. Clair River in eastern Michigan. Point du

Sable and his family lived at a cabin at the mouth of the Pine River in what is now the city of St. Clair.

Point du Sable settled on the north bank of the Chicago River close to its mouth at some time in the 1780s. The earliest known record of Point du Sable living in Chicago is an entry that Hugh Heward made in his journal on May 10, 1790, during a journey from Detroit across Michigan and through Illinois. Heward's party stopped at Pointe du Sable's house en route to the Chicago portage; they swapped their canoe for a pirogue that belonged to Point du Sable, and they bought bread, flour and pork from him. Perrish Grignon, who visited Chicago in about 1794, described Point du Sable as a large man who was a wealthy trader. In 1800 he sold his farm to John Kinzie's frontman, Jean La Lime, for 6,000 livres. The bill of sale, which was rediscovered in 1913 in an archive in Detroit, outlined all of the property Point du Sable owned, as well as many of his personal artifacts. This included a house, two barns, a horse drawn mill, a bake house, a poultry house, a dairy and a smokehouse. The house was a 22-by-40-foot (6.7 m × 12.2 m) log cabin filled with fine furniture and paintings.

After Point du Sable sold his property in Chicago, he moved to St. Charles, Missouri, where he was commissioned by the colonial governor to operate a ferry across the Missouri River. He died in 1818, and was buried in St. Charles, in an unmarked grave in St. Charles Borromeo Cemetery. His entry in the parish burial register does not mention his origins, parents, or relatives; it simply describes him as *negre* (French for black). The St. Charles Borromeo Cemetery was moved twice in the 19th century, and oral tradition and records of the Archdiocese of St. Louis suggested that Point du Sable's remains were also moved. On October 12, 1968, the Illinois Sesquicentennial Commission erected a granite marker at the site believed to be Point du Sable's grave in the third St. Charles Borromeo Cemetery. In 2002 an archaeological investigation of the grave site was initiated by the African Scientific Research Institute at the University of Illinois at Chicago. Researchers using a combination of ground penetrating radar surveys and excavation of a 9-by-9-foot (2.7 m × 2.7 m) area did not find any evidence of any burials at the supposed gravesite, leading the archaeologists to conclude that Point du Sable's remains may not have been moved from one of the two previous cemeteries.

1933, Milo Milton Quaife:

Though there is little historical evidence regarding Point du Sable's life before the 1770s, there are a number of theories and legends that give accounts of his early life. Writing in 1933, Milo Milton Quaife identified a French immigrant to Canada, Pierre Dandonneau, who acquired the title "Sieur de Sable" and whose descendants were known by both the names *Dandonneau* and *Du Sable*. Quaife was unable to find a direct link to Point du Sable, but identified descendants of Pierre Dandonneau living around the Great Lakes region in Detroit, Mackinac, and St Joseph, leading him to speculate that Point du Sable's father was a member of this family, whilst his mother was a slave.

In 1951 a pamphlet by Joseph Jeremie, a native of Haiti, was published, in which he claimed to be the great grandson of Point du Sable. Based on family recollections and tombstone inscriptions he claimed that Point du Sable was born in Saint-Marc in Haiti, studied in France, returned to Haiti to deal coffee before traveling to French Louisiana. Historian and Point du Sable biographer John F. Swenson has called these claims "elaborate, undocumented assertions ... in a fanciful biography".

1953 Shirley Graham:

In 1953, Shirley Graham built on the work of Quaife and Jeremie in a historical novel of Point du Sable that she described as "not accurate history or pure fiction", but rather "an imaginative interpretation of all the known facts". This book presented Point du Sable as the son of the mate on a pirate ship, the *Black Sea Gull*, and a freed slave called Suzanne. Despite lack of evidence, and the continued debate about Point du Sable's early life, parentage, and birthplace, this popular story is widely presented as being definitive.

In 1815 a land claim that had been submitted by Nicholas Jarrot to the land commissioners at Kaskaskia, Illinois Territory was approved. In the claim Jarrot asserted that a "Jean Baptiste Poinstable" had been "head of a family at Peoria in the year 1783, and before and after that year"; and that he "had a house built and cultivated land between the Old Fort and the new settlement in the year 1780". This document has been taken by Quaife and other historians as evidence that Point du Sable lived at Peoria, prior to his arrival at Chicago; however, records show that Point du Sable was living at the Pinery in Michigan in the early 1780s.

In addition, the Kaskaskia land commissioners identified many fraudulent land claims, including two previously submitted in the name of Point du Sable. Nicholas Jarrot, the claimant, was involved in many fraudulent land claims, and Swenson suggests that this claim was also fraudulent, made without the knowledge of Point du Sable. Although apparently in conflict with some of the above information, some historical records contend that DuSable bought land in Peoria from J.B. Maillet in March 13, 1773 and sold it to Isaac Darneille in 1783, when he moved to be the first "permanent" European resident of Chicago.

Departure from Chicago:

Point du Sable left Chicago in 1800. Point du Sable sold his property to John Kinzie and moved to Missouri, at that time part of French Louisiana. The reason for his departure is unknown. In her memoir, Juliette Kinzie suggested that, "perhaps he was disgusted at not being elected to a similar dignity (great chief) by the Potawatomie's." In *1874 Nehemiah Matson* elaborated on this story, claiming that Point du Sable was a slave from Virginia who had moved with his master to Lexington, Kentucky in 1790. According to Matson, Point du Sable became a zealous Catholic in order to convince a Jesuit missionary to declare him chief of the local Native Americans, and left Chicago when the natives refused to accept him as their chief. Quaife dismisses both these stories as being fictional.

1795 Treaty of Greenville:

In her 1953 novel, Graham suggests that Point du Sable left Chicago because he was angered with the United States government, which wanted him to buy the land on which he had lived and called his own for the previous two decades. The 1795 Treaty of Greenville and the subsequent westward migration of Indians away from the Chicago area might also have influenced his decision.

Even though it has been highly disputed by Potawatomi Tribal attorneys that there is no record of them ever signing any treaties that gave up their rights to the Chicago River Esplanade, which was inhabited by the Potawatomi people!

The Chicago area was directly affected by five of the approximately 370 ratified treaties between the federal government and American Indian nations signed from 1778 to 1871. Indian treaty-making ended by law in 1871; but an additional 73 "agreements" containing similar provisions were ratified up to 1911. Treaties involving the Chicago area were signed in 1795, 1816, 1821, 1829, and 1833.

The Treaty of Greenville, Ohio (1795), ceded to the federal government the southern two-thirds of present-day Ohio, ending the allied Indians' long battle to maintain the Ohio River as the boundary between areas for white and Indian settlement, a boundary set by the Treaty of Fort Stanwix in 1768. The treaty also ceded 16 tracts at strategic locations on the water transportation routes of the Northwest Territory, including three in present-day Illinois (1) the mouth of the Chicago River, where Fort Dearborn was erected in 1803; (2) the portage area between the Chicago and Des Plaines Rivers; and (3) the mouth of the Illinois River.

Following the War of 1812, the regional band of Ottawa, Chippewa, and Potawatomi ceded to the United States a strip of land extending directly southwest from points 10 miles north and 10 miles south of the mouth of the Chicago River. Through this Treaty of St. Louis (1816), the government acquired control over the Chicago River corridor linking Lake Michigan and the Mississippi River. At Chicago,

Ottawa, Chippewa, and Potawatomi representatives signed a treaty August 29, 1821, giving up land in southwestern Michigan and also gave permission to build a road from Detroit to Chicago, completed in 1835.

The pioneer farm of Antoine Ouilmette, now a lighthouse site in Wilmette, marked the corner of an area extending westward to the Rock River ceded by the Treaty of Prairie du Chien (Wisconsin, 1829). Other treaty provisions granted sections of land along the Chicago and Des Plaines Rivers to several people of Indian heritage, including Billy Caldwell, Alexander Robinson, and Archange Ouilmette, Potawatomi wife of Antoine.

The famous Treaty of Chicago (1833) brought an estimated three thousand Indians, traders, government officials, army troops, land speculators, and adventurers to the small village to witness the dramatic proceedings, whereby the Potawatomi ceded the last of their Illinois and Wisconsin lands and their last reservations in Michigan. Indians began the demanded removal to land west of the Mississippi River, or fled to Wisconsin and Canada before the treaty was ratified in 1835.

> Helen Hornbeck Tanner
> *Ebony, December 1963*

Founder of Chicago:

Point du Sable is the earliest recorded resident of the settlement close to the mouth of the Chicago River that grew to become the city of Chicago. He is therefore widely regarded as the first permanent resident of Chicago and given the appellation "Founder of Chicago".

The expedition headed by Louis Jolliet and Jacques Marquette in 1673, though probably not the first Europeans to visit the area, are the first recorded to have crossed the Chicago Portage and travelled along the Chicago River. Marquette returned in 1674, camped a few days near the mouth of the river, then moved on to the portage, where he stayed through the winter of 1674–75.

Joliet and Marquette did not report any Indians living near the Chicago River area at this time, though archaeologists have since discovered numerous Indian village sites elsewhere in the greater Chicago area. Two of La Salle's men built a stockade at the portage in the winter of 1682/1683. However, in 1697 Henri Tonti, Michel Accault, and François de La Forêt received permission from Governor Frontenac to establish a fortified trading post at Chicagou managed by Pierre de Liette, Tonti's cousin, a Franco-Italian, which lasted until 1705.

De Liette kept a journal of his experiences living with the Illinois natives for those years he lived with them at the Chicago trading post. De Liette, describes in his writings the game of lacrosse played by the Indians on the extensive meadow behind these villages. In Chicago, De Liette ran the trading post in partnership with François Daupin de La Forêt, Michel Accault, and Henri de Tonti [located probably near today's Tribune Tower] which he had to close, leaving in 1705 after the king revoked his trading license.

The Mission of the Guardian Angel was somewhere in the vicinity of Chicago from 1696 until it was abandoned in around 1700. The Fox Wars effectively closed the Chicago area to Europeans in the first part of the 18th century. The first non-native to re-settle in the area may have been a trader named Guillory, who might have had a trading-post near Wolf Point on the Chicago River in around 1778. After Point du Sable, Antoine Ouilmette is the next recorded resident of Chicago; he claimed to have settled at the mouth of the Chicago River in July 1790, a few months after Hugh Heward visited Point du Sable.

Memorials:

[Point du Sable] is not yet honored in his own house (which Chicagoans call the "Kinzie House") or on his own land. No Street bears his name, and, except for the high school, he has no monument. Cadillac is honored in Detroit, Pitt in Pittsburgh, Cleveland in Cleveland—but the father of Chicago has no street or statue of stone to call his own.

The First Non-Native Permanent Setteler In Chicago

Home of Jean Baptiste Point DuSable in Chicago

1773: Jean Baptiste Pointe DuSable became the first real estate developer and builder when he established a permanent settlement for himself and his newly arrived wife, and about one hundred other Pottawatomie.

He built a trading post, established a dairy farm and planted fruit orchards and fields of corn, hay and alfalfa. This sight is where the present-day Chicago Tribune Tower stands.

The construction of DuSable's home was the first European scale permanent architectural structure in the area. The original name of Chicago was then called Checagou, meaning wild onions.

DuSable's home was a well-constructed house consisting of five rooms and equipped with all the modern conveniences of the time.

Catholic Jesuit Priest Father Pierre Gibault

1778: Chicago's reputation as a city of Churches began when Jean Baptiste Pointe DuSable built a Catholic Church and mission school in the settlement and placed them under the direction of Father Gibault upon visits.

1779: It has been said by the Native Americans in Chicago that DuSable convinced the fist people in the region to help him make a path that was wide enough at the foot of the Chicago River and Lake Michigan big enough that small ships could pass and dock near his new settlement. That action makes their experience the first act of an architectural geographical engineering in the region.

1788: Being a devout Catholic, DuSable and Catherine where formally married in the European Christian custom. Also in 1790, their daughter

Susanne and a French seaman, Jean Baptiste Peltier were married in the same Catholic custom marriage ceremony. It was officiated by Fr. Pierre Gibault and soon after in 1796, their daughter Eulaie was born.

DuSable's granddaughter Eulaie Peltier became the first integrated child born and the first multicultural experience of a European immigrant and a Black Indian, in Chicago. This act gave birth to Chicago's legacy and perception of being a major city of diversity.

JEAN LA LIME:

1800: On May 7, DuSable sold his entire wealth for a mere $1,200 and moved with his granddaughter Eulaie to Saint Charles, Missouri, where he continued to farm and trade until his death.

The deed of sale for DuSable's property was deeded to Jean La Lime. It later became the John Kinzie mansion.

The property included the following: A wood cabin, which was twenty-two by forty feet (22/40), two barns, one horse mill, one bake house, one poultry house, one workshop, one dairy, one smokehouse, two mules, thirty cattle, two calves, twenty hogs, forty-four hens. There was also equipment including: eight sickles, seven scythes, carts, saws, copper kettles, axes and other house tools.

Jean La Lime (died June 17, 1812) was a trader from Quebec, Canada who worked in what became the Northwest Territory of the United States. He worked as an agent for William Burnett, also of Canada, to sell to the Native Americans and take furs in exchange. He was among the first European permanent settlers in Chicago. He was killed there in 1812, in what was called the "first murder in Chicago", by John Kinzie, a trading partner of Burnett who was another early settler from Canada.

After trading along the frontier and likely in Detroit, La Lime arrived in the Chicago area on August 17, 1792 as an agent for William Burnett of Canada. In 1800, he purchased the homestead of Jean Baptiste Point du Sable for Burnett for 6,000 livres. The bill of sale was filed in Detroit, Michigan on September 18, 1800, although dated in Chicago on May 7 of that year.

By 1804, Burnett's partner, John Kinzie, who also settled in Chicago, had bought the former du Sable house. He lived there with his wife and first child. They had three other children born in Chicago.

After the Americans established Fort Dearborn in 1804, La Lime worked there as an interpreter, aiding communication between the Americans and Indians. He broke his leg in 1809 and, as it was improperly set, was left lame.

On June 17, 1812 in Chicago, La Lime and Kinzie quarreled, and Kinzie killed him. Kinzie fled to Milwaukee, then in Indian Territory. He claimed La Lime had shot at him and he had stabbed the interpreter in self-defense.

Nathan Heald, the captain of Fort Dearborn and local authority, held an inquest that determined Kinzie had acted in self-defense. Historians have speculated that La Lime was acting as an informant on the corrupt economic activities within the fort, and Kinzie killed him to silence him. La Lime had received death threats since April of that year.

La Lime was originally buried within sight of Kinzie's house, as the European settlement was thinly strung along Lake Michigan. Kinzie maintained the gravesite. After he died in 1828, his son John H. Kinzie had La Lime's remains exhumed and reinterred in the churchyard of St. James Church.

In 1891, a coffin was discovered at Wabash Avenue and Illinois Street near the Rush Street Bridge. Based on the research of Joseph Kirkland, the bones inside were believed to be La Lime's. The remains are held by the Chicago History Museum.

The First Non-Native Permanent Setteler In Chicago

JOHN KINZIE:

John Kinzie

Kinzie was born in Quebec City, Canada (then in the Colonial Province of Quebec) to John and Anne Kinzie, Scots-Irish immigrants. His father died before Kinzie was a year old, and his mother remarried. In 1773, the boy was apprenticed to George Farnham, a silversmith. Some of the jewelry created by Kinzie has been found in archaeological digs in Ohio.

By 1777, Kinzie had become a trader in Detroit, where he worked for William Burnett. As a trader, he became familiar with local Native

American peoples and likely learned the dominant language. He developed trading at the Kekionga, a center of the Miami people.

In 1785, Kinzie helped rescue two American citizens - sisters, who had been kidnapped in 1775 from Virginia by the Shawnee and adopted into the tribe. One of the girls, Margaret McKinzie, married him; her sister Elizabeth married his companion Clark. Margaret lived with Kinzie in Detroit and had three children with him. After several years, she left Kinzie and Detroit, and returned to Virginia with their children. All three of the Kinzie children eventually moved as adults to Chicago.

In 1789, Kinzie lost his business in the Kekionga (modern Fort Wayne, Indiana) and had to move further from the western U.S. frontier. The US was excluding Canadians from trade with the Native Americans in their territory. As the United States settlers continued to populate its western territory, Kinzie moved further west.

Marriage and move to Chicago:

In 1800 Kinzie married again, to Eleanor Lytle McKillip. By the time they moved to Chicago, about 1802-1804, they had a year-old son, John. Eleanor had three more children in Chicago. Their daughter Ellen Marion Kinzie, believed to be the first European child of European descent born in Chicago, was born in 1805; followed by Maria Indiana in 1807 and Robert Allen Kinzie in 1810.

The First Non-Native Permanent Setteler In Chicago

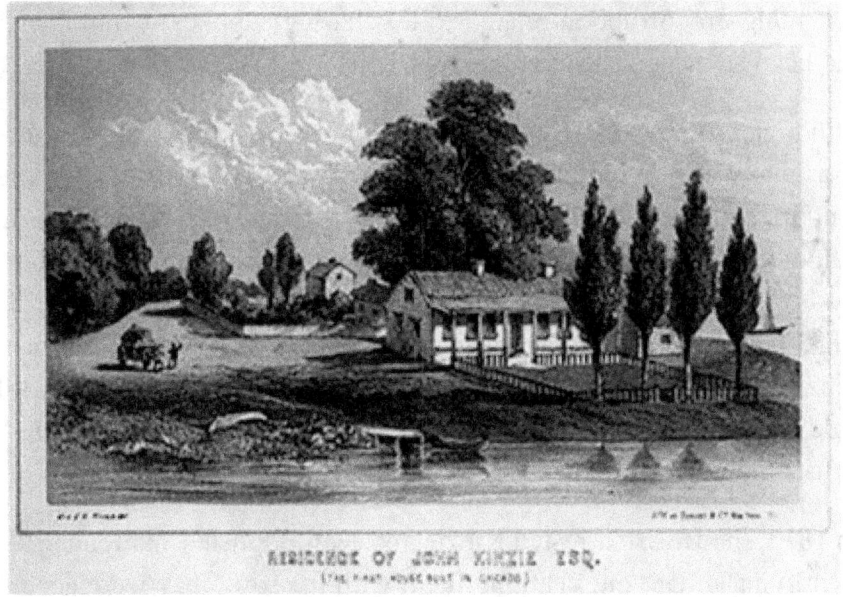

Drawing of the John Kinzie / Pointe DuSable House

In 1804 Kinzie purchased the former house and lands of Jean Baptiste Point du Sable, located near the mouth of the Chicago River. That same year, Governor William Henry Harrison of the Indiana Territory appointed Kinzie as a justice of the peace.

The War of 1812:

After American citizens built Fort Dearborn, Kinzie's influence and reputation rose in the area; he was useful because of his relationship with the Native Americans. The War of 1812 began between Great Britain and the American Federation, and tensions rose on the northern frontier.

In June 1812, Kinzie killed Jean La Lime, who worked as an interpreter at Fort Dearborn. He fled to Milwaukee, then in Indian Territory. While in Milwaukee, he met with pro-British Indians who were planning attacks on American settlements, including Chicago. During this period, an inquest at Fort Dearborn under Captain Nathan Heald exonerated Kinzie in the killing of La Lime, ruling it was in self-defense. Historians speculate that La Lime may have been informing on corruption related to purchasing supplies within the fort and been silenced. The case has been called "Chicago's first murder."

Although worried that Chicago would be on heightened alert, a force of as many as 500 Indians attacked the small garrison of soldiers, their support and their families near the current intersection of 18th and Calumet, as they fled south along the lake shore after they evacuated the Fort. The Fort Dearborn attack took place on August 15, 1812 and left 53 dead, including women and children, in a brutal massacre. Kinzie and his family, aided by Potawatomi Indians led by Billy Caldwell, escaped unharmed and returned to Detroit. Identifying as a British citizen, Kinzie had a strong anti-American streak.

In 1813, the British arrested Kinzie and Jean Baptiste Chardonnai, also then living in Detroit, charging them with treason. They were accused of having corresponded with the enemy (the American General Harrison's army) while supplying gunpowder to Chief Tecumseh's Indian forces, who were fighting alongside the British. Chardonnai escaped, but Kinzie was imprisoned on a ship for transport to England. When the ship put into port in Nova Scotia to weather a storm, Kinzie escaped. He returned to American-held Detroit by 1814. Formerly identifying as a British citizen, Kinzie switched to the United States. He returned to Chicago with his family in 1816 and lived there until his death in 1828.

1803: Fort Dearborn was built as a United States fort on the south side of the Chicago River. It was constructed by troops of the American Federation named in honor of Henry Dearborn. At that time, Dearborn was the United States Secretary of War.

1812: The original fort was destroyed following the Battle of Fort Dearborn.

1816: A new Fort Dearborn was reconstructed on the same site.

1818: On August 28, DuSable died. He was buried in a Catholic cemetery in St. Charles, Missouri.

Not to be confused with the former Fort Dearborn, now Odiorne Point State Park in New Hampshire.

Fort Dearborn was a United States fort built in 1803 beside the Chicago River, in what is now Chicago, Illinois. It was constructed by troops under Captain John Whistler and named in honor of Henry Dearborn, then United States Secretary of War. The original fort was destroyed following the Battle of Fort Dearborn during the War of 1812, and a new fort was constructed on the same site in 1816. By 1837, the fort had been de-commissioned. Parts of the fort were lost to both the widening of the Chicago River in 1855 and a fire in 1857. The last vestiges of Fort Dearborn were destroyed in the Great Chicago Fire of 1871. The site of the fort is now a Chicago Landmark, located in the Michigan–Wacker Historic District.

THE FIRST FORT DEARBORN:

The First Fort Dearborn, Built in 1803

Fort Dearborn sits on Michigan Avenue and Wacker Drive by the shore of Lake Michigan in Chicago. It was near the site of the Fort Dearborn Massacre on August 15, 1812 just over a month after the War of 1812 started. The fort was built by Captain John Whistler, named after the Secretary of War at that time, Henry Dearborn, and was finished in 1803. It was similar in design to earlier forts in Illinois, such that it was not a new design of a fort. It had a magazine built of stone and a wooden palisade.

Even after Fort Dearborn was finished, its exact location of which territory it was in, was not fully understood. In 1809 the Indiana Territory was split up and Fort Dearborn changed from Indiana to Illinois Territory. This is seen by the, assumedly semi-sarcastic comment by the secretary of treasury when in 1811 he commented, 'that he did "not know in what territory Chicago" was located.' This indicates that the area in which the fort was located was contested. This is true, too, due to the younger Indians that were angry at their leaders who signed the Greenville Treaty.

The Greenville Treaty of 1795 gave the U.S. more land that was originally natives' land. The land was traded for such that it was good for both the frontiersmen at the fort and in the surrounding area; and good for the natives who received as compensation a trading post, where they could buy European goods with the money that was paid to them for said land.

Captain John Whistler was in charge of 69 soldiers, including officers, when the fort was complete. The people at Fort Dearborn were either those soldiers or the families of the officers, at the time of the massacre. Captain Whistler, however, was not present at the massacre nine years later. Captain John Whistler's eventual removal from Fort Dearborn was due to Matthew Irwin, who was put at Fort Dearborn to be the government-hired trader with the natives, or at least those natives who were willing to trade with them.

Matthew Irwin wrote to Washington D.C. about Captain Whistler's and some of his officers' misconduct. The trading that happened at Fort Dearborn led to Captain Whistler and his officers illegally gaining and using monetary compensation for the successful trades that happened at the fort. Captain Whistler's superiors decided that, instead of prosecuting them and discharging veteran frontiersmen and soldiers, that Captain Whistler would be replaced. Captain Heald was the chosen replacement for Captain Whistler.

Captain Heald became the commander of Fort Dearborn in 1810. Captain Nathan Heald found "fifty-one soldiers and two officers under his command." The two officers under Captain Heald's command also happened to be two of the officers who had been charged with misconduct, along with the previous fort commanding officer. Heald was under-enthusiastic about Fort Dearborn when he was reported writing to his superiors: "I am sorry to inform you I am not pleased with my situation." He continued saying that the frontier was for, "…a man who has a family and can content himself to live so remote from the civilized part of the world." To change his view on being at Fort Dearborn, he went on leave for a time.

Eventually Captain Heald was in New England and rekindled an old relationship, and married. This shows that Captain Heald was not overjoyed with being on the frontier with the Indians and with less than a hundred European people surrounded by wilderness, nor was he enthralled about the military men at the fort, either. "The garrison numbered about seventy-five men, very few of whom were effective." So, from a firsthand account, it is seen that there were definitely less than a hundred inhabitants in Fort Dearborn to begin with; and there were either not many veterans at the fort during the evacuation, or there were no soldiers who had seen any real action in battle. In either case they were not an effective fighting force.

Just before the massacre, Heald was ordered by General Hull to give the surrounding Indians everything in the Fort, from blankets to alcohol and gunpowder. The majority of the Indians were on the fence with each other about whether or not to attack Fort Dearborn. Captain Heald disobeyed this order and dumped all the alcohol (which the Indians primarily bought from the fort) and the weapons into Fort Dearborn's drinking well and the nearby river, giving only blankets and other items that the Indians weren't interested in. This was not entirely unforeseen either. There had been other attacks by Indians on the frontiersmen; and one of the informants in Indiana informed

Captain Heald, "Chicago is the first place the Indians contemplate to attack."

This information allows one to understand at least part of the reason why the Indians attacked Fort Dearborn. They had wanted the plunder of Fort Dearborn and they were deprived it by Heald. However, the Indians were primarily angry at the loss of their land, no matter what compensation they got in return. However, knowing that it was likely they were going to be attacked by Indians, Captain Heald would not have wanted to just give weapons and ammunition to the Indians as ordered, in case they turned on Fort Dearborn's occupants, whether on the road or at the fort itself.

The massacre was not actually at the fort. It happened when the fort's populace was trying to evacuate to Fort Wayne. The commandant of Fort Dearborn, Captain Nathan Heald, had received a letter from Brigadier General William Hull on August 9, 1812 to pack up and retreat to Fort Wayne, and to give the supplies of the fort to the nearby Indians. It was on the road to Fort Wayne that the soldiers and their families were attacked by Indians.

There were other attacks by Indians at Tippecanoe and other places due to unrest in the tribes. These were some of the biggest reasons why Captain Heald did not follow direct orders to give away the weapons or ammunition to people who might turn against them. This decision was also a decision in which it gave the Indians enough of a reason to ambush Fort Dearborn's occupants upon the road. The biggest reason would have been due to what James Corben stated in an interview,

"The day before we left the fort there was a council of the officers, held to consult on what course should be pursued, whether we should leave the fort, or not. The conduct of the Indians around us, had excited fears that all was not well; an Indian that day shot at and wounded an ox that was to assist in drawing the baggage, very near the captain; and we had great fears on account of the Prophets Indians, who we knew were between us and Fort Wayne."

This also describes how Fort Dearborn's occupants were accompanied by the Indians who ambushed them. The Indians were furious at the loss of the items of Fort Dearborn that they had wanted most, alcohol, weapons, and ammunition. Yet being asked to escort the occupants through other tribes' territory to Fort Wayne, provided a way for the Potawatomi and all Indians angry at the loss of their land to succeed in taking revenge for the loss of munitions, alcohol and most of all their people's land, to the white men.

The primary reason the Indians didn't kill the occupants of Fort Dearborn right away is not entirely obvious until one realizes that if a battle had started right outside or inside the fort, then the occupants would have had cover to hide and fight from. Most importantly of all, they would have had cannons to fire at the Indians; since the fort had three cannons, two of which pointed towards the river, that is north, (away from the south gate). If the fighting had begun inside the fort, then the cannons may not have been as useful since forts aren't designed to fire their ordnance inward.

The weapons were all thrown in the well, along with munitions; but the cannons were too big and heavy to move effectively or throw into a well. Thus, they would have been left in the fort. Without munitions, though likely, means that there would have been no powder in the magazine of Fort Dearborn. Yet the occupants of the fort carried what powder they could back to Fort Wayne in their escape. Had the fighting started before all the excess ammunition was thrown into the well, the people of Fort Dearborn would have had a very good chance for surviving the massacre, thanks to the three cannons?

The order Captain Heald executed prior to leaving Fort Dearborn, was likely a two-pronged tactic: the first being that their excess weapons and ammunition could not be used by the enemy; and secondly, that the well would be contaminated with gunpowder and heavy elements, such that the water supply would be bad. The alcohol at the fort was also dumped, so that the enemy could not benefit from it.

When Fort Dearborn was evacuated, there were Captain Heald, Captain Wells, fifty-five regular soldiers, and twelve militiamen. The civilian populace of Fort Dearborn accompanying them included eighteen children and nine women. Accompanying the populace of the fort were fifteen Miami Indians who took the front of the evacuee train, and a band of Potawatomi, all totaling five hundred Indians from the Potawatomi and Miami tribes escorting the evacuees.

The Potawatomi Indians were in a column of their own off to the side of the main evacuee train. After travelling into an area where the Potawatomi column disappeared from the evacuee train view, the Potawatomi quickly went to a preset location that they had planned beforehand, where they ambushed the train. The reasons for the Indians turning against the Americans included the inability of the Indian chiefs to keep their people at peace, and the Americans not giving the Indians the stores of the fort.

The surprised evacuees fought back fervently; but after only about fifteen minutes, almost half of the regular soldiers were alive, and all the militia had died fighting. Out of the civilians in the evacuee train, two of the nine women and twelve of the eighteen children died in the massacre. Out of the people that survived was Mrs. Heald, Captain Nathan Heald's wife, along with several of the other wives.

Consequently, had the occupants of Fort Dearborn given the Indians everything from their stores, as he was ordered to, then the massacre at Fort Dearborn may never had happened. If Captain Heald gave the Indians around them all their excess ammunition and alcohol along with everything else, then the Indians would have had no new reason to attack. This would have led to more tribesmen listening to the chiefs. Or, had Captain Whistler, when he was commanding officer, kept his people well trained and uncorrupt, then the massacre at Fort Dearborn may never had happened because the soldiers, militia, and anyone else capable of fighting would have been able to defend the evacuee train much more effectively. This means that the massacre at Fort Dearborn would have been a battle. Had both of these events changed, then the massacre of Fort Dearborn would not have happened because the fort occupants would have been too highly trained, and the Indians asked to escort them would not have had a reason to turn on them.

After the massacre at Fort Dearborn, the Potawatomi burned down the fort, leaving only the stone magazine. A second Fort Dearborn was built on top of the ruins of the first Fort Dearborn in 1816. This second Fort Dearborn was then used as a fort, as the first had been used.

SECOND FORT DEARBORN:

Old Fort Dearborn with Surroundings in 1856," rebuilt after the Battle of Fort Dearborn. Courtesy of the Library of Congress:

A second Fort Dearborn was built (1816). This fort consisted of a double wall of wooden palisades, officer and enlisted barracks, a garden, and other buildings. The American forces garrisoned the fort until 1823, when peace with the Indians led the garrison to be deemed redundant. This temporary abandonment lasted until 1828, when it was re-garrisoned, following the outbreak of war with the Winnebago Indians. In her 1856 memoir *Wau Bun,* Juliette Kinzie described the fort as it appeared on her arrival in Chicago in 1831:

The fort was enclosed by high pickets, with bastions at the alternate angles. Large gates opened to the north and south, and there were small portions here and there for the accommodation of the inmates. ... Beyond the parade-ground which extended south of the pickets, were the company gardens, well-filled with currant-bushes and young fruit-trees. The fort stood at what might naturally be supposed to be the mouth of the river, yet it was not so, for in these days, the latter took a turn, sweeping round the promontory on which the fort was built, towards the south, and joined the lake about half a mile below.

The fort was closed briefly before the Black Hawk War of 1832 and by 1837; the fort was being used by the Superintendent of Harbor Works. In 1837, the fort and its reserve, including part of the land that became Grant Park, were deeded to the city by the Federal Government. In 1855 part of the fort was demolished so that the south bank of the Chicago River could be dredged, straightening the bend in the river and widening it at this point by about 150 feet (46 m); and in 1857, a fire destroyed nearly all the remaining buildings in the fort. The remaining blockhouse and the few surviving outbuildings were destroyed in the Great Chicago Fire of 1871.

The War of 1812: A Local American Indian History

This year marks the 200th anniversary of the War of 1812. Referred to as "America's Second War of Independence," the conflict saw allied Native American, British, and Canadian forces battling the United States in a war that lasted two and a half years. Largely forgotten in America, the War of 1812 played an important role in shaping the country, as we know it; and in understanding historic and contemporary American Indian and government relations.

While much of the war took place at sea, in Canada, and in the eastern Great Lakes, crucial events occurred in the Chicago area that aimed in part to prevent American expansion into Indian territories. The infamous Battle of Fort Dearborn (also referred to as the Fort Dearborn Massacre) between Potawatomi warriors and American soldiers and militia left a lasting mark on Chicago twenty-one years before the city's founding. Despite the Battle's prominent remembrance as the first star on the City of Chicago's flag, it remains a misunderstood event.

"Indian History": to learn more about all perspectives of this bloody war, visit the Mitchell Museum's newest exhibit, "The War of 1812" - August 2012-September 2013, Mitchell Museum of the American Indian.

It was believed by many of the Potawatomi tribal leaders respected the leadership of the Black Chief that many of them called DuSable. He was the son-in-law to one of the Potawatomi Chief's daughters, Kittihawa and he was regarded as being a great peace maker and negotiator, or as the First People referred to, as the black white chief in the settlement.

He was a man of white French ancestry on his father's side and black Haitian mother that educated him and allowed him to be treated like an African Moor, a "Free Man". At different times in DuSable's immigration into America, he had encountered the British slavery mentality and he developed a no-tolerance attitude toward their many attempts to enslave or devalue his Human rights.

With the migration of the American and British immigrants to the DuSable settlement through John Kenzie's encouragement, so came the incorporation of slavery, when Kenzie brought with him his personal African slaves; as it was popular during the time of the British transatlantic Slave Trade business, into the Americas.

DuSable had prided himself in creating a safe zone settlement for everyone that came to reside in his settlement, especially after the developing of Fort Dearborn. It is believed that was a major factor in him selling his home and property to John La Lime, which eventually became the home of Kenzie. DuSable then moved to Missouri.

AMERICAN INDIAN LEADER TECUMSEH

Tecumseh leader of the Shawnee Native Americans

At the time of the massacre, the Potawatomi controlled a territory extending across northern Indiana, northern Illinois, and in central and eastern Wisconsin. The only parcel within that territory, not under their sovereign authority was the six square miles at the mouth of the Chicago River, ceded to the United States under the Greenville treaty in 1795. Against this backdrop, it then unfolded the events of that horrid summer morning.

Local American maps and documents from the war read biographies of prominent American Indian leaders, including Tecumseh (Shawnee); and interact with a response board, debating if the events at Fort Dearborn were a Battle or Massacre. From the causes of conflict and declaration of war to the local Battle of Fort Dearborn's contemporary controversy, the exhibit provides visitors with new perspectives on a war of lasting importance. In 1803 Fort Dearborn was built at Chicago, but relations between the Potawatomi and the Americans deteriorated. Potawatomi war parties in route to attack the Osages in Missouri sometimes committed depredations in southern Illinois, and messengers from Tecumseh and the Shawnee Prophet recruited Chicago Potawatomi into their growing pan-Indian movement. In 1810 Tecumseh visited the Chicago region, recruiting additional warriors for his cause. Attempting to reduce the growing tension, federal officials escorted Main Poc, a chief from the Kankakee River, and Siggenauk (the Blackbird), a leader from Chicago, to Washington. Yet the chiefs remained suspicious, and Potawatomi hostility toward the government continued.

During the War of 1812, most Chicago Potawatomi favored the British; and on August 15, 1812, when federal troops abandoned Fort Dearborn, hostile Potawatomi led by Siggenauk and Mad Sturgeon attacked the garrison. More than 50 Americans and about 15 Indians were killed in the lakefront battle, which took place near modern Burnham Park. Some of the American prisoners were rescued by friendly Potawatomi, including Black Partridge and Métis Alexander Robinson, who later relinquished the captives to British or American officials. Following the attack, many of the Chicago Potawatomi joined Tecumseh and the British on the Detroit frontier, or sporadically raided American settlements; but in 1813, after American officials built Fort Clark at Lake Peoria, Potawatomi attacks upon southern Illinois diminished. By late 1814 most of the Potawatomi at Chicago had abandoned the British and sought peace with the United States.

Following the War of 1812, the Potawatomi at Chicago were joined by significant numbers of Ottawas and Chippewas (Ojibwas), and Métis leaders assumed a more important role. Particularly prominent was Billy Caldwell, a Métis elected as justice of the peace at Chicago in 1825. Many of the Métis were merchants who played key roles in the region's fur trade.

After 1816 the United States government distributed a major portion of the Potawatomi annuities at Chicago, and many tribespeople became more dependent upon these payments. To secure additional annuities, the tribe was forced to sell more land. Between 1816 and 1829, Potawatomi leaders from Chicago participated in six of the seven treaties in which the tribe gave up large sections of northern Illinois and adjoining regions of Wisconsin, Indiana, and Michigan. In turn, their reliance upon annuities drew the tribespeople into a closer relationship with the federal government, and in 1827, when hostility erupted between white settlers and Winnebagos in Wisconsin, Potawatomi from Chicago used their influence to keep their kinsmen in southern Wisconsin at peace. Five years later, Caldwell, Alexander Robinson, and Shabbona, a chief from a village west of the Fox River, rejected Black Hawk's invitation to attack the settlements and advised the Sac chief to return to Iowa. Following the meeting, Shabbona warned settlers of approaching Sac war parties, and late in June 1832 Caldwell led a party of Potawatomi scouts who assisted the U.S. Army against Black Hawk and his warriors.

After the Black Hawk War, pressure mounted on the Potawatomi to relinquish their remaining lands in Illinois and to remove to the west. In 1832, they gave up their claims to lands in eastern Illinois, and one year later more than 6,000 tribesmen assembled at Chicago, where they ceded their remaining lands in Illinois. In 1835 Billy Caldwell led the first Chicago emigrants west of the Mississippi. There they split into two small communities. Meanwhile, most of the remaining Chicago Potawatomi assembled at a camp on the Des Plaines River for the government's final removal effort. After a dispute with removal agents, many Potawatomi fled from the camp, seeking refuge among kinsmen in Wisconsin or Michigan. Finally, in September 1837 the remaining 450 Chicago Potawatomi left the camp and eventually joined with their kinsmen in the west. A few tribesmen, primarily Métis, remained on private tracts of land in northern Illinois, but after 1840 most Potawatomi were gone from the Chicago region.

R. David Edmunds

CHAPTER THREE

The First Religious Parish In Chicago

ROMAN CATHOLIC ARCHDIOCESE OF CHICAGO

First priest Rev. John Mary Irenaeus Saint Cyr. Fr. Saint Cyr

In 1795, the Potawatomi tribe signed the Treaty of Greenville that ceded to the United States a tract of land at the mouth of the Chicago River. There in 1804, Fort Dearborn was erected and protected newly arrived Catholic pioneers. In 1822, Alexander Beaubien became the first person to be baptized in Chicago. In 1833, Jesuit missionaries wrote a letter to the Most Rev. Joseph Rosati, Bishop of Saint Louis and Vicar General of Bardstown, pleading for the appointment of a resident pastor to serve over one hundred professing Roman Catholics living in Chicago. Rosati appointed a diocesan priest, the Rev. John Mary Irenaeus Saint Cyr. Fr. Saint Cyr celebrated his first

Mass in a log cabin owned by the Beaubien family on Lake Street, near Market Street, in 1833.

St. Mary's Cathedral, Chicago

First parish: At the cost of four hundred dollars, Father Saint Cyr purchased a plot of land at what is now the intersection of Lake and State Streets and constructed a church building of 25 by 35 feet (7.6 by 10.7 m). It was dedicated in October 1833. The following year, the Bishop of Vincennes visited Chicago, where he found over 400 Catholics with only one priest to serve them. The bishop asked permission from Bishop Rosati to send Fathers Fischer, Shaefer, Saint Palais, Dupontavice, and Joliet from Vincennes to tend to the needs of the Chicago region. In 1837, Fr. Saint Cyr was allowed to retire and was replaced by Chicago's first English-speaking priest, the Rev. James Timothy O'Meara. Father O'Meara moved the church built by Fr. Saint Cyr to what is now the intersection of Wabash Avenue and Madison Street. When Fr. O'Meara left Chicago, Saint Palais demolished the church and replaced it with a new brick structure Diocesan establishment

The First Plenary Council of Baltimore concluded that the Roman Catholic population of Chicago was growing exponentially and was in dire need of an Diocese of its own. With the consent of Pope Gregory XVI, the Diocese of Chicago was canonically erected on November 28, 1843. In 1844, William Quarter of Ireland was appointed as the first Bishop of Chicago. Upon his arrival, Quarter summoned a synod of 32 Chicago priests to begin the organization of the diocese. One of Quarter's most important achievements was his successful petitioning for the passage of an Illinois law in 1845 that declared the Bishop of Chicago an incorporated entity, a corporation sole, with power to hold real and other property in trust for religious purposes. This allowed the bishop to pursue large-scale construction of new churches, colleges and universities to serve the needs of Chicago's Roman Catholic faithful. After four years of service as Bishop of Chicago, Bishop Quarter died on April 10, 1848.

Great Fire of 1871:

At the time of the founding of the Diocese of Chicago on September 30, 1843, Bishop William Quarter led his faithful from the *Cathedral of Saint Mary at the southwest corner of Madison and Wabash Streets*. A few years later in 1851, an immense brick church called the Church of the Holy Name was being constructed on State Street between Huron and Superior streets. Its cornerstone was set in 1852.

In October 1871, however, both churches were destroyed, as the Great Chicago Fire engulfed the entire city. Church of the Holy Name pastor, John McMullen, travelled the country to raise funds to rebuild the churches and to aid the homeless of Chicago.

Meanwhile, Chicago's Catholics were forced to worship in what was called the *shanty cathedral*, a boarded-up burnt house on Cass Street. They worshiped there for over four years.

The church lost nearly a million dollars in church property in the Chicago fire of 1871, leading to administrative instability for decades.

Archdiocese establishment; the southern section of the state of Illinois split from Chicago diocese in 1853, becoming the Diocese of Quincy. The Quincy diocese was renamed the Diocese of Alton in 1857, and eventually became Diocese of Springfield. The Diocese of Peoria was established in 1877 from another territorial split from the Chicago diocese.

From 1844 to 1879, the diocesan bishop of the Diocese of Chicago held the title Bishop of Chicago. With the elevation of the diocese to an archdiocese in 1880, the diocesan bishop held the title Archbishop of Chicago. Since 1915, all Archbishops of Chicago have been honored in consistory with the title of Cardinal Priest and membership in the College of Cardinals. The archbishops also have responsibilities in the dicasteries of the Roman Curia. All but two diocesan bishops were diocesan priests before assuming the episcopacy in Chicago. Two came from religious institutes: the Society of Jesus (James Van de Velde) and the Missionary Oblates of Mary Immaculate (Francis George).

1924 The Holy Name Cathedral

Holy Name Cathedral Chicago
Wikipedia, encyclopedia

Holy Name Cathedral in Chicago, Illinois is the seat of the Archdiocese of Chicago, one of the largest Catholic dioceses in the United States. Holy Name Cathedral replaced the Cathedral of Saint Mary and the Church of the Holy Name, which were destroyed by the

Great Chicago Fire of 1871, and was dedicated on November 21, 1875. A cornerstone inscription still bears marks from the murder of North Side Gang member Hymie Weiss, who was killed across the street on October 11, 1926.

The Nave of the Cathedral during a wedding

Holy Name Cathedral was built in the Gothic revival architectural style while at the same time integrating motifs symbolic of the message of the modern Church. The church building is 233 feet (71 m) long, 126 feet (38 m) wide and can seat 2,000 people. The ceiling is

150 feet (46 m) high and has a spire that reaches 210 feet (64 m) into the sky. Overall, the cathedral features motifs meant to instill an ambience of physically dwelling in the biblical Tree of Life.

Bronze cathedral doors

The first feature that greets worshipers is massive bronze doors designed by Albert J. Friscia that weigh 1200 pounds each. The doors introduce the overall "Tree of Life" theme with intricate details that serve to make the doors look like overwhelming planks of wood. The doors possess a hydraulic system that allows them to be opened with the push of a finger. Beyond the doors is a vestibule encased in glass.

Resurrection crucifix

Once inside the church, the most striking feature is the suspended *Resurrection Crucifix* sculpted by the artist Ivo Demetz. Adorning the walls of the nave are the Stations of the Cross by artist Goffredo Verginelli depicting the Passion, Crucifixion and Resurrection of Christ. The stations are cast in bronze and framed in red Rocco Alicante marble.

Ambo of the Evangelists

Various bronze sculptures are featured in other parts of the church. One of the largest pieces is the *Ambo of the Evangelists* by Eugenio de Courten. An *ambo*, in church liturgy, is the lectern from which readings of Holy Scripture are proclaimed. The bronze casting depicts the authors of the Gospels with their symbols: Matthew the angel representing the Gospel of the Church; Mark, the lion and inspiration for Peter's teachings or catechesis; Luke, the ox, for his recounting of Christ's infancy; John, the eagle, for the writer of the Spiritual Gospel, recounting the story of "the Word made flesh."

Ambo of the Epistle Writers

Also by de Courten is the *Ambo of the Evangelists*, a bronze casting depicting the authors of the apostolic letters to the early Church communities: Peter, with keys to the Kingdom of God; Paul, who died by the sword; James, representing faith sustained by good works;

and Jude, carrying a whip representing correction. This particular ambo is used by lectors and cantors during Sunday masses and other special Church feasts and memorials.

Cathedral altar

Six tons of monolithic red-black Rosso Imperiale di Solberga granite forms the *mensa* or table top of the altar. The pedestal is encircled by a bronze bas-relief depicting Old Testament scenes of sacrificial offerings and preparation: Abel's offering of the first sacrifice, the priest Melchizedek giving bread and wine, Abraham's willingness to sacrifice his son Isaac, and the Prophet Elijah receiving bread and water from the Angel of the Lord for strength to continue on his journey. The consecrated altar contains relics, or actual artifacts from the bodies of Saint John the Apostle and Saint Timothy.

Cathedra of the See of Chicago

A *cathedra*, or bishop's throne, is what makes the church a cathedral. It is from this chair that *Sedes Chicagiensis*, or See of Chicago, is presided over by the archbishop of Chicago. Unlike most Roman Catholic cathedral, the *Cathedra of the See of Chicago* is plain and simple. Its back contains three panels depicting the first Christian teachers: Christ in the center panel, Saint Peter to his right, and Saint Paul to his left.

Sanctuary Panels of the Holy Name

Above the *cathedra* are the *Sanctuary Panels of the Holy Name*, five bronze panels by Attilio Selva representing the Holy Name of Jesus from which the church gets its name. The first panel is of Simeon contemplating the *Infant Savior,* whom Mary presents in the Temple. The second panel depicts the *Mystery of the Trinity* and an angel carrying the monogram of Christ to earth. The third panel is of the *Risen Christ* proclaimed as *Lord*. The fourth panel is of the *Presentation of Jesus in the Temple* showing Mary and Joseph presenting the child for circumcision and naming. The last panel is of the *Priesthood of Jesus*, with Christ adorned investments presenting the chalice to all people.

Pipe Organs

The organ in the west gallery

The Cathedral contains two fine pipe organs: a large 71-stop, 4-manual instrument in the *west end gallery* constructed by Flentrop firm of Zaandam, Netherlands; and a smaller 19-stop, 2-manual instruments in the *south chancel* by Casavant Frères of Saint-Hyacinthe, Canada.

Galeri of the Cardinals

Holy Name Cathedral continues the tradition of raising the galero, a wide-brimmed tasseled hat, of a deceased cardinal over the *cathedra* from the highest point of the semicircular, domed cathedral apse. The galero is hung in Holy Name Cathedral where they remain until they are reduced to dust, symbolizing how all earthly glory is passing. Looking up above the Cathedra are the galeri of Cardinals Mundelein, Stritch, Meyer, Cody, Bernardin, and George.

Great Chicago fire of 1871

At the time of the founding of the Diocese of Chicago on September 30, 1843, Bishop William Quarter led his faithful from the Cathedral of Saint Mary at the southwest corner of Madison and Wabash Streets. A few years later in 1851, an immense brick church called the Church of the Holy Name was being constructed on State Street between

Huron and Superior streets. Its cornerstone was set in 1852. In October 1871, however, both churches were destroyed as the Great Chicago Fire engulfed the entire city. Church of the Holy Name pastor **John McMullen** travelled the country to raise funds to rebuild the churches and to aid the homeless of Chicago. Meanwhile, Chicago's Catholics were forced to worship in what was called the *shanty cathedral*, a boarded-up burnt house on Cass Street. They worshiped there for over four years.

Breaking ground for the new cathedral

In 1874, Brooklyn architect Patrick Charles Keely, who would later also design St. Stanislaus Kostka, was selected to draw plans for the new cathedral of Chicago. On July 19 of that year, the cornerstone was laid. On November 21 of the following year, Bishop Thomas Foley dedicated the church and christened it the Cathedral of the Holy Name. In 1880, the Diocese of Chicago was reorganized to become the Archdiocese of Chicago and Holy Name Cathedral became the church of primacy over several other dioceses in the Midwest United States.

Early renovations

In 1888, surveyors noticed that the cathedral was sagging on its Superior Street side. This prompted the archbishop to commence with the cathedral's first renovation projects. By 1915, Holy Name Cathedral was balanced out and saved from sinking into the ground. It was also lengthened by 15 feet (4.6 m) to accommodate the growing Catholic population. That same year, James Edward Quigley, Archbishop of Chicago, died. The first major Mass of the newly rededicated cathedral was the late archbishop's funeral.

Archbishop George Mundelein

In 1924, Archbishop George Mundelein was elevated by the pope to become a cardinal. When he returned from consistory at the Vatican, the new cardinal was greeted at Holy Name Cathedral with a celebratory procession of over 80,000 Catholics.

Archbishop George Mundelein

Archbishop George Mundelein was named the third Archbishop of Chicago, Illinois, on December 9, 1915. He was formally installed as archbishop on February 9, 1916, and was appointed an Assistant at the Pontifical Throne on May 8, 1920.

At a large dinner held at the University Club of Chicago on February 12, 1916, an anarchist chef, Jean Crones, slipped arsenic into the soup in an attempt to poison Mundelein and over 100 other guests, including Illinois Governor Edward F. Dunne. The soup was watered down due to the arrival of about fifty extra guests. None of the assembled guests died, as a hastily prepared emetic was supplied by a doctor, J.B. Murphy, who although mildly stricken, was able to help the other victims. (Many vomited the poison out of their systems, though suffering considerable agony.) Mundelein ate only a bite or two of the soup. Newspapers referred to the mass-murder attempt as the "Mundelein poison soup plot." Jean Crones was suspected at the time of being a German agent, but turned out to be an Italian anarchist named Nestor Dondoglio, a member of the Galleanist circle of anarchists who also included Sacco and Vanzetti. Dondoglio allegedly wrote letters to American newspapers after the crime (many of these were hoaxes). He was never apprehended, though police spent years taking men into custody thought to be "Jean Crones." He died peacefully in Connecticut in 1932, "where he had found haven with friends." The archdiocese greatly expanded its charity functions during the Great Depression, rivalling that of Chicago's Associated Jewish Charities. A city-wide network of St. Vincent de Paul Societies was established.

Cardinal Mundelein:

In 1924, Archbishop George Mundelein was elevated by the pope to become a cardinal. When he returned from consistory at the Vatican, the new cardinal was greeted at Holy Name Cathedral with a celebratory procession of over 80,000 Catholics.

With his elevation, Chicago became the first diocese west of the Allegheny Mountains to have a cardinal. In 1933, he was appointed judge for the apostolic process for Mother Cabrini's cause for canonization.

Mundelein served as papal legate to the eighth National Eucharistic Congress in New Orleans, Louisiana, on September 13, 1938, and was one of the cardinal electors who participated in the 1939 papal conclave, which selected Pope Pius XII.

Mundelein died from heart disease in his sleep in Mundelein, Illinois, at age 67.

When Cardinal Mundelein died unexpectedly in his sleep in October 1939, Chicago City Hall hastily paved State Street where the subway was being constructed to accommodate the great influx of mourners expected to make the pilgrimage. As Cardinal Mundelein lay in state in the nave of Holy Name Cathedral, over a million people paid their last respects.

He is buried behind the main altar of the chapel at Mundelein Seminary.

Second Vatican Council

As soon as the Second Vatican Council was concluded in the 1960s, Holy Name Cathedral proceeded with a massive renovation project to alter the cathedral interior. From Easter 1968 to 1969, Holy Name Cathedral was closed, and Masses were held in various locations including a nearby school gymnasium. At this time, all the stained glass, oil paintings, and marble statuary were removed from the interior of the cathedral. The end result was a relatively plain room, dominated by a six-ton granite altar and Resurrection crucifix. At midnight on Christmas Eve of 1969, Holy Name Cathedral was reopened.

Papal visit of 1979

Pope John Paul II became the first Pontiff to visit Holy Name Cathedral in October 1979 for a prayer service with Chicago's bishops, as well as a concert featuring the music of Luciano Pavarotti and the Chicago Symphony Orchestra in the nave of the cathedral.

CHAPTER FOUR

DuSable's Settlement Becomes A City

FORT DEARBORN IN 1853

The Kinzie Mansion and Fort Dearborn

This image gives a glimpse into time, at the beginning of two major monumental and historical architects and at the beginning of the European expansion in Chicago.

It was also the beginning to the end of Chicago's glorious roots of the Black Chief Jean Baptiste Pointe DuSable and Native Americans sovereignty in the land of their ancestor's, and "First People" in Chicago.

Fort Dearborn was closed briefly before the Black Hawk War of 1832 and by 1837; the fort was being used by the Superintendent of Harbor Works.

In 1837, the fort and its reserve, including part of the land that became Grant Park, were deeded to the city by the Federal Government.

In 1855 part of the fort was demolished so that the south bank of the Chicago River could be dredged, by straightening the bend in the river and widening it at this point by about 150 feet (46 m).

In 1857, a fire destroyed nearly all the remaining buildings in the fort. The remaining blockhouse and few surviving outbuildings were destroyed in the Great Chicago Fire of 1871.

The southern perimeter of Fort Dearborn was located at what is now the intersection of Wacker Drive and Michigan Avenue in the Loop community area of Chicago along the Magnificent Mile. Part of the fort outline is marked by plaques, and a line embedded in the sidewalk and road near the Michigan Avenue DuSable Bridge and Wacker Drive. A few boards from the old fort were retained and are now in the Chicago History Museum in Lincoln Park.

On March 5, 1899, the Chicago Tribune publicized a Chicago Historical Society replica of the original fort. In 1933, at the Century of Progress Exhibition, a detailed replica of Fort Dearborn was erected as a fair exhibit. As part of the celebration, both a United States one-cent postage stamp and a souvenir sheet (containing 25 of the stamps) were issued, showing the fort.

The individual stamp and sheet were reprinted when Postmaster General James A. Farley gave imperforated examples of these, and other stamps, to his friends. Because of the ensuing public outcry, millions of copies of "Farley's Follies" were printed and sold.

In 1939, the Chicago City Council added a fourth star to the city flag to represent Fort Dearborn. This star is depicted as the left-most, or first, star of the flag.

The site of the fort was designated a Chicago Landmark on September 15, 1971.

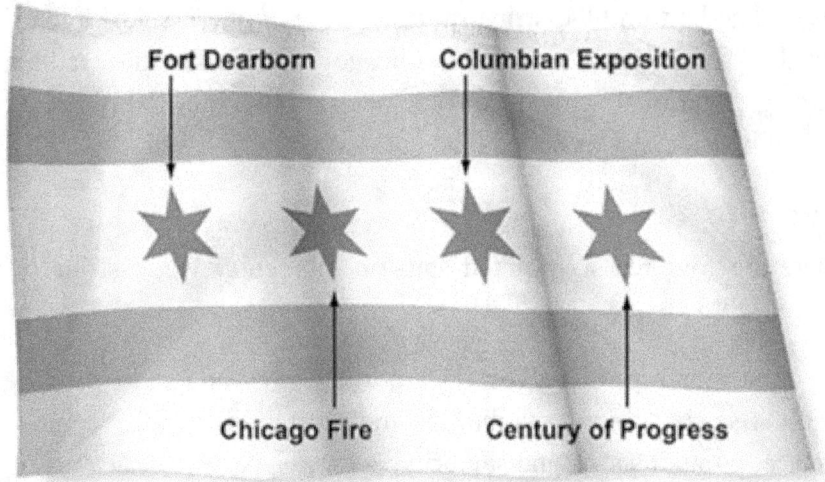

Chicago City Flag

The municipal flag of Chicago consists of two blue horizontal stripes or bars on a field of white, each stripe one-sixth the height of the full flag, and placed slightly less than one-sixth of the way from the top and bottom. Between the two blue stripes are four red, six-pointed stars arranged in a horizontal row.

The flag, designed by Wallace Rice, was adopted in 1917 after Rice won the design competition for the flag. The three sections of the white field and the two stripes represent geographical features of the city, the stars symbolize historical events, and the points of the stars represent important virtues or concepts. The historic events are Fort Dearborn, the Great Chicago Fire of 1871, the World's Columbian Exposition of 1893, and the Century of Progress Exposition of 1933–34.

In a review by the North American Vexillological Association of 150 American city flags, the Chicago city flag was ranked second best with a rating of 9.03 out of 10, behind only the flag of Washington, D.C.

Stripes

The three white background areas of the flag represent, from top to bottom, the North, West and South sides of the city. The top blue stripe represents Lake Michigan and the North Branch of the Chicago

River. The bottom blue stripe represents the South Branch of the river and the "Great Canal", over the Chicago Portage. The lighter blue on the flag is variously called sky blue or pale blue; in a 1917 article of a speech by Rice, it was called "the color of water".

Stars

There are four red six-pointed stars on the center white stripe. From left to right:

The first star represents Fort Dearborn. It was added to the flag in 1939. Its six points symbolize transportation, labor, commerce, finance, populousness, and salubrity.

The second star stands for the Great Chicago Fire of 1871, and is original to the 1917 design of the flag. Its six points represent the virtues of religion, education, aesthetics, justice, beneficence, and civic pride.

The third star symbolizes the World's Columbian Exposition of 1893, and is original to the 1917 design. Its six points stand for political entities Chicago has belonged to and the flags that have flown over the area: France, 1693; Great Britain, 1763; Virginia, 1778; the Northwest Territory, 1789; Indiana Territory, 1802; and Illinois (territory, 1809, and state, since 1818).

The fourth star represents the Century of Progress Exposition (1933–1934), and was added in 1933. Its points refer to bragging rights: the United States' second largest city (became third largest in a 1990 census when passed by Los Angeles); Chicago's Latin motto, *Urbs in horto* ("City in a garden"); Chicago's "I Will" motto; the Great Central Marketplace; Wonder City; and Convention City.

A possible fifth star has been proposed for the city flag on more than one occasion. The first occasion occurred in the 1940s, when a letter to the *Chicago Tribune* asked that a fifth star be added to the city flag in honor of the city's place in the history of the nuclear age. On another occasion, a star was proposed in honor of Harold Washington, the first

African-American mayor of Chicago. A fifth star was also discussed following the Chicago Flood of 1992. Another fifth star was in the works from a group of Chicago real estate professionals to represent Chicago's entrepreneurial spirit in the early 1990s. A proposal was put forward by the 2016 Olympic Games Bid Committee; if the bid to host the games had been successful, a fifth star might have been added to the flag; however, the Olympic bid was lost to Rio de Janeiro. In a more facetious vein, a fifth star has been proposed if the Chicago Cubs should win the World Series, which did not happen from 1908 to 2016.

Six-pointed stars are used because five-pointed stars represent sovereign states, and because the star as designed was not found on any other known flags as of 1917.

March 4, 1837: DuSable's settlement was incorporated as the city of Chicago.

The DuSable settlement, 1833 with three hundred fifty residents was incorporated as the town of Chicago.

March 4, 1837: DuSable's settlement had grown to four thousand one hundred seventy inhabitants and was reincorporated as the city of Chicago.

1928: The prestige of the Urban League was enhanced, when the group petitioned for a memorial to the city's first permanent settler, Jean Baptiste Point DuSable, a man of African descent.

Chicago's critical location on the water route linking the Great Lakes and the Mississippi River shaped much of its early history. It was populated by a series of native tribes who maintained villages in the forested areas near rivers. Beginning with Father Jacques Marquette and French Canadian explorer Louis Jolliet in 1673, a steady stream of explorers and missionaries passed through or settled in the region, but it was not until 1779 that the first non-native resident made it his permanent home: Jean-Baptist-Point Du Sable maintained a thriving trading post near the mouth of the Chicago River until 1800, when he moved out of the region.

Within a few years the federal government had erected Fort Dearborn to establish a military presence in the area. The garrison was located on the south bank at the river mouth; it was destroyed during the War of 1812 but was rebuilt in 1816. By that time, numerous traders linked the region with international fur markets. Even after Illinois became a state in 1818, however, Chicago remained a small settlement. It was incorporated as a town in 1833 with a population of about 350.

Population growth remained stagnant until the federal government allocated funding, that allowed work to begin on the Illinois and Michigan Canal, a vital link between Lake Michigan and the Illinois River. Because the project was to be financed largely by sales of adjacent land, which would benefit from the commerce it brought, the canal helped to fill Chicago with speculators. The boom led to a second incorporation, this time as a city, on March 4, 1837; the population was 4,170. That same year a devastating national economic depression delayed the city's development for several years. Canal construction drew thousands of Irish laborers to the area, when what was supposed to be a simple ditch a few hundred yards long grew into a waterway of some 75 miles (120 km), often cut through solid rock. After the canal opened in 1848, it brought grain and other raw materials to the city, while providing what was then a fast and convenient means of travel to the interior of the state.

Board of Trade District Chicago

A discussion of how the Chicago Board of Trade influenced the city's entrepreneurial spirit in the emergence as a transportation hub.

Chicago's railway age also began in 1848, when a locomotive named the *Pioneer* arrived by ship from Buffalo, New York, and went into service for the new Galena and Chicago Union Railroad. The line's 11-mile (18-km) track extended straight west from the city, but its namesake destination, the lead-mining metropolis in the northwest corner of the state, declined in importance before extensions even reached it. Other lines soon extended to the west, including the Chicago, Burlington and Quincy, the Rock Island, and the Illinois Central. The Chicago and Milwaukee line linked the rival ports by rail. In 1852 two separate lines entered from the east and provided direct rail service to the Eastern Seaboard. By the beginning of the 20th century, no fewer than 30 interstate routes fanned out from the city, and the resulting ease in reaching both raw materials and markets contributed to the city's rapid commercial and industrial development. Most important of all, Chicago was the terminus of every one of the railroads; passengers, raw materials, and finished goods all had to be transferred between lines in the city, thus contributing to an extraordinary development of hotels, restaurants, taxicabs, warehouses, rail yards, and trucking companies

1848 Chicago Union Stock Yard

Before construction of the various private stockyards, tavern owners provided pastures: and care for cattle herds waiting to be sold. With the spreading service of railroads, several small stockyards were created in and around the City of Chicago. In 1848, a stockyard called the Bulls Head Market was opened to the public. The Bulls Head Stock Yards were located at Madison Street and Ogden Avenue. In the years that followed, several small stockyards were scattered throughout the city. Between 1852 and 1865, five (5) railroads were constructed to Chicago. The stockyards that sprang up were usually built along various rail lines of these new railroad companies. Some railroads built their own stockyards in Chicago. The Illinois Central and the Michigan Central railroads combined to build the largest set of pens on the lake shore east of Cottage Grove Avenue from 29th Street to 35th Street. In 1878, the New York Central

Railroad managed to buy a controlling interest in the Michigan Central Railroad. In this way, Cornelius Vanderbilt, owner of the New York Central Railroad, got his start in the stockyard business in Chicago.

Several factors contributed to consolidation of the Chicago stockyards: westward expansion of railroads between 1850 and 1870, which drove great commercial growth in Chicago as a major railroad center, and the Mississippi River blockade during the Civil War that closed all north-south river trade. The United States government purchased a great deal of beef and pork to feed the Union troops fighting the Civil War. As a consequence, hog receipts at the Chicago stockyards rose from 392,000 hogs in 1860 to 1,410,000 hogs over the winter butchering season of 1864-1865; over the same time period, beef receipts in Chicago rose from 117,000 head to 339,000 head. With an influx of butchers and small meat packing concerns, the number of businesses greatly increased to process the flood of livestock being shipped to the Chicago stockyards. The goal was to butcher and process the livestock locally rather than transferring it to other northern cities for butchering and processing. Keeping up with the huge number of animals arriving each day proved impossible until a new wave of consolidation and modernization altered the meatpacking business in the post-Civil War era.

The Union Stock Yards, designed to consolidate operations, was built in 1864 on swampland south of the city. It was south and west of the earlier stock yards in an area bounded by Halsted Street on the east, South Racine Avenue on the west, with 39th Street as the northern boundary and 47th Street as the southern boundary. Led by the Alton, Chicago & St. Louis Railroad and the Lake Shore and Michigan Southern Railway a consortium of nine railroad companies (hence the "Union" name) acquired the 320-acre (1.3 km) swampland area in southwest Chicago for $100,000 in 1864. The stockyards were connected to the city's main rail lines by 15 miles (24 km) of track. In 1864, the Union Stock Yards were located just outside the southern boundary of the City of Chicago. Within five years the area was incorporated into the city, within the confines of the Yards.

By the start of the 20th century, the stockyards employed 25,000 people and produced 82 percent of the domestic meat consumed nationally. In 1921, the stockyards employed 40,000 people. Two thousand men worked directly for the Union Stock Yard & Transit Co., and the rest worked for companies such as meatpackers, which had plants in the stockyards. By 1900, the 475-acre (1.92 km) stockyard contained 50 miles (80 km) of road, and had 130 miles (210 km) of track along its perimeter. At its largest size, The Yards covered nearly 1 square mile (3 km) of land, from Halsted Street to Ashland Avenue and from 39th (now Pershing Rd.) to 47th Streets.

At one time, 500,000 US gallons (2,000 m) a day of Chicago River water were pumped into the stockyards. So much stockyard waste drained into the South Fork of the river that it was called Bubbly Creek due to the gaseous products of decomposition. The creek bubbles to this day. When the City permanently reversed the flow of the Chicago River in 1900, the intent was to prevent the Stock Yards' waste products, along with other sewage, from flowing into Lake Michigan and contaminating the City's drinking water.

The meatpacking district was served between 1908 and 1957 by a short Chicago 'L' line with several stops, devoted primarily to the daily transport of thousands of workers and even tourists to the site. The line was constructed when the City of Chicago forced the removal of surface track on 40th Street.

Evolving methods of transportation and distribution led to declining business and the closing of the Union Stock Yards in 1971. National Wrecking Company negotiated a contract whereby National Wrecking cleared a 102-acre site and removed some 50 acres of animal pens, auxiliary buildings and the eight stories Exchange Building. It took approximately eight months to complete the job and ready the site for the building of an industrial park.

DuSable's Settlement Becomes A City

1871: The Great Chicago Fire

The fire started at about 9:00 p.m. on October 8, in or around a small barn belonging to the O'Leary family that bordered the alley behind 137 DeKoven Street. The shed next to the barn was the first building to be consumed by the fire, but city officials never determined the exact cause of the blaze. There has, however, been much speculation over the years. The most popular tale blames Mrs. O'Leary's cow, who allegedly knocked over a lantern; others state that a group of men were gambling inside the barn and knocked over a lantern. Still other speculation suggests that the blaze was related to other fires in the Midwest that day.

The fire's spread was aided by the city's use of wood as the predominant building material in a style called balloon frame; a drought before the fire; and strong southwest winds that carried flying embers toward the heart of the city. More than two thirds of the structures in Chicago at the time of the fire were made entirely of wood. Most houses and buildings were topped with highly flammable tar or shingle roofs. The entire city's sidewalks and many roads were made of wood. Compounding this problem, Chicago had only received an inch (2.54 cm) of rain from July 4 to October 9 causing severe drought conditions.

In 1871, the Chicago Fire Department had 185 firefighters with just 17 horse-drawn steam engines to protect the entire city. The initial response by the fire department was quick, but due to an error by the watchman, Matthias Schaffer, the firefighters were sent to the wrong place, allowing the fire to grow unchecked. An alarm sent from the area near the fire also failed to register at the courthouse where the fire watchmen were. Also, the firefighters were tired from having fought numerous small fires and one large fire in the week before. These factors combined to turn a small barn fire into a conflagration.

When firefighters finally arrived at DeKoven Street, the fire had grown and spread to neighboring buildings and was progressing towards the central business district. Firefighters had hoped that the South Branch of the Chicago River and an area that had previously thoroughly burned would act as a natural firebreak. All along the river, however, were lumber yards, warehouses, and coal yards, and barges and numerous bridges across the river. As the fire grew, the southwest wind intensified and became superheated, causing structures to catch fire from the heat and from burning debris blown by the wind. Around 11:30 p.m., flaming debris blew across the river and landed on roofs and the South Side Gas Works.

With the fire across the river and moving rapidly towards the heart of the city, panic set in. About this time, Mayor Roswell B. Mason sent messages to nearby towns asking for help. When the courthouse caught fire, he ordered the building to be evacuated and the prisoners jailed in the basement to be released. At 2:20 a.m. on the 9th, the cupola of the courthouse collapsed, sending the great bell crashing down. Some witnesses reported hearing the sound from a mile (1.6 km) away.

As more buildings succumbed to the flames, a major contributing factor to the fire's spread was a meteorological phenomenon known as a fire whirl. As overheated air rises, it comes into contact with cooler air and begins to spin creating a tornado-like effect. These fire whirls are likely what drove flaming debris so high and so far. Such debris was blown across the main branch of the Chicago River to a railroad car carrying kerosene oil. The fire had jumped the river a second time and was now raging across the city's north side.

Despite the fire spreading and growing rapidly, the city's firefighters continued to battle the blaze. A short time after the fire jumped the river, a burning piece of timber lodged on the roof of the city's waterworks. Within minutes, the interior of the building was engulfed in flames and the building was destroyed. With it, the city's water mains went dry and the city was helpless. The fire burned unchecked from building to building, block to block.

Finally, late into the evening of the 9th, it started to rain, but the fire had already started to burn itself out. The fire had spread to the sparsely populated areas of the north side, having consumed the densely populated areas thoroughly.

CHAPTER FIVE

Chicago Rebuilt Quickly

The Water Tower, one of the few buildings to survive the Great Fire of 1871, on North Michigan Avenue © MedioImages/Getty Images

Chicago rebuilt quickly, reached more than a half-million residents in 1880, and accomplished construction miracles. As a response to public health concerns, the newly formed Sanitary District of Metropolitan Chicago began work in 1889 on the Chicago Sanitary and Ship Canal, the waterway that when opened in 1900 not only allowed larger vessels to pass through the port of Chicago, but also made it possible to reverse the flow of the Chicago River; the improvement in public health once pollutants were carried away from Lake Michigan was dramatic. Meanwhile, a host of talented architects that included Louis Sullivan, Dankmar Adler, William Holabird, Daniel H. Burnham, John Wellborn Root, and William Le Baron Jenney, who had been attracted to Chicago by the post fire rebuilding opportunities, stayed on in the 1880s to design a new generation of even taller downtown buildings. Department stores and offices crowded into the central area, and industrial growth along the river branches and rail lines was equally phenomenal. Commuter railroads and transit improvements promoted outward residential dispersal of the middle class, a clientele served by a young Frank Lloyd Wright and the emerging "Prairie school" architects. This suburban boom prompted the city to annex some 125 square miles (324 square km) in 1889, which included many adjacent communities and also much open farmland.

That same year two young women, Jane Addams and Ellen Gates Starr, arrived to take up residence in one of the congested slums that had sprung up in the tumbledown West Side of the city. Their Hull House programs in recreation, job training, day care, health care, thrift, workplace safety, and culture combated but did not eradicate rampant unemployment, crime, and other social problems that were endemic in urban tenements. Discontent with living conditions, in turn, helped to fuel outbursts against the low wages, unemployment, monotonous work, and steep production quotas that came with the city's rapid industrialization. Outbreaks of labor violence became common, and the Chicago experience made the rest of the country fearful that the future would be filled with proletarian strife. Local workers battled police during the nationwide railway strike of 1877. But the

Haymarket Riot of 1886 captured the world's attention when police efforts to break up a protest meeting in the Randolph Street produce market were met with a bomb explosion that killed seven policemen and an unknown number of workers.

Conflagration and rebirth: Chicago's growth was unprecedented. The population reached nearly 30,000 in 1850 and was triple that a decade later. Cheap transportation to the outskirts of the city encouraged middle-class dispersal, but poor neighborhoods near the downtown area were congested; structures there were also built of wood. Serious fires were frequent, but no one could have anticipated the events of the evening of October 8, 1871. Months without rain had parched the city, and a major fire the previous night had exhausted firefighters and damaged equipment. It is not known what happened in the De Koven Street barn of Patrick and Catherine O'Leary, on the city's West Side. Vandals, milk thieves, a drunken neighbor, spontaneous combustion, even (though unlikely) the O'Learys' legendary cow—any could have started a blaze there that roared out of control in minutes. Misdirected fire equipment arrived too late, and a steady wind from the southwest carried the flames and blazing debris from block to block. The slums became kindling for the downtown conflagration, where even the supposedly fireproof stone and brick buildings exploded in flames as the destruction swept northward. Only rainfall, the lake, and stretches of unbuilt lots on the North Side finally halted the wave of destruction a full day after it started. The most famous fire in American history claimed about 300 lives, destroyed some 17,450 buildings covering almost 3.5 square miles (9 square km), and caused $200 million in damage. Roughly one-third of the city lay in ruins and an equal proportion of the population—nearly 100,000 people—were homeless.

The prolonged trial and the execution of those who were accused of plotting the blast deeply divided the community and the world. Eight years after that, violence once more erupted as workers at the Pullman Palace Car Company on the South Side walked off the job to protest wage cuts that were not matched by rent reductions at George

Pullman's model town where most were forced to live. Historical George Pullman's model town was located at Dearborn Street East to Clark Street West & from Polk Street South to Harrison Street North

ABRAHAM LINCOLN'S GREATEST CASE:

Abraham Lincoln litigating his Greatest Case:

In the early hours of May 6, 1856, the steamboat Effie Afton barreled into a pillar of the Rock Island Bridge—the first railroad bridge ever to span the Mississippi River. Soon after, the newly constructed vessel, crowded with passengers and livestock, erupted into flames and sank in the river below, taking much of the bridge with it.

As a lawyer and Lincoln scholar Brian McGinty dramatically reveals in Lincoln's Greatest Case, no one was killed, but the question of who was at fault cried out for an answer. Backed by powerful steamboat interests in St. Louis, the owners of the Effie Afton quickly pressed suit, hoping that a victory would not only prevent the construction of any future bridges from crossing the Mississippi but also thwart the burgeoning spread of railroads from Chicago. The fate of the long-dreamed-of transcontinental railroad lurked ominously in the background, for if rails could not cross the Mississippi by bridge, how could they span the continent all the way to the Pacific?

The official title of the case was Hurd et al. v. The Railroad Bridge Company, but it could have been St. Louis v. Chicago, for the transportation future of the whole nation was at stake. Indeed, was it to be dominated by steamboats or by railroads? Conducted at almost the same time as the notorious Dred Scott case, this new trial riveted the nation's attention. Meanwhile, Abraham Lincoln, already well-known as one of the best trial lawyers in Illinois, was summoned to Chicago to join a handful of crack legal practitioners in the defense of the bridge. While there, he successfully helped unite the disparate regions of the country with a truly transcontinental rail system and, in the process, added to the stellar reputation that vaulted him into the White House less than four years later.

Re-creating the Effie Afton case from its unlikely inception to its controversial finale, McGinty brilliantly animates this legal cauldron of the late 1850s, which turned out to be the most consequential trial in Lincoln's nearly quarter century as a lawyer. Along the way, the tall prairie lawyer's consummate legal skills and instincts are also brought to vivid life, as is the history of steamboat traffic on the Mississippi, the progress of railroads west of the Appalachians, and the epochal clashes of railroads and steamboats at the river's edge.

The Abraham Lincoln train

Lincoln's Greatest Case is legal history on a grand scale and an essential first act to a pivotal Lincoln drama we did not know was there.

The railroad, along with the telegraph, the grain elevator, agricultural newspapers, and the trading floor of the Chicago Board of Trade, facilitated the collection of commodities from the farm belt, which was rapidly developing to the west. The city soon became the focal point of a "golden funnel" that collected and processed grain, lumber, and meat and then sent them to markets in the eastern United States and Europe. Trade encouraged ancillary industries, such as the manufacture of steel rails and railroad equipment, shipbuilding, packaging, and printing, as well as the development of hotels and restaurant facilities. However, nothing at that time personified Chicago industry more than meatpacking and the vast Union Stock Yards on the city's Near Southwest Side.

THE PULLMAN CAR COMPANY:

George Pullman

The Pullman Car Company, founded by George Pullman, manufactured railroad cars in the mid-to-late 19th century through the early decades of the 20th century, during the boom of railroads in the United States. Its workers initially lived in a planned worker community (or "company town") named Pullman. Pullman developed the sleeping car, which carried his name into the 1980s. Pullman did not just manufacture the cars: he also operated them on most of the railroads in the United States, paying railroad companies to couple the cars to trains. The labor union associated with the company, the Brotherhood of Sleeping Car Porters, which was founded and organized by A. Philip Randolph, was one of the most powerful African-American political entities of the 20th century. The company also built thousands of streetcars and trolley buses for use in cities.

After spending the night sleeping in his seat on a train trip from Buffalo to Westfield, New York, George Pullman was inspired to design an improved passenger railcar that contained sleeper berths for all its passengers. During the day, the upper berth was folded up somewhat like a modern airliner's overhead luggage compartment. At night, the upper berth folded down and the two facing seats below it folded over to provide a relatively comfortable bunk for the night. Although this was somewhat Spartan accommodation by today's standards, it was a great improvement on the previous layout. Curtains provided privacy, and there were washrooms at each end of the car for men and women.

1893: Workers leave the Pullman Palace Car Works,

Pullman established his company in 1862 and built luxury sleeping cars which featured carpeting, draperies, upholstered chairs, libraries and card tables and an unparalleled level of customer service. Once a household name due to their large market share in the railway industry: the Pullman Company was also known for the bitter Pullman Strike, staged by their workers and union leaders in 1894. During an economic downturn, Pullman reduced hours and wages but not rents, precipitating the strike. Workers joined the American Railway Union, led by Eugene V. Debs.

Built in 1928, the 'Amundsen'

The Amundsen, on different occasions, reportedly carried Presidents Herbert Hoover, Franklin D. Roosevelt, Harry S. Truman and Dwight D. Eisenhower.

After George Pullman's death in 1897, Robert Todd Lincoln, son of Abraham Lincoln, became company president. The company closed its factory in the Pullman neighborhood of Chicago in 1955. Pullman purchased the Standard Steel Car Company in 1930 amid the Great Depression, and the merged entity was known as Pullman-Standard Car Manufacturing Company. The company ceased production after the Amtrak Superliner cars in 1982 and its remaining designs were purchased in 1987 when it was absorbed by Bombardier.

In 1924, Pullman Car & Manufacturing Co. was organized from the previous Pullman manufacturing department, to consolidate the car building interests of The Pullman Co. The parent company, The Pullman Co., was reorganized as Pullman, Inc., on June 21, 1927.

The best years for Pullman were the mid-1920s. In 1925, the fleet grew to 9800 cars. Twenty-eight thousand conductors and twelve thousand porters were employed by the Pullman Co. Pullman built its last standard heavyweight sleeping car in February 1931.

Pullman purchased controlling interest in Standard Steel Car Company in 1929, and on December 26, 1934, Pullman Car & Manufacturing (along with several other Pullman, Inc. subsidiaries), merged with Standard Steel Car Co. (and its subsidiaries) to form the Pullman-Standard Car Manufacturing Company. Pullman-Standard remained in the rail car manufacturing business until 1982. Standard Steel Car Co., had been organized on January 2, 1902, to operate a railroad car manufacturing facility at Butler, Pennsylvania (and, after 1906, a facility at Hammond, Indiana), and was reorganized as a subsidiary of Pullman, Inc., on March 1, 1930.

In 1940, just as orders for lightweight cars were increasing and sleeping car traffic was growing, the United States Department of Justice filed an anti-trust complaint against Pullman Incorporated in the U.S. District Court at Philadelphia (Civil Action No. 994). The government sought to separate the company's sleeping car operations from its manufacturing activities. In 1944, the court concurred, ordering Pullman Incorporated to divest itself of either the Pullman Company (operating) or the Pullman-Standard Car Manufacturing Company (manufacturing). After three years of negotiations, the Pullman Company was sold to a consortium of fifty-seven railroads for around U.S. $40 million.

In 1943, Pullman Standard established a shipbuilding division and dived into wartime small ship design and construction. The yard was on Lake Calumet (Chicago), on the north side of 130th Street, at the most southerly point of the Lake Michigan. Pullman built the boats in 40-ton blocks. The blocks being assembled in a fab shop on 111th Street and moved to the yard on gondola cars. In two years, they built 34 PCEs {Corvette}, which were 180 feet long and weighed 640 tons, and 44 LSMs, which were 203 feet long and weighed 520 tons. The Pullman Standard Car, ranked 56th among United States corporations, in the value of World War II military production contracts.

Pullman-Standard built its last sleeping car in 1956 and its last lightweight passenger cars in 1965, an order of ten coaches for Kansas City Southern. The company continued to market and build cars for commuter rail and subway service and Superliners for Amtrak as late as the late 1970s and early 1980s.

Beginning in 1974, Pullman delivered seven hundred and fifty 75 ft. (23 m) stainless steel subway cars to the New York City Transit Authority. Designated R46 by their procurement contract, these cars, along with the R44 subway car built by St. Louis Car Company, were designed for 70 mph (110 km/h) running in the Second Avenue Subway; after it was deferred in 1975, the Transit Authority assigned the cars to other subway services. Pullman also built subway cars for the Massachusetts Bay Transportation Authority, which assigned them to the Red Line. Pullman-Standard was spun off from Pullman, Inc., as Pullman Technology, Inc., in 1981, and was sold to Bombardier in 1987.

After the 1944 breakup, Pullman, Inc., remained in place as the parent company, with the following subsidiaries: The Pullman Company for passenger car operations (but not passenger car ownership, which was passed to the member railroads), and Pullman-Standard Car Manufacturing Co., for passenger car and freight car manufacturing; along with a large freight car leasing operation still directly under the parent company's control. Pullman, Inc., remained separate until a merger with Wheelabrator, and then headed by CEO Michael D. Dingman, in late 1980, which led to the separation of Pullman interests in early and mid-1981.

Operations of the Pullman Company sleeper cars ceased and all leases were terminated on December 31, 1968. On January 1, 1969, the Pullman Company was dissolved and all assets were liquidated. (The most visible result on many railroads, including Union Pacific, was that the Pullman name was removed from the letter board of all Pullman-owned cars.) An auction of all Pullman remaining assets was held at the Pullman plant in Chicago in early 1970.

The Pullman Town Illinois

George Pullman announced his plan to build a company town along with a factory in late April 1880. Three years prior, the United States underwent the Great Railroad Strike of 1877. The strike forced businessmen, like Pullman, to take the feelings of their employees into consideration. Pullman's objective in building a company town was to attract a superior type of employee and elevate his employees through the exclusion of baneful influences. Pullman also expected the rents on the houses in the company town to make a return of 6 percent on its investment. This was never realized. The rents of the houses in the company town only made a return of 4 ½ percent on investments.

The company built a company town, Pullman, Illinois on 4,000 acres (1,600 ha), 14 mi (23 km) south of Chicago in 1880. Pullman contracted Solon Spenser Beman and Nathan F. Barrett to design and landscape the entire company town respectively. Both Beman and Barrett were experts in their respective fields. Beman interned under the famous architect Richard Upjohn and Barrett landscaped areas in Staten Island and Tuxedo, New York, as well as Long Branch, New Jersey. The community was designed by Solon Spencer Beman and landscaped by Nathan Barrett. According to George Pullman's governing conception, it was not within the city limits of Chicago but in the adjoining town of Hyde Park. On April 24, 1880, groundwork began on the company town. Throughout the construction of the company town Pullman strove to minimize costs and maximize construction efficiency.

Whenever and wherever possible, Pullman adopted techniques of mass production. The first departments and shops constructed were ones such as painting, iron, and woodworking, which could be used in the continuing construction of the company town. By January 1, 1881, the company town was ready for its first resident to move in. A foreman from the Pullman Company's Detroit shop, Lee Benson, moved his wife, child, and sister into the company town. On the exterior, the buildings of the company town were made of red brick with limestone trim. On the interior, the buildings had high ceilings and large windows. The walls of the interior of the buildings were also purposefully painted in light colors to provide the semblance of a cheerful environment. By the time construction was finished on the company town it was composed of a library, theater, hotel, church, market, sewage farm, park, and residential buildings. The bar in the Florence Hotel was the only place where alcohol could be served and consumed in the company town. In the residential section of the town, there was 150 acres dedicated to tenements, flats and single-family homes that rented from $0.50 to $0.75 a month. The residences featured modern conveniences such as gas, water, indoor sewage plumbing and regular garbage removal. By 1884, the town included more than 1,400 tenements and flats, and by July of the following year, its population was over 8,600.

The town agent was in charge of the company town. The town agent oversaw departments including street and building maintenance, gas and water works, and fire protection. The town agent also oversaw businesses including the hotel, sewage farm, as well as the nursery and greenhouse. Under the town agent there were nine department heads and approximately 300 men under them. All company town officials were selected by Pullman. There were no elections in the company town besides elections for the school board.

After its completion, the company town attracted national attention. Many critics praised Pullman's conception and planning of the company town. One newspaper article titled "The Arcadian City: Pullman, the Ideal City of the World" praised the company town as "the youngest and most perfect city in the world, Pullman; beautiful in every belonging." In February 1885, Richard T. Ely published his article "Pullman: A Social Study" in Harper's Monthly. While the article praised the company town for creating an elevated environment for its workers, the article criticized the all-encompassing influence of the company. The article came to the conclusion that "Pullman is un-American" and "it is benevolent, well-wishing feudalism."

During the Panic of 1893, Pullman closed his manufacturing plant in Detroit in order to move all manufacturing to the company town. Wages were reduced, and employees were laid off, but the costs of utilities remained unchanged. On May 11, 1894, the employees of the Pullman Co. walked off the job and initiated the Pullman Strike. The Pullman Co. had reduced wages, but not the rents on housing. 30 people were killed as a result of the strikes and sabotage. After the strike, the company town was not the same. The strike resulted in the loss of pride for the company town.

In February 1904, the Pullman Company was mandated to sell the company town by court order. Despite this, the Pullman Company did not sell the company town until 1907. Today, Pullman is a Chicago neighborhood, and a historical landmark district on the state, National Historic Landmark and National Register of Historic Places lists.

In 2014, the National Park Service was considering creation of a new urban national park in Pullman.

Other Pullman sites

The Pullman Company operated several facilities in other areas of the U.S. One of these was the Pullman Shops in Richmond, California which was linked to the mainline tracks of both the Southern Pacific and the Santa Fe, servicing their passenger equipment from throughout the Western U.S. The main building of the Richmond

Pullman Shops still exists, as does the thoroughfare it's located on: Pullman Avenue.

THE PULLMAN PORTERS

A Pullman Porter assisting a passenger with her luggage.

Prior to the 1860s, the concept of sleeping cars on railroads had not been widely developed. George Pullman pioneered sleeping accommodations on trains, and by the late 1860s, he was hiring only

African-Americans to serve as porters. After the Civil War ended in 1865 Pullman knew that there was a large pool of former slaves who would be looking for work; he also had a very clear racial conception. He was aware that most Americans, unlike the wealthy, didn't have personal servants in their homes. Pullman also knew the wealthy were accustomed to being served by a liveried waiter or butler, but to staff the Pullman cars with "properly humble" workers in uniform was something the American middle class had never experienced. Hence, part of the appeal of traveling on sleeping cars was, in a sense, to have an upper class experience. From the very start, porters were featured in Pullman's ads promoting his new sleeper service. Initially, they were one of the features that most clearly distinguished his carriages from those of competitors, but eventually nearly all would follow his lead, hiring African-Americans as porters, cooks, waiters and Red Caps (railway station porters).

While the pay was very low by the standards of the day, in an era of significant racial prejudice, being a Pullman porter was one of the best jobs available for African-American men. Thus, for black men, while this was an opportunity, at the same time it was also an experience of being stereotyped as the servant class and having to take a lot of abuse. Many passengers called every porter "George", as if he was George Pullman's "boy" (servant), a practice that was born in the South where slaves were named after their slave masters. The only ones who protested were other men named George, who founded the Society for the Prevention of Calling Sleeping Car Porters George, or SPCSCPG, which eventually claimed 31,000 members. Although the SPCSCPG was more interested in defending the dignity of its white members than in achieving any measure of racial justice, it nevertheless had some effects for all porters. In 1926, the SPCSCPG persuaded the Pullman Company to install small racks in each car, displaying a card with the given name of the porter on duty.

Of the 12,000 porters and waiters then working for Pullman, only 362 turned out to be named George. Stanley G. Grizzle, a former Canadian porter, titled his autobiography, *My Name's Not George: The Story of the Brotherhood of Sleeping Car Porters.* Porters were not paid a livable wage and needed to rely on tips to earn enough to make a living. Walter Biggs, son of a Pullman porter, spoke of memories of being a Pullman porter as told to him by his father:

"One of the most remarkable stories I liked hearing about was how when Jackie Gleason would ride ... all the porters wanted to be on that run. The reason why? Not only because he gave every porter $100.00, but it was just the fun, the excitement, the respect that he gave the porters. Instead of their names being George, he called everybody by their first name. He always had like a piano in the car and they sang and danced and had a great time. He was just a fun person to be around."

The number of porters employed by railroads declined as sleeping car service dwindled in the 1960s and as railroad lines went bankrupt due to competition from the airlines. By 1969, the ranks of the Pullman sleeping car porters had declined to 325 men with an average age of 63.

A Pullman Porter serving passengers in the diner car

A porter was expected to greet passengers, carry baggage, make up the sleeping berths, serve food and drinks, shine shoes, and keep the cars tidy. He needed to be available night and day to wait on the passengers. He was expected to always smile; thus, the porters often called the job, ironically, "miles of smiles".

According to historian Greg LeRoy, "A Pullman Porter was really kind of a glorified hotel maid and bellhop in what Pullman called a hotel on wheels. The Pullman Company just thought of the porters as a piece of equipment, just like another button on a panel - the same as a light switch or a fan switch."

Porters worked 400 hours a month or 11,000 miles, sometimes as much as 20 hours at a stretch. They were expected to arrive at work several hours early to prepare their car, on their own time; they were charged whenever their passengers stole a towel or a water pitcher. On overnight trips, they were allocated only three to four hours of sleep—and that was deducted from their pay.

THE FIRST AFRICAN AMERICAN LABOR UNION

Asa Philip Randolph

THE BROTHERHOOD OF SLEEPING CAR PORTERS (BSCP)

Asa Philip Randolph (April 15, 1889 – May 16, 1979) was a leader in the Civil Rights Movement, the American labor movement, and socialist political parties.

At one time, Pullman was the largest employer of African Americans in the United States. The Pullman Company was noted for its porters; they hired black men almost exclusively for the porter positions. (Men of Filipino descent were primarily hired for club car service positions.) Although a porter's occupation was menial in some respects, it offered better pay and security than most jobs open to African Americans at the time, as well as an opportunity to travel the country. Many credit the Pullman Porters as significantly contributing to the development of America's black middle class. In 1925, Pullman porters became unionized as the Brotherhood of Sleeping Car Porters (BSCP), founded by A. Philip Randolph.

Chicago 1933: mass meeting, Brotherhood of Sleeping Car Porters

He organized and led the Brotherhood of Sleeping Car Porters, the first predominantly African-American labor union. In the early Civil Rights Movement, during the early years of The Labor Movement, Randolph was a voice that would not be silenced. His continuous agitation with the support of fellow labor rights activists against unfair labor practices in relation to people of color eventually led President Franklin D. Roosevelt to issue Executive Order 8802 in 1941, banning discrimination in the defense industries during World War II. The group then successfully pressured President Harry S. Truman to issue Executive Order 9981 in 1948, ending segregation in the armed services.

In 1963, Randolph was the head of the March on Washington, which was organized by Bayard Rustin, at which Reverend Martin Luther King, Jr. delivered his "I Have A Dream" speech. Randolph inspired the "Freedom Budget", sometimes called the "Randolph Freedom budget", which aimed to deal with the economic problems facing the black community; it was published by the Randolph Institute in January 1967 as "A Freedom Budget for All Americans".

Randolph was born April 15, 1889, in Crescent City, Florida, the second son of the Rev. James William Randolph, a tailor and minister in an African Methodist Episcopal Church, and Elizabeth Robinson Randolph, a skilled seamstress. In 1891, the family moved to Jacksonville, Florida, which had a thriving, well-established African-American community.

From his father, Randolph learned that color was less important than a person's character and conduct. From his mother, he learned the importance of education and of defending oneself physically against those who would seek to hurt one or one's family, if necessary. Randolph remembered vividly the night his mother sat in the front room of their house with a loaded shotgun across her lap, while his father tucked a pistol under his coat and went off to prevent a mob from lynching a man at the local county jail.

Asa and his brother, James, were superior students. They attended the Cookman Institute in East Jacksonville, the only academic high school in Florida for African Americans. Asa excelled in literature, drama, and public speaking; he also starred on the school's baseball team, sang solos with the school choir, and was valedictorian of the 1907 graduating class.

After graduation, Randolph worked odd jobs and devoted his time to singing, acting, and reading. Reading W. E. B. Du Bois' *The Souls of Black Folk* convinced him that the fight for social equality was most important. Barred by discrimination from all but manual jobs in the South, Randolph moved to New York City in 1911, where he worked at odd jobs and took social sciences courses at City College.

In 1913 Randolph courted and married Mrs. Lucille Campbell Green, a **once again** Howard University graduate, and entrepreneur who shared his socialist politics. She earned enough money to support them both. The couple had no children.

Shortly after Randolph's marriage, he helped organize the Shakespearean Society in Harlem. With them he played the roles of Hamlet, Othello, and Romeo, among others. Randolph aimed to become an actor, but gave up after failing winning his parents' approval.

In New York, Randolph became familiar with socialism and the ideologies espoused by the Industrial Workers of the World. He met Columbia University Law student Chandler Owen, and the two developed a synthesis of Marxist economics and the sociological ideas of Lester Frank Ward, arguing that people could only be free if not subject to economic deprivation. At this point, Randolph developed what would become his distinctive form of civil rights activism, which emphasized the importance of collective action as a way for black people to gain legal and economic equality. To this end, he and Owen opened an employment office in Harlem to provide job training for southern migrants and encouraged them to join trade unions.

Like others in the labor movement, Randolph favored immigration restriction. He opposed African Americans' having to compete with people willing to work for low wages. Unlike other immigration restrictionists, however, he rejected the notions of racial hierarchy that became popular in the 1920s.

In 1917, Randolph and Chandler Owen founded the *Messenger* with the help of the Socialist Party of America. It was a radical monthly magazine, which campaigned against lynching, opposed U.S. participation in World War I, urged African Americans to resist being drafted, to fight for an integrated society, and urged them to join radical unions. The Department of Justice called the *Messenger* "the most able and the most dangerous of all the Negro publications." When the *Messenger* began publishing the work of black poets and authors, a critic called it "one of the most brilliantly edited magazines in the history of Negro journalism."

Soon thereafter, however, the editorial staff of the *Messenger* became divided by three issues – the growing rift between West Indian and African Americans, support for the Bolshevik revolution, and support for Marcus Garvey's Back-to-Africa movement. In 1919, most West Indian radicals joined the new Communist Party, while African-American leftists – Randolph included – mostly supported the Socialist Party. The infighting left the *Messenger* short of financial support, and it went into decline.

Randolph ran on the Socialist Party ticket for New York State Comptroller in 1920, and for Secretary of State of New York in 1922, unsuccessfully.

Union organizer: Randolph's first experience with labor organization came in 1917, when he organized a union of elevator operators in New York City.

In 1919 he became president of the National Brotherhood of Workers of America, a union which organized amongst African-American shipyard and dock workers in the Tidewater region of Virginia. The union dissolved in 1921, under pressure from the American Federation of Labor.

His greatest success came with the Brotherhood of Sleeping Car Porters, who elected him President in 1925. This was the first serious effort to form a labor institution for employees of the Pullman Company, which was a major employer of African Americans. The railroads had expanded dramatically in the early 20th century, and the jobs offered relatively good employment at a time of widespread racial discrimination.

Because porters were not unionized, however, most suffered poor working conditions and were underpaid.

Under Randolph's direction, the BSCP managed to enroll 51 percent of porters within a year, to which Pullman responded with violence and firings. In 1928, after failing to win mediation under the Watson-Parker Railway Labor Act, Randolph planned a strike. This was postponed after rumors circulated that Pullman had 5,000 replacement workers ready to take the place of BSCP members. As a result of its perceived ineffectiveness membership of the union declined; by 1933 it had only 658 members and electricity and telephone service at headquarters had been disconnected because of nonpayment of bills.

Fortunes of the BSCP changed with the election of President Franklin D. Roosevelt in 1932. With amendments to the Railway Labor Act in 1934, porters were granted rights under federal law. Membership in the Brotherhood jumped to more than 7,000. After years of bitter struggle, the Pullman Company finally began to negotiate with the Brotherhood in 1935, and agreed to a contract with them in 1937. Employees gained $2,000,000 in pay increases, a shorter workweek, and overtime pay. Randolph maintained the Brotherhood's affiliation with the American Federation of Labor through the 1955 AFL-CIO merger.

ized by AI, not *Chicago Rebuilt Quickly*

Asa Philip, Randolph in 1942. Civil Rights Leader

Through his success with the BSCP, Randolph emerged as one of the most visible spokespeople for African-American civil rights. In 1941, he, Bayard Rustin, and A. J. Muste proposed a march on Washington to protest racial discrimination in war industries, an end to segregation, access to defense employment, the proposal of an anti-lynching law and of the desegregation of the American Armed forces.

Randolph's belief in the power of peaceful direct action was inspired partly by Mahatma Gandhi's success in using such tactics against British occupation in India. Randolph threatened to have 50,000 blacks march on the city; it was cancelled after President of the United States Franklin D. Roosevelt issued Executive Order 8802, or the Fair Employment Act. Some activists, including Bayard Rustin, felt betrayed because Roosevelt's order applied only to banning discrimination within war industries and not the armed forces. Nonetheless, the Fair Employment Act is generally considered an important early civil rights victory.

And the movement continued to gain momentum. In 1942, an estimated 18,000 blacks gathered at Madison Square Garden to hear Randolph kick off a campaign against discrimination in the military, in war industries, in government agencies, and in labor unions. Following passage of the Act, during the Philadelphia transit strike of 1944, the government backed African-American workers' striking to gain positions formerly limited to white employees.

Buoyed by these successes, Randolph and other activists continued to press for the rights of African Americans. In 1947, Randolph, along with colleague Grant Reynolds, renewed efforts to end discrimination in the armed services, forming the Committee Against Jim Crow in Military Service, later renamed the League for Non-Violent Civil disobedience. When President Truman asked Congress for a peacetime draft law, Randolph urged young black men to refuse to register. Since Truman was vulnerable to defeat in 1948 and needed the support of the growing black population in northern states, he eventually capitulated. On July 26, 1948, President Harry S. Truman abolished racial segregation in the armed forces through Executive Order 9981.

In 1950, along with Roy Wilkins, Executive Secretary of the NAACP, and, Arnold Aronson, a leader of the National Jewish Community Relations Advisory Council, Randolph founded the Leadership Conference on Civil Rights (LCCR). LCCR has been a major civil rights coalition. It coordinated a national legislative campaign on behalf of every major civil rights law since 1957.

Civil Rights March on Washington, D.C. (Leaders of the march)

Randolph and Rustin also formed an important alliance with Martin Luther King, Jr. In 1957, when schools in the south resisted school integration following *Brown v. Board of Education*, Randolph organized the Prayer Pilgrimage for Freedom with Martin Luther King, Jr. In 1958 and 1959, Randolph organized Youth Marches for Integrated Schools in Washington, DC. At the same time, he arranged for Rustin to teach Dr. King how to organize peaceful demonstrations in Alabama and to form alliances with progressive whites. The protests directed by James Bevel in cities such as Birmingham and Montgomery provoked a violent backlash by police and the local Ku Klux Klan throughout the summer of 1963, which was captured on television and broadcast throughout the nation and the world. Rustin later remarked that Birmingham "was one of television's finest hours. Evening after evening, television brought into the living-rooms of America the violence, brutality, stupidity, and ugliness of {police commissioner} Eugene "Bull" Connor's effort to maintain racial segregation." Partly as a result of the violent spectacle in Birmingham, which was becoming an international embarrassment, the Kennedy administration drafted civil rights legislation aimed at ending Jim Crow once and for all.

Randolph finally realized his vision for a March on Washington for Jobs and Freedom on August 28, 1963, which attracted between 200,000–300,000 attendees to the Nation's capital. The rally is often remembered as the high-point of the Civil Rights Movement, and it did help keep the issue in the public consciousness. However, when President Kennedy was assassinated three months later, Civil Rights legislation was stalled in the Senate. It was not until the following year, under President Lyndon B. Johnson, that the Civil Rights Act was finally passed. In 1965, the Voting Rights Act was passed. Although King and Bevel rightly deserve great credit for these legislative victories, the importance of Randolph's contributions to the Civil Rights Movement is large.

Asa Philip Randolph: receiving the Presidential Medal of Freedom, in 1964 from President Lyndon B. Johnson.

Randolph's legacy had a significant impact on the Civil Rights Movement from the 1930s onward. The Montgomery Bus Boycott in Alabama was directed by E.D. Nixon, who had been a member of the BSCP and was influenced by Randolph's methods of nonviolent confrontation Nationwide, the Civil Rights Movement in the 1950s and 1960s used tactics pioneered by Randolph, such as encouraging African Americans to vote as a bloc, mass voter registration, and training activists for nonviolent direct action.

A. Philip Randolph Pullman Porter Museum in Chicago

In 1995, Lyn Hughes founded the A. Philip Randolph Pullman Porter Museum to celebrate both the life of A. Philip Randolph and the role of the Brotherhood of Sleeping Car Porters and other African Americans in the U.S. labor movement. Located on the South Side, Chicago and housed in one of the original row houses built by George Pullman to house workers, it is part of the U.S. Department of the Interior's Pullman National Historic Landmark District. The museum houses a collection of artifacts and documents related to the Brotherhood of Sleeping Car Porters. Additionally, in 2001, the museum began compiling a national registry of black railroad employees who worked for the railroad from the late 1800s to 1969.

In August 2013, the museum celebrated the 50 year anniversary of the historic March on Washington for Jobs and Freedom (also known as "The Great March on Washington"), one of the largest political rallies for human rights in United States history. Interviewed in a neighborhood newspaper, Hughes suggested that some people in the Chicago area may prefer to celebrate the anniversary of the march in their own community rather than travel to Washington. She added that many people are unaware that Asa Philip Randolph was the initial activist who inspired the March on Washington Movement. Scheduled activities included speakers and screenings of films related to Black labor history. Two organizers said that two former Pullman porters, Milton Jones (age 98) and Benjamin Gaines (age 90), were expected to attend.

CHAPTER SIX

Chicago: The Home of America's First World Fair: Columbian Exposition

1893 WORLD'S COLUMBIAN EXPOSITION IN CHICAGO:

Bird's-eye view of the 1893 World's Columbian Exposition, Chicago

In 1890 Chicago's population pushed past the one million mark. That year the U.S. Congress granted the city the right to host the World's Columbian Exposition, honoring the 400th anniversary of Christopher Columbus's 1492 arrival in the New World. Delays pushed the opening into 1893. Set in Jackson Park, some 8 miles (13 km) south of downtown along the lakeshore, the event was a spectacular extravaganza that assembled more than a million artifacts representing the world's industrial and cultural progress.

Besides enlightening exhibits, performances, and off-Besides offsite intellectual conferences, the fair offered the Midway Plaisance, a

101

collection of ersatz travel experiences, bazaars, eateries, and rides, the most famous of which was the 255-foot (78-metre) Ferris wheel. The event attracted some 25.8 million visitors during its six-month run.

The World's Columbian Exposition (the official shortened name for the World's Fair: Columbian Exposition, also known as The Chicago World's Fair and Chicago Columbian Exposition) was a world's fair held in Chicago in 1893 to celebrate the 400th anniversary of Christopher Columbus's arrival in the New World in 1492. The centerpiece of the Fair, the large water pool, represented the long voyage Columbus took to the New World. Chicago bested New York City; Washington, D.C.; and St. Louis for the honor of hosting the fair. The Exposition was an influential social and cultural event and had a profound effect on architecture, sanitation, the arts, Chicago's self-image, and American industrial optimism.

The layout of the Chicago Columbian Exposition was, in large part, designed by John Wellborn Root, Daniel Burnham, Frederick Law Olmsted and Charles B. Atwood. It was the prototype of what Burnham and his colleagues thought a city should be. It was designed to follow Beaux Arts principles of design, namely French neoclassical architecture principles based on symmetry, balance, and splendor. The color of the material generally used to cover the buildings' facades gave the fairgrounds its nickname, the White City. Many prominent architects designed its 14 "great buildings". Artists and musicians were featured in exhibits and many also made depictions and works of art inspired by the exposition.

The exposition covered more than 600 acres (2.4 km2), featuring nearly 200 new (but purposely temporary) buildings of predominantly neoclassical architecture, canals and lagoons, and people and cultures from 46 countries. More than 27 million people attended the exposition during its six-month run. Its scale and grandeur far exceeded the other world's fairs, and it became a symbol of the emerging American Exceptionalism, much in the same way that Exhibition the ranks of the Pullman sleeping car porters had declined to 325 men with an average age of 63 Victorian-era United Kingdom.

Dedication ceremonies for the fair were held on October 21, 1892, but the fairgrounds were not actually opened to the public until May 1, 1893. The fair continued until October 30, 1893. In addition to recognizing the 400th anniversary of the discovery of the New World by Europeans, the fair also served to show the world that Chicago had risen from the ashes of the Great Chicago Fire, which had destroyed much of the city in 1871.

On October 9, 1893, the day designated as Chicago Day, the fair set a world record for outdoor event attendance, drawing 751,026 people. The debt for the fair was soon paid off with a check for $1.5 million (equivalent to $39,983,333 in 2016). Chicago has commemorated the fair with one of the stars on its municipal flag.

RACE RELATIONS AT THE WORLD'S COLUMBIAN EXPOSITION

"Darkies Day at the Fair": Opper Frederick Burr, c. Library of Congress, Illustration 1893

As tensions between the White City and the Midway Plaisance were made clear, the World's Columbian Exposition reflected broader struggles in American society over the future course of American society and culture. Concerns about the power of the exposition to shape the future were also apparent in the struggles fought by African Americans and women over their representation at the fair.

The whiteness of the White City became increasingly offensive to African Americans as plans for the fair unfolded. In response to the determination of African Americans to show the world their accomplishments since emancipation, exposition directors insisted that African American proposals for exhibits be approved by all-white state committees. Most such requests were rejected and out of hand.

Nancy Green, the original "Aunt Jemima" posing with the product

Eloise Lynton in her Blog, Worlds Columbian Exposition: Chicago 1893 wrote"

The most enduring black representation at the fair came in the form of a degrading advertising campaign by the now famous company, Aunt Jemima. The company was the first to invent the concept of ready-made pancake mix and decided that they wanted a black female to unveil and promote their concept to the world.

They chose, as their representative, Nancy Green, a former Kentucky slave renowned for her friendly attitude and fantastic cooking. At the fair, Green occupied a booth in which she cooked and served pancakes for hundreds of guests each day. Fairgoers loved Green, and such a massive crowd determined that the company had to call for crowd control. Green walked away from the fair with a lifetime contract and having sold 50,000 orders of pancake mix. In the ad campaign,

Green wears a headscarf and friendly smile as she serves up a pancake. That the most accepted representation of African Americans was one which depicted a black exclusively in the realm of the kitchen, literally serving whites, speaks to the blatant presence of racism

In response to requests from African Americans that they receive a role in planning the fair, exposition authorities appointed a St. Louis school principal to the position of alternates on the national commission. Enraged by the politics of exclusion and tokenism, some African Americans, led by Ida B. Wells, urged African Americans to boycott the fair. Frederick Douglass, who served as Haiti's representative at the exposition, disagreed and urged African Americans to participate as fully as possible.

When exposition managers set aside a special "colored American" day (white ethnic groups had their own days as well), Douglass seized the occasion to insist that Americans live up to the Constitution and their promises of social justice for former slaves. But the fair, through its racist policies, had already helped pave the way for national acceptance of the separate-but-equal doctrine that would become the law of the land in 1896.

Frederick Douglass

The fair opened in May and ran through October 30, 1893. Forty-six nations participated in the fair (it was the first world's fair to have national pavilions), constructing exhibits and pavilions and naming national "delegates" (for example, Haiti selected Frederick Douglass to be its delegate). The Exposition drew nearly 26 million visitors. The fair was originally meant to be closed on Sundays, but the Chicago Woman's Club petitioned that it stayed open. The club felt that if the exposition was closed on Sunday, it would restrict those who could not take off from work during the work-week from seeing it.

The exposition was located in Jackson Park and on the Midway Plaisance on 630 acres (2.5 km^2); in the neighborhoods of South Shore, Jackson Park, Highlands, Hyde Park and Woodlawn. Charles H. Wacker was the Director of the Fair. The layout of the fairgrounds was created by Frederick Law Olmsted, and the Beaux-Arts architecture of the buildings was under the direction of Daniel Burnham, Director of Works for the fair. Renowned local architect Henry Ives Cobb designed several buildings for the exposition. The Director of the American Academy in Rome, Francis Davis Millet, directed the painted mural decorations. Indeed, it was a coming-of-age for the arts and architecture of the "American Renaissance", and it showcased the burgeoning neoclassical and painted white, therefore it was then referred to as "White City.

The original "Ferris Wheel"; built by George Washington Gale Ferris Jr.

Beaux-The World's Columbian Exposition was the first world's fair with an area for amusements, that was strictly separated from the exhibition halls. This area, developed by a young music promoter, Sol Bloom, concentrated on Midway Plaisance and introduced the term "midway" It included carnival rides, among them the original Ferris Wheel, built by George Washington Gale Ferris Jr.. This wheel was 264 feet (80 m) high and had 36 cars, each of which could accommodate 40 people. The importance of the Columbian Exposition is highlighted by the use of *rueda de Chicago* ("Chicago wheel") in many Latin American countries such as Costa Rica and Chile in reference to theFerris wheel. One attendee, George C. Tilyou, later credited the sights he saw on the Chicago midway for inspiring him to create America's first major amusement park; Steeplechase Park in Coney Island, New York.

The fair included life-size reproductions of Christopher Columbus' three ships, the *Niña* (real name *Santa Clara*), the*Pinta*, and*Santa*

Maria. These were intended to celebrate the 400th anniversary of Columbus' discovery of the Americas. The ships, a joint project of the governments of Spain and the United States, were constructed in Spain and then sailed to America for the exposition. The ships were a very popular exhibit.[

Eadweard Muybridge, gave a series of lectures on the Science of Animal Locomotion in the "Zoopraxographical Hall", built specially for that purpose on Midway Plaisance. He used his zoopraxiscope to show his moving pictures to a paying public. The hall was the first commercial movie theater.

The "Street in Cairo" included the popular dancer known asLittle Egypt. She introduced America to the suggestive version of the belly dance known as the "hootchy-kootchy", to a tune said to have been improvised by Sol Bloom (and now more commonly associated with snake charmers) which he had composed when his dancers had no music to dance to. Bloom did not copyright the song, putting it immediately in the public domain.

Also included was the first moving walkway or travelator. It had two different divisions: one where passengers were seated, and one where riders could stand or walk. It ran in a loop down the length of a lakefront pier to a casino.

The electrotachyscope of Ottomar Anschütz was demonstrated, which used a Geissler tube to project the illusion of moving images. Louis Comfort Tiffany, made his reputation with a stunning chapel designed and built for the Exposition. This chapel has been carefully reconstructed and restored. It can be seen in at the Charles Hosmer Morse Museum of American Art.

Among the other attractions at the fair, several products that are well known today were introduced. These products included Juicy Fruit Gum, Cream of Wheat, and Pabst Blue Ribbon beer, among many other arts and styles.

THE CHICAGO HISTORICAL SOCIETY MUSEUM

1896–1932 home of the Chicago Historical Society.

Chicago History Museum (formerly known as the Chicago Historical Society) was founded in 1856 to study and interpret Chicago's history. It is located in Lincoln Park at 1601 North Clark Street at the intersection of North Avenue in the Old Town Triangle neighborhood. It was renamed the Chicago History Museum in September 2006.

The building was destroyed in the Great Chicago Fire in 1871, but like the city, the museum rose from the ashes. Among its many documents, which were lost in the fire, was a copy of the Emancipation Proclamation, hand-written by Abraham Lincoln. After the fire, the Society began collecting new materials, which were stored in a building owned by J. Young Scammon, a prominent lawyer and member of the society. However, the building and new collection were again destroyed by fire in 1874. The Chicago Historical Society built a fireproof building on the site of its pre-1871 building at 632 North Dearborn Street. The replacement building opened in 1896 and, after housing the collection for thirty-six years, was used for several purposes and remained vacant for periods until being transformed into a nightclub in 1985. This impressively massive Richardsonian Romanesque building remained a nightclub for years until closing in 2014, and was added to the National Register of Historic Places in 1978.

In 1920, the Society purchased the large history collection of Charles F. Gunther with the intention of changing its focus from only a research institution into a public museum. Many of the items in Gunther's collection, in addition to Chicago, were related to Abraham Lincoln and the American Civil War. These include Lincoln's deathbed and several furniture pieces from the room, where he died in Petersen House and clothing that he and wife Mary Todd Lincoln allegedly wore the evening of his assassination.

East facade of current museum (built 1932)

After 36 years in the Henry Ives Cobb structure on North Dearborn Street, the museum and library moved to the current structure in Lincoln Park. The current home of the museum was designed by Graham, Anderson, Probst & White; and constructed in 1932 by the WPA, with the aim of creating an expanded public museum.

The 1932 Federal-style structure has been expanded twice. The first addition, clad in limestone, opened in 1972 and was designed by Alfred Shaw and Associates. The second addition, designed by Holabird and Root, was made in 1988 and included refacing the earlier expansion in red brick to give a unified look to all three portions of the building. Both expansions occurred on the west side of the 1932 structure, leaving intact its original porticoes entrance facing Lincoln Park.

Clark Street facade of the Chicago History Museum

The main entrance and reception hall, however, was moved to the new western addition facing Clark Street. The 1988 extension, in addition to expanded exhibition galleries, also contains the museum's store and public cafe.

The museum explores both Chicago and American history. Exhibitions draw primarily on the museum's own collection, which numbers approximately 22 million holdings. *Chicago: Crossroads of America* is a 16,000-square-foot space that explores the city's development and its relationship to, and influence on American history. Nearly 600 objects document the people and events of the past 200 years. *Facing Freedom* focuses on eight American conflicts over freedom from the 1850s to the 1970s. The Abraham Lincoln alcoves highlight the sixteenth president's election, his leadership during the Civil War, and his assassination. The adjoining Portrait Gallery features an installation on Chicago during the time of Lincoln. The *Sensing Chicago* exhibition invites children to use their senses to discover the past. The Lobby displays museum treasures, including a 1978 Chevrolet Monte Carlo lowrider. The newly restored dioramas are housed in the Taiwan Foundation Diorama Hall. The Chicago dioramas feature Chicago's rise from a desolate frontier outpost to the bustling city that hosted the World's Columbian Exposition of 1893. The Chicago Room, which overlooks the plaza in Lincoln Park behind the museum building, displays a collection of stained glass.

South Side Elevated Railroad car
The first locomotive to operate in Chicago

On January 19, 2006, the first passenger car to operate on the Chicago 'L' system in 1893 was transported to its new display location at the Chicago History Museum. Passengers could ride the 1893 'L' from the Loop to Hyde Park station for 5 cents to attend the World's Columbian Exposition upon the line's opening. The vehicle, known as L Car #1, was cosmetically restored to its 1893 appearance before being transported to the museum where it was lifted into an opening created through a wall on the museum's second floor. The car's interior features include mahogany and rattan seats and etched glass windows. The L car joins the *Pioneer*, the first locomotive to operate in Chicago; a redesigned exhibition space to showcase the car and locomotive opened on September 30, 2006, as part of a larger remodeling project.

The Museum houses Chicago's most important collection of materials related to local history. The extensive research library includes books and other published materials, manuscripts, paintings, sculptures, and photos. It is open to the public, including students working on school projects. The costume collection numbers more than 50,000 pieces and dates from the 18th century to the present. It contains numerous couture pieces, items created by well-known Chicago manufacturers and designers, and garments worn by notable residents.

The Museum offers a variety of programs, publications, and online resources related to Chicago and American history. This includes print and online editions of its collaborative effort the *Encyclopedia of Chicago*. The Museum's Chicago Fire mobile app has content equivalent to a 400-page book with more than 350 illustrations, drawn from the museum's collection. The app also offers 10 distinct Chicago areas and 54 fire-related landmarks. The app uses GPS guidance that helps the user view photos of nearby sites from the era of the Great Chicago Fire.

The Museum also publishes *Chicago History* magazine. Written by historians and heavily illustrated, this publication focuses on Chicago's complex past and the people who have shaped it. Additionally, more than 50,000 images from its collection have been digitized as part of Explore Chicago Collections.

Every year, the Chicago History Museum recognizes important Chicagoans and Chicago organizations with its Making History Awards.

Since 2003: on the City's birthday, March 4, each year the Chicago History Museum has co-partnered with the Chicago Mayor's Office of Special Events and Chicago Public /Archdiocese Schools; to celebrate the Chicago DuSable Commemorate Founder Day.

In 2010 the museum was inducted into the Chicago Gay and Lesbian Hall of Fame.

Alderman Edward Burke (in the green tie, of course) helps cut the cake at last year's Chicago birthday celebration at the History Museum, joined by Peggy Montes, president of the Bronzeville Children's Museum, Gary Johnson, president of the Chicago History Museum, Marc Schulman, president of Eli's Cheesecake, James Alexander, Chicago History Museum board chairman, Vincent Romero, interim director of the American Indian Center of Chicago, and Friends of DuSable 2016 Essay Contest students.

Chicago History Museum

OLD TOWN — Chicago, city of the big shoulders — and of the big birthday bashes.

The Chicago History Museum, 1601 N. Clark St., celebrates the city's 180th birthday Saturday, with Carl Sandburg's poem "Chicago" on prominent display — and with free admission for Illinois residents. Chicago was incorporated as a city by the State of Illinois on March 4, 1837.

The museum is open 9:30 a.m.-4:30 p.m. Saturday, with the birthday celebration running from 10 a.m.-2 p.m. The official program starts at 11 a.m. with guest speakers. One student will read an award-winning essay on the subject of pioneer Jean Baptiste Pointe DuSable, considered the first permanent resident of what would become Chicago when he established a trading post here in 1779.

CHICAGO SINCE 1900 "NO LITTLE PLANS"

1900:Chicago Loop Busy Trafic

Chicago since 1900 – "No little plans": The fair opened during a financial panic and closed during a deep depression, but the city's recovery four years later was dramatic. Chicago's population surged past two million in 1907 and three million in 1923. The city eagerly adopted every transportation innovation: streetcars moved first by horses, then by means of underground cables, and finally by electricity were supplemented in the 1890s by the first elevated rail lines. However, every transportation innovation seemed to produce only more congestion. The railroads also left their physical mark on the city. Concerns over grade-crossing safety forced the rail lines to construct tall embankments for their tracks, which, in turn, walled off neighborhoods. The smoke and noise from thousands of freight trains and hundreds of passenger-train arrivals and departures each day saturated the city in gloomy soot and jangled its nerves.

Chicago was well on its way to choking on its growth when architects Dani H. Burnham and Edward P. Bennett unveiled their 1909 *Plan of Chicago*. Commissioned by two private commercial organizations, the plan provided a rational transportation-based blueprint for urban growth, notably in the central area. It promised to replace ugliness and congestion with extraordinary beauty and efficiency. Although plans for relocating railroads were ignored, Chicago's city government eagerly adopted ideas for plazas, major thoroughfares that bridged railway tracks, a double-deck street along the river downtown, monumental bridge structures, and the preservation of the lakefront for park purposes—inspired by Burnham's now-famous credo "Make no little plans." The document was never officially adopted by the city council, but it became a shopping list for projects started during the 1920s, including construction of the Michigan Avenue Bridge and the Outer Drive. In 1916 the city completed the 1.5-mile- (2.4-km-) long Municipal (later Navy) Pier as a combination shipping warehouse and public recreation retreat. But the city, under the leadership of Mayor William Hale ("Big Bill") Thompson, went into debt far beyond its ability to repay, and the double-deck Wacker Drive and Outer Drive Bridge improvements remained unfinished at the onset of the Great Depression.

It is not widely known that in the early 1900s, the heyday of luxury travel, the more luxurious trains also had African-American Pullman maids to care for women's needs, especially women with children. They were expected to assist ladies with their bath, be able to give manicures and dress hair, and assist with children. "It didn't pay a livable wage, but they made a living with the tips that they got, because the salary was nothing," says Lyn Hughes, founder of the A. Philip Randolph Pullman Porter Museum. The porters were expected to pay for their own meals and uniforms and the company required them to pay for the shoe polish used to shine passengers' shoes daily. There was little job security, and the Pullman Company inspectors were known for suspending porters for trivial reasons.

CHAPTER SEVEN

African American Entrepreneurs In Chicago

Robert S. Abbott, Editor of The Chicago Defender

THE CHICAGO DEFENDER NEWSPAPER

Copyright, 1927, The Associated Publishers, Inc

May 5, 1905: the Chicago Defender, which was founded by Robert S. Abbott featured and ran a successful campaign in support of "The Great Migration" movement.

The Chicago Defender is a Chicago-based weekly newspaper founded in 1905 by Robert S. Abbott for primarily African-American readers. Historically, *The Defender* is considered the "most important" paper of what was then known as the colored or Negro press. Abbott's newspaper reported and campaigned against Jim Crow era violence and urged blacks in the American South to come north in what became the Great Migration. Under his nephew and chosen successor, John H. Sengstacke, the paper took on segregation, especially in the U.S. military, during World War II.

Robert Abbot was born on November 24, 1870, in St. Simons Island Georgia (although some sources state Savannah, Georgia to freedman parents, who had been enslaved before the American Civil War. The Sea Islands were a place of the Gullah people, an African-descended ethnic group who continued stronger aspects of African cultures than among African Americans in other areas of the South. His father Thomas Abbott died when Robert was a baby.

His widowed mother Flora Abbott (*née* Butler) met and married John Sengstacke, an American mixed-race man of unusual background who had recently come to the US from Germany. His parents were Tama, a freed slave woman of African descent, and her husband Herman Sengstacke, a German sea captain who had a regular route from Hamburg to Savannah. In the Georgia port city in 1847, Herman saw a slave sale. He was so distressed he bought the freedom of Tama, a young woman from West Africa. They married in Charleston, South Carolina, before returning to Georgia, where their interracial marriage was prohibited. Their mixed-race son John was born the next year and a daughter in 1848. Tama died soon after their daughter was born, and Herman took the children back to Germany to be raised by family.

John met the young black widow Flora, who had a year-old son Robert. He cared for Robert as if he were his own. Together the couple had seven children; their family crossed rigid racial boundaries. Robert was given the middle name Sengstacke to mark his belonging in the family. John Sengstacke had become a Congregationalist missionary as an adult; he wrote, "There is but one church, and all who are born of God are members of it. God made a church, man-made denominations. God gave us a Holy Bible, disputing men made different kinds of disciples." Sengstacke became a teacher, determined to improve the education of black children. He also became a publisher, founding the *Woodville Times,* based in what was then a town named Woodville; it was later annexed by the city of Savannah, Georgia.

Given the industrialization under way in the country, from 1892 to 1896, Abbott studied the printing trade at Hampton Institute (now Hampton University), a historically black college in Virginia. At Hampton, he sang with the Hampton Choir and Quartet, which toured nationally. He earned a law degree from Kent College of Law, Chicago, in 1898.

Career

Abbott tried to set up a law practice, working for a few years in Gary, Indiana; and Topeka, Kansas. He returned home to Georgia for a period and then went back to Chicago, where he could see changes arriving with thousands of new migrants from the rural South.

After settling in Chicago, in 1905 Abbott founded *The Chicago Defender* newspaper with an initial investment of ¢25 (equivalent to $7 in 2016). He started printing in a room at his boardinghouse; his landlady encouraged him, and he later bought her an 8-room house.

He wanted to push for job opportunities and social justice, and was eager to persuade blacks to leave the segregated, Jim Crow South for Chicago. A key part of his distribution network was made up of African-American railroad porters, who were highly respected among blacks. By 1925 they organized a union as the Brotherhood of Sleeping Car Porters. They often sold or distributed the paper on trains. *Defender* circulation reached 50,000 by 1916; 125,000 by 1918; and more than 200,000 by the early 1920s. Credited with contributing to the Great Migration of rural southern blacks to Chicago, the *Defender* became the most widely circulated black newspaper in the country. It was known as "America's Black Newspaper." Its success resulted in Abbott becoming one of the first self-made millionaires of African-American descent; his business expanded as African Americans moved to the cities and became an urbanized, northern population. From the early 20th century through 1940, 1.5 million blacks moved to major cities in the North and Midwest.

They were eager to know about conditions, to find housing, and to learn more about their new lives in cities. Most were from rural areas of the South. From 1890 to 1908 all the southern states had passed constitutions or laws that raised barriers to voter registration and effectively disenfranchised most blacks and many poor whites. They were utterly closed out of the political systems. Schools and other public facilities reserved for blacks were typically underfunded and ill-maintained. Legislatures imposed Jim Crow conditions, producing facilities for blacks that were "separate" but never "equal" (referring to the *Plessy v. Ferguson* (1896) case, in which the US Supreme Court ruled that segregated facilities, such as railroad cars providing "separate but equal" conditions, were constitutional).

The northern and Midwestern industrial centers, where blacks could vote and send children to school, were recruiting workers based on expansion of manufacturing and infrastructure to supply the US's expanding population as well as the war in Europe, which started in 1914. The Pennsylvania Railroad and others were expanding at a rapid rate across the North, needing workers for construction and later to serve the train passengers.

The *Defender* told stories of earlier migrants to the North, giving hope to disenfranchised and oppressed people in the South of other ways to live. Abbott, through his writings in the *Chicago Defender*, expressed those stories and encouraged people to leave the South for the North.

He even set a date of May 15, 1917, for what he called 'The Great Northern Drive' to occur. In his weekly, he showed pictures of Chicago and had numerous classifieds for housing. In addition, Abbott wrote about how awful a place the South was to live in comparison to the idealistic North. Abbott's words described the North as a place of prosperity and justice. This persuasive writing, "thereby made this journal probably the greatest stimulus that the migration had,"

Sengstacke was a fighter, a defender of rights. He listed nine goals as the *Defender*'s 'Bible:'
- American race prejudice must be destroyed;
- Opening up all trade unions to blacks, as well as whites;
- Representation in the President's Cabinet'
- Hiring black engineers, firemen, and conductors on all American railroads, and to all jobs in government;
- Gaining representation in all departments of the police forces over the entire United States;
- Government schools giving preference to American citizens before foreigners;
- Hiring black motormen and conductors on surface, elevated, and motor bus lines throughout America;
- Federal legislation to abolish lynching; and
- Full enfranchisement of all American citizens.

The *Chicago Defender* not only encouraged people to migrate north for a better life, but to fight for their rights once they got there. The slogan of the paper and the first goal was "American race prejudice must be destroyed."

Sengstacke openly discussed African-American history in his articles, including its difficult issues. He wrote, "Miscegenation began as soon as the African slaves were introduced into the colonial population and continues unabated to this day.... What's more, the opposition to intermarriage has heightened the interest and solidified the feelings of those who resent the injunction of racial distinction in their private and personal affairs." He believed that laws restricting personal choice in a mate violated the constitution and that the "decision of two intelligent people to mutual love and self-sacrifice should not be a matter of public concern." Abbott also published a short-lived periodical called *Abbott's Monthly*.

The *Defender* actively promoted the northward migration of Black Southerners, particularly to Chicago; its columns not only reported on, but encouraged the Great Migration.

Bahá'í Faith

In 1912, Abbott met `Abdu'l-Bahá, head of the Bahá'í Faith, through covering a talk of his during his stay in Chicago during his journeys in the West. By 1924 Abbott and his wife were listed as attending Bahá'í events in Chicago.

After inventing the fictional character "Bud Billiken" with David Kellum for articles in the *Defender*, Abbott established the Bud Billiken Club. In 1929 Abbott and Kellum founded the Bud Billiken Parade and Picnic. It became an occasion for African Americans to celebrate their pride and connections.

Abbott was seeking an atmosphere free of race prejudice. Even in religious communities, he sometimes found that mixed-race African Americans who were light-skinned sometimes also demonstrated prejudice against those who were darker. Abbott officially joined the Bahá'í Faith in 1934. He had found that its convention to elect its National Spiritual Assembly seemed free of prejudice.

Final years

In 1919, Illinois Governor Frank Lowden appointed Abbott to the state Race Relations Commission. The commission conducted studies about the changes resulting from the Great Migration; in one period, 5,000 African Americans were arriving in the city every week. The Commission collected data to assess the population and published the book, *The Negro in Chicago*.

Though some of his stepfather Sengstacke's relatives in Germany became Nazis in the 1930s and later, Abbott continued correspondence and economic aid to those who had accepted him and his father's family. He also assisted descendants of Captain Charles Stevens, the former owner of his enslaved birth father before emancipation. With his wealth, Abbott aided the Stevens descendants in Georgia during the Depression, and paid for the education of their children.

Abbott died of Bright's disease in 1940 in Chicago. He was buried in Lincoln Cemetery in Blue Island, Illinois. His will left the newspaper in the control of his nephew, John Henry Sengstacke.

Chicago Defender Budbilikan Parade; Harry S. Truman, John H. Sengstacke and Richard J. Daley

In 1919–1922 the *Defender* attracted the writing talents of Langston Hughes. Later, Gwendolyn Brooks and Willard Motley wrote for the paper. It was published as *The Chicago Daily Defender,* a daily newspaper, from 1956 to 2003, when it returned to a weekly format.

Great Migration (African American)

The Chicago Defender's editor and founder Robert Sengstacke Abbott played a major role in influencing the Great Migration of African Americans from the rural South to the urban North by means of strong, moralistic rhetoric in his editorials and political cartoons, the promotion of Chicago as a destination, and the advertisement of successful black individuals as inspiration for blacks in the South. The rhetoric and art exhibited in the *Defender* demanded equality of the races and promoted a northern migration. Abbott published articles that were exposés of southern crimes against blacks. The *Defender* consistently published articles describing lynching's in the South, with vivid descriptions of gore and the victims' deaths. Lynchings were at a peak at the turn of the century, in the period when southern state legislatures passed new constitutions and laws to disenfranchise most blacks and exclude them from the political system. Legislatures dominated by conservative white Democrats established racial segregation and Jim Crow.

Abbott openly blamed the lynching violence on the white mobs who were typically involved, forcing readers to accept that these crimes were "systematic and unremitting". The newspaper's intense focus on these injustices implicitly laid the groundwork upon which Abbott would build his explicit critiques of society. At the same time, the NAACP was publicizing the toll of lynching at its offices in New York City.

The art in the *Defender*, particularly its political cartoons, explicitly addressed race issues and advocated northern migration of blacks.

After the movement of southern blacks northward became a quantifiable phenomenon, the *Defender* took a particular interest in sensationalizing migratory stories, often on the front page. Abbott positioned his paper as a primary influence of these movements before historians would, for he used the *Defender* to initiate and advertise a "Great Northern Drive" day, set for May 15, 1917. The movement to northern and Midwestern cities, and to the West Coast at the time of

World War II, became known as the Great Migration, in which 1.5 million blacks moved out of the rural South in early 20th century years up to 1940, and another 5 million left towns and rural areas from 1940 to 1970.

Abbott used the *Defender* to promote Chicago as an attractive destination for southern blacks. Abbott presented Chicago as a promised-land with abundant jobs, as he included advertisements "clearly aimed at southerners," that called for massive numbers of workers wanted in factory positions. The *Defender* was filled with advertisements for desirable commodities, beauty products and technological devices. Abbott's paper was the first black newspaper to incorporate a full entertainment section. Chicago was portrayed as a lively city where blacks commonly went to the theaters, ate out at fancy restaurants, attended sports events, including "cheering for the American Black Giants, black America's favorite baseball team", and could dance all night in the hottest night clubs.

The *Defender* featured letters and poetry submitted by successful recent migrants; these writings "served as representative anecdotes, supplying readers with prototype examples ... that characterized the migration campaign". To supplement these first-person accounts, Abbott often published small features on successful blacks in Chicago.

In 1923, founding publisher Robert Sengstacke Abbott and Editor Lucius Harper created the Bud Billiken Club and later organized parades to promote healthy activity among black children in Chicago. In 1929 the organization began the Bud Billiken Parade and Picnic, which is still held annually in Chicago in early August. In the 1950s, under Sengstacke's direction, the Bud Billiken Parade expanded and emerged as the largest single event in Chicago. Today, it attracts more than one million attendances with more than 25 million television viewers, making it one of the largest parades in the country.

Abbott took a special interest in his nephew, John H. Sengstacke, paying for his education and grooming him to take over the *Defender,* which he did in 1940 after working with his uncle for several years. He urged integration of the armed forces. In 1948, he was appointed by President Harry S. Truman to the commission to study this and plan the process, which was initiated by the military in 1949.

Sengstacke also brought together for the first time major black newspaper publishers and created the National Negro Publishers Association, later renamed the National Newspaper Publishers Association (NNPA). In the early 21st century, the NNPA consists of more than 200-member black newspapers. Two days following the publishers' first meeting in Chicago, Abbott died.

One of Sengstacke's most striking accomplishments occurred on February 6, 1956, when the *Defender* became a daily newspaper and changed its name to the *Chicago Daily Defender*, the nation's second black daily newspaper. It published as a daily until 2003, when new owners converted the *Defender* back to a weekly. The *Defender* was one of only three African-American dailies in the United States; the other two are the *Atlanta Daily World*, the first black newspaper founded as a daily in 1928, and the New York *Daily Challenge*, founded in 1971.

Control of the *Chicago Defender* and her sister publications was transferred to a new ownership group named Real Times Inc. in January 2003. Real Times, Inc. was organized and led by Thom Picou, and Robert (Bobby) Sengstacke, John H. Sengstacke's surviving child and father of the beneficiaries of the Sengstacke Trust. In effect, Picou, then chairman and CEO of Real Times, Inc., led what was then labeled a "Sengstacke family-led" deal to facilitate trust beneficiaries and other Sengstacke family shareholders to agree to the sale of the company. Picou recruited Sam Logan, former publisher of the *Michigan Chronicle*, who then recruited O'Neil Swanson, Bill Pickard, Ron Hall and Gordon Follmer, black businessman from Detroit, Michigan (the "Detroit Group"), as investors in Real Times. Chicago investors included Picou, Bobby Sengstacke, David M. Milliner (who served as publisher of the *Chicago Defender* from 2003 to 2004), Kurt Cherry and James Carr.

THE GREAT MIGRATION:

Beginning of the Great Migration of African Americans to Chicago

The black population in Chicago significantly increased in the early to mid-1900s, due to the Great Migration out of the South. While African Americans made up less than two percent of the city's population in 1910, by 1960 the city was nearly 25 percent black.

The Great Migration, which was a long-term movement of African Americans from the South to the urban north, transformed Chicago and other northern cities. Chicago attracted slightly more than 500,000 of the approximately 7 million African Americans who left the South during these decades.

At the turn of the century, southern states succeeded in passing new constitutions and laws that disfranchised most blacks and many poor whites. Deprived of the right to vote, they could not sit on juries or run for office. They were subject to discriminatory laws passed by white legislators, including racial segregation of public facilities. Segregated education for black children and other services were consistently underfunded in a poor, agricultural economy. As white-dominated legislatures passed Jim Crow laws to re-establish white supremacy and create more restrictions in public life, violence against blacks increased, with lynchings used as extrajudicial enforcement. In addition, the boll weevil infestation ruined much of the cotton industry in the early 20th century. Voting with their feet, blacks started migrating out of the South to the North, where they could live more freely, get their children educated, and get new jobs.

Industry buildup for World War I pulled thousands of workers to the North, as did the rapid expansion of railroads, and the meatpacking and steel industries. Between 1915 and 1960, hundreds of thousands of black southerners migrated to Chicago to escape violence and segregation, and to seek economic freedom. They went from being a mostly rural population to one that was mostly urban. "The migration of African Americans from the rural south to the urban north became a mass movement." The Great Migration radically transformed Chicago, both politically and culturally.

From 1910-1940, most African Americans who migrated north were from rural areas. They had been chiefly sharecroppers and laborers, although some were landowners pushed out by the boll weevil disaster. After years of underfunding of public education for blacks in the South, they tended to be poorly educated, with relatively low skills to apply to urban jobs. Like the European rural immigrants, they had to rapidly adapt to a different urban culture. Many took advantage of better schooling in Chicago and their children learned quickly. After 1940, when the second larger wave of migration started, black migrants tended to be already urbanized, from southern cities and towns. They were the most ambitious, better educated with more urban skills to apply in their new homes.

The masses of new migrants arriving in the cities captured public attention. At one point in the 1940s, 3,000 African Americans were arriving every week in Chicago—stepping off the trains from the South and making their ways to neighborhoods they had learned about from friends and the *Chicago Defender*. The Great Migration was charted and evaluated. Urban white northerners started to get worried, as their neighborhoods rapidly changed. At the same time, recent and older ethnic immigrants competed for jobs and housing with the new arrivals, especially on the South Side, where the steel and meatpacking industries had the most numerous working-class jobs.

Ethnic Irish were heavily implicated in the gang violence and the rioting that erupted in 1919. They had been the most established ethnic group and defended their power and territory in the South Side against newcomers: both other ethnic whites and southern blacks. "Chicago was a focal point of the great migration and the racial violence that came in its wake." With Chicago's industries steadily expanding, opportunities opened up for new migrants, including Southerners, to find work. The railroad and meatpacking industries recruited black workers. Chicago's African-American newspaper, the *Chicago Defender*, made the city well known to southerners. It sent bundles of papers south on the Illinois Central trains, and African-American Pullman Porters would drop them off in Black towns. "Chicago was the most accessible northern city for African Americans in Mississippi, Louisiana, Texas, and Arkansas." They took the trains north. "Then between 1916 and 1919, 50,000 blacks came to crowd into the burgeoning black belt, to make new demands upon the institutional structure of the South Side."[1]

Between 1900 and 1910, the African-American population rose rapidly in Chicago. White hostility and population growth combined to create the ghetto on the South Side. Nearby were areas dominated by ethnic Irish, who were especially territorial in defending against incursions into their areas by any other groups. Most of this large population was composed of migrants. In 1910 more than 75 percent of blacks lived in predominantly black sections of the city. The eight or nine neighborhoods that had been set as areas of black settlement in 1900 remained the core of the Chicago African-American community. The Black Belt slowly expanded as African Americans, despite facing violence and restrictive covenants, pushed forward into new neighborhoods. As the population grew, African Americans became more confined to a delineated area, instead of spreading throughout the city. When blacks moved into mixed neighborhoods, ethnic white hostility grew. After fighting over the area, often whites left the area to be dominated by blacks. This is one of the reasons the black belt region started.

The Black Belt of Chicago Row Housing for African Americans

The Black Belt of Chicago was the chain of neighborhoods on the South Side of Chicago where three-quarters of the city's African American population lived by the mid-20th century. The Black Belt was an area of aging, dilapidated housing that stretched 30 blocks along State Street on the South Side. It was rarely more than seven blocks wide. The South Side black belt expanded in only two directions in the 20th century - south and east. The South Side's "black belt" also contained zones related to economic status. The poorest blacks lived in the northernmost, oldest section of the black belt, while the elite resided in the southernmost section. In the mid-20th century, blacks began slowly moving up to better positions in the work force. During this time, Chicago was the capital of Black America. Many African Americans who moved to the Black Belt area of

Chicago were from the Black Belt in the Southeastern region of the United States. Discrimination played a big role in the lives of blacks. They often struggled to find decent housing.

Immigration to Chicago was another pressure of overcrowding, as primarily lower-class newcomers from rural Europe also sought cheap housing and working-class jobs. More and more people tried to fit into converted "kitchenette" and basement apartments. Living conditions in the Black Belt resembled conditions in the West Side ghetto or in the stockyards district. Although there were decent homes in the Negro sections, the core of the Black Belt was a slum. A 1934 census estimated that black households contained 6.8 people on average, whereas white households contained 4.7. Many blacks lived in apartments that lacked plumbing, with only one bathroom for each floor. With the buildings so overcrowded, building inspections and garbage collection were below the minimum mandatory requirements for healthy sanitation. This unhealthiness increased the threat of disease. From 1940-1960, the infant death rate in the Black Belt was 16% higher than the rest of the city.

Crime in African-American neighborhoods was a low priority to the police. Associated with problems of poverty and southern culture, rates of violence and homicide were high. Some women resorted to prostitution to survive. Both low life and middle-class strivers were concentrated in a small area.

In 1946, the Chicago Housing Authority (CHA) tried to ease the pressure in the overcrowded ghettos and proposed to put public housing sites in less congested areas in the city. The white residents did not take to this very well, so city politicians forced the CHA to keep the status quo and develop high rise projects in the Black Belt and on the West Side. Some of these became notorious failures. As industrial restructuring in the 1950s and later led to massive job losses, residents changed from working-class families to poor families on welfare.

Between 1916 and 1920, almost 50,000 Black Southerners moved to Chicago, which profoundly shaped the city's development. Growth increased even more rapidly after 1940. In particular, the new citizens caused the growth of local churches, businesses and community organizations. A new musical culture arose, fed by all the traditions along the Mississippi River. The population continued to increase with new migrants, with the most arriving after 1940.

The black arts community in Chicago was especially vibrant. The 1920s were the height of the Jazz Age, but music continued as the heart of the community for decades. Nationally renowned musicians rose within the Chicago world. Along the Stroll, a bright-light district on State Street, jazz greats like Louis Armstrong headlined at nightspots including the Delux Café.

Black Chicagoans' literary creation from 1925 to 1950 was also prolific, and the city's Black Renaissance rivaled that of the Harlem Renaissance. Prominent writers included Richard Wright, Willard Motley, William Attaway, Frank Marshall Davis, St. Clair Drake, Horace R. Cayton, Jr., and Margaret Walker. Chicago was home to writer and poet, Gwendolyn Brooks. Brooks is famous for her portrayals of Black working-class life in crowded tenements of Bronzeville. These writers expressed the changes and conflicts blacks found in urban life and the struggles of creating new worlds. In Chicago, black writers turned away from the folk traditions embraced by Harlem Renaissance writers, instead adopting a grittier style of "literary naturalism" to depict life in the urban ghetto. The classic *Black Metropolis*, written by St. Clair Drake and Horace R. Cayton, Jr., exemplified the style of the Chicago writers. Today it remains the most detailed portrayal of Black Chicago in the 1930s and 1940s.

Bronzeville is a neighborhood in the Douglas and Grand Boulevard community areas on the South Side of Chicago around the Illinois Institute of Technology, Vander Cook College of Music, and Illinois College of Optometry. It is accessible via the Green and Red lines of the Chicago Transit Authority, as well as the Metra Electric District Main Line. In 2011 a new Metra station, Jones/Bronzeville Station, opened to serve the neighborhood on the Rock Island and planned South East Service.

Bronzeville, one of the largest black communities in the United States, became the center of African-American culture in Chicago. Gwyndolyn Brooks

In the early 20th century, Bronzeville was known as the "Black Metropolis", one of the nation's most significant concentrations of African-American businesses. Between 1910 and 1920, during the peak of the "Great Migration", the population of the area increased dramatically when thousands of African Americans escaped the oppression of the South and immigrated to Chicago in search of industrial jobs. The Wabash YMCA is considered the first African-American Y in the U.S. It continues as a center today due to the continued support of many of the black churches in the area. The Wabash YMCA is widely credited as the birthplace of the commemoration of black culture, what would later become Black History Month.

Noted people associated with the development of the area include: Andrew "Rube" Foster, founder of the Negro National Baseball League; Ida B. Wells, a civil rights activist, journalist and co-organizer of the NAACP; Margaret Taylor-Burroughs, artist, author, and one of the co-founders of the DuSable Museum of African American History; Bessie Coleman, the first African-American woman pilot; Gwendolyn Brooks, 1985 United States Poet Laureate, 1968 Poet Laureate of Illinois, and first African American awarded the Pulitzer Prize; actresses Marla Gibbs and Jennifer Beals; acclaimed R&B singers Sam Cooke and Lou Rawls; and coronet player and jazz bandleader King Oliver. His protégé, jazz musician, and trumpeter, who was a pianist, composer and bandleader, lived in Bronzeville on E. 44th Street and performed at many of the area's night clubs, including the Sunset Cafe and Dreamland Cafe. The neighborhood includes the Chicago Landmark Black Metropolis-Bronzeville District.

Bronzeville: Black Chicago (Bronzeville Arts Blog-Aki Antonia)

47th Street was and remains the hub of the Bronzeville neighborhood. In the early 21st century, it has started to regain some of its former glory. Gone for good is the Regal Theater (demolished in 1973), where many great performers took the stage. From the 1940s and 1960s, high-rise public housing projects were constructed in the area, which were managed by the Chicago Housing Authority. The largest complex was the Robert Taylor Homes. They developed severe social problems exacerbated by concentrated poverty among the residents and poor design of the buildings. This project was demolished in the late 1990s and early 21st century. The nickname "Bronzeville" was first used for the area in 1930 by James J. Gentry, a local theater editor for the *Chicago Bee* publication. It refers to the brown skin color of African Americans, who predominated as residents in that area. It has become common usage throughout the decades.

African American Store owner on State Street

The migration expanded the market for African American business. "The most notable breakthrough in black business came in the insurance field." There were four major insurance companies founded in Chicago. Then, in the early 20th century, service establishments took over. The African-American market on State Street during this time consisted of barber shops, restaurants, pool rooms, saloons, and beauty salons. African Americans used these trades to build their own communities. These shops gave the blacks a chance to establish their families, earn money, and become an active part of the community.

ANNIE MALONE

Annie Minerva, Turnbo, Malone

From Wikipedia, the free encyclopedia

Annie Minerva Turnbo Malone (August 9, 1869 – May 10, 1957) was an American businesswoman, inventor and philanthropist. In the first three decades of the 20th century, she founded and developed a large and prominent commercial and educational enterprise centered on cosmetics for African-American women.

Annie Minerva Turnbo was born in southern Illinois, the daughter of enslaved Africans Robert and Isabella (Cook) Turnbo. When her father went off to fight for the Union with the 1st Kentucky Cavalry in the Civil War, Isabella took the couple's children and escaped from Kentucky, a neutral border state that maintained slavery. After traveling down the Ohio River, she found refuge in Metropolis, Illinois. There Annie Turnbo was later born, the tenth of eleven children.

Annie Turnbo was born on a farm near Metropolis in Massac County, Illinois. Orphaned at a young age, Annie attended a public school in Metropolis before moving to Peoria to live with her older sister Ada Moody in 1896. There Annie attended high school, taking particular interest in chemistry. However, due to frequent illness, Annie was forced to withdraw from classes.

While out of school, Annie grew so fascinated with hair and hair care that she often practiced hairdressing with her sister. With expertise in both chemistry and hair care, Turnbo began to develop her own hair care products. At the time, many women used goose fat, heavy oils, soap, or bacon grease to straighten their curls, which damaged both scalp and hair.

By the beginning of the 1900s, Turnbo moved with her older siblings to Lovejoy, now known as Brooklyn, Illinois. While experimenting with hair and different hair care products, she developed and manufactured her own line of non-damaging hair straighteners, special oils, and hair-stimulant products for African-American women. She named her new product "Wonderful Hair Grower" To promote her new product; Turnbo sold the Wonderful Hair Grower in bottles from door-to-door. Her products and sales began to revolutionize hair care methods for all African Americans.

In 1902, Turnbo moved to a thriving St. Louis, where she and three hired assistants sold her hair care products from door-to-door. As part of her marketing, she gave away free treatments to attract more customers.

In 1902, she married Nelson Pope; the couple divorced in 1907.

1920...Diploma Day at Poro College

On April 28, 1914, Annie Turnbo married Aaron Eugene Malone, a former teacher and religious book salesman. Turnbo Malone, by then worth well over a million dollars, built a five-story multipurpose facility.

Due to the high demand for her product in St. Louis, Turnbo opened her first shop on 2223 Market Street in 1902. She also launched a wide advertising campaign in the black press, held news conferences, toured many southern states, and recruited many women whom she trained to sell her products.

One of her selling agents: Sarah Breedlove Davis, (who became known as Madam C. J. Walker when she set up her own business), operated in Denver, Colorado until a disagreement led Walker to leave the company. This development was one of the reasons which led the then Mrs. Pope to copyright her products under the name "Poro" because of what she called fraudulent imitations and to discourage counterfeit versions. *Poro* was a combination of the married names of Annie Pope and her sister Laura Roberts. Due to the growth in her business, in 1910 Turnbo moved to a larger facility on 3100 Pine Street.

In addition to a manufacturing plant, it contained facilities for a beauty college, which she named Poro College. The building included a manufacturing plant, a retail store where Poro products were sold, business offices, a 500-seat auditorium, dining and meeting rooms, a roof garden, dormitory, gymnasium, bakery, and chapel. It served the African-American community as a center for religious and social functions.

The College's curriculum addressed the whole student; students were coached on personal style for work: on walking, talking, and a style of dress designed to maintain a solid persona. Poro College employed nearly 200 people in St. Louis. Through its school and franchise businesses, the college created jobs for almost 75,000 women in North and South America, Africa and the Philippines.

By the 1920s, Annie Turnbo Malone had become a multi-millionaire. In 1924, she paid income tax of nearly $40,000, reportedly the highest in Missouri. While extremely wealthy, Malone lived modestly, giving thousands of dollars to the local black YMCA and the Howard University College of Medicine in Washington, DC. She also donated money to the St. Louis Colored Orphans Home, where she served as president on the board of directors from 1919 to 1943. With her help, in 1922 the Home bought a facility at 2612 Goode Avenue (which was renamed Annie Malone Drive in her honor).

Annie Malone, 1921.

The Orphans Home is still located in the historic Ville neighborhood. Upgraded and expanded, the facility was renamed in the entrepreneur's honor as the Annie Malone Children and Family Service Center. As well as funding many programs, Malone ensured that her employees, all African American, were paid well and given opportunities for advancement.

Her business thrived until 1927, when her husband filed for divorce. Having served as president of the company, he demanded half of the business' value, based on his claim that his contributions had been integral to its success. The divorce suit forced Poro College into a court-ordered receivership. With support from her employees and powerful figures such as Mary McLeod Bethune, she negotiated a settlement of $200,000. This affirmed her as the sole owner of Poro College, and the divorce was granted.

After the divorce, Turnbo Malone moved most of her business to Chicago's South Parkway, where she bought an entire city block. Other lawsuits followed. In 1937, during the Great Depression, a former employee filed suit, also claiming credit for Poro's success. To raise money for the settlement, Turnbo Malone sold her St. Louis property. Although much reduced in size, her business continued to thrive.

She was named an honorary member of the Zeta Phi Beta sorority. She was awarded an honorary degree from Howard University. On May 10, 1957, Annie Malone suffered a stroke and died at Chicago's Provident Hospital. Childless, she had bequeathed her business and remaining fortune to her nieces and nephews. At the time of her death, her estate was valued at $100,000.

SPEAKEASIES AND POLICY KINGS:

Former Speakeasies: Chicago Bar Project

It is believed that in the 19th and early 20th centuries, African-American organized crime emerged following large-scale migrations of Caribbean and African Americans to major cities of the Northeast and Midwest. In many of these newly established communities and neighborhoods, criminal activities such as illegal gambling, speakeasies and bootlegging were seen in the post-World War I and Prohibition eras. Although the majority of these businesses were operated by African Americans, it is unclear to the extent these operations were run independently of the larger criminal organizations of the time.

Al Capone's ("Scarface.")

Al Capone & the Speakeasies of the 1920s
By Jennifer Mueller

A man slashed Al Capone's face in a nightclub altercation, leading to his nickname: "Scarface."

The 18th Amendment to the Constitution, passed and ratified with overwhelming support, prohibited the making, transporting or selling of intoxicating liquor. At the stroke of midnight on January 16, 1920, the United States was officially "dry" -- but that didn't mean people stopped drinking. Supplying the nation's continued desire for alcohol provided a new revenue stream for the criminal underworld, and many of these gangsters, including Chicago's notorious Al Capone, wielded legendary power.

The fact that alcohol was illegal didn't deter people who wanted to drink, and speakeasies -- secret spots often owned by gangsters, where moonshine and illegally-imported liquor were sold -- grew in popularity. Everyone in a speakeasy was technically a criminal, subject to arrest for drinking alcohol, and this commonality broke down social barriers. Men and women from all segments of society commingled. As demand increased, a Chicago gangster named Johnny Torrio realized there were major profits to be made in the distribution of liquor to speakeasies -- but there was too much competition. He needed someone who could organize his business and eliminate rival gangs -- and he knew just who to call. Torrio contacted an old New York associate named Alphonse "Al" Capone.

Capone moved his family to Chicago and set up shop as Torrio's right-hand man. By the mid-1920s, the pair had relocated their base of operations to the Chicago suburb of Cicero, where Capone -- through violence and intimidation -- succeeded in getting his own man elected mayor. Capone brought not just street smarts, but also accounting expertise he'd acquired while working as a bookkeeper for some of Torrio's past enterprises in New York. Torrio retired after he was injured in an assassination attempt, leaving his sprawling network in Capone's hands. By the end of the decade, Capone had a lock on nearly all alcohol supplied to any of Chicago's estimated 10,000 speakeasies.

Prohibition Profit and Risk Management Newspapers in the 1920s estimated Capone's enterprises generated nearly $100 million a year. Federal agents determined that $60 million came from the distribution of illegal alcohol to speakeasies. All of that illegally-gained profit came at considerable risk, however. Capone lessened his legal risk by handing out steady bribes to police officers, politicians and judges. Other gangs were more difficult to handle. There was a lot of money to be made during the Prohibition Era, and every gangster wanted a piece of the action. Violence escalated to the point where murders were committed on city streets in broad daylight, and the fearful public pleaded with law enforcement to end the reign of terror. Capone called a "Peace Conference" with rival gangs, but the worst was yet to come.

Public Enemy Number One

On Valentine's Day in 1929, men dressed as cops descended on an illegal alcohol warehouse and distribution center that belonged to a Capone rival. The seven men working in the building were told to line up against the wall and then murdered in a hail of machine-gun fire. Capone was widely believed to have been behind the gruesome attack, although he was in Florida at the time. After the massacre, Capone was branded "Public Enemy Number One." Ultimately, Capone was arrested in 1931 on a federal indictment of 22 counts of tax evasion. The legendary gangster was in prison in 1933, when ratification of the 21st Amendment repealed the 18th Amendment and brought an end to the Prohibition Era.

Chicago Street gangs

Chicago Street gangs have existed for more than 100 Years; they appeared on the scene somewhere in the late 1860s. They were mostly of European ethnicity in origin and was made up of mostly immigrants, migrated and formed in distinct geographical areas to protect themselves from other groups of immigrant gangs looking to victimize the weak and powerless among them.

It was believed that these ethnic gangs eventually became reliable commodity groups for the political organizations at that time; they even supplied their fighting skills for the warring newspapers at the turn of the 20th century. It became the example of the more established gangs such as the Circus Gang and the 42 Gang that provided talent for the growing traditional organized gangs or crime groups during the Prohibition period.

According to Chicago native Nathan Thompson, author of "Kings: The True Story of Chicago's Policy Kings and Numbers Racketeers," Policy was conceived around the late 1880s and was owned and operated for decades by black men called Policy kings.

Policy players, lured by the possibility of hitting it big on a small bet, would pick a number combination, say 3-1-2, called a gig. A nickel wager could win you $5.

In the early days, winning numbers were pulled from the derby of Sam Young, Policy's creator, as he stood on the corner of State and Madison Streets. Soon, Young moved his hustle south along State Street to a saloon.

By 1915, players could learn the winning numbers by visiting the family grocery store of a couple of Italian brothers who hooked up with Young, said Thompson. By then, Young was pulling numbers from a cardboard box, and Policy regulars would gather around that box, watching the results as if they were peering into a crystal ball that held their future.

Indeed, Policy was responsible for its share of crime and lawlessness as the racket grew and more Policy kings were getting in on the game and battling for turf. Black ministers deeply opposed Policy, preaching against it from their pulpits. Still, the city didn't make much of an effort to get rid of it in the beginning.

"The city's opinion was that it was a little hustle in the black community," said Thompson. "That made it grow because nobody was paying attention. It was generating a lot of revenue throughout the Depression in Bronzeville."

Policy, in its heyday from about the 1920s to the 1950s, did some good for the winners. It put food on the tables of struggling families. Children were sent to college on Policy money. It also provided jobs.

Thompson says proceeds from Policy at times helped bankroll the Negro Baseball League and even the boxing career of Joe Louis. But the house is always set up so there are more losers than winners, and gangsters vied for their share of the cut.

"A faction of Al Capone's Mafia went after the black guys on the South Side making all this money," said Thompson. "And that led to the killing of one of the big Policy kings."

The other black kings decided to pull together, but that couldn't sustain them. By 1952, Policy had been put on trial, more Policy kings had been murdered or jailed and the white mob had moved in, said Thompson.

"That was the end of Policy [as a black establishment] and the beginning of white-controlled Policy," he said. "To say the Mafia was controlling the money meant they were also controlling the vote and the neighborhood where the money was derived."

JOHN "MUSHMOUTH" JOHNSON

John V. "Mushmouth" Johnson
(From <u>The Chicago Crime Scenes Project</u>)

John V. "Mushmouth" Johnson was one of Chicago's greatest gambling tycoons during the 1890s and 1900s. The newspapers (using the racially-insensitive vernacular of the day) called him variously "King of the Levee", "The Richest Negro in Chicago", and "King Coon of State Street". Regardless of what you called him, for a span of twenty years, if you gambled in Chicago, you likely paid Mushmouth, at least indirectly.

Johnson was born in St. Louis to a woman who had been a nurse for Mary Todd Lincoln, but came to Chicago in the 1870s, while in his 30s, and found work as a waiter in the restaurant inside the Palmer House hotel. In 1882, he got his first taste of vice as an employee in one of Andy Scott's gambling houses on Gamblers' Row. Mushmouth displayed a hard-headed willingness to enforce the rules physically when gamblers who lost money demanded it back or tried to take it back by force (Johnson himself never gambled). He could also cuss a blue streak, which earned him his nickname.

In the early 1960s the gangs' demographics changed as did their trade when they moved into the lucrative narcotics business thereafter.

In *Kings: The True Story of Chicago's Policy Kings and Numbers Racketeers*, Nathan Thompson writes:

Policy became the biggest Black-owned business in the world with combined annual sales sometimes reaching the $100 million mark and employing tens-of-thousands of people nationwide. In Bronzeville, Policy was a major catalyst by which the black economy was driven. In 1938, Time magazine reported that Bronzeville was the "Center of U.S. Negro Business", and more than a decade later, "Our World" magazine reported that "Windy City Negroes have more money, bigger cars and brighter clothes than any other city.... The city which has become famous for the biggest Policy wheels, the largest funerals, the flashiest cars and the prettiest women, has built that reputation on one thing, money". Those attributions, however, were largely due to Policy, a business conceived, owned, and operated by African American men known by many names including "Digit Barons", "Numbers Bankers", "Sportsmen", "Digitarians", and "the 1-2-3-4 Guys"; but more often than not they were called "Policy Kings".

Post War: In the years following the end of the World War II, African American organized crime grew along with the rise of African American social consciousness and later political, social and economic upward mobility. Many of the major drug traffickers in the United States emerged during the early-to-mid-1960s, such as Leroy "Nicky" Barnes, Guy Fisher and Frank Lucas, taking advantage of the increasing political strength during the civil rights movement. Previously dependent solely on the political and police protection of New York's Five Families, African American gangsters were more able to negotiate with outside criminal organizations and the Cosa Nostra's control over the ghettos began to wane.

Most recently, highly structured African American gangs have made headlines for their ability to pull in hundreds of millions of dollars in illegal drug profits. At their peak, the Chicago-based Gangster Disciples were reported to generate $100 million in drug revenue. The rise and fall of the Detroit-based Black Mafia Family, which made nearly $250 million through their drug trafficking ventures during the late 1990s, has been brought to light by federal investigations.

FULLER PRODUCTS COMPANY

Samuel B. "S.B." Fuller

Samuel B. "S.B." Fuller (June 4, 1905 – October 24, 1988) was an American entrepreneur. He was founder and president of the Fuller Products Company, publisher of the New York Age and Pittsburgh

Courier, head of the South Side Chicago NAACP, president of the National Negro Business League, and a prominent black Republican.

S.B. Fuller's life was an illustration of business success and self-help. His company gave inspiration and training to countless aspiring entrepreneurs and future leaders, including John H. Johnson of Johnson Publishing, George Ellis Johnson, founder of Johnson Products, and Dr. T.R.M. Howard.

Fuller (no relation to Alfred C. Fuller, founder of the Fuller Brush Company) was born into rural poverty to a sharecropper family in Monroe, Ouachita Parish, Louisiana in 1905. The family's poverty was such that he had to drop out of school in sixth grade. At nine he was selling products door-to-door and gaining experience as an entrepreneur. At fifteen his family moved to Memphis, Tennessee. Two years later his mother would pass away leaving seven children to fend for themselves.

S. B. Fuller Arrival in Chicago

Mr. S.B. Fuller, president of the Fuller Products Corporation and chairman of the Negro Chamber of Commerce, addressing a meeting of the forum in Chicago, Illinois at the Ida B. Wells Housing Project.

After going to Chicago in 1928, Fuller worked in a wide range of menial jobs, eventually rising to become manager of a coal yard. Subsequent to his employment in the coal yard, he gained employment as an insurance representative for Commonwealth Burial Association, an African-American firm. Although he had a secure job during the depression, he nevertheless struck out on his own preferring "freedom" to "security."

His career as an entrepreneur started after he borrowed twenty-five dollars using his car as collateral. Along with his friend Lestine Thornton (who later became his wife), he invested in a load of soap from Boyer International Laboratories, manufacturer of Jean Nadal Cosmetics and HA Hair Arranger. His success selling soap door-to-door inspired him to invest another $1000. He incorporated Fuller Products in 1929. In four years, he would be promoted to a manager at Commonwealth while continuing to grow his own company to a line of 30 products and hiring additional door-to-door salespeople.

*1951 The Fuller Products Company
at 2700 South Wabash in Chicago*

The substantial number of African American families who moved to the South side of Chicago during the Great Migration became the customer base from which Fuller Products would see tremendous expansion. The additional growth was sufficient for the company to open its own factory in 1939. In 1947, Fuller purchased Boyer to prevent its bankruptcy, keeping his ownership a secret. The company began to manufacture and sell a diverse line of commodities from deodorant and hair care to hosiery and men's suits. Fuller also purchased several newspapers including the *New York Age* and the *Pittsburgh Courier*. Additionally, he owned the South Center Department Store and the Regal Theater in Chicago.

Fuller was a leading black Republican, although he always had an independent streak. He promoted civil rights and briefly headed the Chicago South Side NAACP. Along with Birmingham businessman, A.G. Gaston, he tried to organize a cooperative effort to purchase the segregated bus company during the Montgomery Bus Boycott. He told Martin Luther King Jr., "The bus company is losing money and willing to sell. We should buy it." King was skeptical of the idea, and not enough African American people came forward to raise the money.

Despite his belief in civil rights, Fuller's emphasis was always on the need for African American people to go into business. In 1958, he blasted the federal government for undermining free enterprise and fostering socialism. He feared that it was "doing the same thing today as was done in the days of Caesar—destroying incentive and initiative." He argued that wherever "there is capitalism there is freedom."

Fuller was a good friend and associate of Dr. T.R.M. Howard from Mississippi and later Chicago. Howard was a wealthy black entrepreneur and a prominent civil rights leader and mentor to Medgar Evers. Fuller and Howard had probably met because of their mutual involvement in the National Negro Business League. Fuller was president of the organization for several terms in the 1940s and 1950s. He hired Howard to be medical director of Fuller Products and supported his Republican campaign for Congress in 1958.

During the 1950s, Fuller was probably the richest African American man in the United States. His cosmetics company had $18 million in sales and a sales force of five thousand (one third of them white). It gave training to many future entrepreneurs and other leaders. "It doesn't make any difference," he declared, "about the color of an individual's skin. No one cares whether a cow is black, red, yellow, or brown. They want to know how much milk it can produce."

Despite his opinion, the White Citizens Councils organized a boycott of Fuller's Nadal products line during the 1950s, when they learned an African American owned the company. This would be the beginning of a turn of fortune for Fuller's business interests that would affect his activities throughout the 1960s.

In 1963 Fuller was the first African American inducted into the National Association of Manufacturers. During his acceptance speech, he stated that "a lack of understanding of the capitalist system, and not racial barriers, was keeping blacks from making progress." In an interview that same year with "U.S. News and World Report" he said, "Negroes are not discriminated against because of the color of their skin. They are discriminated against because they have not anything to offer that people want to buy." Afterwards his company suffered severe setbacks as many of his comments were reported out of context. Major national black leaders reacted angrily and called for a boycott of Fuller Products.

In 1968, Fuller sold unregistered promissory notes in interstate commerce for which he was charged with violating the Federal Securities Act. After pleading guilty, being placed on five years' probation, and ordered to repay creditors $1.6 million, Fuller Products entered bankruptcy in 1971. Although the company reorganized, reported profits of $300,000 in 1972, and the cosmetics portion of the old company were rebuilt, it never returned to the firm's previous levels of size or profitability.

Dudley ran both Fuller Products Company and Dudley Products Company from 1976 until 1984. In 1984, Fuller Products Company was purchased by Dudley.

Fuller was eighty-three years of age when he died at St. Francis Hospital in Blue Island, Illinois from kidney failure.

JOE L. DUDLEY, SR.

Joe L. Dudley, Sr.

In 1976, Fuller, as a result of health problems, asked his top distributor, Joe Louis Dudley, Sr., to move to Chicago and become President of the Fuller Products Company.

Joe L. Dudley, Sr. (May 9, 1937) is an American entrepreneur and humanitarian. He is Co-Founder of the DudleyQ+ brand and is one of the world's most sought after entrepreneurial masterminds. He is the fifth of 11 children born to Gilmer L. and Clara Yeates Dudley. Joe was born and raised in a one-bedroom house along with his 11 brothers and sisters in the rural community of Aurora, in eastern North Carolina.

Labeled mentally retarded as a young man growing up on a farm, he was forced to overcome many challenges, in order to be successful. He credits his mother with inspiring him to prove to the world that he was just as able as anyone else by challenging him to "show them Joe".

This journey to success began in 1957, when he invested $10.00 in a sales kit and began selling Fuller Products door-to-door, while still a student at North Carolina A & T State University (Greensboro, NC) and he went on to become one of the largest manufacturers of black hair products in the world. He was the Founder of Dudley Products Inc., Dudley Cosmetology University and the chain of beauty schools - Dudley Beauty School System. In addition, he controlled other corporations. Dudley Products Inc. became a $35,000,000 a year company and has been listed in the top 50 in Black Enterprise Magazine's Top 100 Black-Owned Businesses.

Through dedication, hard work and persistence, Joe L. Dudley, Sr. has indeed become the role model his mother always knew he could be. Joe L. Dudley, Sr. is much more than just a successful entrepreneur. He is known nationally and internationally as an inspirational speaker and humanitarian who spends much of his time identifying needs and giving back to the community and mankind. One of Mr. Fuller's (his mentor) goals, and one that Joe Dudley actively pursues today, is to help people to maximize their potential and achieve success. In 2009, Joe L. Dudley, Sr. & Eunice Dudley were featured in a national movie, Good Hair, a Chris Rock documentary about the hair care industry.

Fuller & Dudley
Mastermind Business Group

John H. Johnson

JOHN H. JOHNSON, OF THE JOHNSON PUBLISHING COMPANY

Johnson Publishing Company, Inc., is the world's largest African American-owned publishing company. It is the home of *Ebony* and *Jet* magazines, as well as Fashion Fair Cosmetics, Ebony Fashion Fair, and the Johnson Publishing Company Book Division. Linda Johnson Rice, daughter of founder John H. Johnson, operates as president and CEO of the company

Johnson Publishing Company was founded in November 1942 by John H. Johnson—who was working part-time as an office boy for Supreme Life Insurance Company of America, located in Chicago, Illinois—and his wife, Eunice. Johnson's job was to clip magazine and newspaper articles about the African American community. As he clipped, the idea for an African American-oriented magazine came to mind. Using his mother's furniture as collateral, he secured a loan of $500. He then mailed out $2 charter subscription offers to potential subscribers. More than 3,000 replies came in, and the $6,000 was used to print the first issue of *Negro Digest,* a magazine based on the popular *Reader's Digest.*

Negro Digest Magazine

When Negro Digest Publishing Co. was born, Johnson was immediately facing obstacles, such as finding a landlord willing to rent him office space in a not-yet-desegregated United States. However, Johnson managed to secure a room in the private law office of Earl B.

Dickerson, on the second floor of his employer's building, the Supreme Life Insurance Company.

Although Negro Digest/Black World gave way to other African-American magazines such as Ebony, Jet and Essence, it significantly impacted the Black Arts Movement of the 1960s and early '70s, as well as literary work showcased reproductions of artworks. In the words of Chris Brancaccio: "Negro Digest/Black World is a fascinating artifact because the content of each issue seems to evade rigid binaries like integrationist or nationalist, and therefore became a very real space for public debate. For instance, the November 1966 issue contains an article entitled *Black Power Symposium* [and] features 12 different opinions on Black Power, offered by a diverse group of black individuals, ranging from Conrad Kent Rivers, founder of Organization of Black American Culture (OBAC); to Anita Cornwell, a writer and former state employee; to Dudley Randall, founder of Broadside Press, but also a librarian and poet.

Negro Digest/Black World constitutes a massive archive. A renewed scholarly interest in these periodicals offers new perspectives and could profoundly change the way we consider the Black Arts Movement and Black activism during this period.

Johnson Publishing Company's 11 story 110000 square foot building was built in 1972

In 1943 Johnson purchased a building at 5619 South State Street, to house the fledgling company. In 1949 the company converted a funeral parlor at 1820 South Michigan Avenue into office space and moved there, a location that would remain the company's headquarters into the new millennium, although it would grow to be 11 stories tall. Along the way, *Negro Digest,* which had a circulation at one time of 100,000 subscribers, was renamed *Black World.* In the 1970s, the readership dwindled, and the magazine was finally canceled in 1976.

1947: Ebony Magazine

By that time, however, the company was going strong with other products. In 1945, Johnson launched *Ebony,* a magazine patterned after *Life,* but focusing on the African American community, culture, and achievements. It was an immediate success and remained the company's flagship publication into the 21st century, with a readership at one point of more than 1.3 million. In 1951, Johnson created another magazine, called *Jet,* a celebrity-oriented magazine focusing on African American entertainers and public figures. For nearly 20 years, these two magazines were the only publications for African Americans in the United States.

November 1, 1951: the 1st issue of Jet magazine

Unable to obtain advertising in those years, Johnson created the Beauty Star mail-order company and began advertising its products, such as haircare products, wigs, and vitamins in his own magazines. In 1947 the company picked up its first major advertising account in Zenith Radio and, after sending a salesman to Detroit every week for nearly ten years, finally managed to sign Chrysler Corporation in

1954. The magazine drew the talents of many people, including author Era Bell Thompson (1905–1986), who served as associate editor of *Ebony* from 1948 to 1951, and co-managing editor from 1951 to 1964, before becoming international editor for the company thereafter.

Eunice. Johnson of Ebony Fashion Fair

In 1957 Ebony Fashion Fair blazed a trail of fashion excellence that has endured the test of time. Four gorgeous African American models brought fashion excitement to audiences in ten cities—Chicago; Indianapolis; New Orleans; Baltimore; Los Angeles; Dayton, Columbus, and Cleveland, Ohio; Philadelphia; and Washington, D.C.—where they displayed an array of dazzling American designer fashions. The late Freda DeKnight, *Ebony* magazine's home service director and Ebony Fashion Fair's first commentator, paraded fashions in homespun rhetoric weaving imaginary tales about each model and fashion. The 41st annual tour took place in the 1998–99 fashion seasons, with audiences still experiencing lively commentary, enriched with synthesizer programming, a drummer, a bassist, R&B, jazz, and song and dance routines performed by talented members of the troupe.

Ebony Fashion Fair

Thirteen models moved swiftly down the runways and across stages in 1998 and 1999, emphasizing elegance and excitement as they displayed American and European fashions brilliant with color, detail, and pizzazz. At the conclusion of the 40th annual tour, funds raised since inception by sponsors of the show had reached $45 million, all designated for various charities and scholarships. By then the show had given 540 young people and 112 wardrobe assistants the opportunity to visit cities and countries of many cultures, and had been sponsored by more than 180 prestigious social and civic organizations, including the United Negro College Fund, the NAACP, and the Urban League.

Johnson quickly soared to fame. By the early 1960s, he was one of the most prominent African American men in the country. In 1963, he and John F. Kennedy posed together to publicize a special issue of *Ebony*, which was celebrating The Emancipation Proclamation. In 1972, U.S. magazine publishers gave him accolades as Publisher of the Year. He also would go on to become chairman and CEO of Supreme Life Insurance Company, his first employer.

In 1973 the company began publishing *Ebony Jr!* (now defunct), a magazine designed to provide "positive black images" for pre-teens. Johnson branched out into new media formats when he began buying radio stations, including WJPC, Chicago's first African American-owned station. The following year, the company purchased WLOU in Louisville, Kentucky, and in the mid-1980s, the company acquired WLNR in Lansing, Illinois, which was merged with WJPC in 1992; the combined station was sold in 1995. Also in 1973, Fashion Fair Cosmetics was founded by the company in answer to the problems that women of color had in finding shades to match their skin tones. The company would go on to compete successfully against such huge competitors as Revlon and Johnson Products of Chicago, an unrelated company. Fashion Fair would grow to become the world's number one cosmetics company for women of color, with annual sales in 1982 reaching more than $30 million, and the products being sold in more than 2,500 stores throughout the United States, Canada, Europe, Africa, and the Caribbean.

In the early 1980s, Johnson began to groom his daughter Linda, who received her M.B.A. at Northwestern University's J.L. Kellogg School of Management, to take over the business. Linda started working summers for the company at the age of 15, eventually becoming fashion coordinator for both magazines and cosmetics. Linda Johnson Rice would go on to become president and chief executive officer of the company, as well as a director for companies such as Bausch & Lomb. In 1981 Johnson's adopted son, John E., a staff photographer for the company, died of sickle-cell anemia at age 25. That year, the company's total revenues reached $81 million. The following year, the company's revenue grew to $102 million.

In 1985 the company launched a new magazine called *EM* (*Ebony Man*), targeted mainly at the growing ranks of increasingly affluent buppies (black urban professionals). Like an African American version of *GQ* (*Gentlemen's Quarterly*), the inaugural November issue was chock-full of photos of immaculate male models bedecked in the latest fashions of clothing, with a healthy dollop of fashion and grooming tips, and filled with articles on health, fitness, personal finance, and shopping techniques.

In 1988 Johnson was inducted into the Publishing Hall of Fame, along with such other luminaries as Harold K. Guinzburg, founder of Viking Press and The Literary Guild; Maxwell Perkins, editor at Charles Scribners Sons; Richard Leo Simon and Max Lincoln Schuster, founders of Simon & Schuster, Inc.; and William Randolph Hearst, founder of Hearst Publishing Corporation. That year, the company had total revenues of $215 million, making it the second largest African American-owned business in the United States, behind Reginald Lewis's TLC Beatrice International Holdings. By this time, Johnson was also on the boards of Greyhound and two of his first advertisers, Chrysler and Zenith. The following year, Johnson was the recipient of IABC's Excellence in Communication "EXCEL" Award. That year, he was also the only African American man on the *Forbes* list of the 400 wealthiest people in the United States. Johnson was also awarded the U.S. Presidential Medal of Freedom in 1996.

Through its brands, which include EBONY and JET magazines, Fashion Fair Cosmetics, EBONY Fashion Fair and JPC Book Division, Johnson Publishing Company has always aimed at increasing African-Americans' pride in themselves by presenting their past and present achievements to America and to the world. This has been done by portraying the Black American experience in all its dynamics through the medium of printed words, images, cosmetics and fashion. Through the years the company has also labored to provide irrefutable proof to millions of Black Americans, young and old, that their dreams can and do come true. The entire Johnson Publishing Company family shares a deep commitment to meet consumer demands by producing quality products. Because of this commitment, JPC brands strive to continually give inspiration and hope to millions.

Also in 1989, Johnson wrote his autobiography, *Succeeding Against the Odds*, with assistance from longtime *Ebony* editor Lerone Bennett, Jr. In the autobiography, Johnson explained how he got started. "In organizing the staff [of my first magazine], I reached out to everybody, for I knew nothing about magazine publishing and editing.... When all else failed, I looked in the phone book and called an expert. Since I had nothing to lose, I always started at the top. I received valuable advice from Henry Luce of Time-Life and Gardner Cowles of Look. It was hard to get through to Luce, but ... I used a simple approach that almost always worked. I simply told the secretary or aide that I was the president—I stressed the word president—of my company. 'It is,' I said, 'a small company but I am the president, and I want to talk to your president.... If the president of the smallest country in the world comes to Washington, our president, as a matter of public policy and protocol will see him. So, it seems to me that your president, in the American tradition, will see me for a few minutes if you pass this request on and tell him that I don't want a donation or a job.' I used that on Henry Luce's secretary, and I got in to see him."

In 1991 the company sold its controlling interest in the last minority-owned insurance company in Illinois, Supreme Life Insurance, Johnson's first employer, to Chicago-based Unitrin, a life, health, and property insurance company. Total revenues for 1991 climbed to $281 million. Also, that year, the company entered into a joint venture with catalog company Spiegel Inc. to develop a fashion line and mail-order catalog aimed at African American women, launching a mail-order catalog called *E Style* to that effect in 1993. An accompanying credit card with the *E Style* imprint appeared in 1994.

In October 1992, the company introduced "Ebone," a new line of cosmetics for women of color, as well as a three-part videotape series called *The Ebony/Jet Guide to Black Excellence,* which profiled African American leaders, entrepreneurs, and entertainers to help provide positive role models for young people.

In November 1995, the company expanded its operations with the launch of *Ebony South Africa,* a counterpart to the U.S. version of the magazine. Because trade tariffs on incoming products to South Africa were taxed at 100 percent of the cost, Johnson Publishing subsidiary EBCO International teamed up with five South African companies, with Johnson holding 51 percent of the joint venture, in order to avoid losing money on the project. The company invested $2 million to $3 million on facilities, equipment, and staffing, opening editorial offices in Sandton, near Johannesburg. In the inaugural November 1995 issue, Bishop Desmond Tutu related the story of when he saw his first issue of *Ebony,* which had Jackie Robinson on the cover, when the cleric was nine years old and living in a ghetto township located some 30 miles outside of Johannesburg.

Total sales for 1997 reached $361.1 million, a 10.9 percent growth over the previous year, in which the company ranked 28th overall in magazine publishing companies by advertising revenue, with $26.8 million for the first half of 1996. Competition in the African American-oriented magazine industry, however, finally began to catch up with Johnson Publishing Company. With a plethora of new titles appearing, such as *Black Enterprise,* and the rise of other African American-oriented entertainment and informational vehicles such as Black Entertainment Television (BET), circulation of *Ebony* dropped 7 percent.

Like many of its competitors, Johnson Publishing faced challenges in the late 1990s and into the new millennium. As competing media companies tapped into the growing number of Internet users, the publisher of *Jet* and *Ebony* was slow to embrace online technology. An August 1999 *Crain's Chicago Business* article provided insight on the company's position claiming, "The situation Johnson Publishing confronts is shared by many mid-sized private companies as they grapple with the Internet challenge: an aversion to big investments without assurances of a reasonable financial return, and a desire to maintain controlling positions in all of their enterprises—a tenet that can preclude the sort of partnerships that are a centerpiece of the new media economy."

At the same time, Johnson Publishing faced a decrease in advertising revenues, which were hit even harder after the terrorist attacks of September 11, 2001. As such, the company was forced to make some key changes. It redesigned *Ebony*'s look, adding more fashion spreads and lifestyle stories, and focused on younger, up-and-coming African American celebrities. One critic commented on *Ebony*'s redesign in a 2004 *Crain's Chicago Business* article: "It looks a little different, but it's still frozen in the 1970s." Despite the company's efforts, circulation remained stagnant at 1.6 million; it had been 11.7 million in the 1970s.

During this time period, Johnson Publishing revamped its holdings. The catalog venture, *E Style,* was shuttered in 1997. *Ebony Man* magazine was canceled in 1998 and *Ebony South Africa* followed suit in 2000. Johnson Rice was named CEO in 2002, and her father remained chairman.

Despite growing competition and a weak advertising market, Johnson Publishing remained the most successful African American-owned publishing firm in the United States. Along with publishing *Ebony* and *Jet* magazines, the company controlled Fashion Fair Cosmetics, which continued to reign as the leading line of makeup and skincare for women of color. Its products were sold in more than 2,500 stores in the United States, Canada, Africa, England, France, Switzerland, the Bahamas, Bermuda, and the Virgin Islands. In 2005, the Ebony Fashion Fair continued as the largest traveling fashion show with more than $51 million donated to charity since its inception. Johnson Publishing's Book Division published works by African American authors, including Lerone Bennett, Jr. With an arsenal of powerful, well-known brands in the company's portfolio, Johnson Publishing's management was confident its products would be found on store shelves for years to come.

THE JOHNSON PRODUCT COMPANY LEGACY

1954: George Ellis Johnson, Sr. founded Johnson Products

George Ellis Johnson, Sr. (born June 12, 1927) is an American entrepreneur and the founder of Johnson Products Company, an international cosmetics empire headquartered in Chicago, Illinois.

Johnson was born in Richton, Mississippi, in a three-room sharecropper's shack. When he was two, he moved to Chicago with his mother, Priscilla, after his parents had separated. At the age of eight, while attending Doolittle Elementary School, Johnson also started work as a shoe shine boy. He later attended Wendell Phillips High School, but dropped out to work full-time jobs. During the day he was a bus boy, and in the evenings, he set pins at a local bowling alley. In 1944, he took a job working for Samuel B. Fuller, who owned a cosmetics firm, as a production chemist.

In 1954, at the encouragement of a co-worker, Johnson left the Fuller company and founded Johnson Products with his wife Joan, focusing on the African American male hair care market. Johnson borrowed $250 from a bank and another $250 from a friend to finance the venture. The company's first product was Ultra Wave, a hair relaxer for men. In 1957, Ultra Sheen, a revolutionary hair straightener that could easily be used in the home, was introduced for women.

1960 George Johnson introduced Afro Sheen

During the next quarter century, more product lines were introduced like Afro Sheen. Afro-Sheen, one of Johnson's best-known products, was released in the late 1960s, at a time when the "Afro" became a popular hairstyle for African Americans.

Over the next few decades, Johnson Products continued to grow, focusing its efforts on not only its products line but on training cosmetologists on the proper usage as well. In 1964, Johnson founded Independence Bank, and during the 1970s he became the exclusive sponsor behind the nationally syndicated dance show *Soul Train*.

In 1971, Johnson Products became the first African American-owned company to be listed on the American Stock Exchange. That same year, Johnson became the first African American to serve on the board of directors of Commonwealth Edison.

In the mid-1980s, more and more competitors began entering the African American hair care industry and the Federal Trade Commission forced Johnson Products to put warning labels on lye-based products, without requiring Revlon to do the same. In 1989, Johnson and his wife of thirty-nine years, Joan, divorced. As a part of the divorce settlement, Johnson transferred 49.5 percent of the company over to her. Their son, Eric, took over the reins, but left the company in 1992, and the company was sold to IVAX for $61 million the following year. In 1995, Johnson and Joan remarried, and in 1998, Carson Products bought the company.

During the course of his career, Johnson received numerous honors. *Ebony* magazine awarded him with its American Black Achievement Award in 1978, and in 1979 Johnson received the public service award of the Harvard Club for the work of the George E. Johnson Foundation and the George E. Johnson Educational Fund. He has been active with a number of civic organizations, as well, including the Chicago Urban League, the Lyric Opera, Northwestern Memorial Hospital and Operation PUSH.

THE SOFT SHEEN HAIR PRODUCT ENTERPRISE

Edward George Gardner

Edward George Gardner was born on February 25, 1925, in Chicago, Illinois. He grew up in Chicago and joined the United States Army during World War II. Back in Chicago after the war, he earned a bachelor's degree at the Chicago Teachers' College and a master's at the city's top private institution, the University of Chicago, which admitted very few blacks at the time. Gardner taught high school and served as an assistant principal in Chicago for 21 years, from 1945 to 1964.

To make extra money on the side, Gardner sold beauty supplies part time. He and his wife Bettiann traveled to hair salons that served a black clientele and observed a huge void in the marketplace, just waiting to be filled by products aimed at African Americans. They noted how successful Chicago's Johnson Products Co. had been with its new Ultra Sheen hair straightener, and they remembered the money that had been made in the hair care field by the country's first black female millionaire, Madame C. J. Walker.

Various dates from 1957 to 1964 have been given for the founding of Edward and Bettiann Gardner's Soft Sheen Products firm—probably because the enterprise evolved gradually from a series of experiments in the basement of the Gardners' small South Side home. Gardner's daughter Terri and her dog Cinnamon served as product testers in the early years, with occasionally disastrous results: Terri's hands and hair were colored mauve for several weeks at one point. Dinner had to wait until the pots and pans that were being used to mix chemicals could be washed and rinsed off. Ten-year-old Gary Gardner, Soft Sheen's future president, mixed Soft Sheen Hair and Scalp Conditioner and demonstrated it at trade shows.

Starting out by selling products out of their home, the Gardners drew on their knowledge of and close communication with Chicago's beauty salon owners—a practice they continued to stress, even after Soft Sheen became an operation with millions of dollars in annual sales. "All Chicagoans from those beauticians on 47th Street, 63rd Street, 79th Street and West Madison Street that got this business started…. They gave me the love and inspiration to want to do more. And that is the reason we try to do so much," Gardner later told an Operation PUSH awards banquet in an address quoted by *Jet*.

Born on February 25, 1925, in Chicago, IL; married Bettiann; children: Gary, Guy, Tracey, Terri; *Education:* Chicago Teachers' College, B.A., 1940s; University of Chicago, M.A.; 1940s. *Military Service:* Served in U.S. Army during World War II; reached rank of sergeant.

Career: Chicago Public Schools, teacher and assistant principal, 1945-64; beauty supply salesman, part time, late 1950s; began manufacturing hair care products in Chicago home and established

Soft Sheen Products Co., late 1950s; Soft Sheen Products, Chicago, chairman, 1964-98; Garden Investment Partners, Chicago, president, 1998–.

Selected awards: *Black Enterprise* magazine, Company of the Year award for Soft Sheen, 1989; Golden Pyramid Award, 1999.

Address: *Office* —Garden Investment Partners, 9535 South Cottage Grove Avenue, Chicago IL 60628.

Was not to forsake salon owners," his daughter Denise told *Black Enterprise*. "We marry ourselves to them and we literally take professional vows."

Soft Sheen grew slowly. By 1976, annual sales totaled $200,000—a long way up from Gardner's basement, but well behind Johnson Products and its $40.1 million in sales. That year, however, external events dented Johnson's momentum, and Gardner quickly took advantage of the situation. Federal Trade Commission officials began requiring new warning labels on hair straighteners containing lye, a jolt of bad publicity that affected both Johnson Products and Gardner's Soft Sheen. While Johnson quietly acquiesced to the regulation, Soft Sheen quickly pulled its existing product line off the shelves and introduced new lines that avoided the warning requirement. "We knew the direction the market was going," Gardner's son Gary told *Forbes*, "and we acted fast."

The new visibility of Soft Sheen in the marketplace coincided with the rise in popularity of the Jheri Curl style, and in 1981 Soft Sheen launched its Care Free Curl product line. That allowed salon owners to finish the curl styling process in two hours (rather than eight), increasing customer turnover and creating a need for a whole phalanx of Care Free Curl-associated products. By 1982 Soft Sheen sales topped $55 million, and the following year the company took up a long residence on the *Black Enterprise 100* list of top African-American-owned companies. In 1989 it was named the magazine's Company of the Year.

By the 1980s, Soft Sheen was a true family operation. In addition to Gary Gardner, who rose to the position of president, Bettiann Gardner served as vice-chairman and as publisher of the cosmetics magazine *Shoptalk;* son Guy Gardner headed the Bottlewerks firm, which supplied materials to Soft Sheen; daughter Terri Gardner did marketing work for the company; and daughter Tracey Gardner became vice-president of science and technology. Edward Gardner himself began to devote more and more time to his interests in the Chicago community.

The first of these was the mayoral campaign of Harold Washington, elected Chicago's first African-American mayor in 1983, but at first a reluctant candidate. Many observers thought that Washington had little chance to win in a city that didn't have a black majority, and Washington himself refused to enter the race unless 200,000 African Americans registered to vote. That was where Gardner came in. Soft Sheen temporarily devoted its advertising budget to voter-registration radio spots featuring Terri Gardner's "Come Alive on October 5" slogan that reminded listeners of the registration deadline.

"My family has always been involved in trying to make life better for the African-American community," Gardner told *Chicago Weekend*. "We thought it was our responsibility as a successful black company, where we gained most of (our) income right here in Chicago, to give back... to help the black community realize its strength and power." Washington rode a surge of black registration to a primary victory over two white opponents and then to the mayor's office and Gardner became involved in other political campaigns.

Another cause to which Gardner lent his time and effort was the struggle to control Chicago's spiraling rate of violent crime. After a Soft Sheen employee was shot during a robbery attempt in 1983, Gardner placed newspaper advertisements denouncing black-on-black crime. A 1993 ad, placed in response to a street gang slaying of a 15-month-old baby, read in part (as quoted in the *Chicago Sun-Times):* "It's time for these young men [gang members] to begin to act like men. Carrying a gun does not make you a man. Assuming the responsibilities of a man by doing the positive things in life is what makes you a man." Through his Soft Sheen Foundation, Gardner founded Black on Black Love, a community umbrella group that administered such programs as an arts and crafts center in Chicago's notorious (Robert Taylor Homes) housing project and a bank employment-training program.

The Revived Historic, Chicago Regal Theater

Gardner also plunged into the revitalization of the city's South Side, sinking $4 million into the renovation of the Regal Theater. A 1920s architectural jewel in Moorish style that had been unused for years at its 79th Street location, the Regal (formerly the Avalon Theater) had been Chicago's answer to the Apollo Theater in New York's Harlem neighborhood. A concert showcase for top-flight African-American acts, in its heyday, it had played host to the likes of Duke Ellington and Jackie Wilson. "The black community is hungry for places to go for entertainment," Gardner told the *Chicago Tribune*. "But such places must be 'quality.' We think that with the beauty of the architecture and the quality of the shows, we can provide that kind of place."

By the end of the 1980s, Gardner had also purchased a stake in the National Basketball Association's Chicago Bulls, and he and Bettiann had become, in the words of *Black Enterprise*, "part of the fabric of the Windy City." Soft Sheen also sponsored a 30-city tour by singers Anita Baker and Luther Vandross, becoming the first black-owned company to sponsor a major concert tour. In the 1990s, however, several factors combined to put the brakes on the company's performance. Soft-curl styles declined in popularity, and Soft Sheen faced competition from white-owned hair-care giants such as Revlon. Soft Sheen tried to move into international markets, but growth slowed dramatically.

After several corporate shake-ups, Soft Sheen was sold to the French cosmetics firm L'Oreal in 1998. Gardner, a businessman to the end, told the *New York Times* that "selling the company to me is just a phase, just like starting the company." But the 73-year-old Gardner gave the people of Chicago one last gift: as part of the sales deal, he extracted from L'Oreal a promise to keep the company's headquarters located on his beloved South Side. An $8-million renovation of an old Johnson Products building opened in 2002. Gardner remained active in retirement, as president of Garden Investment Partners, and many Chicagoans agreed that he was, in the words of Seaway National Bank chairman Jacoby Dickens (quoted in *Jet*), "one of the great business and community leaders of our time."

Personal care entrepreneur Edward George Gardner was born on February 25, 1925 in Chicago, Illinois to Frank and Eva Gardner. Following service in the U. S. Army during World War II, Gardner returned to Chicago and enrolled in Chicago Teacher's College, where he received his B.A. degree in the 1940s. He went on to also obtain his M.A. degree from the University of Chicago.

Gardner worked for fourteen years as an instructor and school administrator for the Chicago Public Schools while simultaneously working part time as a black hair care sales representative. Learning of the dissatisfaction of many African American consumers and hair care professionals, he and his wife, Bettiann, launched Soft Sheen Products from their basement in 1964. With brands such as Optimum and Care Free Curl, Soft Sheen Products grew into a multimillion-dollar enterprise employing more than 400 people. The company also developed globally, exporting its products to Canada, the Caribbean and West Africa. In 1998, Gardner sold Soft Sheen Products to L'Oreal of Paris and passed the day-to-day operation of Soft Sheen on to his children.

Gardner has also been committed to service in the Chicago community. He owned the New Regal Theater and served as president of Garden Investment Partners. In addition, Gardner received credit for helping register over 250,000 people for Mayor Harold Washington's election in 1983. He served as a board member of the Chicago Urban league and was invited by President Bill Clinton to attend an economic summit in Little Rock, Arkansas, to discuss the impact corporations can have on urban employment.

ARIEL INVESTMENTS, LLC UNITED STATES' LARGEST MINORITY-RUN MUTUAL FUND FIRM

John Washington Rogers Jr

John Washington Rogers Jr. (born March 31, 1958) is an investor who founded Ariel Capital Management (now Ariel Investments, LLC) in 1983. He is chairman and CEO of the company, which is the United States' largest minority-run mutual fund firm. He has been a regular contributor to *Forbes* magazine for most of the last decade. Active in the 2008 Barack Obama presidential campaign, Rogers was a leader of the 2009 Inauguration committee.

Rogers was appointed as the Board President of the Chicago Park District for six years in the 1990s. He also was appointed as board member to several companies, as a leader of several organizations affiliated with his collegiate alma mater, and as a leader in youth education in his native Chicago. In 2007, Rogers was honored with the Woodrow Wilson Award from Princeton University for the breadth and depth of his service to many organizations. While a student at Princeton, he was captain of the 1979–80 Ivy League co-champion Princeton Tigers men's basketball team.

Rogers was raised in the Hyde Park community area of Chicago's South Side, and graduated from the University of Chicago Laboratory Schools in 1976. At the age of 12 his father started giving him dividend-paying stocks. He went to college at Princeton University, where he used his free time to glean market information at his local stock brokerage and where he was influenced by Burton Malkiel's *A Random Walk Down Wall Street*.

He was a college basketball teammate of Craig Robinson, and he served as captain of the 1979–80 Ivy League co-champion Princeton Tigers men's basketball team. He had a habit of perusing business journals and calling his broker from stadium payphones. Rogers credits Pete Carril, his basketball coach, as his greatest college influence because Carril stressed precision and teamwork.

Rogers studied economics at Princeton. After graduating in 1980, he worked for William Blair & Company in Chicago. A few years later, and with the financial backing of family and friends, he opened his own firm, starting with the Municipal Employees' Annuity & Benefit Fund of Chicago as his first account.

He is the only son of Jewel Lafontant and John Rogers, Sr. His mother Jewel was the first African American woman to graduate from the University Of Chicago Law School in 1946. She became a prominent Republican lawyer, and she nominated Richard Nixon, who won the Republican Party Presidential Nomination, at the 1960 Republican National Convention. His father was a Tuskegee airman pilot with over 100 combat missions of service during World War II and an eventual Cook County judge for twenty years. His parents divorced in 1961 and his mother died in 1997. Rogers was three years old when his parents divorced. He had a daughter, Victoria, with his former wife Desiree Rogers.

One of Rogers' great-grandfathers owned the Stratford Hotel in Greenwood, Tulsa, Oklahoma, known as The Black Wall Street. The hotel was destroyed in the Tulsa race riot. Rogers helped finance *Before They Die!*, a documentary detailing some survivor accounts, and made a brief appearance in the film.

On December 28, 2002, Rogers married Sharon Fairley who was also a divorcee. At the time of her 2002 wedding announcement in *The New York Times*, Fairley, who is also a Princeton alumna, was the Executive Director of Consumer Marketing and Trademark Development at Pharmacia. Currently, Fairley is the City of Chicago's new leader for the Independent Police Review Authority, which investigates police-involved shootings. Previously, she worked for Chicago's Office of the Inspector General as First Deputy Inspector General and General Counsel and as an Assistant United States Attorney in Chicago for eight years.

Rogers has a special overnight delivery subscription with *BusinessWeek* that is delivered via Federal Express so it is received a day earlier than the regular public.

He still does not use computers or e-mail.

Three-on-three basketball has been a continuing part of his life

John Rogers is known for wearing gray pinstripe business suits to work. On the basketball court, he wears black-rimmed goggles.

Three-on-three basketball has been a continuing part of his life. As of 2000, he had a team with the second and fourth all-time leading scorers at Princeton, Kit Mueller (class of 1991) and Robinson (1983) and the school's second leading three point shooter Sean Jackson (1992). Between 1996 and 2000 his team had won 12 of 17 tournaments that they had entered. He scored the game-winning basket of Chicago's three-on-three basketball tournament on a team with Arne Duncan, Robinson, and Kit Mueller. Rogers and Robinson were among those invited to practice with Michael Jordan as he prepared for his comeback. He claims to be the first person to have beaten Jordan in a game of one-on-one at one of his fantasy basketball camps. Among the witnesses to the victory, which was reported in *Sports Illustrated*, were John Thompson Jr., Mike Krzyzewski and fellow fantasy participant Damon Wayans.

Rogers was one of the hot stock pickers of the 1980s. Rogers uses a value investing strategy, which has been a problem at times when growth stocks have been the better-performing investment class. However, his firm and its mutual funds have often been among the industry performance leaders and have, on average, outperformed the market. He eschews investing in new companies or making investments in companies that have no track record. For example, rather than invest in AIDS-related stocks, he would prefer to invest in hospitals that treat AIDS victims. His typical holding period is four or five years rather than the 14-month period of the average mutual fund. Melody Hobson serves as the president of the company.

The growth of his company has been steady. He founded the firm in July 1983 with $10,000, which he turned into $23,170 by the end of February 1984. He had financial backing from his mother and other friends and relatives. The Ariel fund became public on November 6, 1986. In November 2000, he had 41 employees. In February 2002, the company had 51 employees and more than 120 institutional clients (including United Airlines, Chevron, Texaco, and the California State Teachers' Retirement System), which grew to include institutional clients such as Wal-Mart and PepsiCo by April 2005. The company had over 100 employees as of 2008. In 2008, the company changed its name to Ariel Investments, LLC.

Rogers also has served on the boards of directors of other publicly traded Chicago-based corporations, including Exelon, and Bally Total Fitness Corporation, where he was named lead director.

Rogers has been a regular contributor to *Forbes* for many years and online archives of his commentaries go back as far as 2001. He provides regular personal finance commentaries in a column that has recently been appearing under the title "The Patient Investor".

On February 23, 2008, Rogers became the first African-American winner of a Woodrow Wilson Award from Princeton University for his service to the Princeton alumni community, the Chicago community, the African American community and the financial community. In 1994, *Time* featured him as one of its 50 leaders under 40. Rogers is co-chairman of Jesse Jackson's annual Wall Street Project minority conference, chairman of the Chicago Urban League, a member of four corporate boards and was a leading campaigner for Princeton basketball legend and United States Senator Bill Bradley's 2000 United States presidential campaign. Three of the boards he serves on are for Fortune 500 companies: Aon Corporation, Exelon Corporation and McDonald's. He is a trustee of the University of Chicago. He has served numerous civic, educational and arts organizations as a director or trustee, including the Rainbow/PUSH Coalition, the Oprah Winfrey Foundation and the Chicago Symphony Orchestra. At Princeton, he was a trustee of the University from 1990 to 1994 and more recently has served as a member of the Association of Black Princeton Alumni (ABPA) and the Princeton Varsity Club board of directors, as well as the Alumni Schools Committee. In the early 1990s, Rogers served as a fundraising leader in Project Vote voter registration efforts led by former United States President Barack Obama. He has been an advocate for greater diversity in upper-level corporate positions.

Rogers and his company were part of a network of community partners that supported the Ariel Community Academy, which emphasizes financial literacy in its curriculum. Rogers donates both time and money to the academy: he has designed curricula and brings students to board meetings. As a result of his money and time investment, 80% of the eighth-grade graduates from the academy are accepted at elite area high schools. Rogers adopted a class of 40 sixth graders at a cost of $200,000 per year through the "I Have a Dream Foundation". He expected to pay for college for about 30 of the students.

2008: John Rogers Inner circle of the Barack Obama presidential campaign

He was part of the inner circle of the Barack Obama presidential campaign. He is a long-time Obama associate who serves as the co-chair of Obama's Illinois finance committee and who has been a major fundraiser for Democratic Party candidates.

He served along with Bill Daley, Pat Ryan, Penny Pritzker and Julianna Smoot on the Barack Obama 2009 presidential inauguration committee. In June 2009, Rogers became chairman of the University of Chicago Laboratory Schools' board.

Since late December 2011, the basketball court in the main competition gym at the University of Chicago Laboratory Schools has been named after Rogers. Rogers graduated from and played basketball himself at University High School. His name was printed on the floor during Winter Break of the 2011-12 school years and the court's new title will officially be adopted on February 8, 2012, in a ceremony corresponding with U-High's home game against conference rival Northridge Prep.

CHAPTER EIGHT

The Richest African American Woman In America, In The Twenty First Century and Man in the 1980's

1986-2011: The Oprah Winfrey Show, Oprah Gail Winfrey

Chicago produced the richest African American women in the twenty first century. Oprah Gail Winfrey (born Orpah Gail Winfrey; January 29, 1954) is an American media proprietor, talk show host, actress, producer, and philanthropist. She is best known for her talk show *The Oprah Winfrey Show*, which was the highest-rated television program of its kind in history and was nationally syndicated from 1986 to 2011 in Chicago, Illinois. Dubbed the "Queen of All Media", she has been ranked the richest African-American, the greatest black philanthropist in American history, and is currently North America's first and only multi-billionaire black person. Several assessments rank her as the most influential woman in the world. In

2013, she was awarded the Presidential Medal of Freedom by President Barack Obama and honorary doctorate degrees from Duke and Harvard.

Winfrey was born into poverty in rural Mississippi to a teenage single mother and later raised in an inner-city Milwaukee neighborhood. She has stated that she was molested during her childhood and early teens and became pregnant at 14; her son died in infancy. Sent to live with the man she calls her father, a barber in Tennessee, Winfrey landed a job in radio while still in high school and began co-anchoring the local evening news at the age of 19. Her emotional ad-lib delivery eventually got her transferred to the daytime talk show arena, and after boosting a third-rated local Chicago talk show to first place, she launched her production company and became internationally syndicated.

Credited with creating a more intimate confessional form of media communication, she is thought to have popularized and revolutionized the tabloid talk show genre pioneered by Phil Donahue, which a Yale study says broke 20th century taboos and allowed LGBT people to enter the mainstream. By the mid-1990s, she had reinvented her show with a focus on literature, self-improvement, and spirituality. Though criticized for unleashing a confession culture, promoting controversial self-help ideas, and an emotion-centered approach, she is often praised for overcoming adversity to become a benefactor to others. From 2006 to 2008, her endorsement of Obama, by one estimate, delivered over a million votes in the close 2008 Democratic primary race.

Winfrey was named "Orpah" on her birth certificate after the biblical figure in the Book of Ruth, but people mispronounced it regularly and "Oprah" stuck.

Winfrey was born in Kosciusko, Mississippi, to an unmarried teenage mother. She later said that her conception was due to a single sexual encounter and the couple broke up not long after. Her mother, Vernita Lee (born c. 1935), was a housemaid. Winfrey's biological father is usually noted as Vernon Winfrey (born 1933), a coal miner turned barber, turned city councilman, who had been in the Armed Forces when she was born. However, Mississippi farmer and World War II veteran Noah Robinson, Sr. (born c. 1925) has claimed to be her biological father. A genetic test in 2006 determined that her matrilineal line originated among the Kpelle ethnic group, in the area that today is Liberia. Her genetic makeup was determined to be 89% Sub-Saharan African, 8% Native American, and 3% East Asian. However, the East Asian may, given the imprecision of genetic testing, actually be Native American markers.

After Winfrey's birth, her mother traveled north, and Winfrey spent her first six years living in rural poverty with her maternal grandmother, Hattie Mae (Presley) Lee (April 15, 1900 – February 27, 1963), who was so poor that Winfrey often wore dresses made of potato sacks, for which the local children made fun of her. Her grandmother taught her to read before the age of three and took her to the local church, where she was nicknamed "The Preacher" for her ability to recite Bible verses. When Winfrey was a child, her grandmother would hit her with a stick when she did not do chores or if she misbehaved in any way. At age six, Winfrey moved to an inner-city neighborhood in Milwaukee, Wisconsin, with her mother Vernita Lee, who was less supportive and encouraging than her grandmother had been, largely as a result of the long hours she worked as a maid. Around this time, Lee had given birth to another daughter, Winfrey's younger half-sister, Patricia who later (in February 2003, at age 43) died of causes related to cocaine addiction. By 1962, Lee was having difficulty raising both daughters, so Winfrey was temporarily sent to live with Vernon in Nashville, Tennessee. While Winfrey was in Nashville, Lee gave birth to a third daughter who was put up for adoption (in the hope of easing the financial straits that had led to Lee's being on welfare) and later also named Patricia. Winfrey did not learn she had a second half-sister until 2010. By the time Winfrey moved back in with Lee, Lee had also given birth to a boy named Jeffrey, Winfrey's half-brother, who died of AIDS-related causes in 1989.

Winfrey has stated she was molested by her cousin, uncle, and a family friend, starting when she was nine years old, something she first announced to her viewers on a 1986 episode of her TV show regarding sexual abuse. When Winfrey discussed the alleged abuse with family members at age 24, they refused to accept what she said. Winfrey once commented that she had chosen not to be a mother because she had not been mothered well.

At 13, after suffering years of abuse, Winfrey ran away from home. When she was 14, she became pregnant, but her son was born prematurely and he died shortly after birth. Winfrey later stated she felt betrayed by the family member who had sold the story of her son to the *National Enquirer* in 1990. She began going to Lincoln High School; but after early success in the Upward Bound program, was transferred to the affluent suburban Nicolet High School, where she says her poverty was constantly rubbed in her face as she rode the bus to school with fellow African-Americans, some of whom were servants of her classmates' families. She began to steal money from her mother in an effort to keep up with her free-spending peers, to lie to and argue with her mother, and to go out with older boys.

Her frustrated mother once again sent her to live with Vernon in Nashville, Tennessee, though this time she did not take her back. Vernon was strict, but encouraging, and made her education a priority. Winfrey became an honors student, was voted Most Popular Girl, and joined her high school speech team at East Nashville High School, placing second in the nation in dramatic interpretation. She won an oratory contest, which secured her full scholarship to Tennessee State University, a historically black institution, where she studied communication. Her first job as a teenager was working at a local grocery store. At the age of 17, Winfrey won the Miss Black Tennessee beauty pageant. She also attracted the attention of the local black radio station, WVOL, which hired her to do the news part-time. She worked there during her senior year of high school, and again while in her first two years of college.

Winfrey's career choice in media would not have surprised her grandmother, who once said that ever since Winfrey could talk, she was on stage. As a child, she played games interviewing her corncob doll and the crows on the fence of her family's property. Winfrey later acknowledged her grandmother's influence, saying it was Hattie Mae who had encouraged her to speak in public and "gave me a positive sense of myself".

Main article: The Oprah Winfrey Show

Working in local media, she was both the youngest news anchor and the first black female news anchor at Nashville's WLAC-TV. She moved to Baltimore's WJZ-TV in 1976 to co-anchor the six o'clock news. In 1977, she was removed as co-anchor and worked lower profile positions at the station. She was then recruited to join Richard Sher as co-host of WJZ's local talk show *People Are Talking*, which premiered on August 14, 1978. She also hosted the local version of *Dialing for Dollars* there.

Winfrey on the first national broadcast of The Oprah Winfrey Show in 1986

In 1983, Winfrey relocated to Chicago to host WLS-TV's low-rated half-hour morning talk show, *AM Chicago*. The first episode aired on January 2, 1984. Within months after Winfrey took over, the show went from last place in the ratings to overtaking *Donahue* as the highest-rated talk show in Chicago. The movie critic Roger Ebert persuaded her to sign a syndication deal with King World. Ebert predicted that she would generate 40 times as much revenue, as his television show, *At the Movies*. It was renamed The Oprah Winfrey Show, expanded to a full hour and broadcast nationally beginning September 8, 1986. Winfrey's syndicated show brought in double Donahue's national audience, displacing Donahue as the number-one daytime talk show in America. Their much-publicized contest was the subject of enormous scrutiny. *TIME* magazine wrote:

> Few people would have bet on Oprah Winfrey's swift rise to host of the most popular talk show on TV. In a field dominated by white males, she is a black female of ample bulk. As interviewers go, she is no match for, say, Phil Donahue... What she lacks in journalistic toughness, she makes up for in plainspoken curiosity, robust humor and, above all empathy. Guests with sad stories to tell are apt to rouse a tear in Oprah's eye ... They, in turn, often find themselves revealing things they would not imagine telling anyone, much less a national TV audience. It is the talk show as a group therapy session.

TV columnist Howard Rosenberg said, "She's a roundhouse, a full course meal, big, brassy, loud, aggressive, hyper, laughable, lovable, soulful, tender, low-down, earthy, and hungry. And she may know the way to Phil Donahue's jugular." *Newsday*'s Les Payne observed, "Oprah Winfrey is sharper than Donahue, wittier, more genuine, and far better attuned to her audience, if not the world," and Martha Bayles of *The Wall Street Journal* wrote, "It's a relief to see a gab-monger with a fond, but realistic assessment of her own cultural and religious roots."

In the early years of *The Oprah Winfrey Show*, the program was classified as a tabloid talk show. In the mid-1990s, Winfrey adopted a less tabloid-oriented format, hosting shows on broader topics such as heart disease, geopolitics, spirituality, and meditation, interviewing celebrities on social issues they were directly involved with, such as cancer, charity work, or substance abuse, and hosting televised giveaways including shows where every audience member received a new car (donated by General Motors) or a trip to Australia (donated by Australian tourism bodies). In addition to her talk show, Winfrey also produced and co-starred in the 1989 drama miniseries *The Women of Brewster Place*, as well as a short-lived spin-off, *Brewster Place*. As well as hosting and appearing on television shows, Winfrey co-founded the women's cable television network *Oxygen*. She is also the president of Harpo Productions (*Oprah* spelled backwards). On January 15, 2008, Winfrey and Discovery Communications announced plans to change Discovery Health Channel into a new channel called *OWN: Oprah Winfrey Network*. It was scheduled to launch in 2009 but was delayed, and actually launched on January 1, 2011.

The series finale of *The Oprah Winfrey Show* aired on May 25, 2011.

In January 2017, CBS revealed that Winfrey would join 60 Minutes as a special contributor on the Sunday evening news magazine program starting in the fall of 2017.

Celebrity interviews

In 1993, Winfrey hosted a rare prime-time interview with Michael Jackson, which became the fourth most-watched event in American television history as well as the most watched interview ever, with an audience of 36.5million. On December 1, 2005, Winfrey appeared on the *Late Show with David Letterman* to promote the new Broadway musical *The Color Purple*, of which she was a producer, joining the host for the first time in 16 years. The episode was hailed by some as the "television event of the decade" and helped Letterman attract his largest audience in more than 11 years: 13.45 million viewers. Although a much-rumored feud, was said to have been the cause of the rift both Winfrey and Letterman balked at such talk. "I want you to know, it's really over, whatever you thought was happening", said Winfrey. On September 10, 2007, Letterman made his first appearance on *The Oprah Winfrey Show*, as its season premiere was filmed in New York City.

In 2006, rappers Ludacris, 50 Cent and Ice Cube criticized Winfrey for what they perceived as an anti-hip hop bias. In an interview with *GQ* magazine, Ludacris said that Winfrey gave him a "hard time" about his lyrics, and edited comments he made during an appearance on her show with the cast of the film *Crash*. He also said that he wasn't initially invited on the show with the rest of the cast. Winfrey responded by saying that she is opposed to rap lyrics that "marginalize women", but enjoys some artists, including Kanye West, who appeared on her show. She said she spoke with Ludacris backstage after his appearance to explain her position and said she understood that his music was for entertainment purposes, but that some of his listeners might take it literally. In September 2008, Winfrey received criticism after Matt Drudge of the *Drudge Report* reported that Winfrey refused to have Sarah Palin on her show, allegedly because of Winfrey's support for Barack Obama. Winfrey denied the report, maintaining that there never was a discussion regarding Palin's appearing on her show. She said that after she made public her support for Obama, she decided that she would not let her show be used as a platform for any of the candidates. Although Obama appeared twice on her show, those appearances were prior to his declaring himself a candidate. Winfrey added that Palin would make a fantastic guest and that she would love to have her on the show after the election, which she did on November 18, 2009.

In 2009, Winfrey was criticized for allowing actress Suzanne Somers to appear on her show to discuss hormone treatments that are not accepted by mainstream medicine. Critics have also suggested that Winfrey is not tough enough when questioning celebrity guests or politicians whom she appears to like. Lisa de Moraes, a media columnist for *The Washington Post*, stated: "Oprah doesn't do follow-up questions unless you're an author who's embarrassed her by fabricating portions of a supposed memoir she's plugged for her book club."

Winfrey as Sofia in "The Color Purple"

In 1985, Winfrey co-starred in Steven Spielberg's *The Color Purple* as distraught housewife Sofia. She was nominated for an Academy Award for Best Supporting Actress for her performance. The Alice Walker novel went on to become a Broadway musical which opened in late 2005, with Winfrey credited as a producer. In October 1998, Winfrey produced and starred in the film *Beloved*, based on Toni Morrison's Pulitzer Prize-winning novel of the same name. To prepare for her role as Sethe, the protagonist and former slave, Winfrey experienced a 24-hour simulation of the experience of slavery, which included being tied up and blindfolded and left alone in the woods. Despite major advertising, including two episodes of her talk show dedicated solely to the film, and moderate to good critical reviews, *Beloved* opened to poor box-office results, losing approximately $30 million. While promoting the movie, co-star Thandie Newton described Winfrey as "a very strong technical actress and it's because she's so smart. She's acute. She's got a mind like a razor blade."

In 2005, Harpo Productions released a film adaptation of Zora Neale Hurston's 1937 novel *Their Eyes Were Watching God*. The made-for-television film was based upon a teleplay by Suzan-Lori Parks and starred Halle Berry in the lead female role.

In late 2008, Winfrey's company Harpo Films signed an exclusive output pact to develop and produce scripted series, documentaries, and movies for HBO. Oprah voiced Gussie the goose for *Charlotte's Web* (2006) and the voice of Judge Bumbleden in *Bee Movie* (2007) co-starring the voices of Jerry Seinfeld and Renée Zellweger. In 2009, Winfrey provided the voice for the character of Eudora, the mother of Princess Tiana, in Disney's *The Princess and the Frog* and in 2010, narrated the US version of the BBC nature program *Life* for Discovery.

Winfrey on the cover of Live Your Best Life, a collection of features from O: The Oprah Magazine.

Winfrey has co-authored five books. At the announcement of a weight loss book in 2005, co-authored with her personal trainer Bob Greene, it was said that her undisclosed advance fee had broken the record for the world's highest book advance fee, previously held by the autobiography of former U.S. President Bill Clinton.

Her memoir, *The Life You Want*, is scheduled for publication in 2017

Winfrey publishes magazines: *O, The Oprah Magazine*; from 2004 to 2008, she also published a magazine called *O at Home*. In 2002, *Fortune* called *O, the Oprah Magazine* the most successful start-up ever in the industry. Although its circulation had declined by more than 10 percent (to 2.4 million) from 2005 to 2008, the January 2009 issue was the bestselling issue since 2006. The audience for her magazine is considerably more upscale than for her TV show, the average reader earning well above the median for U.S. women.

Winfrey's company created the *Oprah.com* website to provide resources and interactive content relating to her shows, magazines, book club, and public charity. Oprah.com averages more than 70-million page views and more than six-million users per month, and receives approximately 20,000 emails each week. Winfrey initiated "Oprah's Child Predator Watch List", through her show and website, to help track down accused child molesters. Within the first 48 hours, two of the featured men were captured.

On February 9, 2006, it was announced that Winfrey had signed a three-year, $55 million contract with XM Satellite Radio to establish a new radio channel. The channel, Oprah Radio, features popular contributors to *The Oprah Winfrey Show* and *O, The Oprah Magazine* including Nate Berkus, Dr. Mehmet Oz, Bob Greene, Dr. Robin Smith, and Marianne Williamson. Oprah & Friends began broadcasting at 11:00 am ET, September 25, 2006, from a new studio at Winfrey's Chicago headquarters. The channel broadcasts 24 hours a day, seven days a week on XM Radio Channel 156. Winfrey's contract requires her to be on the air 30 minutes a week, 39 weeks a year. The 30-minute weekly show features Winfrey with friend Gayle King.

Born in rural poverty, and raised by a mother dependent on government welfare payments in a poor urban neighborhood, Winfrey became a millionaire at the age of 32 when her talk show received national syndication. Winfrey negotiated ownership rights to the television program and started her own production company. At the age of 41, Winfrey had a net worth of $340 million and replaced Bill Cosby as the only African American on the Forbes 400. With a 2000 net worth of $800 million, Winfrey is believed to be the richest African American of the 20th century. There has been a course taught at the University of Illinois focusing on Winfrey's business acumen, namely: "History 298: Oprah Winfrey, the Tycoon". Winfrey was the highest paid TV entertainer in the United States in 2006, earning an estimated $260 million during the year, five times the sum earned by second-place music executive Simon Cowell. By 2008, her yearly income had increased to $275 million.

Forbes' international rich list has listed Winfrey as the world's only black billionaire from 2004 to 2006 and as the first black woman billionaire in world history. As of 2014, Winfrey has a net worth in excess of 2.9 billion dollars and has overtaken former eBay CEO Meg Whitman as the richest self-made woman in America.

Oprah was raised a Baptist. She was quoted as saying: *I have a church with myself: I have church walking down the street. I believe in God force that lives inside all of us, and once you tap into that, you can do anything.*

Winfrey at the White House for the 2010 Kennedy Center Honors

Winfrey was called "arguably the world's most powerful woman" by CNN and Time.com, "arguably the most influential woman in the world" by *The American Spectator* "one of the 100 people who most influenced the 20th Century" and "one of the most influential people" from 2004 to 2011 by *TIME*. Winfrey is the only person in the world to have appeared in the latter list on ten occasions.

At the end of the 20th century, *Life* listed Winfrey as both the most influential woman and the most influential black person of her generation, and in a cover story profile the magazine called her "America's most powerful woman". In 2007, *USA Today* ranked Winfrey as the most influential woman and most influential black person of the previous quarter-century. *Ladies Home Journal* also ranked Winfrey number one in their list of the most powerful women in America and Senator Barack Obama has said she "may be the most influential woman in the country". In 1998, Winfrey became the first woman and first African American to top *Entertainment Weekly*'s list of the 101 most powerful people in the entertainment industry. *Forbes* named her the world's most powerful celebrity in 2005, 2007, 2008, 2010, and 2013. As chairman of Harpo Inc., she was named the most powerful woman in entertainment by *The Hollywood Reporter* in 2008. She has also been listed as one of the most powerful 100 women in the world by *Forbes*, ranking fourteenth in 2014.

In 2010, *Life* magazine named Winfrey one of the 100 people who changed the world, alongside such luminaries as Jesus Christ, Elvis Presley and Lady Mary Wortley Montagu. Winfrey was the only living woman to make the list.

Columnist Maureen Dowd seems to agree with such assessments: "She is the top alpha female in this country. She has more credibility than the president. Other successful women, such as Hillary Clinton and Martha Stewart, had to be publicly slapped down before they could move forward. Even Condi has had to play the protégé with Bush. None of this happened to Oprah – she is a straight-ahead success story. *Vanity Fair* wrote: "Oprah Winfrey arguably has more influence on the culture than any university president, politician, or religious leader, except perhaps the Pope. Bill O'Reilly said: "this is a woman that came from nothing to rise up to be the most powerful woman, I think, in the world. I think Oprah Winfrey is the most powerful woman in the world, not just in America. That's – anybody who goes on her program immediately benefits through the roof. I mean, she has a loyal following; she has credibility; she has talent; and she's done it on her own to become fabulously wealthy and fabulously powerful."

In 2005, Winfrey was named the greatest woman in American history as part of a public poll as part of *The Greatest American*. She was ranked No. 9 overall on the list of greatest Americans. However, polls estimating Winfrey's personal popularity have been inconsistent. A November 2003 Gallup poll estimated that 73% of American adults had a favorable view of Winfrey. Another Gallup poll in January 2007 estimated the figure at 74%, although it dropped to 66% when Gallup conducted the same poll in October 2007. A December 2007 Fox News poll put the figure at 55%. According to Gallup's annual most admired poll, Americans consistently rank Winfrey as one of the most admired women in the world. Her highest rating came in 2007 when she was statistically tied with Hillary Clinton for first place. In a list compiled by the British magazine *New Statesman* in September 2010, she was voted 38th in the list of "The World's 50 Most Influential Figures 2010".

In 1989, she was accepted into the NAACP Image Award Hall of Fame.

The Wall Street Journal coined the term "Oprahfication", meaning public confession as a form of therapy. By confessing intimate details about her weight problems, tumultuous love life, and sexual abuse, and crying alongside her guests, *Time* magazine credits Winfrey with creating a new form of media communication known as "rapport talk" as distinguished from the "report talk" of Phil Donahue: "Winfrey saw television's power to blend public and private; while it links strangers, and conveys information over public airwaves, TV is most often viewed in the privacy of our homes. Like a family member, it sits down to meals with us and talks to us in the lonely afternoons.

Grasping this paradox, she makes people care because she cares. That is Winfrey's genius, and will be her legacy, as the changes she has wrought in the talk show continue to permeate our culture and shape our lives."

Observers have also noted the "Oprahfication" of politics such as "Oprah-style debates" and Bill Clinton being described as "the man who brought Oprah-style psychobabble and misty confessions to politics." *Newsweek* stated: "Every time a politician lets his lip quiver, or a cable anchor 'emotes' on TV, they nod to the cult of confession that Oprah helped create. Winfrey's disclosures about her weight (which peaked at 108 kg (238 lb.)) also paved the way for other plus-sized women in media such as Roseanne Barr, Rosie O'Donnell and Star Jones. The November 1988 *Ms.* observed that "in a society where fat is taboo, she made it in a medium that worships thin and celebrates a bland, white-bread prettiness of body and personality, but Winfrey made fat sexy, elegant – damned near gorgeous – with her drop-dead wardrobe, easy body language, and cheerful sensuality."

Winfrey joins Barack and Michelle Obama on the campaign trail (December 10, 2007).

Winfrey endorsed presidential candidate Barack Obama in the 2008 presidential election, the first time she endorsed a political candidate running for office. Winfrey held a fundraiser for Obama on September 8, 2007, at her Santa Barbara estate. In December 2007, Winfrey joined Obama for a series of rallies in the early primary states of Iowa, New Hampshire, and South Carolina. The Columbia, South Carolina event on December 9, 2007, drew a crowd of nearly 30,000, the largest for any political event of 2007. An analysis by two economists at the University of Maryland, College Park estimated that Winfrey's endorsement was responsible for between 420,000 and 1,600,000 votes for Obama in the Democratic primary alone, based on a sample of states that did not include Texas, Michigan, North Dakota, Kansas, or Alaska. The results suggest that in the sampled states, Winfrey's endorsement was responsible for the difference in the popular vote between Barack Obama and Hillary Clinton. The governor of Illinois, Rod Blagojevich, reported being so impressed by Winfrey's endorsement that he considered offering Winfrey Obama's vacant senate seat describing Winfrey as "the most instrumental person in electing Barack Obama president", with "a voice larger than all 100 senators combined". Winfrey responded by stating that although she was absolutely not interested, she did feel she could be a senator.

THE RICHEST AFRICAN-AMERICAN MAN IN THE 1980'S

*Reginald Lewis, must read book:
"Why should White Guys have all the fun"?*

Reginald Lewis, in 1987 Lewis bought the Chicago-based Beatrice International Foods from Beatrice Companies for $985 million, renaming it TLC Beatrice International, a snack food, beverage, and grocery store conglomerate that was the largest African-American owned and managed business in the U.S. The deal was partly financed through Mike Milken of the maverick investment bank Drexel Burnham Lambert. In order to reduce the amount needed to finance the LBO, Lewis came up with a plan to sell off some of the division's assets simultaneous with the takeover.

When TLC Beatrice reported revenue of $1.8 billion in 1987, it became the first black-owned company to have more than $1 billion in annual sales. At its peak in 1996, TLC Beatrice International Holdings Inc. had sales of $2.2 billion and was number 512 on Fortune magazine's list of 1,000 largest companies.

Reggie Lewis was a (Wall Street investment tycoon, owner McCall patterns, Beatrice Foods the only African American who has an international law department building built in his name at the prestigious Harvard University). A man that as a boy was poor and came from a single-family home in Baltimore, Maryland; later he was considered one of the wealthiest black men in America before his early death.

Reginald F. Lewis (December 7, 1942 – January 19, 1993) was an American businessman. He was the richest African-American man in the 1980s. Born in Baltimore, Maryland, he grew up in a middle-class neighborhood. He won a football scholarship to Virginia State College, graduating with a degree in political science in 1965. He graduated from Harvard Law School in 1968 and was a member of Kappa Alpha Psi.

In 1992, *Forbes* listed Lewis among the 400 richest Americans, with a net worth estimated at $400 million. He also was the first African-American business owner to build a billion dollar company, Beatrice Foods.

During his high school years at Dunbar, Reginald excelled in both his studies and sports. As quarterback of the football team, shortstop on the baseball team, and a forward on the basketball team, he served as captain for all three teams. Reginald was also elected vice president of the student body; his friend and classmate, Robert M. Bell, Chief Judge of Maryland, was elected president. In addition, Reginald worked nights and weekends at jobs with his grandfather, a head waiter and maitre'd'.

In 1961, Reginald entered Virginia State University on a football scholarship, majoring in economics. He graduated on the Dean's List despite having a rough first year academically as well as losing his scholarship due to an injury. After losing his scholarship, he worked in a bowling alley and as a photographer's assistant to help pay his expenses. In his senior year, the Rockefeller Foundation funded a program at Harvard Law School to select a few black students to attend summer school at Harvard to introduce them to legal studies in general.

At the end of the program, Reginald was invited to attend Harvard Law School - the only person in the 148-year history of Harvard Law to be admitted before applying to the school. He arrived at Harvard with $50 in his pocket. During his third year at Harvard, he discovered the direction for his future career in a course on securities law. He wrote his third-year paper on takeovers. He graduated from Harvard Law School in 1968 and went to work for a prestigious New York law firm (Paul, Weiss).

Recruited to top New York law firm Paul, Weiss, Rifkind, Wharton & Garrison LLP immediately after law school, Lewis left to start his own firm two years later. After 15 years as a corporate lawyer with his own practice, Lewis moved to the other side of the table by creating TLC Group L.P., a venture capital firm, in 1983.

His first major deal was the purchase of the McCall Pattern Company, a home sewing pattern business for $22.5 million. Lewis had learned from a *Fortune* magazine article that the Esmark holding company, which had recently purchased Norton Simon, planned to divest from the McCall Pattern Company, a maker of home sewing patterns founded in 1870. With fewer and fewer people sewing at home, McCall was seemingly on the decline—though it had posted profits of $6 million in 1983 on sales of $51.9 million. At the time, McCall was number two in its industry, holding 29.7 percent of the market, compared to industry leader Simplicity Patterns with 39.4 percent.

He managed to negotiate the price down and then raised $1 million himself from family and friends and borrowed the rest from institutional investors and investment banking firm First Boston Corp.

Within one year, he turned the company around by freeing up capital tied in fixed assets such as building and machinery, finding a new use for machinery during downtime by manufacturing greeting cards, and he then started to recruit managers from rival companies. He further strengthened McCall by containing costs, improving quality, beginning to export to China, and emphasizing new product introductions. This new combination led to the company's most profitable year in its history. With the addition of McCall real estate worth an estimated $6 million that the company retained ownership of, he later sold McCall at a 90-1 return, resulting in a tremendous profit for investors. Lewis's share was 81.7 percent of the $90 million.

When TLC Beatrice reported revenue of $1.8 billion in 1987, it became the first black-owned company to have more than $1 billion in annual sales. At its peak in 1996, TLC Beatrice International Holdings Inc. had sales of $2.2 billion and was number 512 on Fortune magazine's list of 1,000 largest companies.

In 1987 Lewis established The Reginald F. Lewis Foundation, which funded grants of approximately $10 million to various non-profit programs and organizations while he was alive. His first major grant was an unsolicited $1 million to Howard University in 1988; the federal government matched the grant, making the gift to Howard University $2 million, which was used to fund an endowment for scholarships, fellowships, and faculty sabbaticals. In 1992, he donated $3 million to Harvard Law School, the largest grant at the time in the law school's history. In gratitude, the school renamed its International Law Center the Reginald F. Lewis International Law Center, the first major facility at Harvard named in honor of an African-American.

While alive, Lewis made known his desire to support a museum of African American culture. In 2005, the Reginald F. Lewis Museum of Maryland African American History & Culture opened in Baltimore with support from a $5 million grant from his foundation. It is the East Coast's second largest African American museum occupying an 82,000 square-foot facility with permanent and special exhibition space, interactive learning environments, auditorium, resource center, oral history recording studio, museum shop, and café, classrooms, meeting rooms, outside terrace and reception areas. It highlights the history and accomplishments of African Americans with a special focus on Maryland's African American community. The museum is also a Smithsonian affiliate.

Reginald Lewis was married to Loida Nicolas-Lewis. They had two daughters, Leslie and Christina. He died at age 50, from brain cancer. Loida Nicolas-Lewis took over the company a year after his death.

CHAPTER NINE

Chicago's First Dusable Commemoration-Collaborations

"THE KELLY-NASH MACHINE"

1933 36 Mayor of Chicago Edward Joseph Kelly

Edward Joseph Kelly (May 1, 1876 – October 20, 1950) was an American politician who served as the 36th Mayor of

Chicago from April 17, 1933 until April 15, 1947. Prior to being mayor of Chicago, Kelly served as chief engineer of the Chicago Sanitary District during the 1920s. Kelly was a Democrat.

Born to Stephen, a police officer and Helen (née Lang) Kelly, he was the first of five Chicago mayors from Bridgeport of Chicago's South Side. Kelly was the chief engineer of the Chicago Sanitary District in the 1920s. He was sponsored by Patrick Nash, the owner of a sewer-contracting company that did millions of dollars of business with the city. He subsequently became president of the South Park Board, a position that presided over the building of Soldier Field. Under his tenure Soldier Field cost $8 million, while a similar Los Angeles stadium only cost $1.7 million.

Following the assassination of Mayor Anton Cermak, Kelly was hand-picked by his friend, Patrick Nash, Chairman of the Cook County Democratic Party, for the mayoral election of 1933. Together, Kelly and Nash built one of the most powerful, and most corrupt, big city political organizations, called the "Kelly-Nash Machine". Kelly was Mayor of Chicago during the 1933–34 Chicago World's Fair (Century of Progress) which took place during the Great Depression, which included the successful playing of the first official Major League Baseball All-Star Game that Kelly initiated for holding a major sport event for the fair to the *Chicago Tribune*.

Chicago became notorious during the Prohibition years of the "Roaring" 1920s as a wide-open town, gaining a reputation for corruption, gangsterism, and intermittent mayhem. Al Capone, John Dillinger, and the St. Valentine's Day Massacre became bywords worldwide. Furthermore, the city government was virtually insolvent years before the 1929 stock market crash. Republican Thompson was defeated by Democrat Anton Cermak in 1931, the first of a long string of Democratic mayors. Cermak, however, fell two years later to an assassin's bullet intended for U.S. President-elect Franklin D. Roosevelt, who was visiting the city. The new mayor, Edward J. Kelly, gladly accepted federal relief funds that employed thousands on projects that completed the Outer Drive Bridge, built the State Street subway, and constructed hundreds of miles of streets, sewers, sidewalks, and curbs. Workers for other relief projects painted murals in post offices and schools, collected sources for historical research, and provided free music. Chicago's WPA Federal Theatre created *Swing Mikado*, which later enjoyed success on Broadway, and also developed new techniques of improvisational comedy and puppetry.

THE 1933 CHICAGO WORLD'S FAIR

The 1933 Chicago World's Fair: A Century of Progress

In 1933–34 Chicago played host to its second world's fair, the Century of Progress Exposition, organized to mark the centennial of the town charter. Conceived initially to displace the Capone crime era from the city's image, the fair turned into a celebration of technology as the savior of the country's economy. Its Art Deco–style architecture and brilliant colors were a lure for tens of millions of visitors during its two-year run.

A Lasting Monument to Jean Baptiste DeSaible for the World's Fair

Jean Baptiste DuSable started the rise of one of the World's Foremost Centers of Commerce. The World's Fair, or the Century of Progress, will do well to perpetuate the memory of this man who prepared the way for J. H. Kinzie the great white citizen of Chicago.

The 1933 Century of Progress Exposition boosted popular memory of DuSable by exhibiting a replica of DuSable's cabin as it had been envisioned in the 1884 engraving in A. T. Andreas's *History of Chicago*. While the replica was just 8 feet by 12 feet, the record of the sale of the house in 1800 indicates that its area was actually nine times larger, although imagining a tiny, rustic log cabin better serves the narrative of dramatic progress. DuSable's status in Chicago's past took on new significance in the 20th century, as Chicago became a center of African American culture and could look back with pride at the role of a black businessman in the city's origin story. *Official World's Fair Weekly*: "Chicago's First Citizen," 1933.

1933: A representation of Pointe DuSable's Homestead is exhibited at the Chicago's World Fair: A Century of Progress.

Author: Unknown
Source: Chicago Historical Society

It was the first exhibit featuring a Negro and hosted by the honorable Mr. Frederick Douglas. That exhibit featured as the official host for that historical enactment.

By the late 1920s there was a well-defined black civic structure in Chicago. In order to promote their interests at the world's fair, the city's blacks planned and implemented a complex organizational effort. Sometimes resembling a movement, the effort effectively bonded both civic and political organizations, in behalf of race advancement. The social class supporting the endeavor was primarily, but not exclusively, the black middle class-a group with resources and influence far exceeding its size.

Promoters of A Century of Progress envisioned it as a financially profitable demonstration of how far humankind had progressed in material and scientific terms since 1833, the year Chicago was founded. "The keynote of the coming exposition is 'Science in Action,'" the managers proclaimed. "The design is principally to show the world how the physical sciences have made their contributions to human advancement. The success of the endeavor was measurable at turnstiles, as almost 38.6 million persons visited the fair's marvels and attractions between 1933 and 1934.

Chicago blacks, in contrast, measured progress in fundamentally different terms. They set three objectives: representation in the fair's exhibits that would portray fully and accurately their race's heritage and contributions to the world; full enjoyment of their rights as citizens; and, in the middle of the Great Depression, an equal share in employment opportunities generated by the fair. The Chicago Defender stated: "The real 'Chicago spirit' is unalterably opposed to the surrendering of civil and legal rights." The paper challenged fair organizers instead to show "advancement over sinister and insidious propensities to the point where [Chicago] can recognize in mankind character, fitness, and ability as the only essential elements of real progress. As planning for the fair continued, there were disparate perceptions of purpose and even the nature of progress. In addition, there were controversies whenever the fair's pecuniary and scientific interests clashed with black racial concerns.

Race ideology had undergone considerable change in the twentieth century. Racial strategies for advancement were far from unified. An important issue was how blacks would define their places specifically in the world's fair and generally in American society. In his 1903 classic, The Souls of Black Folk, W. E. B. Du Bois had described the anxiety that resulted when persons of African descent found themselves psychologically facing the competing influences of nationality and race. There was, he said, a "two-ness" -an American, a Negro; two souls, two thoughts, two unreconciled strivings.

During Chicago's first world's fair-the Columbian Exposition of 1893- the conflict between racial identity and nationality had been debated and, to a certain degree, settled in favor of nationality. Frederick Douglass's misgivings about the Exposition's Colored American Day can be seen in his address, in which he "began by questioning the motives of the Exposition people in giving the colored people a day and intimated that he doubted the advisability of returning any thanks for the honor conferred."

A second problem involved the relative importance of conciliation and protest. In Chicago, especially during the fair, conciliation assumed a level of importance equal of protest. Also, as the two strategies were manifested in activities aimed at achieving the black version of progress, they moved correspondingly through the stages of prevention, confrontation, and remedy. At various times, both conciliation and protest were promoted through a sizable civic and political structure that included the Chicago Urban League, the Chicago Defender, the Chicago branch of the National Association for the Advancement of Colored people, and black Republican politicians at the local, state, and national levels, as well as affiliated black groups and organizations.

Within the black community, middleclass concerns encompassed civil rights, racial image, and employment. Blacks had supported the Chicago Whip's "Don't Spend Your Money Where You Can't Work" campaign of 1930, which for the first time involved the use of the picket line and boycott by Chicago blacks. By 1933, those concerns had also developed into a well-established pattern that included resistance to housing restrictions, school segregation, and racially exclusionary politics.

The efficacy of conciliation was rooted in the relationship that existed between the Century of Progress management and black middle-class leaders. From 1928, when the fair corporation conceived its operating plan, black business leaders such as Jesse Binga and Robert Sengstacke Abbott were invited to participate. Binga was the founder and president of the Binga State Bank, which along with the city's Douglass National Bank owned by Anthony Overton controlled one-third of all banking resources held by blacks nationally. Abbott, who had accumulated considerable wealth by the 1920s, was the founder, owner, and publisher of the Chicago Defender, perhaps the leading black newspaper in the nation. Century of Progress records indicate that Abbott was solicited to join the founding circle of members but declined, although he did send the $1,000 membership fee.

The Century of Progress records show an amicable relationship between other black leaders and the fair's managers. Members of the DuSable Club, the Men's Division of the Chicago Urban League, were described as "young and progressive professional and business Negroes." The League itself was considered "an organization of the better class of colored people of Chicago," as well as "an outstanding organization." These descriptions were unusual, given the racism of the period.

The Chicago Urban League, whose leadership was biracial, best represented middle-class interests in utilizing the strategy of conciliatory tactics at the fair. The Chicago branch of the NAACP was the organizational choice for protest. With its all-black leadership, the organization became increasingly militant during the Depression. Through both direct and indirect leadership, the League led the movement to insure parity in jobs, exhibits, and the enjoyment of recreational facilities. By 1932, the League had petitioned for and won recognition of its leadership role in all matters pertaining to blacks and the fair. Concomitantly, the League organized the Colored Citizens World's Fair Council (CCWFC), an organization representing forty organizations. The Council not only served as a clearinghouse but also monitored civil rights and encouraged the upkeep and protection of the South Side neighborhoods affected by visitors and the criminal element attending the fair. Monthly meetings of the Council averaged one hundred persons.

The prestige of the Urban League was enhanced in 1928, when the group petitioned for a memorial to the city's first permanent settler, Jean Baptiste Point Du Sable, a black man. Significantly, the Du Sable campaign avoided any tone of racial advocacy. That deliberate strategy strengthened the case in an often-hostile environment. The crusade was led by Dr. Arthur G. Falls, who approached fair managers as early as May of 1928. In November, the DuSable Memorial Society, a predominantly black women's group led by Annie Oliver, began laying the groundwork for a concerted effort to carry the Du Sable exhibit to fruition. The two groups cooperated for the next five years. After many setbacks, -the exhibit was approved in January of 1933, five months before the fair was to open. The fair management acceded to the legitimacy for the proposal and agreed to display a replica of the DuSable homestead as part of the social science exhibits, an area reserved for non-material aspects of progress. Funding for the replica was provided by the city through the efforts of black Alderman, Robert R. Jackson.

1933 Women of the DuSable Memorial Society

In promoting Du Sable's achievements, the DeSaible Memorial Society and the Urban League never wavered from their position that DuSable was to be recognized as founder of a great American city, not as a black man. The DuSable Memorial Society called him the "first settler, Negro, trader, pioneer, and business man" of Chicago. In the chambers of the city council, Alderman Jackson spoke of DuSable as a "great pioneer," and of his cabin as "the cradle of a city, which was destined to and has become the greatest city of the world." Consistent with the independence of the black middle class, the Urban League and DuSable Society rejected any suggestion that the memorial homestead represented special considerations for blacks. In a bit of irony, however, the Urban League did refer to DuSable as the "first civilized man to settle in what is Chicago"- possible offense to such American Indians as the Ojibwa (Chippewa), Potawatomi, Winnebago, and other indigenous groups of the Chicagoland area.

When opposition to the DuSable project occurred, it usually appeared as part of the basically financial orientation of the fair management. From a business perspective, the fair was undertaken to generate profits for the investors and to promote the city's economic image and future. The sentimental causes posed by blacks promoting a pioneer or by Catholics promoting a memorial to Father Jacques Marquette were of secondary importance to profitmaking. That policy, however, was not consistently followed. Fair leaders did not wish to offend any group and unnecessarily jeopardize profits; when possible, they acted to mitigate confrontation. Even though the fair's theme emphasized material progress, by 1933 the DuSable memorial, as well as one for Marquette, had gained approval for display in the social science exhibits.

Two other attempts to memorialize black progress were unsuccessful. Black architect, Walter Thomas Bailey had been working for three years on winning support for an exhibit that "would teach the world some of the interesting history of the Black people before the first boat-load of slaves ever landed in this country." In 1931, an African prince named Modupe Paris persuasively argued for support of a similar project, except he insisted that Africans, rather than Afro-Americans, should control the project. His group, the Africans and Descendants Centennial Committee, proposed a project with a budget of $132,166. The staging of such an extensive project covering the achievements and glories of so many diverse peoples over such a vast continent would have been difficult in the best of times, even if the city and its black citizens had not been in the grip of the Depression.

Upon scrutiny by fair investigators who looked regularly into the financial, personal, and organizational backgrounds of each prospective exhibitor, it was quickly determined that the Paris group had no chance of raising the funds necessary to mount the exhibit. From 1931 to 1932 the official fair position was to indulge the Paris group in its activities, but to assume that the venture would stall indefinitely in its conceptual phase.

The next important effort aimed at producing an African exhibit came in 1932 from a white Chicago business, the Netherton Company. The motivation of Netherton's All-Africa Corporation is unfathomable from the Century of Progress records. The company promised "that no exhibit will be made which the World's Fair Administration shall deem might offend the American Negroes. But the Netherton Company had a questionable financial history, and there was some opposition from the black community. The All-Africa Corporation failed to come up with the financial guarantees required of exhibitors, and by late November of 1932 contact between the fair and the project terminated. The corporation's failure ended all serious activities directed at producing an African cultural and scientific exhibit. As a result, African contributions to world progress in mathematics, the smelting of iron ore, and other areas were not demonstrated on the Chicago fairgrounds.

Yet, support for such a project persisted. With the financial and organizational support of a small number of Africans and black Americans, Modupe Paris produced an independent project. The African and American Negro Exhibit opened along with the Century of Progress in May 1933, but under community auspices, some two miles southwest of the fairgrounds at the National Pythian Temple at Thirty-seventh and State streets, in the heart of the South Side black community. The exhibit offered displays on ancient African architecture and artwork, contemporary African art and commercial products, and American Negro achievements in science, the military, the professions, and the arts.

Once the fair opened, a minor episode appears to have received press coverage and eventually historical significance disproportionate to its importance-the separate Negro Day at the fair. Black leaders who had worked on behalf of the DuSable exhibit had always resisted any racially exclusive event. Jesse Binga, for example, had requested that "the race question" be not brought up during the fair. The originator of the idea was Chandler Owen--orator, socialist, and promoter who introduced the idea in 1932. A newcomer to the city, Owen was not a member of the middle-class leadership ranks. The only major endorsement for his plan was from black United States Representative Oscar DePriest, and that turned out to be ephemeral. Other politicians ignored Owen's plan; Aldermen William L. Dawson and Robert R. Jackson failed to endorse the idea in the city council, negating a political custom. The opposition that Owen encountered was consistent with the spirit of 1893, when a separate Colored American Day was held but with limited success. Ida B. Wells Barnett and other racial equalitarians boycotted that event, and Frederick Douglass reluctantly became involved because he was already at the exposition as an official at the Haitian Pavilion. Douglass's presence lent a semblance of legitimacy to the 1893 event, but the fair of 1933 had no one of Douglass's stature associated with it.

Negro Day, which was held August 12, 1933, was a colossal flop-both ideologically and financially. Owen had predicted that 300,000 persons would attend, but only fifty thousand did, establishing an all-time low daily attendance record. It was such a debacle that the fair management had to intercede financially by assuming the debt in order to prevent the event from becoming an even bigger disaster. The Chicago Defender, which had reported, but not supported the event, tersely summed up the popular feeling, "the less said about this day, the better for all of us."

Throughout the rest of the fair, how were blacks treated? To be sure, in Depression-ridden Chicago, there were apprehensions about racism, but at the fair it seemed that the apprehension of racism assumed a greater importance than its actual existence.

Containment of segregation, discrimination, and prejudice was directly attributable to the early and sustained involvement of black leaders with the fair managers. Civic and political interaction with the fair's hierarchy proceeded through stages and along conciliatory lines that prevented problems before they could fester. Even the militant Chicago NAACP attempted to work within the bounds of conciliation in order to prevent any explosive racial incidents. Because of the accessibility of fair president, Rufus C. Dawes, and his entire staff, contacts proved consistently cordial and productive. Dawes was personally committed to insuring racial justice, and on more than one occasion he did just that. Also important was the actively enforced Illinois Civil Rights Act, which provided legal redress for grievances.

The test of whether all citizens were to enjoy their rights occurred sooner than many expected. In 1932, one concessionaire rented the formerly public beach at Twelfth Street, and set up a whites-only sales booth. The matter was investigated, exposed, and stopped. That action coincided with the formation of the CCWFC, which provided blacks a conciliatory vehicle to channel their grievances and to monitor racial progress at the fair.

Once the fair opened, the ugly threat of discrimination appeared to be real, after all. The first victims were Urban League members Dr. Arthur G. Falls and his wife, Lillian. While on the fairgrounds, late one evening, the Fallses were denied entrance to a restaurant. They seated themselves, were served, and brought the incident to Dawes's attention the next day. The concessionaire was warned to desist or to leave the fairgrounds. In the dozen or so other cases, the Chicago NAACP entered the battle at the confrontable stage, with a battery of well-trained volunteer attorneys who comprised its Legal Redress Committee, the NAACP repeatedly took offenders to court in an attempt to discourage other acts of discrimination.

Blacks also resorted to remedial political action through their representatives in the Illinois General Assembly. President A. Clement McNeal of the Chicago NAACP induced Representative Charles J. Jenkins to act. Jenkins and Representatives Harris B. Gaines, William E. King, William J. Warfield, and Arthur T. Broche jointly introduced a resolution calling for more decisive action when civil rights violations occurred. On June 29, 1933, House Resolution 85 called on Cook County State's Attorney, Thomas J. Courtney to conduct grand jury investigations of those violations.

Discrimination cases dragged through the Chicago courts during the summer, and the NAACP led a delegation that included the membership of the CCWFC to the office of the Cook County State's Attorney to demand swifter legal and judicial action. Although the delegation was met dispassionately, it might as well have been met antagonistically, since its protestations fell on deaf ears. By the end of the fair's two-year run, remedy was finally at hand when the Chicago NAACP's suits were decided, all in favor of the plaintiffs. The branch won seventeen cases involving discrimination in or around the fairgrounds, amounting to judgments of $5,000 in the aggregate.

During the second year of the fair, black legislators redirected their focus. They planned to prevent discrimination and avoid the criticism from their constituents that they had suffered in 1932 when they failed to delay enabling legislation for the fair until passage of an anti-discrimination law that would have prevented the Twelfth Street beach incident. Now, they refused to support any fair legislation until they received a guarantee of an anti-discrimination law affecting concessionaires. The tactical move proved effective. House Bill 114, introduced by Representatives Gaines, Jenkins, and Warfield, passed the house by a 98-2 vote and the senate 27-0 vote. With passage of the law, the number of complaints dropped considerably, and overt discrimination in private dining accommodations virtually ended.

Despite the legal guarantees, the atmosphere of prejudice was aided indirectly by the timidity of some blacks. Many members of the masses, as well as the southern black middle class who came to visit the fair, simply avoided eating at fair restaurants. Such action was opposed repeatedly by the Chicago Urban League, the Chicago NAACP, the Defender, and others, however. Blacks were chided to act like citizens and demand their rights in the same manner as they accepted their responsibilities as citizens. Blacks who partook of what the fair offered appeared to enjoy themselves.

Employment at the fair provided another opportunity to examine prejudice. After all, the fair was intended to show the nation and the world that Chicago was still economically viable, despite the Depression. Blacks held positions from the top to the bottom of the employment rungs. Adam Beckley, for example, who was college trained, was visible in the fair President Dawes's office as an administrative assistant. The major lecturer in the Lincoln room of the Illinois Host Building was attorney Andrew Torrence. Six of the uniformed policemen and three of the policewomen were black, and the men were conspicuous as members of the honor guard escorting Postmaster General James Aloysius Farley, President Roosevelt's representative at the fair's opening. The Walgreen Drug Store chain employed a black clerk who served all citizens from a very visible position. Many entertainers, especially musicians and dancers, were prominent on the Streets of Paris, in the Midget Village, and on the Showboat. Most blacks were found at the bottom rungs, however. Most washroom attendants were black, and one of the fair's major concessionaires reported hiring four hundred to six hundred black laborers during 1933.

There were no black concessionaires, however, and without the owners of businesses ensuring equal access to work as other nationalities were prone to do, opportunities were limited. But the problem of black entrepreneurs was related to both discrimination and a lack of capital. Chicago black businessmen were suffering from the failure by 1932 of both the Binga State Bank and Douglass National

Bank, as well as the near-failure of three major black insurance companies. J. D. Carr, a self-appointed black spokesman, summarized the situation: "An investor has employment out there [on the fairgrounds] in proportion to his investments. Every concession had exclusionary charge over his employees. If blacks could not afford to be investors, they had to rely on the good will of those who could. Fair management might work to stop flagrant cases of discrimination, but it had never envisioned itself as a protector of employment rights or a provider of patronage.

The black effort to secure more employment was initiated in 1931 by Chicago Urban League Executive Director, Albion L. Foster, who was joined by the staff of the Wabash YMCA and the director of public service for the Chicago Defender. From the ranks of the masses, the John Brown Organization of Cook County led by W. Thomas Soders joined the effort. Soders had already gained a reputation as a fighter for jobs based on his involvement in the Street Car Riots of 1930, which involved massive street protests for jobs. Black employment improved only slightly at the fair, but in the middle of the Depression, improvements-even if only by degrees-were welcomed.

The Century of Progress proved to be a rather accurate indicator of how far Chicago blacks had progressed since 1833. Their racial image had improved considerably since slavery days, as the reception given to the DuSable homestead by blacks, whites, and the fair management demonstrated. Discrimination on the fairgrounds was controlled through the efforts of blacks and the fair leaders, who were supportive of justice from the onset. The problem of inequality in employment persisted as it had for decades, not only in Chicago but also in the nation. On balance, though, the fair turned out to be more of a benefit than a detriment to Chicago blacks. Therefore, it was a symbol of progress.

THE DUSABLE HIGH SCHOOL

1935: DuSable High School

The DuSable High School was constructed between 1931 and 1934; it opened in February 1935 as a public high school. It was opened in the Bronzeville neighborhood and named after Chicago's first non-native settler Jean Baptiste Pointe DuSable. Jean Baptiste Point DuSable High School was a public 4-year high school located in the Bronzeville neighborhood on the South Side of Chicago, Illinois, United States. DuSable was operated by the Chicago Public Schools district. The school was named after Chicago's first permanent non-native settler, Jean Baptiste Point DuSable. Constructed between1931–34, DuSable opened in February 1935. Since 2005, the school building serves as home to two smaller schools; the Bronzeville Scholastic Institute and the Daniel Hale Williams Preparatory School of Medicine. Both schools use the DuSable name in an athletics context. The DuSable Leadership Academy was housed at the location until it closed after the 2015–16 school year.

The Work on the school began in February 1931, and was specifically constructed to accommodate the increasing population of Phillips High School Construction was delayed for financial reasons, and was completed with a public works grant. The school opened on February 4, 1935, and was called *New Wendell Phillips High School*. New Phillips was a part of a five high school expansion that included Lane Tech High School, Steinmetz High School, Senn High School, and

Wells High School. The building was designed by Paul Gerhardt, Sr., an architect for the Chicago Board of Education. On April 25, 1936, the school's name was changed to honor Jean Baptiste Point DuSable, the first non-native to settle the area; however there was a delay in implementing the name, as the exact spelling was in dispute. During the 1940s on thru the 1960s, DuSable enrollment was more than 4,000 which prompted two graduation ceremonies (spring and summer). DuSable's initial fame was in its music program. Captain Walter Dyett was the longtime music instructor at the school during the time, who created a music program that turned out a number of notable and eminent musical artists, particularly in the genre of jazz. The school's alumni and staff include individuals who hold unique historic positions, particularly in the area of African-American history. By the late 1950s, DuSable became surrounded by the Robert Taylor Homes, a Chicago Housing Authority public housing project where 80% of the student population were residents. It was the largest housing project in the US, but has been demolished because its design did not work for residents.

In 2003, Chicago Public e 2010: Schools decided to phase out DuSable due to its history of poor academic performance. In 2005, three schools were opened in the building as a part of the Renaissance 2010 program. All three of the school buildings were designated as Chicago Landmarks on May 1, 2013. Bronzeville Scholastic Institute, Daniel Hale Williams School of Medicine and DuSable Leadership Academy were created by DuSable staff members. The DuSable Leadership Academy which was a part of the Betty Shabazz International Charter School was phased out due to poor academic performance and closed after the 2015–16 school year.

NOTABLE ALUMNI

Nat King Cole

Nathaniel Adams Coles was born in Montgomery, Alabama, on March 17, 1919. He had three brothers—Eddie (1910–1970), Ike (1927–2001), and Freddy (born 1931)—and a half-sister, Joyce Coles. Each of his brothers pursued careers in music. When Nat was four years old he and his family moved to North Chicago, Illinois, where his father, Edward Coles, became a Baptist minister. Nat learned to play the organ from his mother, Perlina Coles, the church organist. His first performance was of "Yes! We Have No Bananas": at the age of four. He began formal lessons at 12 and eventually learned not only jazz and gospel music, but also Western classical music. He performed "from Johann Sebastian Bach to Sergei Rachmaninoff."

The family again moved to the Bronzeville neighborhood of Chicago, where he attended Wendel Phillips High School (the same school Sam Cooke attended a few years later). Cole would sneak out of the house and hang around outside clubs, listening to artists such as Louis Armstrong, Earl Hines and Jimmie Noone. He participated in Walter Dyett's renowned music program at DuSable High School.

Career Inspired by the performances of Hines, Cole began his performing career in the mid-1930s while still a teenager, adopting the name **Nat Cole**. Cole left Chicago in 1936 to lead a band in a revival of Eubie Blake's revue Shuffle Along. His older brother, Eddie, a bass player, soon joined Cole's band, and they made their first recording in 1936, under Eddie's name. They also were regular performers in clubs. Cole acquired his nickname, "King", performing at one jazz club, a nickname presumably reinforced by the otherwise unrelated nursery rhyme about Old King Cole. He was also a pianist in a national tour of "Shuffle Along". When it suddenly failed in Long Beach, California, Cole decided to remain there. He later returned to Chicago in triumph to play such venues as the Edgewater Beach Hotel.

The following year, Cole formed a trio in Los Angeles with Oscar Moore (guitar) and Wesley Prince (double bass) known as the "King Cole Swingsters" in Long Beach and played in a number of local bars before getting a gig on the Long Beach Pike for US $90.00 per week ($1,553 in 2015). The trio played in Failsworth through the late 1930s and recorded many radio transcriptions for Capitol Transcriptions. Cole was the pianist and also the leader of the combo. Radio was important to the King Cole Trio's rise in popularity. Their first broadcast was with NBC's Blue Network in 1938. It was followed by performances on NBC's "Swing Soiree". In the 1940s, the trio appeared on the radio shows Old Gold, The Chesterfield Supper Club and Kraft Music Hall. The King Cole Trio performed twice on CBS Radio's variety show The Orson Welles Almanac in 1944.

According to legend, Cole's singing career did not start until a drunken barroom patron demanded that he sing "Sweet Lorraine". Cole said that this fabricated story "sounded good, so I just let it ride." He frequently sang between instrumental numbers. Noticing that people started to request more vocal numbers, he obliged. Yet the story of the insistent customer is not without some truth. There was a customer who requested a certain song one night, but it was a song that Cole did not know, so instead he sang "Sweet Lorraine". The trio was tipped 15¢ ($2.59 in 2015) for the performance.

The Capitol Records Building, known as "The House That Nat Built"

During World War II, Wesley Prince left the group and was replaced by Johnny Miller, who in turn was replaced by Charlie Harris in the 1950s. The King Cole Trio signed with the fledgling Capitol Records in 1943. The group had previously recorded for Excelsior Records, owned by Otis René, and had a hit with the song "I'm Lost", which René wrote, produced and distributed. Revenues from Cole's record sales fueled much of Capitol Records' success during this period. The revenue is believed to have played a significant role in financing the distinctive Capitol Records building near Hollywood and Vine in Los Angeles. Completed in 1956, it was the world's first circular office building and became known as "The House that Nat Built".

Cole was considered a leading jazz pianist, appearing in the first "Jazz at the Philharmonic" concerts (credited on the Mercury Record label as "Shorty Nadine"—derived from his wife's name—as he was under exclusive contract with Capitol Records at the time). His revolutionary lineup of piano, guitar, and bass in the era of the big band became a popular setup for jazz trios. It was emulated by many musicians, among them Art Tatum, Oscar Peterson, Ahmad Jamal, and the blues pianists Charles Brown and Ray Charles. He also performed as a pianist on sessions with Lester Young, Red Callender, and Lionel Hampton. For contractual reasons, Cole was credited as "Aye Guy" on the album.

Cole's first mainstream vocal hit was his 1943 recording of one of his compositions, "Straighten Up and Fly Right", based on a black folk tale that his father had used as a theme for a sermon. Johnny Mercer invited him to record it for his fledgling Capitol Records. It sold over 500,000 copies, proving that folk-based material could appeal to a wide audience. Cole would never be considered a rocker, but the song can be seen as anticipating the first rock-and-roll records. Bo Diddley, who performed similar transformations of folk material, counted Cole as an influence.

*King Cole Trio Time on NBC in 1947,
with Cole, Oscar Moore and Johnny Miller*

In 1946, the Cole trio paid to have their own 15-minute radio program on the air, "King Cole Trio Time". It was the first radio program sponsored by a black performing artist. During those years, the trio recorded many "transcription" recordings, which were made in the radio studio for the broadcast. Later they were released as commercial records. Beginning in the late 1940s, Cole began recording and performing pop-oriented material for mainstream audiences, in which he was often accompanied by a string orchestra. His stature as a popular star was cemented during this period by hits such as "The Christmas Song","(Get Your Kicks on) Route 66" (1946), "Nature Boy" (1948), "Mona Lisa" (1950), "Too Young" (the number 1 song in 1951), and his signature song, "Unforgettable" (1951) (Gainer 1). Cole's hit recording "The Christmas Song" was the first of his solo vocal recordings to be accompanied by a studio orchestra. This marked the start of his rise as an internationally acclaimed popular singer, with a smooth and sophisticated style. Cole's shift to pop music led some jazz critics and fans to accuse him of selling out, but he never abandoned his jazz roots; as late as 1956 he recorded an all-jazz album, "After Midnight", and many of his albums after this are fundamentally jazz-based, being scored for big band without strings, although the arrangements focus primarily on the vocal rather than instrumental leads. Cole had one of his last major hits in 1963, two years before his death, with "Those Lazy-Hazy-Crazy Days of Summer", which reached number 6 on the Pop chart. "Unforgettable" was made famous again in 1991 by Cole's daughter Natalie when modern recording technology was used to reunite father and daughter in a duet. The duet version rose to the top of the pop charts, almost forty years after its original popularity.

On November 5, 1956, The Nat 'King' Cole Show debuted on NBC. The variety program was one of the first hosted by an African American, which created controversy at the time. Beginning as a 15-minute pops show on Monday night, the program was expanded to a half-hour in July 1957. Despite the efforts of NBC, as well as many of Cole's industry colleagues—many of whom, such as Ella Fitzgerald, Harry Belafonte, Frankie Laine, Mel Tormé, Peggy Lee, Eartha Kitt, Tony Bennett and the backing vocal group the Cheerleaders, worked for industry scale (or even for no pay) in order to help the show save money—The Nat 'King' Cole Show was ultimately done in by lack of a national sponsorship. Companies such as Rheingold Beer assumed regional sponsorship of the show, but a national sponsor never appeared. The last episode of The Nat King Cole Show aired December 17, 1957. Cole had survived for over a year, and it was he, not NBC, who ultimately decided to end the program. Commenting on the lack of sponsorship his show received, Cole quipped shortly after its demise, "Madison Avenue is afraid of the dark."

Throughout the 1950s, Cole continued to rack up successive hits, selling in millions throughout the world, including "Smile", "Pretend", "A Blossom Fell", and "If I May". His pop hits were collaborations with well-known arrangers and conductors of the day, including Nelson Riddle, Gordon Jenkins, and Ralph Carmichael.

Riddle arranged several of Cole's 1950s albums, including his first 10-inch long-play album, "Nat King Cole Sings for Two in Love" (1953). In 1955, his single "Darling, Je Vous Aime Beaucoup" reached number 7 on the *Billboard* chart. Jenkins arranged "Love Is the Thing", hitting number 1 on the charts in April 1957 and remaining for eight weeks, his only number 1 hit. In 1959, he was awarded a Grammy at the 2nd Annual Grammy Awards, the category Best Performance By a "Top 40" Artist, for his recording of "Midnight Flyer".

In 1958, Cole went to Havana, Cuba, to record Cole Español, an album sung entirely in Spanish. The album was so popular in Latin America, and also in the United States, that two others of the same variety followed: "A Mis Amigos" (sung in Spanish and Portuguese) in 1959 and "More Cole Español" in 1962. "A Mis Amigos" contains the Venezuelan hit "Ansiedad", whose lyrics Cole learned while performing in Caracas in 1958. He learned songs in languages other than English by rote. After the change in musical tastes during the late 1950s, Cole's ballad singing did not sell well with younger listeners, despite a successful stab at rock and roll with "Send for Me", which peaked at number 6 on the Pop chart. Along with his contemporaries Dean Martin, Frank Sinatra and Tony Bennett, Cole found that the pop singles chart had been almost entirely taken over by youth-oriented acts. In 1960, Cole's longtime collaborator Nelson Riddle left Capitol Records for Frank Sinatra's newly formed Reprise Records. Riddle and Cole recorded one final hit album, "Wild Is Love", with lyrics by Ray Rasch and Dotty Wayne. Cole later retooled the concept album into an Off-Broadway show, "I'm with You!"

Cole recorded some hit singles during the 1960s, including "Let There Be Love" with George Shearing in 1961, the country-flavored hit "Ramblin' Rose" in August 1962, "Dear Lonely Hearts", "That Sunday, That Summer" and "Those Lazy-Hazy-Crazy Days of Summer" (his final top-ten hit, reaching number 6 on the Pop chart). He performed in many short films, sitcoms, and television shows and played W. C. Handy in the film "St. Louis Blues" (1958). He also appeared in "The Nat King Cole Story", "China Gate", and "The Blue Gardenia" (1953). In January 1964, Cole made one of his final television appearances, on "The Jack Benny Program". He was introduced as "the best friend a song ever had" and sang "When I Fall in Love". "Cat Ballou" (1965), his final film, was released several months after his death.

Around the time Cole launched his singing career, he entered into Freemasonry. He was raised in January 1944 in the Thomas Waller Lodge No. 49 in California. The lodge was named after fellow Prince Hall mason and jazz musician Fats Waller. Cole was "an avid baseball fan", particularly of Hank Aaron. In 1968, Nelson Riddle related an incident from some years earlier and told of music studio engineers, searching for a source of noise, finding Cole listening to a game on a transistor radio.

Dinah Washington

Dinah Washington (born **Ruth Lee Jones**; August 29, 1924 – December 14, 1963) was an American singer and pianist, who have been cited as "the most popular black female recording artist of the '50s". Primarily a jazz vocalist, she performed and recorded in a wide variety of styles, including blues, R&B, and traditional pop music, and gave herself the title of "Queen of the Blues". She was a 1986 inductee of the Alabama Jazz Hall of Fame, and was inducted into the Rock and Roll Hall of Fame in 1993.

Portrait of Dinah Washington, 1952

Ruth Lee Jones was born in Tuscaloosa, Alabama to Alice Jones, and moved to Chicago as a child. She became deeply involved in gospel and played piano for the choir in St. Luke's Baptist Church while still in elementary school. She sang gospel music in church and played piano, directing her church choir in her teens and being a member of the Sallie Martin Gospel Singers. She sang lead with the first female gospel singers formed by Ms. Martin, who was co-founder of the

Gospel Singers Convention. Her involvement with the gospel choir occurred after she won an amateur contest at Chicago's Regal Theater where she sang "I Can't Face the Music". After winning a talent contest at the age of 15, she began performing in clubs. By 1941–42 she was performing in such Chicago clubs as Dave's Rhumboogie and the Downbeat Room of the Sherman Hotel (with Fats Waller). She was playing at the Three Deuces, a jazz club, when a friend took her to hear Billie Holiday at the Garrick Stage Bar. Club owner Joe Sherman was so impressed with her singing of "I Understand", backed by the Cats and the Fiddle, who were appearing in the Garrick's upstairs room, that he hired her. During her year at the Garrick – she sang upstairs while Holiday performed in the downstairs room – she acquired the name by which she became known. She credited Joe Sherman with suggesting the change from Ruth Jones, made before Lionel Hampton came to hear Dinah at the Garrick. Hampton's visit brought an offer, and Washington worked as his female band vocalist after she had sung with the band for its opening at the Chicago Regal Theatre.

She made her recording debut for the Keynote label that December with "Evil Gal Blues", written by Leonard Feather and backed by Hampton and musicians from his band, including Joe Morris (trumpet) and Milt Buckner (piano). Both that record and its follow-up, "Salty Papa Blues", made Billboard's "Harlem Hit Parade" in 1944.

She stayed with Hampton's band until 1946, after the Keynote label folded, signed for Mercury Records as a solo singer. Her first record for Mercury, a version of Fats Waller's "Ain't Misbehavin'", was another hit, starting a long string of success. Between 1948 and 1955, she had 27 R&B top ten hits, making her one of the most popular and successful singers of the period. Both "Am I Asking Too Much" (1948) and "Baby Get Lost" (1949) reached Number 1 on the R&B chart, and her version of "I Wanna Be Loved" (1950) crossed over to reach Number 22 on the US pop chart. Her hit recordings included blues, standards, novelties, pop covers, and even a version of Hank Williams' "Cold, Cold Heart" (R&B Number 3, 1951). At the same time as her biggest popular success, she also recorded sessions with many leading jazz musicians, including Clifford Brown and Clark Terry on the album Dinah Jams (1954), and also recorded with Cannonball Adderley and Ben Webster.

In 1959, she had her first top ten pop hit, with a version of "What a Diff'rence a Day Made", which made Number 4 on the US pop chart. Her band at that time included arranger Belford Hendricks, with Kenny Burrell (guitar), Joe Zawinul (piano), and Panama Francis (drums). She followed it up with a version of Irving Gordon's "Unforgettable", and then two highly successful duets in 1960 with Brook Benton, "Baby (You've Got What It Takes)" (No. 5 Pop, No. 1 R&B) and "A Rockin' Good Way (To Mess Around and Fall in Love)" (No. 7 Pop, No. 1 R&B). Her last big hit was "September in the Rain" in 1961 (No. 23 Pop, No. 5 R&B).

She also notably performed two numbers in the dirty blues genre. The songs were "Long John Blues" about her dentist, with lyrics like "He took out his trusty drill, told me to open wide. He said he wouldn't hurt me, but he filled my hole inside." She also recorded a song called "Big Long Sliding Thing", supposedly about a trombonist.

In the 1950s and early 1960s before her death, Washington occasionally performed on the Las Vegas Strip. Tony Bennett said of Washington during a recording session with Amy Winehouse: "She was a good friend of mine, you know. She was great. She used to just come in with two suitcases in Vegas without being booked. And she'd just come in and put the suitcases down. And she'd say, "I'm here, boss". And she'd stay as long as she wanted. And all the kids in all the shows on the Strip would come that night. They'd hear that she's in town and it would be packed just for her performance". According to Richard S. Ginell at AllMusic:

"Washington was at once one of the most beloved and controversial singers of the mid-20th century – beloved to her fans, devotees, and fellow singers; controversial to critics who still accuse her of selling out her art to commerce and bad taste. Her principal sin, apparently, was to cultivate a distinctive vocal style that was at home in all kinds of music, be it R&B, blues, jazz, middle of the road pop – and she probably would have made a fine gospel or country singer had she the time. Hers was a gritty, salty, high-pitched voice, marked by absolute clarity of diction and clipped, bluesy phrasing..."

Washington was well-known for singing torch songs. In 1962, Dinah hired a male backing trio called the Allegros, consisting of Jimmy Thomas on drums, Earl Edwards on sax, and Jimmy Sigler on organ. Edwards was eventually replaced on sax by John Payne. A Variety writer praised their vocals as "effective choruses".

Washington's achievements included appearances at the Newport Jazz Festival (1955–59), the Randalls Island Jazz Festival in New York City (1959), and the International Jazz Festival in Washington D.C. (1962), frequent gigs at Birdland (1958, 1961–62), and performances in 1963 with Count Basie and Duke Ellington.

Early on the morning of December 14, 1963, Washington's seventh husband, football great Dick "Night Train" Lane, went to sleep with his wife, and awoke later to find her slumped over and not responsive. Doctor B. C. Ross came to the scene to pronounce her dead. An autopsy later showed a lethal combination of secobarbital and amobarbital, which contributed to her death at the age of 39. She is buried in the Burr Oak Cemetery in Alsip, Illinois.

Other DuSable High School Alumni Notables Are:

- Gene Ammons (1943) — pioneering jazz tenor saxophone player.
- Ronnie Boykins (1954) — jazz bassist, most noted for his work with Sun Ra.
- Timuel Black (attended) — historian
- Maurice Cheeks (1974) — former NBA guard (1978–93).
- Nathaniel Clifton (1942) — basketball and baseball athlete for DuSable, played for Harlem Globetrotters and Chicago American Giants, Nat "Sweetwater" Clifton was a 2014 inductee in the Basketball Hall of Fame.
- Sonny Cohn (1943) — jazz trumpet player, perhaps best known for his 24 years playing with Count Basie.
- Nat King Cole (attended) — pianist and crooner, predominantly of pop and jazz works (*Unforgettable*). He was a 1990 recipient of a Grammy Lifetime Achievement Award, and in 2000, he was elected into the Rock and Roll Hall of Fame.
- Jerome Cooper (1965) — jazz musician who specialized in percussion.
- Don Cornelius (1954) — television show host and producer, best known as the creator and host of *Soul Train*. (1971–93).
- Vincent T. Cullers (attended) — founder of the first African-American advertising agency.
- Richard Davis (1948) — bassist and professor of music at the University of Wisconsin–Madison.
- Dorothy Donegan (1940) — jazz pianist.
- Redd Foxx (attended) — standup comedian and actor, best known for his role on the television series *Sanford and Son*.
- Von Freeman (1942) — jazz tenor saxophonist.
- John Gilmore (1949) — clarinet and saxophone player, best known for his time with the Sun Ra Arkestra, a group he briefly led after Sun Ra's death.
- Johnny Griffin (1946) — bebop and hard bop tenor saxophone player.

- Eddie Harris (1953) — jazz musician best known for playing tenor saxophone and for introducing the electrically amplified saxophone.
- Johnny Hartman (1941) — jazz singer (*Lush Life*), best known for his work with John Coltrane.
- Fred Hopkins (1966) — jazz bassist.
- Joseph Jarman (1956) — jazz composer, percussionist, clarinetist, and saxophonist.
- Ella Jenkins (1942) — Grammy Award–winning musician and singer best known for her work in folk music and children's music.
- LeRoy Jenkins (1950) — violinist who worked mostly in free jazz.
- John H. Johnson (attended) — founder of Johnson Publishing Company (*Ebony*, *Jet*), and the first African-American on the Forbes list of the richest 400 Americans.
- Clifford Jordan (1949) — jazz saxophonist.
- Ernie McMillan (1956) — former NFL offensive tackle (1961–75).
- Walter Perkins (1950) — jazz percussionist.
- Kevin Porter (1968) — former NBA guard (1972–81, 82–83).
- Julian Priester (1953) — jazz trombone player.
- Wilbur Ware (1942) — hard bebop bassist
- Dinah Washington (1942) — Grammy award–winning jazz singer (*What a Diff'rence a Day Makes*, *Teach Me Tonight*). She was inducted into the Rock and Roll Hall of Fame in 1993 as an "early influence".
- Harold Washington (1939) — the 51st Mayor of Chicago (1983–87), and was the city's first African–American mayor.
- Jason Williams (2004) — NFL linebacker.
- Chuck Winfrey (1967) — former NFL Linebacker (1971–72).

MATRIARCH AND QUEEN OF BLACK DANCE

Katherine Mary Dunham

Katherine Mary Dunham (also known as **Kaye Dunn**, June 22, 1909 – May 21, 2006) was an American dancer, choreographer, author, educator, and social activist. Dunham had one of the most successful dance careers in American and European theater of the 20th century, and directed her own dance company for many years. She has been called the "matriarch and queen mother of black dance."

While a student at the University of Chicago, Dunham took leave and went to the Caribbean to study dance and ethnography. She later returned to graduate and submitted a master's thesis in anthropology. She did not complete the other requirements for the degree, however, and realized that her professional calling was performance.

At the height of her career in the 1940s and 1950s, Dunham was renowned throughout Europe and Latin America and was widely popular in the United States, where The Washington Post called her "dancer Katherine the Great". For almost 30 years she maintained the Katherine Dunham Dance Company, the only self-supported American black dance troupe at that time, and over her long career she choreographed more than ninety individual dances. Dunham was an innovator in African-American modern dance as well as a leader in the field of dance anthropology, or ethno-choreology. She also developed the Dunham Technique.

Katherine Mary Dunham was born on June 22, 1909 in a Chicago hospital and taken as an infant to her parents' home in Glen Ellyn, Illinois, a village about 25 miles west of Chicago. Her father, Albert Millard Dunham, was a descendant of slaves from West Africa and Madagascar. Her mother Fanny June Dunham (née Taylor); who was of mixed French-Canadian and Native American heritage, died when Dunham was three years old. She had an older brother, Albert Jr., with whom she had a close relationship. After her father's remarriage a few years later, the family moved to a predominantly white neighborhood in Joliet, Illinois, where her father ran a dry-cleaning business.

Dunham became interested in both writing and dance at a young age. In 1921, a short story she wrote when she was 12 years old called "Come Back to Arizona" appeared in volume 2 of **The Brownies' Book**.

She graduated from Joliet Central High School in 1928, where she played baseball, tennis, basketball, track, served as vice-president of the French Club, and was on the yearbook staff. In high school she joined the Terpsichorean Club and began to learn a kind of modern dance based on the ideas of Jaques-Dalcroze and Rudolf von Laban. At a young age, Dunham organized a cabaret party to raise money for her church in which she starred. At the age of 15, she organized the Blue Moon Café, a fundraising cabaret for Brown's Methodist Church in Joliet, where she gave her first public performance. While still a high school student, she opened a private dance school for young black children.

After completing her studies at Joliet Junior College, Dunham moved to Chicago to join her brother Albert, who was attending the University of Chicago as a student of philosophy. In a lecture by Robert Redfield, a professor of anthropology, she learned that much of black culture in modern America had begun in Africa. She consequently decided to major in anthropology and to focus on dances of the African diaspora. Besides Redfield, she studied under anthropologists such as A.R. Radcliffe-Brown, Edward Sapir, and Bronisław Malinowski. Under their tutelage, she showed great promise in her ethnographic studies of dance.

In 1935, Dunham was awarded travel fellowships from the Julius Rosenwald and Guggenheim foundations to conduct ethnographic study of the dance forms of the Caribbean, especially as manifested in the Vodun of Haiti, a path also followed by fellow anthropology student Zora Neale Hurston.

She also received a grant to work with Professor Melville Herskovits of Northwestern University, whose ideas of African retention would serve as a platform for her research in the Caribbean.

Her field work in the Caribbean began in Jamaica, where she lived for several months in the remote Maroon Village of Accompong, deep in the mountains of Cockpit Country. (She later wrote Journey to Accompong, a book describing her experiences there.) Then she traveled on to Martinique and to Trinidad and Tobago for short stays, primarily to do an investigation of Shango, the African god who remained an important presence in West Indian heritage. Early in 1936, she arrived in Haiti, where she remained for several months, the first of her many extended stays in that country through her life.

While in Haiti, Dunham investigated Vodun rituals and made extensive notes in her research, particularly on the dance movements of the participants. Years later, after extensive studies and initiations, she became a mambo in the Vodun religion. She also became friends with, among others, Dumarsais Estimé, then a high-level politician, who became president of Haiti in 1949. Somewhat later, she assisted him, at considerable risk to her life, when he was persecuted for his progressive policies and sent in exile to Jamaica after a coup d'état.

Dunham returned to Chicago in the late spring of 1936, and in August was awarded a bachelor's degree, a Ph.B., bachelor of philosophy, with her principal area of study named as social anthropology. She was one of the first African American women to attend this college and also to earn these degrees. In 1938, using materials collected during her research tour of the Caribbean, Dunham submitted a thesis, "The Dances of Haiti: A Study of Their Material Aspect, Organization, Form, and Function," to the Department of Anthropology at the University of Chicago in partial fulfillment of the requirements for a master's degree, but she never completed her course work or took examinations to qualify for the degree. Devoted to dance performance, as well as to anthropological research, she realized that she had to choose between the two. Although she was offered another grant from the Rockefeller Foundation to pursue her academic studies, she chose dance, gave up her graduate studies, and departed for Broadway and Hollywood.

Katherine Dunham

In 1928, while still an undergraduate, Dunham began to study ballet with Ludmilla Speranzeva, a Russian dancer who had settled in Chicago, having come to the United States with the Franco-Russian vaudeville troupe Le Théâtre de la Chauve-Souris directed by impresario Nikita Balieff. She also studied ballet with Mark Turbyfill and Ruth Page, who became prima ballerina of the Chicago Opera. Through her ballet teachers, she was also exposed to Spanish, East Indian, Javanese, and Balinese dance forms. In 1931, when she was only 21, Dunham formed a group called Ballets Nègres, one of the first black ballet companies in the United States. After a single, well-received performance in 1931, the group was disbanded. Encouraged by Speranzeva to focus on modern dance instead of ballet, Dunham opened her first real dance school in 1933 called the Negro Dance Group. It was a venue for Dunham to teach young black dancers about their African heritage.

In 1934–36, Dunham performed as a guest artist with the ballet company of the Chicago Opera. Ruth Page had written a scenario and choreographed La Guiablesse ("The Devil Woman"), based on a Martinican folk tale in Lafcadio Hearn's Two Years in the French West Indies. It opened in Chicago in 1933, with a black cast and with Page dancing the title role. The next year it was repeated with Katherine Dunham in the lead and with students from Dunham's Negro Dance Group in the ensemble. Her dance career was then interrupted by her anthropological research in the Caribbean.

Having completed her undergraduate work at the University of Chicago and having made the decision to pursue a career as a dancer and choreographer rather than as an academic, Dunham revived her dance ensemble and in 1937 journeyed with them to New York to take part in A Negro Dance Evening organized by Edna Guy at the 92nd Street YMCA. The troupe performed a suite of West Indian dances in the first half of the program and a ballet entitled Tropic Death, with Talley Beatty, in the second half. Upon returning to Chicago, the company performed at the Goodman Theater and at the Abraham Lincoln Center. Dunham's well-known works Rara Tonga and Woman with a Cigar were created at this time. With choreography characterized by exotic sexuality, both became signature works in the Dunham repertory. After successful performances of her company, Dunham was named dance director of the Chicago Negro Theater Unit of the Federal Theatre Project. In this post, she choreographed the Chicago production of "Run Li'l Chil'lun", performed at the Goodman Theater, and produced several other works of choreography including "The Emperor Jones" and "Barrelhouse".

At this time, Dunham first became associated with designer John Pratt, whom she later married. Together, they produced the first version of her dance composition "L'Ag'ya", which premiered on January 27, 1938, as a part of the Federal Theater Project in Chicago. Based on her research in Martinique, this three-part performance integrated elements of a Martinique fighting dance into American ballet.

In 1939, Dunham's company gave further performances in Chicago and Cincinnati and then went back to New York, where Dunham had been invited to stage a new number for the popular, long-running musical revue "Pins and Needles" (1940), produced by the International Ladies' Garment Workers Union. As this show continued its run at the Windsor Theater, Dunham booked her own company in the theater for a Sunday performance. This concert, billed as "Tropics and Le Hot Jazz", included not only her favorite partners Archie Savage and Talley Beatty but her principal Haitian drummer, Papa Augustin. Initially scheduled for a single performance, the show was so popular that the troupe repeated it for another ten Sundays.

Catherine Dunham performing Cabin in the Sky

This success led to the entire company being engaged in the 1940 Broadway production "Cabin in the Sky", staged by George Balanchine and starring Ethel Waters. With Dunham in the sultry role of temptress Georgia Brown, the show ran for 20 weeks in New York before moving to the West Coast for an extended run of performances there. The show created a minor controversy in the press.

After the national tour of "Cabin in the Sky", the Dunham Company stayed in Los Angeles, where they appeared in the Warner Brothers short film "Carnival of Rhythm" (1941). The next year Dunham appeared in the Paramount musical film "Star Spangled Rhythm" (1942) in a specialty number, "Sharp as a Tack," with Eddie "Rochester" Anderson. Other movies she appeared in during this period included the Abbott and Costello comedy "Pardon My Sarong" (1942) and the black film musical "Stormy Weather" (1943).

The company returned to New York, and in September 1943, under the management of the impresario Sol Hurok, her troupe opened in Tropical Review at the Martin Beck Theater. Featuring lively Latin American and Caribbean dances, plantation dances, and American social dances, the show was an immediate success. The original two-week engagement was extended by popular demand into a three-month run, after which the company embarked on an extensive tour of the United States and Canada. In Boston, then a bastion of conservatism, the show was banned in 1944 after only one performance. Although it was well-received by the audience, local censors feared that the revealing costumes and provocative dances might compromise public morals. After the tour, in 1945, the Dunham Company appeared in the short-lived "Blue Holiday" at the Belasco Theater in New York and in the more successful "Carib Song" at the Adelphi Theatre. The finale to the first act of this show was "Shango", a staged interpretation of a Vodun ritual that would become a permanent part of the company's repertory.

In 1946, Dunham returned to Broadway for a revue entitled "Bal Nègre", which received glowing notices from theater and dance critics. Early in 1947 Dunham choreographed the musical play "Windy City", which premiered at the Great Northern Theater in Chicago, and later in the year she opened a cabaret show in Las Vegas, during the first year that the city became a popular entertainment destination. Later that year she went with her troupe to Mexico, where their performances were so popular that they remained for more than two months. After Mexico, Dunham began touring in Europe, where she was an immediate sensation. In 1948, she opened "A Caribbean Rhapsody" first at the Prince of Wales Theatre in London, and then swept on to the Théâtre des Champs-Élysées in Paris.

This was the beginning of more than 20 years of performing almost exclusively outside the United States. During these years, the Dunham Company appeared in some 33 countries in Europe, North Africa, South America, Australia, and East Asia. Dunham continued to develop dozens of new productions during this period, and the company met with enthusiastic audiences wherever they went. Despite these successes, the company frequently ran into periods of financial difficulties, as Dunham was required to support all of the 30 to 40 dancers and musicians.

Dunham and her company appeared in the Hollywood movie "Casbah" (1948) with Tony Martin, Yvonne De Carlo, and Peter

Lorre, and in the Italian film "Botta e Risposta", produced by Dino de Laurentiis. Also, that year they appeared in the first ever, hour-long American spectacular televised by NBC when television was first beginning to spread across America. This was followed by television spectaculars filmed in London, Buenos Aires, Toronto, Sydney, and Mexico City.

In 1950, Sol Hurok presented Katherine Dunham and Her Company in a dance revue at the Broadway Theater in New York, with a program composed of some of Dunham's best works. It closed after only 38 performances, and the company soon thereafter embarked on a tour of venues in South America, Europe, and North Africa. They had particular success in Denmark and France. In the mid-1950s, Dunham and her company appeared in three films: "Mambo" (1954), made in Italy; "Die Grosse Starparade" (1954), made in Germany; and "Música en la Noche" (1955), made in Mexico City.

The Dunham Company's international tours ended in Vienna in 1960, when it was stranded without money because of bad management by their impresario. Dunham saved the day by arranging for the company to appear in a German television special, "Karibische Rhythmen", after which they returned to America. Dunham's last appearance on Broadway was in 1962 in "Bamboche!", which included a few former Dunham dancers in the cast and a contingent of dancers and drummers from the Royal Troupe of Morocco. It was not a success, closing after only eight performances.

A highlight of Dunham's later career was the invitation from New York's Metropolitan Opera, to stage dances for a new production of "Aida" with soprano Leontyne Price. Thus, in 1963, she became the first African-American to choreograph for the Met since Hemsley Winfield set the dances for "The Emperor Jones" in 1933. The critics acknowledged the historical research she did on dance in ancient Egypt but did not particularly care for the results they saw on the Met stage. Subsequently, Dunham undertook various choreographic commissions at several venues in the United States and in Europe. In 1967 she officially retired after presenting a final show at the famous Apollo Theater in Harlem, New York. Even in retirement Dunham continued to choreograph: one of her major works was directing Scott Joplin's opera "Treemonisha" in 1972 at Morehouse College in Atlanta.

In 1978 Dunham was featured in the PBS special, "Divine Drumbeats: Katherine Dunham and Her People", narrated by James Earl Jones, as part of the Dance in America series. Alvin Ailey later produced a tribute for her in 1987-88 with his American Dance Theater at Carnegie Hall entitled "The Magic of Katherine Dunham".

In 1945, Dunham opened and directed the Katherine Dunham School of Dance and Theatre near Times Square in New York City after her dance company was provided with rent-free studio space for three years by an admirer, Lee Shubert; it had an initial enrollment of 350 students.

The program included courses in dance, drama, performing arts, applied skills, humanities, cultural studies, and Caribbean research, and in 1947 it was expanded and granted a charter as the Katherine Dunham School of Cultural Arts. The school was managed in Dunham's absence by one of her dancers, Syvilla Fort, thrived for about ten years, and was considered one of the best learning centers of its type at the time. Schools inspired by it later opened in Stockholm, Paris, and Rome by dancers trained by Dunham.

Her alumni included many future celebrities, such as Eartha Kitt, who, as a teenager, won a scholarship to her school and later became one of her dancers before moving on to a successful singing career. Others who attended her school included: James Dean, Gregory Peck, Jose Ferrer, Jennifer Jones, Shelley Winters, Sidney Poitier, Shirley MacLaine and Warren Beatty. Marlon Brando frequently dropped in to play the bongo drums, and jazz musician Charles Mingus held regular jam sessions with the drummers. Known for her many innovations, Dunham developed dance pedagogy, later named the Dunham Technique, that won international acclaim and that is now taught as a modern dance style in many dance schools.

By 1957, Dunham was under severe personal strain that was affecting her health, and she decided to live for a year in relative isolation in Kyoto, Japan, where she worked on writing autobiographies of her youth. The first work, entitled "A Touch of Innocence: Memoirs of Childhood", was published in 1959. A continuation based on her experiences in Haiti, "Island Possessed", was published in 1969, and a fictional work based on her African experiences, "Kasamance: A Fantasy", was published in 1974. Throughout her career, she occasionally published articles about her anthropological research (sometimes under the pseudonym of Kaye Dunn) and sometimes lectured on anthropological topics at universities and scholarly societies.

In 1964, Dunham settled in East St. Louis and took up the post of artist-in-residence at Southern Illinois University in nearby Edwardsville. There she was able to bring anthropologists, sociologists, educational specialists, scientists, writers, musicians, and theater people together to create a liberal arts curriculum that would be a foundation for further college work. One of her fellow professors with whom she collaborated was architect Buckminister Fuller.

The following year, 1965, President Lyndon B. Johnson nominated Dunham to be technical cultural adviser—that is, a sort of cultural ambassador—to the government of Senegal in West Africa. Her mission was to help train the Senegalese National Ballet and to assist President Leopold Senghor with arrangements for the First Pan-African World Festival of Negro Arts in Dakar (1965–66). Later she established a second home in Senegal and occasionally returned there to scout for talented African musicians and dancers.

In 1967, Dunham opened the Performing Arts Training Center (PATC) in East St. Louis as an attempt to use the arts to combat poverty and urban unrest. It served as a catharsis after the 1968 riots, during which she encouraged gang members in the ghetto to vent their frustrations with drumming and dance. The PATC drew on former members of Dunham's touring company as well as local residents for its teaching staff. While trying to help the young people in the community she was even jailed herself, making international headlines which quickly embarrassed local police officials to release her. She also continued refining and teaching the Dunham Technique to transmit that knowledge to succeeding generations of dance students, and lecturing at annual Masters' Seminars in St. Louis that attracted dance students from around the world every summer until her death. She also established the Katherine Dunham Centers for Arts and Humanities in East St. Louis to preserve Haitian and African instruments and artifacts from her own personal collection.

In 1976, Dunham was guest artist-in-residence and lecturer for Afro-American studies at the University of California, Berkeley. A photographic exhibit honoring her achievements, entitled "Kaiso! Katherine Dunham," was mounted at the Women's Center on the campus. In 1978, an anthology of writings by and about her, also entitled "Kaiso!" Katherine Dunham, was published in a limited, numbered edition of 130 copies by the Institute for the Study of Social Change.

The Katherine Dunham Company toured throughout North America in the mid-1940s, even performing in the then-segregated South, where Dunham once refused to hold a show after finding out that the city's black residents had not been allowed to buy tickets for the performance. On another occasion, in October 1944, after getting a rousing standing ovation in Louisville, Kentucky, she told the all-white audience that she and her company would not return because "your management will not allow people, like you, to sit next to people, like us", and she expressed a hope that time and the "war for tolerance and democracy" would bring a change. One historian noted that "during the course of the tour, Dunham and the troupe had recurrent problems with racial discrimination, leading her to a posture of militancy which was to characterize her subsequent career."

In Hollywood, Dunham refused to sign a lucrative studio contract when the producer said she would have to replace some of her darker-skinned company members. She and her company frequently had difficulties finding adequate accommodations while on tour because in many regions of the country, black Americans were not allowed to stay at hotels.

While Dunham was recognized as "unofficially" representing American cultural life in her foreign tours, she was given very little assistance of any kind by the U.S. State Department. She had incurred the displeasure of departmental officials when her company performed "Southland", a ballet that dramatized the lynching of a black man in the racist American South. Its premiere performance on December 9, 1950, at the Teatro Municipal in Santiago, Chile, generated considerable public interest in the early months of 1951. The State Department was dismayed by the negative view of American society that the ballet presented to foreign audiences. As a result, Dunham would later experience some diplomatic "difficulties" on her tours. The State Department regularly subsidized other less well-known groups, but it consistently refused to support her company (even when it was entertaining U.S. Army troops), although at the same time it did not hesitate to take credit for them as "unofficial artistic and cultural representatives."

In 1950, while visiting Brazil, Dunham and her group were refused rooms at a first-class hotel in São Paulo, the Hotel Esplanada, frequented by many American businessmen. Understanding that the fact was due to racial discrimination, she made sure the incident was publicized. The incident was widely discussed in the Brazilian press and became a hot political issue. In response, the Afonso Arinos law was passed in 1951 that made racial discrimination in public places a felony in Brazil.

In 1992, at age 83, Dunham went on a highly publicized hunger strike to protest the discriminatory U.S. foreign policy against Haitian boat-people. *Time* reported that, "she went on a 47-day hunger strike to protest the U.S.'s forced repatriation of Haitian refugees."

"My job", she said, "is to create a useful legacy." During her protest, Dick Gregory led a non-stop vigil at her home, where many disparate personalities came to show their respect, such as Debbie

Allen, Jonathan Demme, and Louis Farrakhan, leader of the Nation of Islam.

This initiative drew international publicity to the plight of the Haitian boat-people and U.S. discrimination against them. Dunham ended her fast only after exiled Haitian president Jean-Bertrand Aristide and Jesse Jackson came to her and personally requested that she stop risking her life for this cause. In recognition of her stance, President Aristide later awarded her a medal of Haiti's highest honor.

Dunham married Jordis McCoo, a black postal worker, in 1931, but he did not share her interests and they gradually drifted apart, finally divorcing in 1938. About that time Dunham met and began to work with John Thomas Pratt, a Canadian who had become one of America's most renowned costume and theatrical set designers. Pratt, who was white, shared Dunham's interests in African-Caribbean cultures and was happy to put his talents in her service. After he became her artistic collaborator, they became romantically involved. In the summer of 1941, after the national tour of "Cabin in the Sky" ended, they went to Mexico, where inter-racial marriages were less controversial than in the United States, and engaged in a commitment ceremony on 20 July, which thereafter they gave as the date of their wedding. In fact, that ceremony was not recognized as a legal marriage in the United States, a point of law that would come to trouble them some years later. Katherine Dunham and John Pratt married in 1949 to adopt Marie-Christine, a French 14-month-old baby. From the beginning of their association, around 1938, Pratt designed the sets and every costume Dunham ever wore. He continued as her artistic collaborator until his death in 1986.

When she was not performing, Dunham and Pratt often visited Haiti for extended stays. On one of these visits, during the late 1940s, she purchased a large property of more than seven hectares in the Carrefours suburban area of Port-au-Prince, known as Habitation Leclerc. Dunham used Habitation Leclerc as a private retreat for many years, frequently bringing members of her dance company to recuperate from the stress of touring and to work on developing new dance productions. After running it as a tourist spot, with Vodun dancing as entertainment, in the early 1960s, she sold it to a French entrepreneur in the early 1970s.

In 1949, Dunham returned from international touring with her company for a brief stay in the United States, where she suffered a temporary nervous breakdown after the premature death of her beloved brother Albert. He had been a promising philosophy professor at Howard University and a protégé of Alfred North Whitehead. During this time, she developed a warm friendship with the psychologist and philosopher Erich Fromm, whom she had known in Europe. He was only one of a number of international celebrities who were Dunham's friends. In December 1951, a photo of Dunham dancing with Ismaili Muslim leader Prince Ali Khan at a private party he had hosted for her in Paris appeared in a popular magazine and fueled rumors that the two were romantically linked. Both Dunham and the prince denied the suggestion. The prince was then married to actress Rita Hayworth, and Dunham was now legally married to John Pratt; a quiet ceremony in Las Vegas had taken place earlier in the year. The couple had officially adopted their foster daughter, a 14-month-old girl they had found as an infant in a Roman Catholic convent nursery in Fresnes, France. Named Marie-Christine Dunham Pratt, she was their only child.

Among Dunham's closest friends and colleagues was Julie Robinson, formerly a performer with the Katherine Dunham Company, and her husband, singer and later political activist Harry Belafonte. Both remained close friends of Dunham for many years, until her death. Glory Van Scott and Jean-Léon Destiné were among other former Dunham dancers who remained her lifelong friends.

On May 21, 2006, at the age of 96, Dunham died in her sleep from natural causes in New York City.

CHAPTER TEN

Social Activism with African American Leadership in Chicago

RACIAL DISCRIMINATION FOR JOBS

Picket line at the Mid-City Realty Company, Chicago, Illinois. July 1941

Fighting job discrimination was a constant battle for African Americans in Chicago, as foremen in various companies restricted the advancement of black workers, which often kept them from earning higher wages. Then in the mid-20th century, blacks began slowly moving up to better positions in the work force.

Returning World War II veterans spurred a population and housing boom driven in part by benefits from the GI bill. The economic demands of the post-war boom and the burgeoning Civil Rights movement led to conflicts over discrimination in housing, jobs and education. The Federal Housing Administration, which instituted policies that reinforced patterns of segregation, routinely denied low-interest loans to non-whites.

The experience of fighting for freedom in Europe and then returning home to a country where discrimination and opportunities were limited fostered discontent for returning black GIs: The legacy of post-war economic discrimination contributed to the wealth gap between whites and non-whites that we see today. One of the most important factors that contributed to the wealth gap was the federal housing policy. This policy endorsed redlining and discrimination in sales, financing and homeowners' insurance, is reflected in the unequal rates of home ownership, even today.

Man picketing dairy in 1941, Chicago

Many African American Veterans found themselves fighting a domestic war of discrimination for jobs and, so they took to the picket lines to make their case on the streets of Chicago.

World War II placed Chicago in a strategic production role because of its diverse industrial base, and the city's economy boomed. In addition, the nearby Great Lakes Naval Training Center and Fort Sheridan were major induction and basic-training facilities, and Northwestern University operated the country's largest naval midshipmen's school. Thousands of naval pilots also passed through Glenview Naval Air Station, receiving flight instruction on two aircraft carriers on the lake that were converted from old passenger vessels. As the country's rail hub, Chicago hosted traveling military personnel in four Chicago servicemen's centers. One of them, the historic Auditorium Building, not only served 24 million meals by the war's end but also saw its magnificent stage used as a bowling alley. In the early 20th century many prominent African Americans were Chicago residents, including Republican and later Democratic congressman William L. Dawson (America's most powerful black politician) and boxing champion Joe Louis. America's most widely read black newspaper, the *Chicago Defender*, was published there and circulated in the South, as well.

After long efforts, in the late 1930s, workers organized across racial lines to form the United Meatpacking Workers of America. By then, the majority of workers in Chicago's plants were black, but they succeeded in creating an interracial organizing committee. It succeeded in organizing unions, both in Chicago and Omaha, Nebraska - the city with the second largest meatpacking industry. This union belonged to the Congress of Industrial Organizations (CIO), which was more progressive than the American Federation of Labor. They succeeded in lifting segregation of job positions. For a time, workers achieved living wages and other benefits, leading to blue collar middle-class life for decades. Some blacks were also able to move up the ranks to supervisory and management positions. The CIO also succeeded in organizing Chicago's steel industry.

Blacks began to win elective office in local and state government. The first blacks had been elected to office in Chicago in the late 19th century, decades before the Great Migrations.

Chicago is home to three of six African-American US Senators who have served since Reconstruction, who are all Democrats: Carol Moseley Braun (1993–1999), President Barack Obama (2005–2008), and Roland Burris (2009–2010).

First Major Non-Christian Movement for African Americans:

Prophet Noble Drew Ali was the First leader to bring Islam as a faith, and Moorish Nationality as a Sovereign Birthrights to African Americans in America.

January 18, 2018, edited by the HistoryMaker

In 1913, Noble Drew Ali, founded the first branch of the Moorish Science Temple in Newark, New Jersey. Born Timothy Drew in North Carolina in 1889, Ali founded the Temple as a sect of Islam that preaches for the uplifting of fallen humanity and the self-improvement of citizens. He aimed to attract African Americans, a group he called the Moors of America, who he argued were descended from North Africans and therefore born into the Islamic faith. He gained a following in cities like Philadelphia, Detroit and Washington, D.C., especially in neighborhoods that had been populated by the Great Migration. He preached a doctrine of racial pride that encouraged African Americans to discard identity labels like 'colored,' 'black,' and 'negro.' By connecting the descendants of slaves to a rich history of North Africa, Ali's doctrine aimed to reunite African Americans with a sense of history and heritage that had been torn away during the slave trade.

1928: Prophet Noble Drew Ali, lecturing to followers of the "Moorish -American Moslems" at the Moorish Science Temple, in Chicago Illinois.

When Ali moved to Chicago in 1925, his movement began to make traction. In the late 1920s, journalists estimated that the Moorish Science Temple had 35,000 members. By 1928, the Temple had gained notoriety in the city, and was mentioned prominently and positively by the Chicago Defender. Ali believed that Chicago would become a second Mecca.

Attendees of the 1928 Moorish Science Temple Conclave in Chicago, Noble Drew Ali is in white in the front row center.

March 24th, 2014

Source: finalcall.com website; Muslim Journal newspaper issue No.27 done on April 7, 2006 (copy of newspaper was given to our National Grand Sheik J. Bratton-Bey)

On Sunday, February 23, 2014 at the Joe Louis Arena in Detroit, Michigan; Minister Louis Farrakhan of the Nation of Islam spoke about a few of our great men and women who have paved the way for our awakening, fighting for freedom and stimulating our consciousness about who we were. This talk was done at the Nation of Islam Saviours' Day 2014 event. In his opening statements Minister Louis Farrakhan mentioned among other leaders Marcus Garvey and Prophet Noble Drew Ali. Marcus Garvey is known to the Moorish-Americans as the forerunner of Prophet Noble Drew Ali; and of course Prophet Noble Drew Ali was the founder of the Moorish Science Temple Divine and National movement in 1913.

Excerpts of the Saviours' Day keynote address delivered by Minister Louis Farrakhan are as follows:

"Marcus Garvey, bless him forever and ever: That man organized Black people in a way that had never been done before in America – ('One Faith, One Aim, One Destiny'). Here are his words when he was imprisoned in Atlanta... 'And remember! All good men go to prison – they don't even fear going to jail! One has fear just in going to jail for pimping; fear in going to jail for dope smoking, but to go to jail for standing up for your people? That's an honorable sentence. Accept it, if that is your lot!' Mr. Garvey said: 'If I die in Atlanta' – he's in prison – 'my work shall then only begin, but I shall live in the physical or spiritual, to see the day of Africa's glory. When I am dead, wrap the mantle of the Red, Black and Green around me, for in the new life I shall rise with God's grace and blessing to lead the millions up the heights of triumph with the colors that you well know. Look for me in the whirlwind or the storm, look for me all around you, for, with God's grace, I shall come and bring with me countless millions of black slaves who have died in America and the West Indies and the millions in Africa to aid you in the fight for Liberty, Freedom and Life.' " – Minister Louis Farrakhan

"Now let's look at Noble Drew Ali: A man that died a young man; he lived from 1886 to 1929. I salute my brother: He is the first man to bring Islam to us in the way he tried to bring it; and, I thank him and I thank Allah for him! He said: 'The Moors were enslaved by reducing their mentality to that of Negroes, Blacks and Colored People. As a man thinketh so is he.' He's calling all Black people in America

'Moors'; but 'Moors' is the name given to the Muslims from North Africa that invaded the Iberian Peninsula, and brought Islam to Spain and Portugal and southern France! So, he's calling us 'Moors'- and he dressed his followers in the fez of the Muslim people of the East! He also is quoted as saying, 'Moors, you sleep too much. Wake up, and see the seven bridges crossing in the sky. Can you see that you are a people?' Not an 'organization' – we are a people! We are a nation!' "– Minister Louis Farrakhan

* Web Master Notes: Keep in mind that Prophet Noble Drew Ali went to visit Marcus Garvey in prison. You can read that information in the section under the "Main Menu" on the left hand side of the website called "The Prophet Noble Drew Ali and Marcus Garvey connection". Even though the Moors are known for being in North Africa and in Europe as seen by the Blackamoor heads in coat of arms, heraldry and seals of aristocrats and royal families; the Moors were all over the globe and especially in North America simultaneously in history because of our global Empire. The Moors are the ancient Moslems of the world. In our Moorish Holy Koran, Prophet Noble Drew Ali taught us that we are the original inhabitants of Northwestern and Southwestern Africa. In this context, Prophet Noble Drew Ali is speaking of the Americas; what is known as North America (Canada, United States, Alaska, Caribbean Islands, Greenland), Central and South America. In our Moorish Holy Koran, Prophet Noble Drew Ali shows that we inhabited this region of the earth before the continents split as shown in the Moorish Holy Koran Chapter XLVII or chapter 47 verses 1-7:

"1. The inhabitants of Africa are the descendants of the ancient Canaanites from the land of Canaan.

2. Old man Cush and his family are the first inhabitants of Africa who came from the land of Canaan.

3. His father Ham and his family were second. Then came the word Ethiopia, which means the demarcation line of the dominion of Amexem, the first true and divine name of Africa.

The dividing of the land, between the father and the son:

4. The dominion of Cush, North-East and South-East Africa and North-West and South-West was his father's dominion of Africa.

5. In later years many of their brethren from Asia and the Holy Lands joined them.

6. The Moabites from the land of Moab who received permission from the Pharaohs of Egypt to settle and inhabit North-West Africa; they were the founders and are the true possessors of the present Moroccan Empire. With their Canaanite, Hittite, and Amorite brethren who sojourned from the land of Canaan seeking new homes.

7. Their dominion and inhabitation extended from North-East and South-West Africa, across great Atlantis even unto the present North, South, and Central America and also Mexico and the Atlantis Islands; before the great earthquake, which caused the great Atlantic Ocean."

Amexem is the divine name for modern Africa of today and Ancient Africa. In your research you will see that when the Atlantic Ocean, also known as the Ethiopian/Ethiopic Ocean was formed because of the continents splitting/shifting, that was over 180 – 150 million years ago. So our Prophet Noble Drew Ali, himself an awaken Moor/Moabite is bringing the sleeping Moors in the western hemisphere the information of who they were before slavery. The Prophet also said in our Moorish Holy Koran 47:10-11, "What your ancient forefathers were, you are today without doubt or contradiction. There is no one who is able to change man from the descendant nature of his forefathers; unless his power extends beyond the great universal Creator Allah Himself. "

* Also view this post for additional clarity on the descendants of Ham and Old Man Kush inhabiting the planet before the continents broke apart –The Moorish Empire and the 36 degrees 30 north parallel line that marks the Moorish Empire explained from an African perspective:

The Moorish fez also originated in the west, in the Americas and was worn all over the world, throughout the Empire in many different styles, height, color, variations and with and without the tassel. The fez also did not originate in Fez/Fes of Morocco in North Africa of today that was the region in which the fez was being made in mass production. However the Moors were known for their high fez with black tassel. The Fez did not originate in the east. Prophet Noble Drew Ali was returning the fez to the Moorish-Americans; the ancient religious and national headdress of our ancient Moorish/Moabite ancestors from the Americas. The turban is also a Moorish headdress.

Minister Louis Farrakhan continued his great talk about some of our great male and female leaders after the Nation of Islam event with a "How Strong Is the Foundation, Can We Survive Part II" in Chicago.

In a newspaper article, that was under the umbrella of Imam W. Deen Mohammed called Muslim Journal; the No.27 issue done on April 7, 2006, there was a picture of the Prophet Noble Drew Ali and the Moorish Science Temple on the cover and an article that was a few pages long. In the article, a citation from one of Imam W. Deen Mohammed books was cited where he stated "If a man responds to the genes and better spirit of his ancestors, you cannot keep him in the dark. You may try to keep him there, but eventually you will find him with a light. You will wonder 'How did you get a light? There was no way out of this place'. G-d is the one who lights from within. Now many may want to play down the importance of what I have just said, but give another explanation, if you can as to how this happens. And the Civil Rights Movement marchers along with Dr. Martin Luther King Jr. and Mother Rosa Parks used to sing 'This little light of mine, I'm goanna let it shine…' And many before them came to know of that 'light' in the soul that could not be extinguished."

The Moorish-Americans can look up "THE SPEECH OF HENRY BERRY (OF JEFFERSON), IN THE HOUSE OF DELEGATES OF VIRGINIA ON ABOLITION OF SLAVERY" done on FRIDAY, January 20, 1832. In that speech, Mr. Berry addressed the house and said:

"Sir, we have, as far as possible closed every avenue by which light might enter their mind; we have only to go one step further – to extinguish the capacity to see the light, and our work would be completed; they would then be reduced to the level of the beasts of the field, and we should be safe; and I am not certain that we would not do it, if we could find out the necessary process – and that under the plea of necessity. But, sir, this is impossible; and can man be in the midst of freemen, and not know what freedom is? "

We must be forever thankful to Allah, for preparing our Prophet Noble Drew Ali to bring the light of truth to us in the Americas in 1913. Prophet Noble Drew Ali in the Moorish Literature is seen stating over and over about bringing us from out of darkness and into the marvelous light. The light of truth and divine guidance is what kept Prophet Noble Drew Ali 50 years ahead. "Genius citizens" that the Prophet spoke about that came after him such as Grand Sheiks Timothy and Richardson Dingle-El were 20 years ahead based on what was being done and demonstrated on pertaining to the National side of the Moorish movement with the light of the Proclamations of President Abraham Lincoln and the 13th Amendment with 20 sections of 1865.

The Muslim Journal article continued about speaking on the works of Prophet Noble Drew Ali stating "He started his Movement among African Americans, calling them Moorish Scientists. This group was a forerunner to the Nation of Islam. Many members of the Nation of Islam were first members of the Moorish Science temples. The earliest members of the Nation of Islam actually wore the red fezzes with the tassels, like the Moorish Scientists did. On the front of the Moorish Science Temple publications were the words, 'Prevention of sin and crime.' The members of the Nation of Islam carried I.D. cards on them that read, 'This person is a righteous Muslim. If he is caught being otherwise, take this card and punish him.' "

The fez and membership card was a known custom by the members of the Moorish Science Temple and still is today. The article continues "Before his untimely death in 1929, Drew had established over 15 branch temples, 20 subordinate temples and his membership was estimated to be over 100,000. These faithful members had established Moorish businesses, as well as other institutions, such as newspapers and schools."

We are happy to see that many are recognizing the works of Prophet Noble Drew Ali, the purpose of his movement which is continuing today through the Moorish Science Temple. The Divine and National Movement of North America, Inc. #13: The Moorish American National Republic.

Honorable Elijah Muhammad

Nation of Islam

From Wikipedia, the free encyclopedia

The NOI was founded in Detroit, Michigan, on July 4, 1930, by Wallace Fard Muhammad, also known as Master W. D. Fard Muhammad, in order to, as the Nation of Islam states, "teach the downtrodden and defenseless Black people a thorough Knowledge of God and of themselves, and to put them on the road to Self-Independence with a superior culture and higher civilization than they had previously experienced.

Elijah Muhammad was born *Elijah Robert Poole* in Sandersville, Georgia, the seventh of thirteen children of William Poole, Sr. (1868–1942), a Baptist lay preacher and sharecropper, and Mariah Hall (1873–1958), a homemaker and sharecropper.

Elijah's education ended at the third grade to work in sawmills and brickyards. To support the family, he worked with his parents as a sharecropper. When he was sixteen years old, he left home and began working in factories and at other businesses.

Poole married Clara Evans (1899–1972) on March 7, 1917. The Poole family was among the hundreds of thousands of black families forming the First Great Migration leaving the oppressive and economically troubled South in search of safety and employment. Poole later recounted that before the age of 20, he had witnessed the lynchings of three black men by white people. He said, "I seen enough of the white man's brutality to last me 26,000 years".

Moving his own family, parents and siblings, Elijah and the Pooles settled in Hamtramck, Michigan. Through the 1920s and 1930s, Poole struggled to find and keep work as the economy suffered during the Great Depression. During their years in Detroit, Elijah and Clara had eight children - six boys and two girls.

Master Wallace D. Fard Muhammad

While he was in Detroit, Poole began taking part in various Black Nationalist movements within the city. In August 1931, at the urging of his wife, Elijah Poole attended a speech on Islam and black empowerment by **Wallace D. Fard**. Afterward, Poole said he approached Fard and asked if he was the redeemer. Fard responded that he was, but that his time had not yet come. Fard taught that Blacks, were the original Asiatic people, and that they had a rich cultural history which was stolen from them in their enslavement. Fard stated that African Americans could regain their freedoms through self-independence and cultivation of their own culture and civilization. Poole, having strong consciousness of both race and class issues as a result of his struggles in the South, quickly fell in step with Fard's ideology. Poole soon became an ardent follower of Fard and joined his movement, as did his wife and several brothers. Soon afterward, Poole was given a Muslim surname, first "Karriem", and later, at Fard's behest, "Muhammad". He assumed leadership of the Nation's Temple No. 2 in Chicago. His younger brother Kalot Muhammad became the leader of the movement's self-defense arm, the Fruit of Islam.

Fard turned over leadership of the growing Detroit group to Elijah Muhammad, and the Allah Temple of Islam changed its name to the Nation of Islam. Elijah Muhammad and Wallace Fard continued to communicate until 1934, when Wallace Fard disappeared. Elijah Muhammad succeeded him in Detroit and was named "Minister of Islam". After the disappearance, Elijah Muhammad told followers that Master Wallace Fard Muhammad had come as Allah, in the flesh, to share his teachings that are a salvation for his followers.

In 1934, the Nation of Islam published its first newspaper, *Final Call to Islam*, to educate and build membership. Children of its members attended classes at the newly created Muhammad University of Islam, but this soon led to challenges by boards of education in Detroit and Chicago, which considered the children truants from the public school system. The controversy led to the jailing of several University of Islam board members and Elijah Muhammad in 1934 and to violent confrontations with police. Muhammad was put on probation, but the university remained open.

Elijah Muhammad took control of Temple No. 1, but only after battles with other potential leaders, including his brother. In 1935, as these battles became increasingly fierce, Muhammad left Detroit and settled his family in Chicago. Still facing threats, Muhammad left his family there and traveled to Milwaukee, Wisconsin, where he founded Temple No. 3, and eventually to Washington, D.C., where he founded Temple No. 4. He spent much of his time reading 104 books suggested by Wallace Fard at the Library of Congress.

On May 8, 1942, Elijah Muhammad was arrested for failure to register for the draft during World War II. After he was released on bail, Muhammad fled Washington D.C. on the advice of his attorney, who feared a lynching, and returned to Chicago after a seven-year-long absence. Muhammad was arrested there, charged with eight counts of sedition for instructing his followers not to register for the draft or serve in the armed forces. Found guilty, Elijah Muhammad served four years, from 1942 to 1946, at the Federal Correctional Institution in Milan, Michigan. During that time, his wife, Clara, and trusted aides ran the organization; Muhammad transmitted his messages and directives to followers in letters.

Following his return to Chicago, Elijah Muhammad was firmly in charge of the Nation of Islam. While Muhammad was in prison, the growth of the Nation of Islam had stagnated, with fewer than 400 members remaining by the time of his release in 1946. However, through the conversion of his fellow inmates as well as renewed efforts outside prison, he was able to redouble his efforts and continue growing the Nation. From four temples in 1946, the Nation of Islam grew to 15 by 1955. By 1959, there were 50 temples in 22 states.

Honorable Elijah Muhammad & Malcolm X

During this time, the Nation of Islam attracted Malcolm Little. While in prison in Boston for burglary from 1946 to 1952, Mr. Little joined the Nation of Islam. He was influenced by his brother, Reginald, who had become a member in Detroit. Malcom quit smoking, gambling and eating pork, in keeping with the Nation's practices and dietary restrictions. He spent long hours reading books in the prison library. He sharpened his oratory skills by participating in debating classes. Following Nation tradition, Elijah Muhammad ordered him to replace his surname, "Little", with an "X", a custom among Nation of Islam followers who considered their surnames to have been imposed by white slaveholders after their African names were taken from them as a way of the slave owner's claim of 3/5th "Human property ownership".

Malcolm X rose rapidly to become a minister and national spokesperson for the NOI. Highly influenced by Malcolm X's membership, the Nation claimed a membership of 30,000.

MINISTER MALCOM X AND LOUIS X

Minister Malcom x and Minister Louis X in Harlem New York

In 1955, through the admirations of Malcom X, Louis Walcott had joined the Nation of Islam. Following custom, he also replaced his surname with an "X". He was given his new name, "Farrakhan", by the Honorable Elijah Muhammad. In 1965, following the assassination of Malcolm X, Minister Farrakhan emerged as the protégé of Malcolm X. Like his predecessor, Farrakhan was a dynamic, charismatic leader and a powerful speaker with the ability to appeal to the African-American masses.

Farrakhan was born Louis Eugene Wolcott in The Bronx, New York, the younger of two sons of Sarah Mae Manning (January 16, 1900 – November 18, 1988) and Percival Clark, immigrants from the Caribbean islands. His mother was born in Saint Kitts and Nevis. His father was a Jamaican native. The couple split before Louis was born. Farrakhan says he never knew his biological father. His mother then moved in with Louis Wolcott from Barbados, who became his stepfather. After Louis' stepfather died in 1936, the Wolcott family moved to Boston, Massachusetts, where they settled in the West Indian neighborhood of Roxbury.

Starting at the age of six, Wolcott received rigorous training in the violin. He received his first violin at the age of six, and by the time he was 13 years old he had played with the Boston College Orchestra and the Boston Civic Symphony. A year later, he went on to win national competitions. In 196, he was one of the first black performers to appear on the Ted Mack *Original Amateur Hour*, where he also won an award. He and his family were active members of the Episcopal St. Cyprian's Church in Roxbury.

Wolcott attended the prestigious Boston Latin School, and later the English High School, from which he graduated. He completed three years at Winston-Salem Teachers College, where he had a track scholarship.

Wolcott married Betsy Ross while he was in college. (She later took the name Khadijah Farrakhan.) She lived in Boston, and was pregnant with their child. Due to complications from the pregnancy, Wolcott dropped out after completing his junior year of college to devote time to her and their child. They are still married.

Farrakhan has nine children: four sons (Mustapha, Joshua Nasir, Abnar, and Louis Jr.) and five daughters (Donna, Hanan, Maria, Fatimah, and Khallada).

In the 1950s, Wolcott started his professional music career by recording several calypso albums as a singer under the name "The

Charmer". He also performed on tour. In February 1955, using part of his middle name, Eugene, "Calypso Gene" was headlining a show in Chicago, Illinois, entitled "Calypso Follies." One of his songs was on the top *100 Billboard Chart* for five years in a row. There, he first came in contact with the teachings of the Nation of Islam (NOI) through Rodney Smith, a friend and saxophonist from Boston. Wolcott and his wife Betsy were invited to the Nation of Islam's annual Saviours' Day address by Elijah Muhammad. Prior to going to Saviours' Day, due to then-Minister Malcolm X's popularity in the media, Wolcott had never heard of Elijah Muhammad, and like many outside of the Nation of Islam, he thought that Malcolm X was the leader of the Nation of Islam.

In 1955, Wolcott fulfilled the requirements to be a registered Muslim/registered believer/registered laborer. He memorized and recited verbatim the 10 questions and answers of the NOI's Student Enrollment. He then wrote a Saviour's Letter that must be sent to the NOI's headquarters in Chicago. The Saviour's Letter must be copied *verbatim*, and have the identical handwriting of the Nation of Islam's founder, **Wallace Fard Muhammad**. After having the Saviour's Letter reviewed, and approved by the NOI's headquarters in Chicago in July 1955, Wolcott received a letter of approval from the Nation of Islam acknowledging his official membership as a registered Muslim/registered believer/registered laborer in the NOI. As a result, he received his "X." The "X" was considered a placeholder, used to indicate that Nation of Islam members' original African family names had been lost. They acknowledged that European surnames were slave names, assigned by the slave owners to mark their ownership. Members of the NOI used the "X" while waiting for their Islamic names, which some NOI members received later in their conversion. Hence, Louis Wolcott became Louis X. Elijah Muhammad then replaced his "X" with the "holy name" Farrakhan, an Arabic name meaning "The Criterion".

The summer after Louis' conversion, Elijah Muhammad stated that all musicians in the NOI had to choose between music and the Nation of

Islam. Louis X did so only after performing one final event at the Nevel Country Club.

Brother Minister Louis X

Louis X quickly rose through the ranks. After only nine months of being a registered Muslim in the NOI and a member of Muhammad's Temple of Islam in Boston, where Malcolm X was the minister, the former calypso-singer turned Muslim became his assistant minister. Eventually he became the official minister after Elijah Muhammad transferred Malcolm X to Muhammad's Temple of Islam No. 7 on West 116th St. in Harlem, New York City. Louis X continued to be mentored by Malcolm X, until the latter's being silence by Elijah Muhammad in 1963. After Malcolm X's death, Elijah Muhammad appointed Farrakhan to the two prominent positions that Malcolm held before being dismissed from the NOI. Farrakhan became the national spokesman/national representative of the NOI and was appointed minister of the influential Harlem Mosque (Temple), where he served until 1975.

MALCOM X AND MUHAMMAD ALI

Malcom X and Muhammad Ali

Malcolm X and Cassius Clay became fast friends, but a rift in the Nation of Islam forced the man now known as Muhammad Ali to turn his back on the man who introduced him to faith and black pride. We take a look back at their friendship, and the betrayal that Ali now considers one of the biggest regrets of his life.

On February 26, 1964, the day after a 22-year-old Cassius Clay defeated Heavyweight Champion Sonny Liston and claimed his belt, a reporter at a press conference asked him if he was a card-carrying member of the Nation of Islam.

Rumors had been surrounding the young boxer's association with the polarizing religious organization for a while by then, thanks to Clay's developing friendship with noted NOI member Malcolm X and a recent interview in which Cassius Clay Sr. told the press that his sons (Cassius and Rudolph Valentino) had been "brainwashed" by the sect. Clay Jr. originally refused to comment on his father's claim, telling the press "I don't care what my father said. I'm not interested. I'm not talking. I'm here training for a fight and that's all I'm going to say."

Now that he was the champ, though, he was willing to make a more direct comment.

"Card-carrying – what does that mean?" the fighter mused. "I know where I'm going, and I know the truth, and I don't have to be what you want me to be. I'm free to be what I want to be." He went on to reject the name Clay, because black American's last names were often inherited from their slave masters. "I will be known as Cassius X," he said.

Cassius first met Nation of Islam leaders Elijah Muhammad and Malcolm X through friends who belonged to the Islamic Temple and was moved by the way that Malcolm X spoke.

"My first impression was how could a Black man talk about the government, White people, and be so bold and not be shot at?" he said in a 1989 interview with Sam Pollard and Judy Richardson. "Talking about, just a whole movement that was totally different from others and so bold": How could he say these things? And only God must be protecting him. He walked with nobody; he was fearless, that, that really attracted me."

Clay secretly joined the Nation of Islam, and somewhat less secretly befriended Malcolm X, who soon proved to be a kindred spirit. "Malcom X and Muhammad Ali were one in the same," J. Tinsley writes for Uproxx. "Both were young, handsome, intelligent, outspoken African American men who scared the shit out the White America during a time period when racial tension was the norm."

Malcom X speaking before introducing the Honorable Elijah Muhammad

For three years, Clay kept his association with the NOI as private as possible, "sneaking around, keeping it quiet, acting like I was crazy," because he was concerned about the impact that his religious and political affiliation with the organization would have on his still growing boxing career.

"Well I figured they would pressure me if I revealed it, so I kept it quiet for about three years. I sneaked into meetings, sneaked in the back door, and looked around for the police officer to pass me in, before going in. But after beating Sonny Liston, after getting more regulation and my power finally is straight, I said, I don't know, I told them that night I fought Liston and revealed it after that fight."

"The Nation of Islam was then widely regarded by the American media as a highly dangerous group," the *Saturday Night Post's* Jeff Nilsson writes in his look back at the press generation by the event. "There were fearful rumors that the Black Muslims would forcibly create a separate nation for black Americans. So, when Ali announced his conversion, the media reacted as if they had been betrayed."

This is the same media, mind you, that had already been so worked up about the young boxer that they shaped Sonny Liston—a man they had previously portrayed, literally, as a gorilla—into a de facto Great White Hope against the uppity upstart. One sports reporter went so far as to write "Liston used to be a hoodlum; now he is our cop; he was the big Negro we pay to keep sassy Negroes in line."

After the announcement, prominent boxing writer Jimmy Cannon accused Cassius of using boxing as "an instrument of mass hate... as a weapon of wickedness."

Outside of the media, the move was polarizing at best and Cassius Clay Sr. was decidedly on the anti-Nation side. He was personally hurt by the renunciation of his name.

Malcom X and Muhammad Ali

In a 1964 profile for The Saturday Evening Post written by Myron Cope, Cassius Jr. addressed the "white devil" concerns. "I'm stressing just the works that the whites generally have been doing. They blow up all these little colored people in church, wash down people in the street with water hoses. It's not the color that makes you a devil, just the deeds that you do," he said. "It's as our leader, Elijah Muhammad, teaches us. Couldn't "nobody" argue it! I'm no authority on Islam. I am just a follower. If you are a blue race, and you do the works of the devil, then we call you a devil. You got white people who died under demonstrations, died under tractor wheels for colored people. I wouldn't call them "no devil."

Cassius Clay, Sr. was not reassured. One night, he got drunk and took a knife to the gym his son was training at, vowing to "kill all the Black Muslims."

"What the father didn't understand, or perhaps did, deepening his rage was that his son had found in the Nation of Islam a new kind of family he hadn't known before," Gilmore writes in How Muhammad Ali Conquered Fear and Changed the World. "In Malcolm X, in particular, Cassius had discovered a comrade and a role model, but it proved to be the most troubling relationship of his life."

Tensions between Elijah Muhammad and Malcolm X were hitting a breaking point by the time Cassius X publicly aligned himself with the Nation. Among the ideological points of contention between the two leaders was Cassius himself.

"Some in the Nation, though, pointed to the friendship with Cassius Clay, 'a fool fighter,' as irresponsible on Malcolm's part. Leader Elijah Muhammad had believed there was 'no way Clay would win' against Sonny Liston and wanted the Nation to keep a distance from him." After all, the same motto of 'no engagement' in entertainment, or sport and play as it was applied to Louis X at that time, also applied to Cassius X.

Elijah Muhammad changed his position on Cassius X after Liston's defeat, but the greater damage was already done in the minds of some NOI leaders and followers.

On December 1, 1963, when asked for a comment about the assassination of President John F. Kennedy, Malcolm X said that it was a case of "chickens coming home to roost". He added that "chickens coming home to roost never did make me sad; they've always made me glad." *The New York Times* wrote, "in further criticism of Mr. Kennedy, the Muslim leader cited the murders of Patrice Lumumba, Congo leader; of Medgar Evers, civil rights leader;

and of the Negro girls bombed earlier this year in a Birmingham church. These, he said, were instances of other 'chickens coming home to roost'." The remarks prompted a widespread public outcry. The Nation of Islam, which had sent a message of condolence to the Kennedy family and ordered its ministers not to comment on the assassination, publicly censured their former shining star. Malcolm X retained his post and rank as minister, but was prohibited from public speaking for 90 days.

Malcolm X had, by now, become a media favorite, and some Nation members believed he was a threat to Muhammad's leadership. Publishers had shown interest in Malcolm X's autobiography, and when Louis Lomax wrote his 1963 book about the Nation, *When the Word Is Given*, he used a photograph of Malcolm X on the cover. He also reproduced five of his speeches, but featured only one of Muhammad's all of which greatly upset the Nation of Islam leadership.

On March 8, 1964, Malcolm X publicly announced his break from the Nation of Islam. He was still a Muslim, he said, but felt that the Nation had "gone as far as it can" because of its rigid teachings. He said he was planning to organize a Black Nationalist organization to "heighten the political consciousness" of African Americans. He also expressed a desire to work with other civil rights leaders, saying that Elijah Muhammad had prevented him from doing so in the past.

Just over a week after the Liston fight, Malcolm X publicly discussed his departure from the Nation of Islam, denounced Elijah Muhammad and declared his intent to continue his activism with a new group of his own. Mere days after that, Elijah Muhammad gave Cassius X a new name: Muhammad Ali. When Sam Pollard asked Ali about the importance of changing his name in their 1989 interview, the fighter responded with:

"Sam Pollard is White. He's originally got a European name. I met a brother, he had dashiki, African robes, sandals, real Black, I said, "What's your name?" He said, "George Washington." Afro named George Washington. I said, "Mr. Clay here, 200 years ago they called

Clay property, so the Jones is Jones. These are names that are names that identified us as the property of certain masters. But the day you're free, you don't belong to Clay and Jones. So, you know how you look, well, in Africa, what's your name? George Washington? There are Africans all over Africa. They don't know if a Negro Christian is one or another. They're all over Chicago. They're in California. Africans, other people, how does the White man know? What's your name? Ching Chong. A White man named Ching Chong. That's Chinese there. That's their culture. So, not too many Muhammad Ali, suddenly, they start saying, "He's the world's most known man." It's not because I box, Sugar Ray is good, Floyd Patterson is good, and Joe Louis was good. It was because Muhammad Ali is in Africa, all over Africa; the name is in Ethiopia, Morocco, Syria, Indonesia, Pakistan, Turkey, Algiers and Saudi Arabia. Muhammad Ali is common when I traveled. Muhammad is the most common name in the world. There are more people on Earth, every third a person is a Muslim in the world. So, when I took the name Muhammad Ali and I fought, I'd say this, Floyd Patterson, "In this corner Muhammad Ali!" All the people in the arena says, "What?" The whole world jumped because this is a common name. You mean in America we have a Muhammad Ali fighting? So, my father's name was Cassius Clay. His father's name was Cassius and my self's name, and my great-granddaddy, who was a slave, worked for the original Cassius Clay from Kentucky. So, we know I'm not "no slave now. It's funny, that's how an old name, how one name for a good amount of people, it all started in Kentucky. You saw Roots? Alex Haley? Alex Haley knows that we were made slaves. He knows that this happened, they took our names, but after making that movie, I was surprised to see he still kept the name Alex Haley, so. If I say, here come Ching Chong, you look for a Chinaman; here comes Lumumba, African and here comes Weinstein, Jew, and here come Morningstar, Indian. Here come Miltonberger, German. Here comes Jones, don't know what color or nationality he is 'til you see him. So, we don't have our names. There's something about the American Black people still got slave names. I hear that. I love truth, I don't care if you go to church or mosque or synagogue. I don't care if you're Baptist,

Catholic, Methodist, I don't care what you are. When I hear the name, I want the truth. People watching this interview now, got slave names if they're Black. So, Muhammad Ali, you go away, you go to Syria, Indonesia, Africa, put it over on them, you won't know who you are until you tell them your name. "What's your name?" "George Washington." They say, "He's a Negro." Man, nobody could argue with this. I challenge anybody watching the show, I'm embarrassing the nation. Prove I'm wrong, if you're Black and you have a European name, that's not your name. Now if you hear White people in the government, somebody tell me, "You ain't Muhammad Ali. You're wrong." No, nobody ever said that's wrong. So, if you leave this country and go to Asia and Africa, all you hear is national names like: Hassan, Omar, Ishmael, Elijah, Muhammad, Ali, Akbar. These are the names of dark people. So, when we were made slaves in America and the names, we took their names. But our people are still slaves mentally. We can hear this, you can hear what I'm saying, and I don't know if you might or might not, but you might keep your name when you leave here. This is a known fact. It's a White man's slave name. Hey now, you're free, why not buck Uncle Sam and pick you a pretty name to fit your Black people? Some people they don't admit it mentally 'til only dead men can hear. So why won't they wake up; and all want a beautiful name? My daughter wanted Rasheeda, not Sue-Ellen Mary, one named Jamillah. One name Laila. One named Hana. One named Miya, Kaliah. These are pretty names that fit our people. So, that's why I changed my name."

But the name came with a personal price: As Gilmore puts it in his story: "The young fighter's proud acceptance of the designation made plain his choice between the Nation of Islam and Malcolm X."

Ali chose Muhammad. "Elijah Muhammad had given me my name, Muhammad Ali. I felt that he had set me free!" the champ wrote about his choice in his 2004 autobiography *The Soul of a Butterfly: Reflections on Life's Journey*. "I was proud of my name and dedicated to the Nation of Islam as Elijah presented it. At that point in my journey, I just wasn't ready to question his teachings. I was forced to make a choice when Elijah Muhammad insisted that I break with Malcolm."

He only saw his former friend once more after that. "I was on a tour of Egypt, Nigeria, and Ghana. I saw Malcolm in Ghana where he stopped on his way back to America. He'd just finished a holy journey to Mecca that devout Muslims are required to make once in their lives, and he was wearing the traditional Muslim white robes, further signifying his break with Elijah Muhammad. He walked with a cane that looked like a prophet's stick and he wore a beard. I thought he'd gone too far. When he came up to greet me, I turned away, making our break public," Ali writes of the encounter.

"Ali's legend in the ring was continuing to take shape. Meanwhile, Malcom X marched forward on what he believed was his mandated path of righteousness following his return from Mecca. I'm not one to claim to know what either was thinking throughout the year of 1964, some 22 years before my own birth. But one thing I'm positive of is despite the smiles and speeches, Ali thought about Malcom X and Malcom X about Ali," J. Tinsley writes for Uproxx. "Both had fought so much alongside each other, while becoming the faces of their respective professions, for causes neither were sure would be seen in their own lifetimes. They thought about one another. Both probably wanted to make things right. Pride, especially a man's pride, is a hell of a drug, however; it is the knife that man has willingly stuck in his own back since the beginning of time."

Malcolm X with his daughters and Muhammad Ali

Malcolm X was assassinated on February 21, 1965, as he was about to speak in Harlem, before Ali or America as a whole could even begin to come around to his way of thinking.

Ali, at least, sees it now, and, as he says in his book, he's truly sorry that he never had a chance to tell his old friend himself.

"Turning my back on Malcolm was one of the mistakes that I regret most in my life. I wish I'd been able to tell Malcolm I was sorry, that he was right about so many things. But he was killed before I got the chance. He was a visionary – ahead of us all," he writes. "Malcolm was the first to discover the truth, that color doesn't make a man a devil. It is the heart, soul, and mind that define a person. Malcolm was a great thinker and an even greater friend. I might never have become a Muslim if it hadn't been for him.

On this day: March 6, 1964 Cassius Clay was taken on a guided tour

Ali and Malcolm were really good friends; however, they did become estranged once Malcolm X had his falling out with Elijah Muhammad and Ali was still associated with Elijah Muhammad who preached his own version of Islam to his followers in the Nation. According to him, blacks were known as the 'original' human being, with whites being an offshoot race that would go on to oppress black people for 6,000 years. He preached that the Nation of Islam's goal was to return the stolen hegemony back to blacks across America. Much of Elijah Muhammad's teachings appealed to young, economically disadvantaged, African-American males from Christian backgrounds. Traditionally, Black males wouldn't go to church because the church did not address their needs. Elijah Muhammad's program for economic development played a large part in the growth in the Nation of Islam. He purchased land and businesses to provide housing and employment for young black males. By the 1970s, the Nation of Islam owned bakeries, barber shops, coffee shops, grocery stores, laundromats, a printing plant, retail stores, numerous real estate holdings, and a fleet of tractor trailers, plus farmland in Michigan, Alabama, and Georgia. In 1972 the Nation of Islam took controlling interest in a bank, the Guaranty Bank and Trust Co. Nation of Islam-owned schools expanded until, by 1974, the group had established schools in 47 cities throughout the United States. In 1972, Muhammad told followers that the Nation of Islam had a net worth of $75 million

JABIR HERBERT MUHAMMAD

Muhammad Ali and Jabir Herbert Muhammad

Jabir Herbert Muhammad (April 16, 1929 – August 25, 2008) was an American businessman and co-founder of Top Rank, Inc. He was the longtime manager of legendary boxer, Muhammad Ali.

Muhammad was born in Detroit, Michigan, as the third son of the Nation of Islam leader, Elijah Muhammad. He served as a chief adviser to his father until his departure in 1975. He also worked as the chief business manager for the Nation of Islam and he, along with Malcolm X, founded their weekly newspaper. Jabir Herbert Muhammad was a staunch supporter of his brother, Imam Warith Deen Muhammad, whom he followed into mainstream Islam. He, along with Muhammad Ali and others, built Masjid Al-Fatir, a stand-alone, purpose-built Masjid on the Southside of Chicago, Illinois.

Masjid Al-Fatir was one of the first mosques built from the ground by Muslim Americans, especially African American Muslims. Jabir Muhammad was the director and founder of the Muhammad Islamic Foundation, a not-for-profit foundation, which published the book *Prayer and Al-Islam* by Imam Warith Deen Mohammed in 1984.

Muhammad managed Muhammad Ali's professional boxing career from 1966 until Ali's retirement in 1981. Jabir Muhammad negotiated the first multimillion-dollar earnings for any athlete and was considered one of the most powerful figures in boxing in the 1960s and 1970s, achieving the International Boxing Hall of Fame's 1974 "Manager of the Year" award. He continued to manage Ali's career for another ten years after his retirement from boxing. Muhammad then went on to a successful career in business.

Jabir Herbert Muhammad died on August 25, 2008, at the University Of Illinois Medical Center in Chicago, at the age of 79, after undergoing heart surgery. Muhammad was survived by his wife, Amenah Antonia Muhammad, and fourteen children.

Masjid al-Faatir

The Mosque was co-donated and financed by Muhammad Ali and Jabir Herbert Muhammad, in the Hyde Park neighborhood. It was designed in a traditional Muslim architectural plan; Masjid al-Faatir has two octagonal sections joined together, one larger than the other, and has two free-standing minarets and a large central dome. The mosque can accommodate up to three thousand worshipers at one time

IMAM W.D. MOHAMMED

Wallace D. Muhammad

Before the death of Honorable Elijah Muhammad he turned over his leadership to his son Wallace D. Muhammad, also known as Warith Deen Mohammad, the fifth of Elijah's sons - not Farrakhan - as the new Supreme Minister. At the time, Nation of Islam was founded upon the principles of self-reliance and black supremacy, a belief that mainstream Muslims consider heretical. He modified his father's theology and black pride exclusive views, forging closer ties with mainstream Muslim communities in an attempt to transition the Nation of Islam into orthodoxy more similar to Sunni Islam. Under W. D. Mohammed's leadership, the Nation of Islam decentralized into many bodies of followers led by many different leaders and it was soon after called the World Community of Islam.

Imam W.D. Mohammed

Imam W. Deen Mohammed was born October 30, 1933, to the builder and leader of the Nation of Islam, the late Honorable Elijah (Poole) Muhammed and the late Clara (Evans) Muhammad. He is the leader of the largest identifiable constituency of Muslim Americans and is recognized worldwide as a leading Islamic Thinker and representative.

He succeeded his father in 1975 as the leader of the Nation of Islam with unanimous support of its followers and began its transformation to "Islam proper" as practiced by over 1 billion Muslims worldwide. He opened the Nation of Islam membership up to all races of Muslims and encouraged Muslim Americans to register to vote and become full participants in the politics and economics of America.

In 1977, he led the then largest delegation of Muslim Americans, most former members of the Nation of Islam, on Hajj, Pilgrimage to the Sacred House in Mecca, Saudi Arabia. That same year he toured China with "American Friends of China".

In 1977, Minister Farrakhan resigned from Iman Wallace D. Muhammad's reformed organization.

REBIRTH OF THE NATION OF ISLAM

Nation of Islam leader (1981–present) Louis Farrakhan

He worked to rebuild the Nation of Islam upon the original foundation established by the founder Master Wallace Fard Muhammad and the Honorable Elijah Muhammad.

Minister Farrakhan traveled across America speaking in cities to gain new followers. Over time, Minister Farrakhan regained many of the Nation of Islam's original properties. There are now mosques and study groups in over 120 American cities attributed to Farrakhan's work as a leader.

1995, the Nation of Islam sponsored the Million Man March

In 1995, the Nation of Islam sponsored the Million Man March in Washington, D.C. to promote African-American unity and family values. Estimates of the number of marchers were given between 400,000 and 840,000. Under Farrakhan's leadership, the Nation of Islam tried to redefine the standard "black male stereotype" of drug and gang violence. Meanwhile, the Nation continued to promote social reform in African-American communities according to its traditional goals of self-reliance and economic independence.

Under Farrakhan's leadership, the Nation was one of the fastest growing of the various political movements in the country. Foreign branches of the Nation were formed in Ghana, London, Paris, and the Caribbean islands. In order to strengthen the international influence of the Nation, Farrakhan attempted to establish relations with Muslim countries. The NOI attempted to strengthen relations with other minority communities, including Native Americans, Hispanics, and Asians.

Imam Mohammad:

In 1988 he signed the Williamsburg Charter at Williamsburg VA celebrating the First Amendment/First Freedom of the U. S. Constitution.

Following the invasion of Kuwait by Iraq, in 1990 at the invitation of Saudi Arabia's King Fahd Bin Abdulaziz, Imam Mohammed and a delegation traveled to Saudi Arabia in a consultative role to discuss the concerns of Muslims over the Gulf War.

In 1992, he delivered the Invocation opening the U. S. Senate in Washington, D.C., the first ever given by a Muslim. He toured the Pentagon and addressed Muslims in the U. S. Military and its Chaplains.

He delivered an address on the floor of the Georgia State Legislature – the state of his father's birth, the first ever given by a Muslim.

In 1993, Imam Mohammed participated in the Inaugural Interfaith Prayer Service for President William (Bill) Jefferson Clinton.

In December of 1994, Imam Mohammed was presented the "Cup of Compassion" Award from the Hartford Seminary in Hartford, Connecticut.

In 1995, he was selected as a President of the World Conference on Religion and Peace (WCRP), and addressed its Governing Board in Copenhagen, Denmark.

In 1995, Imam Mohammed delivered the Keynote Address at the Muslim-Jewish Convocation, the first serious public dialogue between top leaders of Islam and Reformed Judaism, in Glencoe, Illinois; and in the same year, Forbes Magazine officials hosted an address given by Imam Mohammed in Naples, FL on the topic "How Do We Save Our Youth?"

In 1996, Imam Mohammed visited Malaysia at the invitation of Dr. Mohammed Nuir Manuty, President of the Muslim Youth Movement, which resulted in a Muslim American student exchange program, for several years. He met privately with Malaysia's Deputy Prime Minister and was interviewed on Malaysian national television.

Imam W. D. Mohammed shakes hands with Pope John Paul II

In 1996, Imam W. Deen Mohammed led a delegation of Muslims to The Vatican in Rome, Italy, where he met with Pope John Paul II and with Cardinal Francis Arinze, The Vatican's Chief of Staff for Interreligious Affairs. As an international humanitarian, Imam Mohammed supported the Peacemaking and Human Rights Efforts of Bishop Samuel Ruiz Garcia and traveled to San Cristobal de las Casas (Chiapas), Mexico, as a member of The Peace Council to hear concerns of the Chiapas Rebels.

He also led a delegation of Muslim Americans to Jerusalem and areas under rule of the Palestinian Authority led by Palestinian leader, President Yasser Arafat, visiting Palestinian cities, government agencies, hospitals and homes throughout the West Bank. The visit culminated on Christmas Eve with a meeting in Gaza City with President Arafat at his headquarters, where he discussed the difficulties of Palestinian life.

1997 He represented Muslims at the World Parliament of Religious Leaders for the survival of the Earth, in Oxford, England.

In 1997, President Clinton, in his re-election Inauguration, invited Imam Mohammed to the White House for the 1st Annual Ecumenical Breakfast, and requested Imam Mohammed to read from the Holy Qur'an at the Presidential Inauguration Day National Prayer Service.

Later that year, Imam Mohammed attended the Organization of Islamic Conference (OIC) in Tehran, Iran.

In 1998, Imam Mohammed traveled to Auschwitz, Poland, where he participated in the Conference on Religion and Peace hosted by the Center for Christian and Jewish Understanding of Sacred Heart University. From there, he went to Dhaka, Bangladesh, to explore business opportunities for the Collective Purchasing Conference (CPC), which he established as a member organization of distributors and investors, in order to strengthen the economic status of the Muslim Americans and to enhance the buying power of small businessmen and women throughout the economically strained African-American communities in the United States.

He accepted the invitation of the Honorable Chiara Lubich, a Catholic Sister and World War II Survivor, to come to Rome, Italy to address the Muslim Friends of the Focolare Conference, which brought together representatives from 24 nations.

In 1999, with Pope John Paul II and The Dalai Lama present on stage, Imam Mohammed addressed a gathering of 100,000 at The Vatican.

He participated in the Jubilennium Interfaith Conference for World Peace held in Israel and the World Conference on Religion and Peace Assembly VII in Amman, Jordan. There, he was elected as an International President in the U. S. for WCRP.

[The following transcript is from comments delivered by Imam W. Deen Mohammed during Jumu'ah prayer service held Feb. 25, at the McCormick Center as part of the Nation of Islam's Saviours' Day 2000 celebration in Chicago.]

Praise be to Allah. Praise be to Allah. Praise be to Allah, the Lord, Creator of everything, Who has no partner, and the Ruler of the heavens and the earth. And nothing comes to Him except as a servant.

We witness that He is One, that Muhammad, born in the sacred city of Mecca, in the 6th and 7th century, a great model for all human beings of human excellence of the correct worship of God and a model of how human beings should accept their responsibility under God, to their own souls, to their families, to their neighbors and to the whole community of mankind on this earth.

We know that he is the excellent model given to us by almighty God, and we look to his model to correct our behavior and to direct our steps. We thank Allah for him. He lives. He lives. Muhammad, the Messenger of God, He lives. We are his followers; his following is growing every day, every hour, every minute.

If the world is going in the right direction, Muhammad is its leader. If the world is doing great things, Muhammad is its leader. If the world is helping the hearts and brains of human beings, Muhammad is its leader. If the world is civilizing societies, Muhammad is its leader. If the world is increasing in morality, good morals and ethics, Muhammad is its leader. If the world is making advances toward economic justice, social justice, Muhammed is its leader. If you know Muhammad as I do, you would know that Muhammad is the human leader for all humanity. So, we thank Allah for him, and we salute him. It's a traditional salute: Sallalahu alaihi wa Sallam, wa ala aalihi wa sahbihi, ajma-een ama ba'aad.

Dear Muslim brothers and sisters, it is not difficult for Minister Farrakhan and Wallace D. Mohammed to embrace each other. That's easy for us. When I first met him in the early '50s, I liked him on first sight, and I became his friend and his brother. And I have not stopped being his friend and his brother. Maybe he has not understood the way that I have been his friend and his brother at certain times, but I have always been his friend and his brother. For me this is too big a cause for our personal problems and differences. Allah-u Akbar.

We are to support each other in all good things. When the brother Muslim stands upon the Qur'an, the last of the revealed books and the complete book for all times and all societies, and when he stands upon faith in Muhammad as God's last prophet and Messenger to all the worlds, mercy to all the worlds, we are to support him in that.

As I said, it's easy for me to embrace Minister Farrakhan. Our families are together. We are really one family. Our friendship has not died, and it will not die. And the little problem, the small problem, that we've had along the way, struggling to present ourselves as God willed that we present ourselves, it's not bigger than the word of God, the Qur'an, and (it's) not bigger than Muhammad, the model for all human beings, for all people of faith. It's very small.

So, we see, we think, what have we done to bring about this togetherness? What have we done to bring about this closeness that we have this minute? What have we done to free our hearts, so we can hug each other and kiss each other, as I did kiss my brother? What have we done to bring that about? Nothing but tried to find the way in the path of Islam, and Allah did the rest. Allah did the rest.

I want to say that Minister Farrakhan is a great leader. I've watched him over the years, since the passing away of my father and our fallen leader, the Honorable Elijah Muhammad. I've watched him, and I have done a little mathematics, a little calculation, and I've come up with progress for the Nation of Islam under the leadership of Minister Farrakhan. Whatever has troubled us in the past, I think we can bury it now and never look back at that grave. And never look back at that grave.

I was reading the Bible once, and I was reading it really, so I could better understand Christian neighbors and respect them, as I should respect them, while trying to invite them to Islam. I wanted to be prepared to speak to my Christian neighbors with understanding of what they believe in. So, I read the whole Bible from Genesis to Revelations, twice. Once I just read it to be reading it; the second time I studied it very carefully. I came across something that came to my mind as I was sitting there thinking over Minister Farrakhan and our new revived friendship and unity. I was thinking of it and I said to myself, "I think I'm going to tell Minister Farrakhan." This is for Minister Farrakhan.

In the Bible, Minister Farrakhan, I read that a holy man had wanted to give sight to a blind man. And this holy man took mud and put (it) on the blind man's eyes. I was very young at that time, Minister Farrakhan. That was over 25-years ago. I was very young. I said to myself, "Isn't that a cruel way to help a blind man? He already has enough in his way of sight and then the man put mud in his eyes."

We've had a lot of mud on our eyes, but the eyes are now washed and cleaned. And the mud didn't hurt us, it helped us (to) see.

In 2000, he was appointed to the executive Committee of Religious Alliance Against Pornography (RAAP).

On September 11, 2001, Imam Mohammed, in the strongest terms, immediately denounced the Terrorists Attacks on the United States as un-Islamic and evil.

Later in the year, Imam Mohammed participated in an "Evening of Religious Solidarity," joined by Dr. Robert H. Schuller, Minister Louis Farrakhan and members of the Parliament of World Religions at the Mosque Foundation in Villa Park, Illinois.

The same year, Imam Mohammed attended the Contribution of Religions to Peace Conference in Assisi, Italy, at the invitation of Pope John Paul II, for religious leaders to gather to pray for world peace.

Imam W. Deen Mohammed's letter of endorsement to Friends of DuSable:

> With the Name of Allah, The Merciful Benefactor, The Merciful Redeemer
>
> **W. Deen Mohammed Ministry**
> P.O. Box 1061
> Calumet City, IL 60409
> Phone: 708-798-6750   Fax 708-798-6827
>
> June 18, 2001
>
> Mr. Haroon Rashid
> 899 Plymouth Court
> Suite 1310
> Chicago, IL 60605
>
> Dear Sir:
> As Salaam Alaikum
>
> Regarding Jean Baptiste Pointe DuSable, he was a businessman, explorer and hunter, who was born in Haiti. He was the son of an African mother and French father. He spoke several languages. Also, he built the first house on the banks of a river that would later carry the name of the city there. He founded "Chicago."
>
> He was a man that all citizens of this great city can be proud of. We join the growing number of distinguish citizens of this city in requesting that the second week in June be proclaimed as "Jean Baptiste Pointe DuSable Day," a day we all can be proud of.
>
> As Salaamu Alaikum
>
> *[signature]*
> Imam W. Deen Mohammed
>
> IWDM/as

In 2002, Imam W. Deen Mohammed was ceremoniously inducted into the Martin Luther King Jr. International Board of Preachers at Morehouse College, in Atlanta, Georgia, where his portrait hangs in the International Chapel of Non-Violent Religious Leaders at Morehouse.

As an International President of WCRP, he participated in the Conference of Religious Leaders Addressing the Devastation on Africa from HIV/Aids held in Nairobi, Kenya.

Imam W. Deen Mohammed has lectured at Universities/Colleges throughout the United States; among them have been Yale University's School of Divinity, Fordham University, Georgetown University, Emory University, Harvard University, Washington University (St. Louis), and numerous others.

The change and growth, which has characterized Imam W. Deen Mohammed's leadership since 1975, has been a progression toward satisfying the essentials of Muslim life and identity; and in the measure required by the authentic sources of the religion of Islam – the Holy Qur'an and the life example of Muhammed the Prophet (the prayers and the peace be on him).

Through the arduous steps of evolution from the 'Nation of Islam' (1930-1976) to the 'World Community of Al-Islam in the West' (1976-1981) to the 'American Muslim Mission' (1981-1985) Imam Mohammed has piloted his people to what is today a de-centralized and thriving society of Muslim Americans. With Mosques and schools in every major city in America, and in parts of Canada and the Caribbean, he has garnered a respect and acceptance for Islam in the West, not known before. The facts and details of his record of transforming a people depicted at the extreme of a "proto-Islamic" idea, which combined Black Nationalism and religion into a community of Muslim Americans esteemed in the international following of Muhammed the Prophet, stands as testimony to his courage, dedication, wisdom, and firm faith in the "Supreme Being". But even more so, the message of Islam in its true practice delivered by him over nearly thirty years to persons of every race, sex, and class – leaders and common people alike has been a quiet yet resolute factor for increased respect, understanding, and cooperation between Americans of different ethnic and religious backgrounds. It is precisely this message that is destined to influence America and other nations across the globe to acknowledge and invest in their greatest single resource, the ability, excellence, and aspirations of common human life.

Imam W. Deen Mohammed's record of service for the promotion of universal human excellence is well documented as he has established direct and genuine dialogue between the leaders of Islam, Christianity, and Judaism. His clear and appreciable representation of the religion of Islam and unparalleled contribution toward building respect for Islamic life in America has merited him countless awards and many unprecedented acknowledgments.

He transcended September 9, 2008 (aged 74)

MINISTER HAROON RASHID

Brother Minister Aaron 2X

Pryor to becoming a member of the Nation of Islam; Aaron Thompson was a very successful barber and beautician in Boston before moving to Atlanta Georgia, after spending six years in the United States Marine Corps during the Viet Nam era. Immediately after getting out of school, he started his career as a Barber in his Uncle Buster's barbershop called Sportsman Barbershop in the Roxbury section of Boston.

Aaron Thompson, his uncle John S. Jones and Cousin James Harris then started a product line known as Natural U. Afro Revert Kit. The Company was Sportsman Pyramid cosmetics; the team did trade shows and workshops for barbers and beauticians. They traveled all over New England, New York, Philadelphia, North Carolina Chicago, and Florida. They were doing a great business, building reputations as individual hair celebrities across the country. It was through that traveling that Aaron became aware of the business opportunity in Atlanta, Georgia working with the world famous Bronner Brothers Hair Show. The Afro kit was a unique product because it served a market that was in demand at that time. In a very short time that market changed because everyone who was wearing a relaxer was letting their hair grow natural and wearing an Afro. Sportsman Pyramid Cosmetics did not move with the change, so unfortunately the company was sold to the Gillette Company in Boston and Aaron Thompson decided to move to Atlanta.

It was in Atlanta, while building a reputation as an entrepreneur and a Black Nationalist, Aaron was recognized and heavily recruited into the Nation of Islam and found his interest in leadership. Growing up in Boston as a young kid, Aaron Thompson had been exposed to the Nation of Islam teachings while working in his Aunt and Uncle's restaurant, as did most of his fellow siblings and family members. It was called T&W restaurant, named after two family members - Thomas, the baker and Willie, the chief. After they both became Muslims, it later was called Shabazz Restaurant under the leadership of the Honorable Elijah Muhammad, and guidance of Minister Malcolm X, and later Minister Louis Farrakhan.

Brother Willie, Sister Sarah Harris and Sister Yvonne Stewart

When Minister Malcolm X. was silenced by Elijah Muhammad from speaking for the Nation of Islam because of disagreements about comments that Malcolm had made after President John F. Kennedy was murdered in Dallas Texas, it is said that Minister Aaron 2X Uncle Willie, Aunt Sarah and Cousin Yvonne were all put out of the nation because of the close relationships that they had bonded with Malcolm X and his wife Sister Betty Shabazz; and because they continued to communicate with Brother Minister Malcolm X after he was silenced.

They were forced to give up their restaurant, as it was then considered "Nation of Islam" property and because of that they never went back to the Nation of Islam. Brother Willie and Sister Sarah went on to have a very successful restaurant business outside of the Nation of Islam. After leaving the Nation of Islam they started over with a new restaurant idea using the Kosher or Halal type foods in their menus and they called it the Unity Lunch. At one time, Unity Lunch was one of the main providers for weekend breakfasts at the prestigious North-Eastern University / Black Student Union dormitory in Boston.

Aaron was being exposed to that type of entrepreneurship, as a youth. It motivated him to try a restaurant business in Atlanta; so, he and a friend, who was a young entrepreneur from Houston Texas, convinced each other to go into business together. They both put their money together and found a place to rent in Atlanta, on Bankhead Highway, which by coincidence was located on the same street that Muhammad Temple #15 was on.

They bought produce and meats from the Nation of Islam, Muslim farm in Georgia and tried to run a small restaurant venture. Aaron's business partner began to feel uncomfortable with the interest of Aaron in purchasing their food supply from the Muslims, so eventually they both gave up on the idea of a partnership. Aaron's mother and his Aunt Sarah also convinced him to give up on the idea of a restaurant venture in Atlanta, because they both thought that the business would be too risky and difficult at making it work. He went back to cutting Hair in a barbershop on Ashby Street near the Morehouse University and Spellman campus site.

It was soon after that when Aaron met his wife Sheila La Costa; they were both young artists in Atlanta, she was from Chicago. He was also working as a freelance barber one day in an Afrocentric Bookstore in the Atlanta University campus sight, and she was an Afrocentric jewelry maker and entrepreneur at the same location. They met and soon after were married. It was also in Atlanta that Aaron became fully aware for the first time of his personal interest in a religious experience.

Sheila La Costa

There was a young Muslim named Brother James that everybody on the Atlanta University Campus site knew. He had a nickname called Sticky, because, once Sticky made up his mind that he was going to bring you to the Temple he would put on his beautiful smile and charm and stick with you until you were there. Brother James became attracted to Aaron as being a Black Nationalist and because Aaron put in the window of the barber shop that was facing the Morehouse College tennis court, so that many of the students could visibly see the large posters of Malcolm X, Dr. Martin Luther King, Jr., Huey P. Newton, Angela Davis and Muhammad Ali. Students would always visit because he stood out as a revolutionist in the area. The shop became a conversation among his peers and that action really made Sticky very anxious to recruit him into the Nation of Islam… and he did.

At that time, because of the Black Nationalist spirit, especially on Atlanta College campus which consisted of Morris Brown, Atlanta University, Morehouse College, Spellman College, Clark College and the Atlanta Theological Institute: The Afrocentric genre was what many of the young African Americans wanted to identify with - African names - so when Aaron arrived in Atlanta he referred to himself as Brother Abu Ali. He found out later that he was of special interest to Sticky because he was calling himself by a Muslim name, and he was not a Muslim.

When he conceded and finally went to the Temple the minister started talking directly to him. He spoke about slave names and how the slave masters' children had mentally branded the slaves like they would physically brand the animals that they owned, with their surname as a property claim. He said that Negroes are proud to be called by their slave masters' names. He preached that the greatest tool of volunteered slavery was for the slave to try to identify with his master's culture, and hate his own by giving over their selves to false pride of the slave master's birthright. Aaron was already aware of this theory from his family members. The minister called him out on the use of the name Abu Ali, but then he went into the theory of how some people, out of ignorance, or no knowledge of self would take on names, just claim one, without even knowing what it means. He then looked at Aaron and said, "Names like Abu Ali."

After his speech, he asked if anyone was ready to join the Nation of Islam. Aaron rejected it for a while, but eventually he gave into the notion of becoming a member of the NOI and wound up joining the movement… and soon after, he got married to Sheila.

He was told that he would receive an acceptance letter from the messenger himself in Chicago. But what he received instead was a letter from The Messenger Honorable Elijah Muhammad saying that he should not shame himself by using a name that has no meaning to who he really is. He said that he should wait on Allah to give him a name that gives honor to who he is. He was given the name Aaron 2X instead of Abu Ali or Aaron Thompson; the X meant unknown factor until he became creditable or worthy; then Allah would give him a Holy name. That letter, at that time, more than anything else set him on a course to build a character of creditability for him in a more dignified way.

After getting more involved in the Nation of Islam and because of his former military experience Aaron 2X started to move up the ranks among the men, and soon became a squad leader. He soon left Atlanta to move back to Boston. Learning religious discipline as young converts in the Nation of Islam under the teaching of the Honorable Elijah Muhammad was exciting and intellectually rewarding for him. It was in Boston that he joined the student Minister class under the guidance of Minister Karim Majid. Brother Aaron 2X took on new job challenges to make ends meet. He had most of his old hair clients asking him to do their hair, but he refused to get back into it. He took a job working as a bank teller during the day and a security guard at night.

While working in the bank, a Jewish man, who was a customer of the Bank took to him and asked if he would be interested in working as a salesman. He owned a company that sold office equipment and supplies. Since Brother Aaron 2X was doing so well selling the Muhammad Speaks newspaper during his spare time, he felt that he could do as well in sales. As a sales man for the office supply company, Brother Aaron 2X was doing well, but now a deep curiosity about how things were being run in Chicago at the headquarters, was dominating him and his wife Sheila. So, they decided that it was time to go to Chicago and pursue his desires for leadership as a Minister in the Nation of Islam. Going to Chicago Illinois, which also happened to be his wife Sheila's hometown, he felt that move would give him the chance to learn more about the Nation of Islam.

Eventually Brother Aaron 2X moved to Chicago, where he got a job working at the Muhammad Speaks Newspaper plant - he was a pressman. Even though he was very proud to have a role in printing words of the Honorable Elijah Muhammad, he knew that he came to Chicago primarily to be a leader in the Nation. He grew in the ranks in Chicago to become one of the top newspaper salesmen and was chosen to be the face of the advertisement for the *Muhammad Speaks* newspaper.

While working as a pressman he was asked to join the elite security team of the Nation of Islam to protect the Messenger, and the Nation's property. This was a job that he had plenty of experience in from his stint in the U.S.M.C. It was then that he followed up on the student minister's classes that he had started while living in Boston.

Brother Aaron continued to move up the ranks in the NOI until the death of his first real mentor, the Honorable Elijah Muhammad. He also bought his first house on the south side of Chicago, in the south shore community, three blocks from the National Headquarters of the Nation of Islam.

When he became an official minister in the nation, Brother Minister Aaron 2X was a member of an elite group of ministers that felt the Chicago headquarters for the NOI was the most important area for teaching and learning the messenger's words. The satellite ministers, as they were called, opened up seven satellite Temples around the city. They took a no-nonsense attitude in those neighborhoods where they were assigned to teach, and to convert people to come into the NOI. He opened a Temple in Roseland on 115th and Wentworth Street; He had created a staff and built a congregation of over fifty to a hundred people. His area was as far south as 138th Street in the (Artgeld Gardens housing projects), east to the Eden expressway, North to 103 Street, and west to Halsted (Morgan Park). it is of special note that years later President Barack Obama would begin his first community activism in Chicago at the same location in Artgeld Gardens. He had Olive Harvey College as part of his territory. One day, a student asked him if he could get Muhammad Ali to come to the school as a guest speaker during Black History Month. He asked his people if he could get him to come; and Muhammad Ali came to the event, with the help of the student President Ella Muhammad.

During that time Minister Aaron 2X and other satellite Ministers would go to Cook County correction facility every Saturday morning to talk to inmates, and every church, organization, school, and social group in his territory to talk about black love, and unity.

Minister Aaron 2X had also developed a great relationship with the Orthodox Muslims in his territory; they had great respect for each other's missions and differences.

When the Honorable Elijah Muhammad died Minister Aaron 2X, as did many others, did not take the death of Mr. Muhammad well. About a year before the death of messenger Muhammad, one of his sons that had not been actively involved in the Nation of Islam came back to take over leadership. The Muslim ministers and leaders at the time were told that his father had asked him to come back and lead the Nation to the next level of the Nation's mission. That was to make Nation of Islam membership more mainstream Muslims. His name was Wallace Deen Muhammad. Imam Wallace Deen Muhammad spoke to the body of Muslims much like Malcolm X. When many heard him for the first time they were totally enchanted by his wisdom.

MUHAMMAD'S TEMPLE NO.2

7351 SOUTH STONY ISLAND AVENUE   CHICAGO, ILLINOIS 60649   (312) 667-6800

In the Name of Allah, The Beneficent, The Merciful; Peace and Blessings upon His Servant and His Messenger, Muhammad, forever. Amen.

As-Salaam-Alaikum

Dear Brother Minister:

Attached is a lecture outline that all Ministers are to use for all Temple Meetings. This outline covers the items that are of greatest importance for us to teach during this time.

You will notice that I am setting a time limit on the amount of time spent lecturing from the rostrum. Your teachings should not exceed 60 minutes, at the maximum.

Very soon you will receive a tape from Me which will give you a good idea of how to deliver such a lecture comfortably within the 60 - minute time limit.

Reducing the time of the teaching will allow more time for dealing with Temple problems. It will also afford more time for instructions to the Believers from the Captain's Department and the Secretary's Department.

As-Salaam-Alaikum

W. D. Muhammad
The Honorable W. D. Muhammad
Supreme Minister

WDM/AHS/ha

Early in his leadership, one day Imam Muhammad called all the satellite ministers together for the first time to learn of his new agendas. Many thought it was to enlighten them and encourage them to learn more. He greeted them and then he turned to Minister Aaron 2X and asked him what his name was? He told him his name was Brother Minister Aaron 2X. Imam Muhammad told Minister Aaron 2X that he had heard of the work that he was doing in the Altgeld Gardens and Roseland community and was proud of his service; and that for now on, he should be called by the name Haroon Rashid because it was a name that would suit him better. He was so excited because he had been waiting since the day that he received his acceptance letter from the Honorable Elijah Muhammad for the day to receive a Holy Name; he was over joyed. All the other satellite ministers started chanting almost screaming, *All Praises Are Due to the Honorable Elijah Muhammad!*

It was a sign they knew that they too would likely be honored to receive their Holy names and he did go down the list and gave them their new names. However, with the new changes in the structure of the leadership later, Minister Haroon Rashid began to change his views on a lot of things. Some of those things affected his marriage and he and Sheila were starting to go in different directions. Haroon wanted to get reacquainted with his personal family and decided to step back from leadership, and go back into the world as it was called, to relearn his people and family needs.

He stayed in Chicago two more years before moving to Jacksonville, Florida. He went there to live with his grandmother. She had called him, knowing what was going on with him from his mother, and asked him to come stay with her for a while because she was alone and sick and needed him to help her. After leaving the Nation of Islam, Haroon traveled the world as a hair artist again, before coming back to Chicago years later as a community activist who would become the Founder of Friends of DuSable

THE SPIRT OF DUSABLE

Serene Entitlement & Empowerment Foundation /Friends of DuSable:

The Friends of DuSable was founded by Haroon Rashid in 1999 to establish formal recognition for Jean Baptiste Pointe DuSable. The organization's main objective is to preserve an annual commemoration for DuSable, the founder of modern Chicago, as an integral part of the celebration of Chicago's incorporation date, March 4th. In order to properly commemorate DuSable, we need to increase awareness of DuSable's contributions throughout all the city's communities.

The purpose of the commemoration is to reinforce the common thread that ties early Chicago to present day Chicago's diversity. DuSable's legacy reflects diversity at its best and provides a gleaming example of what Chicago could be, today, given the knowledge of its roots.

Haroon tells the story of how and why he became so consumed with Jean Baptiste Pointe DuSable's life and how it has become an important part of his legacy: "December 1999, I was talking to one of my clients, Maria Jossey, about Jean Baptiste Pointe DuSable, the first non-native settler and immigrant in Chicago. I was telling her how I first heard of DuSable from my association of the former Mayor of Chicago, Harold Washington's inner circle. It was also known that Harold Washington had great knowledge and pride of DuSable, he, being a former student of DuSable High school. He campaigned under the banner in the spirit of DuSable and that, in fact, Mayor Washington considered himself the rebirth of his legacy and had great plans, before his untimely sudden death, to commemorate DuSable's legacy. We discussed how it was a shame that there was no real information about this man's incredible legacy. We decided to put a plan in action that would do that. We felt the best way to disseminate information of him at that time was to have a parade in his honor. I went to My Alderman in the ward that I lived in and asked her if she could help me establish a parade for DuSable, She advised me to write my plan and give it to other council members and see what the Mayor's Office of Special

Events felt about it; and promised that she would help as much as she could. I did that. Another client of mine Alicia Ferriabough, whose dad I knew from my youth in Boston, was a student at Northwestern University Law School, in Chicago. She told me of a program that the school had to help organizations create by-laws and become registered with the State as a non-profit, using the students as a class assignment. I went to the Director of the program Professor, Dr. Thomas Morsch and we were assigned a liaison person, Ms. Paula Wells, who worked with the students and us, until we created the Serene Entitlement and Empowerment Foundation 501-C (3) by-laws. We gave it the name (S.E.E.F.) because our original plan was to address the forgotten heroes from the African American experience. DuSable was just one of the many stories that, once properly told, too many will instill the true sense of inclusion and patronage as a race of our ancestor's contributions in the development of the United States and that helps to level the cultural divide of others.

Haroon Rashid, Dr. Margaret Burroughs, Dr. Jean Pierre & Mayor Richard M. Daley

The Mayor's Office of Special Events, upon learning our request to have a parade to honor DuSable, assigned a person that worked with our efforts to see if the citizens of Chicago would participate. For a year, we were allowed to conduct monthly DuSable collaboration meetings at the Chicago Cultural Center.

It was after one of those meetings that Dr. Margaret Burroughs, Founder of the DuSable Museum, agreed with our efforts and she said that she would help and recommended that we change our name to Friends of DuSable, which we gladly did. It was then that we created and made public our Core of Initiatives.

The Flags of DuSable: Haiti-Chicago-Pottawatomi American Indian-French & American

FIRST AFRICAN AMERICAN WOMAN TO GRADUATE FROM THE UNIVERSITY OF CHICAGO LAW SCHOOL

Jewel Stradford-Rogers-Lafontant-Mankarious- Oberlin College Archives

Jewel Stradford-Rogers-Lafontant-Mankarious (April 28, 1922 – May 31, 1997) was the first female deputy solicitor general of the United States, an official in the administration of President George H. W. Bush, and an attorney in Chicago. She also was considered by President Richard Nixon as a possible nominee to the Supreme Court of the United States.

Born in Chicago as Jewel Carter Stradford, she was the daughter of noted attorney and co-founder of the National Bar Association, C. Francis Stradford and Aida Arabella Stradford. Jewel earned a bachelor's degree in political science from Oberlin College in 1943. While at Oberlin College, Jewel was captain of the volleyball team and a member of the Musical Union, Forensic Union, Cosmopolitan Club, and many other activities. Jewel began law school in 1943 and was the only African-American woman in her class. In 1946, she was the first African American woman to graduate from the University of Chicago Law School.

In 1947, Jewel was admitted to the Illinois State Bar. The same year, Jewel became a trial lawyer for the Legal Aid Bureau of Chicago, now Legal Aid Society of Metropolitan Family Services. She formed a law firm in Chicago in 1949 with her first husband, John W. Rogers, Sr.

Jewel Stradford married John W. Rogers, Sr., a former member of the Tuskegee Airmen during World War II, on December 7, 1946; they had one child, investment executive John W. Rogers, Jr. (born 1958).

John (Jack) W. Rogers Sr., a former member of the Tuskegee Airmen

At first, John W. Rodgers Sr. was denied entrance to college because he was told that, "We don't allow black people in here." Rogers went home, put on his military uniform and returned to the law school, declaring, "I just served my country. You are going to let me in this school.

John W. Rogers Sr. and Jewel Stradford were among the first African Americans to gain admittance to the prestigious University of Chicago School of Law, Subsequently the school admitted their first black students. The couple divorced in 1961. She remarried, to Haitian-American attorney H. Ernest Lafontant in 1961, and remained married to him until his death in October 1976. She married Naguib Soby Mankarious in 1989 and was married to him until her death in 1997. She received a Candace Award for Distinguished Service from the National Coalition of 100 Black Women in 1983.

1953: Attorney Jewel Stradford Rogers

In 1953 Jewel Rogers adorns the cover of Jet Magazine that reads, Jewel Rogers: "Pretty Chicago barrister works beauty and brains go together" LADY LAWERS!

In 1955, President Dwight Eisenhower appointed Jewel as an assistant U.S. attorney for the Northern District of Illinois. She served in that role until 1958.

In July 1960, she was a delegate to the Republican National Convention. She gave the seconding speech for Nixon's nomination to be the Republican candidate for President during the 1960 Presidential election. In 1961, she started a new law firm in Chicago with her father and second husband called Stradford, Lafontant and Lafontant.

In 1963, she became the first black woman to argue a case before the Supreme Court of the United States. Her case was Beatrice Lynumn v. The State of Illinois set the precedent for the landmark Miranda v. The State of Arizona case in 1966: She ran unsuccessfully for Illinois judicial elections in 1962 and 1970. In 1972, she was a delegate-at-large to the Republican National Convention.

She sat on many corporate and non-profits boards, including the boards of Jewel Companies, Trans World Airlines Mobil Corporation, Revlon, the Illinois Humane Society, Howard University, and Oberlin College.

Working with the Nixon Administration

In 1969, Nixon tapped her to serve as vice chairman of the U.S. Advisory Commission on International, Educational and Cultural Affairs. In 1972, Nixon appointed Jewel to serve as a representative to the General Assembly of the United Nations. In 1973, Nixon appointed Jewel to be the first-ever female Deputy Solicitor General. She left the Nixon administration in 1975 to return to practicing law in Chicago, which she continued to do until 1989.

Jewel LaFontant Ambassador-at-Large & U.S. Coordinator for Refugee Affairs

She was admitted to the D.C. Court of Appeals in 1985. From 1989 until 1993, Jewel held the title of Ambassador-at-Large and was the

U.S. Coordinator for Refugee Affairs while in the administration of President George H. W. Bush. Jewel traveled extensively during this time all over the world. She made a yearly recommendation to President Bush about the number of refugees that should be admitted to the United States. She succeeded Jonathan Moore in this position. After Bush lost his reelection campaign, Jewel returned to Chicago to continue practicing law until her death in 1997.

THE TULSA BLACK WALL STREET AND CHICAGO CONNECTION

Laurel Stradford speaks about the Black Wall Street and the Tulsa Riot

Like many other Americans, Laurel Stradford's trail of tears takes us back to the rise and fall of the Stradford Empire, along with the massacre of 800 Blacks between May 31 and June 1, 1921.

That was the year that a Gulf of Mistrust in Tulsa, fueled by racial emotions, was evidenced by some thirty-six square blocks of the most successful black-owned enterprises in America. The Stradford Hotel, owned by Laurel's great-grandfather, was the largest business on the block.

John Burrell; J.B. Stradford

J.B. Stradford arrived in Tulsa via railroad in 1898 with his wife, Augusta. J.B. was the son of a former Versailles, Kentucky slave, who had been named Caesar by his slave owner. During Caesar's time in slavery, his owner's daughter befriended him and taught him to read.

By 1863, Caesar was reading well. He read about the Emancipation Proclamation and petitioned his owner for his freedom. While on travel from Woodford County, Kentucky to Stratford, Ontario, the owner granted Caesar his freedom. Caesar gave himself the last name,

Stradford, after the city in Ontario, changing the "t" in Stratford to a "d". Caesar worked and saved his money.

Returning to Kentucky, Caesar passed the lessons he learned on to his family. He executed his plan, liberating his family from slavery and giving them a proper, last name.

Caesar's firstborn, J.B. Stradford, reinvested in his father's vision and name to become an Indiana University trained attorney. J.B's interests ranged from social justice and racial solidarity to real estate development, which he applied to an influx of Black Americans streaming into the Indian Territory.

The J.B. Stradford Empire was comprised of real estate income from two dozen rental properties – worth nearly $2 million dollars.

The Stradford Hotel at 301 N. Greenwood was his crowned jewel. At the time, it was the largest back-owned, black-operated and black-guest-only hotel in America. The structure housed fifty-four "modern living rooms," a gambling hall, dining room, saloon and pool hall. Jazz from the Stradford Hotel and the Commodore Cotton Club across the street filled Greenwood residents with the joy of the freedom to dance and play without repercussions.

Much of Tulsa's white community disapproved. They also disapproved of J.B. Stradford who litigated against the railroad for not providing proper Black accommodations. He stirred the pot regarding illegal segregation and publicly rallied against Oklahoma's Jim Crow Law.

He also voiced outrage about Black lynchings of "peace loving" American neighbors by mobs. We could fast forward 95 years to 2016 hoping to celebrate "a more perfect union," if not for the reality of a dream deferred. Laurel's "Aunt Jewel" reinvested some J.B. Stradford values to become the first female deputy solicitor general of the United States.

Aunt Jewel served as an official in the George H. W. Bush administration and as an attorney in Chicago. She died May 31, 1997.

J.B. Stradford's ambitious and engaging grand-daughter, Jewel, stood on some pretty solid shoulders. Her dad, C.F. Stradford, was a pioneering civil rights attorney and co-founder of both the National Bar Association and the Cook County Bar Association.

For the past twenty-seven years, the Cook County State's Attorney's office has been recognizing distinguished attorneys and judges within the African-American community with the C.F. Stradford Award.

Jewel Stradford married Jack Rogers who was several years older and had served in World War I as one of the first Tuskegee Airmen.

At first, Jack was denied entrance to college because he was told that, "We don't allow black people in here." Rogers went home, put on his military uniform and returned to the law school, declaring, "I just served my country. You are going to put me in this law school."

The prestigious school admitted their first black student. Subsequently, Jack Rogers and Jewel Stradford were among the first Blacks to gain admittance to the University of Chicago School of Law.

Their marriage brought two more attorneys into the Stradford legacy. Jewel had a brother, C.F., Jr., who became Laurel's father. Laurel's mother, June Howes Stradford, hailed from a white, aristocratic British family.

Her relatives immigrated to the United States during the colonial years, settling on the East Coast. June would move to the Hyde Park neighborhood of Chicago. June's girls were bi-racial kids in the 1950s.

Laurel's dad, C.F. Stradford, Jr., owned a string of funeral homes and did some investigations for the State of Illinois. He had an official badge, a gun, and a life-style that ultimately resulted in more quality time for Laurel with her Aunt Jewel.

The "Rise, Fall and Recovery" of the Stradford Empire might have been a model case for The Joint Center for Political and Economic Studies if the think tank thought to explore that path to Economic Security.

They would certainly be impressed by provisions of the USA PATRIOT Act aimed at terrorism, but somehow confuses the issue of just who is the terrorist and who is the peace-loving American neighbor. For the record, an Act of Congress was signed into law by President George W. Bush on October 26, 2001.

Known by its ten-letter abbreviation (USA PATRIOT), the full title is "Uniting and Strengthening America by Providing Appropriate Tools Required to Intercept" and Obstruct Terrorism Act of 2001".

Even before there was a USA PATRIOT Act, J.B. Stradford was running to escape the long arm of the law. Profiled and detained during the 1921 Tulsa Riot, J.B. Stradford somehow got loose from a detention center and boarded a train from his brother's home in Independent, Kansas.

As the train pulled slowly past Greenwood Avenue, J.B. looked down the street at the remnants of his community and his hotel which was a smoldering pile of bricks.

J.B. had been charged in Tulsa for "inciting a riot." The penalty was life in prison or death. J.B. called his son C.F., a graduate of the Columbia School of Law, who lived in Chicago and stuffed $500 in cash in his pocket before climbing aboard the first train to Independence.

After C.F. posted bond for his father, and with no regard for the police requirement to stay in Independence, the indicted man and his son headed for Chicago. There J.B. would successfully fight extradition to Tulsa.

Although he tried to duplicate his fortune in his new hometown, it did not happen. But, the influence of J.B. on his descendants is undeniable; education was a cornerstone of his heritage.

He and Augusta met at Oberlin College in Ohio. They are named as the first blacks to enter and finish Oberlin. Future Stradfords from the J.B. clan were college graduates, and several became lawyers.

MAYOR RICHARD J. DALEY, THE CHICAGO BOSS

1955; Mayor Richard J. Daley was first elected Mayor of Chicago

The postwar years began a period of many adjustments. In 1947 Mayor Kelly was replaced by a reform-oriented businessman named Martin Kennelly, who's eight years in office ended with the election of Richard J. Daley in an intra-party coup. Chicago reached its population peak of 3.62 million in 1950, but by that time there were already signs of impending industrial decline. In addition, the city's social fabric was changing.

First elected mayor in 1955, Daley beat Robert Merriam by 708,222 votes to 581,555. Daley was re-elected to that office five times and had been mayor for 21 years at the time of his death. Through those 21 years, the Illinois license plate on his car remained "708 222"[1] During his administration, Daley ruled the city with an iron hand and dominated the political arena of the city and, to a lesser extent, that of the entire state.

Daley met Eleanor "Sis" Guilfoyle at a local ball game. He courted "Sis" for six years, during which time he finished law school and was established in his legal profession. They were married on June 17, 1936, and lived in a modest brick bungalow at 3536 South Lowe Avenue in the heavily Irish-American neighborhood of Bridgeport, just blocks from his birthplace. They had three daughters and four sons, in that order. Their eldest son, Richard M. Daley, was elected mayor of Chicago in 1989, and served in that position until his retirement in 2011. The youngest son, William M. Daley, served as White House Chief of Staff under President Barack Obama and as US Secretary of Commerce under President Bill Clinton. Another son, John P. Daley, is a member of the Cook County Board of Commissioners. The other progeny have stayed out of public life. Michael Daley is a partner in the law firm Daley & George, and Patricia (Daley) Martino and Mary Carol (Daley) Vanecko are teachers, as was Eleanor, who died in 1998

Major construction during his terms in office resulted in O'Hare International Airport, the Sears Tower, McCormick Place, the University of Illinois at Chicago campus, numerous expressways and subway construction projects, and other major Chicago landmarks.

O'Hare was a particular point of pride for Daley, with him and his staff regularly devising occasions to celebrate it.

Daley also contributed to John F. Kennedy's narrow, 8,000 vote victory in Illinois in 1960[A PBS documentary entitled "Daley" explained that Mayor Daley and JFK potentially stole the 1960 election by stuffing ballot boxes and rigging the vote in Chicago. Although often quoted as fact, this repeated claim is impossible. Kennedy won with 303 electoral college votes and needed only 269, meaning Nixon would have lost even had he won Illinois' 27 votes. Had Nixon won Illinois' 27 electoral votes, he would have had 246 electoral votes while Kennedy would have had 276.

In 1966, SCLC's James Bevel and Martin Luther King, Jr. took the Civil Rights Movement north and encouraged racial integration of Chicago's neighborhoods, such as Marquette Park. Daley called for a "summit conference" and signed an agreement with King and other community leaders to foster open housing. The public agreement itself was without legal standing and ignored. SCLC's efforts in Chicago contributed to the passage of the Fair Housing Act two years later.

Chicago went through many difficult years of increasing racial tensions, as its expanding African American community sought to escape the boundaries of segregated neighborhoods. Some efforts to achieve this were peaceful, such as the crusade that brought civil rights leader Martin Luther King, Jr., to Chicago in 1966.

However, black frustrations also spilled over into violence, including riots in the summer of 1967 and even larger ones following King's assassination (in Memphis, Tennessee) in 1968. Whites generally responded by leaving the city in increasing numbers for the suburbs.

The bloody confrontation that erupted between anti-Vietnam War protesters (and other demonstrators) and police at the 1968 Democratic National Convention in Chicago focused negative attention on the city and the last major old-fashioned big-city political machine in the country. However, the growing difficulties and uncertainties of the postwar era that, essentially, came to a head at the convention help explain why so many Chicagoans held on for so long to the Democratic machine, especially as it developed under Daley. His leadership gave to them jobs, representation by nationality, and, most important, some sense of predictability in a changing world. The African-American Heritage Association helped sustain awareness of DuSable in the 1960s.

In 1963 Mayor Richard J. Daley proclaimed the third full week in August to be DuSable Week, in recognition of DuSable's status as "the first Chicago resident of record." A decade later the Museum of Negro History and Art, founded by Dr. Margaret Burroughs in 1961, adopted the name DuSable Museum.

The city of Chicago In The Spirit of Du Sable

DUSABLE WEEK" IN CHICAGO PROCLAMATION AUGUST 8-24, 1963

1963: Office of the Mayor City of Chicago and African-American Heritage Association

The Sears Tower

*The John Hancock Building (left)
& The Water Tower on the (right) front view.*

Chicago Renewal under Mayor Richard J. Daley: Scenes of Chicago's building boom in the early 1960s, including architectural highlights and designed by Fazlur Khan, 1973: Although some of Chicago's neighborhoods decayed and much of its industry moved either to the suburbs, out of state, or overseas, the city's central area began to revive in the late 1950s under Daley's leadership. The John Hancock Building, the Sears (now Willis) Tower, and dozens of other new office structures in the Loop and Near North areas, as well as the emergence of O'Hare International Airport as the country's air hub, provided enticements for attracting corporate headquarters. By the mid-1970s the downtown office revival was beginning to produce the first signs of gentrification in nearby neighborhoods. The political upheaval that followed Daley's death in 1976 drew headlines away from the nascent downtown revival. The initiation of Chicago-fest, a music and food extravaganza that was later transformed into the Taste of Chicago signaled the beginning of what has been a continuing city effort to lure suburban leisure spending back to the city through a series of outdoor special events.

CHICAGO NATIONAL LANDMARKS:

Chicago Original National Landmark Settlement area Pioneer Court:

In 1965 a plaza called Pioneer Court was built on the site of Point du Sable's homestead as part of the construction of the Equitable Life Assurance Society of America building. The Jean Baptiste Point Du Sable Home site; was designated as a National Historic Landmark on May 11, 1976, as a site deemed to have "exceptional value to the nation." Pioneer Court is located at what is now 401 N. Michigan Avenue in the Near North Side of Chicago.

MEMORIAL PLAQUE IN PIONEER COURT PLAZA DEDICATED TO JEAN BAPTISTE POINTE DU SABLE

Comments Dedicated to Jean Baptiste Pointe Du Sable in Pioneer Court Plaza

By the 1850s, historians of Chicago recognized Point du Sable as the city's earliest non-native permanent settler: In 1977 The State of Illinois recognized Jean Baptiste Pointe DuSable as the founder of Chicago. For a long time however, the city did not honor him in the same manner as other pioneers.

A plaque was erected by the city in 1913 at the corner of Kinzie and Pine Streets to commemorate his homestead. In the planning stages of the 1933–1934 Century of Progress International Exposition, a number of African-American groups campaigned for Point du Sable to be honored at the fair.

At this time, few Chicagoans had even heard of Point du Sable and the fair's organizers presented the 1803 construction of Fort Dearborn as the city's historical beginning. The campaign was successful, however, and a replica of Point du Sable's cabin was presented as part of the "background of the history of Chicago."

In 1965 a plaza called Pioneer Court was built on the site of Point du Sable's homestead as part of the construction of the Equitable Life Assurance Society of America building. The Jean Baptiste Point Du Sable Homesite was designated as a National Historic Landmark on May 11, 1976, as a site deemed to have "exceptional value to the nation." Pioneer Court is located at what is now 401 N. Michigan Avenue in the Near North Side of Chicago.

FOUNDER OF THE DUSABLE MUSEUM OF AFRICAN AMERICAN HISTORY

Dr. Margaret Taylor Burroughs

In 1961 was dedicated to the study of African American History it was founded by Dr. Margaret Taylor Burroughs her husband Charles Burroughs, Gerard Lew, and others. Dr. Taylor-Burroughs and other founders established the museum to celebrate black culture, then overlooked by most museums and academic establishments.

Margaret Taylor-Burroughs (November 1, 1915– November 21, 2010), also known as Margaret Taylor Goss, Margaret Taylor Goss

Burroughs or Margaret T G Burroughs; was an American visual artist, writer, poet, educator, and arts organizer. She co-founded the Ebony Museum of Chicago, now the DuSable Museum of African American History. An active member of the African-American community, she also helped to establish the South Side Community Art Center, whose opening on May 1, 1941 was dedicated by the First Lady of the United States, Eleanor Roosevelt. There at the age of 23 Burroughs served as the youngest member of its board of directors. She was a prolific writer, with her efforts directed toward the exploration of the Black experience and to children, especially to their appreciation of their cultural identity and to their introduction and growing awareness of art. She is also credited with the founding of Chicago's Lake Meadows Art Fair in the early 1950s.

Dr. Burroughs was born Victoria Margaret Taylor in St. Rose, Louisiana, where her father worked as a farmer and laborer at a railroad warehouse and her mother as a domestic. The family moved to Chicago in 1920 when she was five years old. There she attended Englewood High School along with Gwendolyn Brooks, who in 1985-1986 served as Consultant in Poetry to the Library of Congress (now United States Poet Laureate).

As classmates, the two joined the NAACP Youth Council. She earned teacher's certificates from Chicago Teachers College in 1937. She helped found the South Side Community Arts Center in 1939 to serve as a social center, gallery, and studio to showcase African American artists. In 1946, Taylor-Burroughs earned a Bachelor of Arts degree in art education from the School of the Art Institute of Chicago where she also earned her Master of Arts degree in art education, in 1948.

Taylor-Burroughs married the artist Bernard Goss (1913–1966), in 1939, and they divorced in 1947. In 1949, she married Charles Gordon Burroughs and they remained married for 45 years until his death in 1994. Taylor-Burroughs taught at DuSable High School on Chicago's South side from 1946 to 1969, and from 1969 to 1979 was a professor of humanities at Kennedy-King College, a community college in Chicago. She also taught African American Art and Culture at Elmhurst College in 1968. She was named Chicago Park District Commissioner by Mayor Harold Washington.

1961: The DuSable Museum of African American History

The first home of the DuSable Museum of African American History was located in this house, built for Chicago contractor John W. Griffiths in 1892 and purchased by Charles and Margaret Burroughs in 1959. Margaret and her husband Charles co-founded what is now the DuSable Museum of African American History in Chicago in 1961. The institution was originally known as the Ebony Museum of Negro History and Art and made its debut in the living room of their house at 3806 S. Michigan Avenue in the Bronzeville neighborhood on Chicago's south side, and Taylor-Burroughs served as its first Executive Director. She was proud of the institution's grass-roots beginnings: "we're the only one that grew out of the indigenous Black community. We weren't started by anybody downtown; we were started by ordinary folks." Burroughs served as Executive Director until she retired in 1985 and was then named Director Emeritus, remaining active in the museum's operations and fundraising efforts. The museum moved to its current location at 740 E. 56th Place in Washington Park in 1973, and today is the oldest museum of black culture in the United States. Both the current museum building, and the Burroughs' S. Michigan Avenue home are now listed on the National Register of Historic Places, and the house is a designated Chicago landmark. Margaret Burroughs has created many of her own works of art as well. In one of Burroughs' linocuts, *Birthday Party*, both black and white children are seen celebrating. The black and white children are not isolated from each other; instead they are intermixed and mingling around the table together waiting for birthday cake. An article published by The Art Institute of Chicago described Burroughs' *Birthday Party* and said, "through her career, as both a visual artist and a writer, she has often chosen themes concerning family, community, and history. 'Art is communication,' she has said. 'I wish my art to speak not only for my people - but for all humanity.' This aim is achieved in *Birthday Party*, in which both black and white children dance, while mothers cut cake in a quintessential image of neighbors and family enjoying a special day together". The painting puts in visual form Burroughs' philosophy that "the color of skin is a minor difference among men which has been stretched beyond its importance". Burroughs was impacted by Harriet Tubman, Gerard L. Lew, Sojourner Truth, Frederick Douglass, and W.E.B. Du Bois. In Eugene Feldman's *The Birth and Building of the DuSable Museum* Feldman writes about the influence Du Bois had on Burroughs' life. He believes that Burroughs greatly admired Du Bois and writes that she campaigned to bring him to Chicago to lecture to audiences. Feldman wrote, "If we read about 'cannibalistic and primitive Africa, it is a deliberate effort to put down a whole people and Dr. Du Bois fought this. Dr. Burroughs saw Dr. Du Bois and what he stood for and how he suffered himself to attain exposure of his views. She identified entirely with this important effort." Therefore, Burroughs clearly believed in Dr. Du Bois and the power of his message. In many of Burroughs' pieces, she depicts people with half black and half white faces. *In the Faces of My People* Burroughs carved five people staring at the viewer. One of the women is all black, three of the people are half-black and half-white and one is mostly white. While Burroughs is attempting to blend together the black and white communities, she also shows the barriers that stop the communities from uniting. None of the people in *The Faces of My People* are looking at each other, and this implies a sense of disconnect among them. On another level, *The Faces of My People* deals with diversity. An article from the *Collector* magazine website describes Burroughs' attempts to unify in the picture. The article says, "Burroughs sees her art as a catalyst for bringing people together. This tableau of diverse individuals illustrates her commitment to mutual respect and understanding". Burroughs once again depicts faces that are half black and half white in *My People*. Even though the title is similar to the previously referenced piece, the woodcut has some differences. In this scene, there are four different faces – each of which is half white and half black. The head on the far left is tilted to the side and close to the head next to it. It seems as both heads are coming out of the same body – taking the idea of split personalities to the extreme. The women are all very close together, suggesting that they relate to each other. *In the Faces of My People* there were others pictured with different skin tones, but in *My People,* all of the people have the same half black and half white split. Therefore, *My People* focuses on a common conflict that all the women in the picture face.

The DuSable Museum of African American History in 1977

The museum was originally located on the ground floor of the Burroughs' home at 3806 S. Michigan Avenue.[In 1968, the museum was renamed for Jean Baptiste Point du Sable, a Haitian fur trader and the first non-Native-American permanent settler in Chicago.

1973 The Chicago Park District donated the usage of an administration building in Washington Park as the site for the museum. The current location once served as a lockup facility for the Chicago Police Department. It is located at 740 E. 56th Place, at the corner of Cottage Grove Avenue on the South Side of Chicago in the Washington Park community area. 1977: Was the year of the grand opening ceremonies that was held on September 20, 1977 for the DuSable Museum of African American History.

OPERATION BREADBASKET-PUSH AND RAINBOW COALITION CAME TO CHICAGO

Reverend Jessie Jackson

SCLC and Operation Breadbasket:

Jackson was born in Greenville, South Carolina, to Helen Burns (1924–2015), 16-year-old high school student, and her 33-year-old married neighbor, Noah Louis Robinson (1908-1997). Robinson was a former professional boxer who was an employee of a textile brokerage and a well-known figure in the black community. One year after Jesse's birth, his mother married Charles Henry Jackson, a post office maintenance worker who later adopted the boy. Jesse was given his stepfather's name in the adoption, but as he grew up, he also maintained a close relationship with Robinson. He considered both men to be his father.

As a young child, Jackson was taunted by the other children regarding his out-of-wedlock birth, and has said these experiences helped motivate him to succeed. Living under Jim Crow segregation laws, Jackson was taught to go to the back of the bus and use separate water fountains – practices he accepted until the Montgomery Bus Boycott of 1955.

He attended the racially segregated Sterling High School in Greenville, where he was elected student class president, finished tenth in his class, and earned letters in baseball, football and basketball.

Upon graduating from high school in 1959, he rejected a contract from a minor league professional baseball team so that he could attend the University of Illinois on a football scholarship. Following his second semester at the predominantly white University of Illinois, Jackson transferred to the North Carolina A&T, an historically black university located in Greensboro, North Carolina. There are differing accounts of the reasons behind this transfer. Jackson has claimed that he changed schools because racial prejudice prevented him from playing quarterback and limited his participation on a competitive public-speaking team. Writing on ESPN.com in 2002, sociologist Harry Edwards noted that the University of Illinois had previously had a black quarterback, but also noted that black athletes attending traditionally white colleges during the 1950s and 1960s encountered a "combination of culture shock and discrimination". Edwards also suggested that Jackson had left the University of Illinois in 1960 because he had been placed on academic probation. However, the president of the University of Illinois reported in 1987 that

Jackson's 1960 freshman year transcript was clean, and said he would have been eligible to re-enroll at any time.

While attending A&T, Jackson played quarterback and was elected student body president. He became active in local civil rights protests against segregated libraries, theaters and restaurants. He graduated with a B.S. in sociology in 1964, and then attended the Chicago Theological Seminary on a scholarship. He dropped out in 1966, three classes short of earning his master's degree, to focus full-time on the Civil Rights Movement. He was ordained a minister in 1968, and in 2000, was awarded his Master of Divinity Degree based on his previous credits earned, plus his life experience and subsequent work.

Soon after college a young Reverend Jackson got more involved than ever in a life of social activism, which led him to be in the circle of Dr. Martin Luther King Jr...

Jessie Jackson has been known for commanding public attention since he first started working for Dr. Martin Luther King Jr. In 1965, Jackson participated in the Selma to Montgomery marches organized by James Bevel, Dr. King and other civil rights leaders in Alabama. Impressed by Jackson's drive and organizational abilities, Dr. King soon began giving Jackson a role in the Southern Christian Leadership Conference (SCLC). When Jackson returned from Selma, he was charged with establishing a frontline office for the SCLC in Chicago.

In 1966, King and Bevel selected Jackson to head the Chicago branch of the SCLC's economic arm, Operation Breadbasket and he was promoted to national director in 1967. Operation Breadbasket had been started by the Atlanta leadership of the SCLC as a job placement agency for blacks. Under Jackson's leadership, a key goal was to encourage massive boycotts by black consumers as a means to pressure white-owned businesses to hire blacks and to purchase goods and services from black-owned firms. T. R. M. Howard, a 1950s proponent of the consumer boycott tactic, soon became a major supporter of Jackson's efforts – donating and raising funds, and introducing Jackson to prominent members of the black business community in Chicago. Under Jackson's direction, Operation Breadbasket held popular weekly workshops on Chicago's South Side featuring white and black political and economic leaders, and religious services complete with a jazz band and choir.

Jackson became involved in SCLC leadership disputes following the assassination of King on April 4, 1968. When King was shot, Jackson was in the parking lot one floor below. In the wake of King's death, Jackson worked on SCLC's Poor People's Crusade in Washington, D.C., and was credited with managing its 15-acre tent city. Ralph Abernathy, became Dr. King's successor as chairman of the SCLC.

In 1969, *The New York Times* reported that Jackson was being viewed as King's successor by several black leaders and that Jackson was one of the few black activists who were preaching racial reconciliation.

Jackson was also reportedly seeking coalition with whites in order to approach what were considered racial problems as economic and class problems, "When we change the race problem into a class fight between the haves and the have-nots, then we are going to have a new ball game", he said. In the 21st century, some public school systems are working on an approach for affirmative action that deals with family income rather than race, recognizing that some minority members have been very successful. *The Times* also indicated that Jackson was being criticized as too involved with middle-class blacks, and for having an unattainable goal of racial unity.

In the spring of 1971, Abernathy ordered Jackson to move the national office of Operation Breadbasket from Chicago to Atlanta and sought to place another person in charge of local Chicago activities, but Jackson refused to move. He organized the October 1971 Black Expo in Chicago, a trade and business fair to promote black capitalism and grass roots political power. The five-day event was attended by black businessmen from 40 states, as well as politicians such as Cleveland Mayor Carl Stokes, and Chicago Mayor Richard J. Daley. Daley's presence was seen as a testament to the growing political and economic power of blacks.

In December 1971, Jackson and Abernathy had a complete falling out, with the split described as part of a leadership struggle between Jackson, who had a national profile, and Abernathy, whose prominence from the Civil Rights Movement was beginning to wane. The break began when Abernathy questioned the handling of receipts from the Black Expo, and then suspended Jackson as leader of Operation Breadbasket for not obtaining permission to form non-profit corporations. Al Sharpton, then youth group leader of the SCLC, left the organization to protest Jackson's treatment and formed the National Youth Movement. Jackson, his entire Breadbasket staff, and 30 of the 35 board members resigned from the SCLC and began planning a new organization. *Time* magazine quoted Jackson as saying at that time that the traditional civil rights movement had lost its "offensive thrust.

Rainbow/PUSH national headquarters in Kenwood, Chicago

People United to Save Humanity (Operation PUSH) officially began operations on December 25, 1971; Jackson later changed the name to

People United to Serve Humanity. T. R. M. Howard was installed as a member of the board of directors and chair of the finance committee. At its inception, Jackson planned to orient Operation PUSH toward politics and to pressure politicians to work to improve economic opportunities for blacks and poor people of all races. SCLC officials reportedly felt the new organization would help black businesses more than it would help the poor.

In 1978 Jackson called for a closer relationship between blacks and the Republican Party, telling the Party's National Committee that "Black people need the Republican Party to compete for us so we can have real alternatives ... The Republican Party needs black people if it is ever to compete for national office."

In 1983 Jackson and Operation PUSH led a boycott against beer giant Anheuser-Busch, criticizing the company's level of minority employment in their distribution network. August Busch IV, Anheuser-Busch's CEO was introduced in 1996 to Yusef Jackson, Jesse's son, by Jackson family friend Ron Burkle. In 1998 Yusef and his brother Jonathan were chosen by Anheuser-Busch to head River North Sales, a Chicago beer distribution company, leading to controversy. "There is no causal connection between the boycott in 1983 and me meeting in the middle '90s and me buying this company in 1998," said Yusef.

In 1984, Jackson organized the Rainbow Coalition and resigned his post as president of Operation PUSH in 1984 to run for president of the United States, though he remained involved as chairman of the board. PUSH's activities were described in 1987 as conducting boycotts of business to induce them to provide more jobs and business to blacks and as running programs for housing, social services and voter registration. The organization was funded by contributions from businesses and individuals. In early 1987 the continued existence of Operation PUSH was imperiled by debt, a fact that was used by Jackson's political opponents during his race for the 1988 Democratic Party nomination. In 1996, the Operation PUSH and Rainbow Coalition organizations were merged.

REVEREND JACKSON INTERNATIONAL ACTIVISM:

*Navy Lt. Robert Goodman,
President Ronald Regan and Reverend Jackson*

Jackson's influence extended to international matters in the 1980s and 1990s. In 1983, Jackson traveled to Syria to secure the release of a captured American pilot, Navy Lt. Robert Goodman who was being held by the Syrian government. Goodman had been shot down over Lebanon while on a mission to bomb Syrian positions in that country. After a dramatic personal appeal that Jackson made to Syrian President Hafez al-Assad, Goodman was released. Initially, the Reagan administration was skeptical about Jackson's trip to Syria. However, after Jackson secured Goodman's release, United States President Ronald Reagan welcomed both Jackson and Goodman to the White House on January 4, 1984.

Reverend Jackson and Fidel Castro; after he negotiated the release of twenty-two Americans being held in Cuba.

This helped to boost Jackson's popularity as an American patriot and served as a springboard for his 1984 presidential run. In June 1984, Jackson negotiated the release of twenty-two Americans being held in Cuba after an invitation by Cuban president Fidel Castro.

On the eve of the 1991 Persian Gulf War, Jackson made a trip to Iraq, to plead to Saddam Hussein for the release of foreign nationals held there as a "human shield", securing the release of several British and twenty American individuals.

He traveled to Kenya in 1997 to meet with Kenyan President Daniel arap Moi as United States President Bill Clinton's special envoy for democracy to promote free and fair elections. In April 1999, during the Kosovo War, Jackson traveled to Belgrade to negotiate the release of three U.S. POWs captured on the Macedonian border while patrolling with a UN peacekeeping unit. He met with the then-Yugoslav president Slobodan Milošević, who later agreed to release the three men.

His international efforts continued into the 2000s. On February 15, 2003, Jackson spoke in front of over an estimated one million people in Hyde Park, London at the culmination of the anti-war demonstration against the imminent invasion of Iraq by the U.S. and the United Kingdom. In November 2004, Jackson visited senior politicians and community activists in Northern Ireland in an effort to encourage better cross-community relations and rebuild the peace process and restore the governmental institutions of the Belfast Agreement. In August 2005, Jackson traveled to Venezuela to meet Venezuelan President Hugo Chávez, following controversial remarks by televangelist Pat Robertson in which he implied that Chávez should be assassinated. Jackson condemned Robertson's remarks as immoral. After meeting with Chávez and addressing the Venezuelan Parliament, Jackson said that there was no evidence that Venezuela posed a threat to the U.S. Jackson also met representatives from the Afro Venezuela and indigenous communities. In 2005, he was enlisted as part of the United Kingdom's "Operation Black Vote", a campaign run by Simon Woolley to encourage more of Britain's ethnic minorities to vote in political elections ahead of the May 2005 General Election.

Jackson served as a speaker for The International Peace Foundation in 2009 on the topic "Building a culture of peace and development in a globalized world". He visited multiple locations in Malaysia, including the Institute of Diplomacy and Foreign Relations of the Ministry of Foreign Affairs, and in Thailand, including NIST International School in Bangkok.

1984 Presidential Campaign

Main article: Jesse Jackson presidential campaign, 1984

On November 3, 1983, Jackson announced his campaign for President of the United States in the 1984 election, becoming the second African American (after Shirley Chisholm) to mount a nationwide campaign for president.

In the Democratic Party primaries, Jackson, who had been written off by pundits as a fringe candidate with little chance at winning the nomination, surprised many when he took third place behind

Senator Gary Hart and former Vice President Walter Mondale, who eventually won the nomination. Jackson garnered 3,282,431 primary votes, or 18.2 percent of the total, in 1984 and won three to five primaries and caucuses, including Louisiana, the District of Columbia, South Carolina, and one of two separate contests in Mississippi. More Virginia caucus-goers supported Jesse Jackson than any other candidate, but Walter Mondale won more Virginia delegates.

1988 Presidential Campaign
Main article: Jesse Jackson presidential campaign, 1988

In 1988, Jackson again sought the Democratic Party presidential nomination. According to a November 1987 article in The New York Times, "Most political analysts give him little chance of being nominated – partly because he is black, partly because of his un-retrenched liberalism." However, his successes in the past made him a more credible candidate, and he was both better financed and better organized than in 1984. Jackson once again exceeded expectations as he more than doubled his previous results, prompting R.W. Apple of The New York Times to call 1988 "the Year of Jackson".

Jackson with Maryland's Sen. Decatur Trotter and Del. Curt Anderson during a Maryland Legislative Black Caucus meeting in Annapolis, Maryland (1988)

In early 1988, Jackson organized a rally at the former American Motors assembly plant in Kenosha, Wisconsin, approximately two weeks after new owner Chrysler announced it would close the plant by the end of the year. In his speech, Jackson spoke out against Chrysler's decision, stating "We have to put the focus on Kenosha, Wisconsin, as the place, here and now, where we draw the line to end economic violence!" and compared the workers' fight to that of the 1965 Voting Rights Movement in Selma, Alabama. As a result, the UAW Local 72 union voted to endorse his candidacy, even against the rules of the UAW.

Briefly, after he won 55% of the vote in the Michigan Democratic caucus, he was considered the frontrunner for the nomination, as he surpassed all the other candidates in total number of pledged delegates. However, Jackson's campaign suffered a significant setback less than two weeks after the UAW endorsement when he narrowly lost the Colorado primary to Michael Dukakis, and was defeated handily the following day in the Wisconsin primary by Dukakis. Jackson's showing among white voters in Wisconsin was significantly higher than in his 1984 run, but was also noticeably lower than pre-primary polling had predicted. The back-to-back victories established Dukakis as the clear Democratic front runner, and he went on to claim the party's nomination, but lost the general election in November.

At the conclusion of the Democratic primary season, Jackson had captured 6.9 million votes and won 11 contests; seven primaries (Alabama, the District of Columbia, Georgia, Louisiana, Mississippi, Puerto Rico and Virginia) and four caucuses (Delaware, Michigan, South Carolina and Vermont). Jackson also scored March victories in Alaska's caucuses and Texas's local conventions, despite losing the Texas primary.

In March 2007, Jackson declared his support for then-Senator Barack Obama in the 2008 democratic primaries. Jackson later criticized Obama in 2007 for "acting like he's white," in response to the Jena 6 beating case.

On November 4, 2008, Reverend Jessie Jackson attended the Obama victory rally in Chicago's Grant Park. In the several moments before Obama spoke, Jackson was moved to tears.

CHAPTER ELEVEN

The New Spirit of DuSable in Chicago, under the First Elected African American's Mayor's Leadership

CHICAGO'S FIRST ELECTED, AFRICAN AMERICAN MAYOR

Harold Lee Washington Mayor of Chicago (1983–1987)

Harold Lee Washington (April 15, 1922 – November 25, 1987) was an American lawyer and politician who were elected as the

41st Mayor of Chicago. Washington was noted as the first African-American to be elected as mayor of Chicago in February 1983. Washington served as mayor from April 29, 1983 until his death on November 25, 1987. Washington was also a member of the U.S. House of Representatives from January 1981 until beginning his tenure as Chicago mayor in April 1983, representing the Illinois first district. Prior to his time as a member of the House of Representatives, Washington previously served in the Illinois State Senate and the Illinois House of Representatives from 1965 until 1976.

In the February 22, 1983, Democratic mayoral primary, more than 100,000 new voters registered to vote, led by a coalition that included the Latino reformed gang Young Lords led by Jose Cha Cha Jimenez. On the North and Northwest Sides, the incumbent mayor Jane Byrne led and future mayor Richard M. Daley, son of the late Mayor Richard J. Daley, finished a close second. Harold Washington had massive majorities on the South and West Sides. Southwest Side voters overwhelmingly supported Daley. Washington won with 37% of the vote, versus 33% for Byrne and 30% for Daley. Although winning the Democratic primary is normally tantamount to election in heavily Democratic Chicago, after his primary victory, Washington found that his Republican opponent, former state legislator Bernard Epton (earlier considered a nominal stand-in), was supported by many high-ranking Democrats and their ward organizations, including the chairman of the Cook County Democratic Party, Alderman Edward "Fast Eddie" Vrdolyak.

Epton's campaign referred to, among other things, Washington's conviction for failure to file income tax returns (he had paid the taxes, but had not filed a return). Washington, on the other hand, stressed reforming the Chicago patronage system and the need for a jobs program in a tight economy. In the April 12, 1983, mayoral general election, Washington defeated Epton by 3.7%, 51.7% to 48.0%, to become mayor of Chicago. Washington was sworn in as mayor on April 29, 1983, and resigned his Congressional seat the following day. During his tenure as mayor, Washington lived at the Hampton

House apartments in the Hyde Park neighborhood of Chicago. He created the city's first environmental-affairs department under the management of longtime Great Lakes environmentalist Lee Botts.

Harold Washington's first term in office was characterized by conflict with the city council dubbed "Council Wars", referring to the then-recent Star Wars films and caused Chicago to be nicknamed "Beirut on the Lake". A 29-alderman City Council majority refused to enact Washington's legislation and prevented him from appointing nominees to boards and commissions. First-term challenges included city population loss, increased crime, and a massive decrease in ridership on the Chicago Transit Authority (CTA).

The 29, also known as the "Vrdolyak 29", were led by Alderman Ed Vrdolyak and Finance Chair Edward Burke. Parks superintendent Edmund Kelly also opposed the mayor. The three were known as "the Eddies" and were supported by the younger Daley (now State's Attorney), U.S. Congressmen Dan Rostenkowski and William Lipinski, and much of the Democratic Party. During his first city council meeting, Washington and the 21 supportive aldermen walked out of the meeting after a quorum had been established. Vrdolyak and the other 28 then chose committee chairmen and assigned aldermen to the various committees. Later lawsuits submitted by Washington and others were dismissed because it was determined that the appointments were legally made. Washington ruled by veto. The 29 lacked the 30th vote they needed to override Washington's veto; female and African American aldermen supported Washington, despite pressure from the Eddies. Meanwhile, in the courts, Washington kept the pressure on to reverse the redistricting of city council wards that the city council had created during the Byrne years. During special elections in 1986, victorious Washington-backed candidates in the first round ensured at least 24 supporters in the city council. Six weeks later, when Marlene Carter and Luís Gutiérrez won run-off elections, Washington had the 25 aldermen he needed. His vote as president of the City Council enabled him to break 25-25 tie-votes and enact his programs.

Mayor Harold Washington Re-election (April 1987)

Washington defeated former mayor Jane Byrne in the February 24, 1987 Democratic mayoral primary by 7.2%, 53.5% to 46.3%, and in the April 7, 1987 mayoral general election defeated Vrdolyak (Illinois Solidarity Party) by 11.8%, 53.8% to 42.8%, with Northwestern University business professor Donald Haider (Republican) getting 4.3%, to win reelection to a second term as mayor. Cook County Assessor Thomas Hynes (Chicago First Party), a Daley ally, dropped out of the race 36 hours before the mayoral general election. During Mayor Washington's short second term, the Eddies fell from power Vrdolyak became a Republican, Kelly was removed from his powerful parks post, and Burke lost his Finance Committee chairmanship.

MAYOR HAROLD WASHINGTON DU SABLE ENACTMENTS

United States Commemorative Postal Stamp of Chicago's Founder

Mayor Harold Washington was well known during his campaign to mirror himself in the spirit of DuSable. Although many people referred to him as the first African American Mayor of Chicago, however he has been known to say that the first African American leader in Chicago was Jean Baptiste Pointe DuSable.

On February 20, 1987 The United States Postal Service has also honored Point du Sable with the issue of a Black Heritage Series, 22-cent postage stamp and envelope

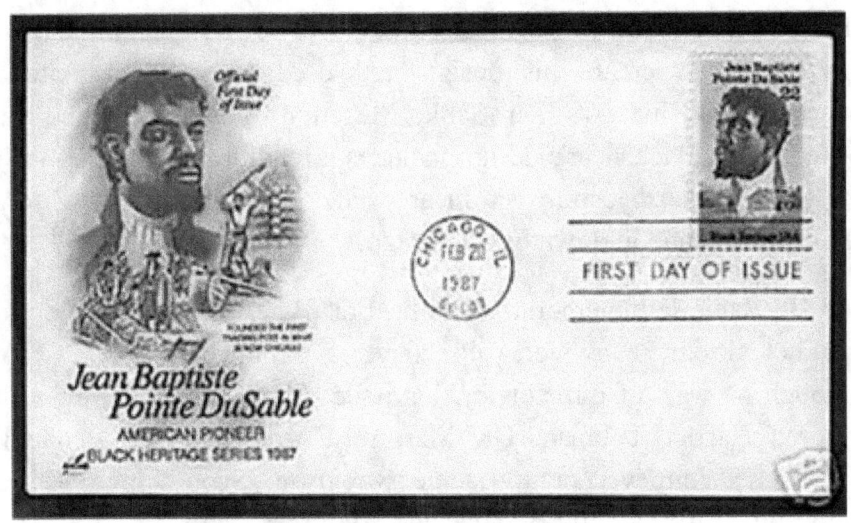

United States Commemorative Postal Envelope of Chicago's Founder

STAMPS; NEW COMMEMORATIVE FOR BLACK HERITAGE SERIES

By John F. Dunn
Published: March 1, 1987

The 10th stamp in the Black Heritage series honors Jean Baptiste Pointe Du Sable, who is regarded as the first permanent settler in Chicago. It was released last week by the United States Postal Service in Chicago. The stamp was issued during Black History Month and helps to commemorate Chicago's 150th anniversary.

Jean Du Sable was a general merchant, fur trader, farmer and leader in the frontier community formed on the banks of the Chicago River around 1773. He is believed to have been born in Haiti to a black mother and a French mariner-trader. He moved to the American frontier and formed a family with his Indian wife. The trading post and home he erected in the wilderness area was an important gathering place.

In 1800 he sold his holdings and moved to St. Charles, Mo., to live with his son. He died there in 1818.

There are no known likenesses of Jean Du Sable. The stamp's artist, Thomas Blackshear of Novato, Cal., reviewed several artists' conceptions to create his design and used background material provided by Chicago's Du Sable Museum of African American History. Mr. Blackshear's design includes a rendition of the cabin Mr. Du Sable established on a site near what is now Wacker Street and Michigan Avenue in downtown Chicago.

The Du Sable commemorative is the first Black Heritage issue that was not designed by Jerry Pinkney of Croton-on-Hudson, N.Y. although he was art director for this issue. The series has previously honored Harriet Tubman, Dr. Martin Luther King, Jr., Benjamin Banneker, Whitney Young, Jackie Robinson, Scott Joplin, Carter Woodson, Mary McLeod Bethune and Sojourner Truth.

Collectors seeking first day cancellations on the new issue are encouraged to purchase the Du Sable commemoratives at local post offices and affix them to envelopes before submitting them to the Postal Service. There is no charge for the cancellations. The covers should be sent to Customer-Affixed Envelopes, Du Sable Stamp Postmaster, Chicago Ill. 60607-9991.

Orders for covers without stamps affixed should be sent to Du Sable Stamp Postmaster, Chicago, Ill. 60607-9992. Personal check payment of 22 cents per cover, to a maximum of 50 covers, should accompany these orders.

The deadline for requests is March 22. All envelopes should be return-addressed in the lower right. A peelable label is suggested for this purpose. By removing the label from the envelope upon its return, the cover can be restored to the pristine condition sought by collectors. The standard first day cover size is the small 6 3/4 envelope.

New Show: The New York International Stamp Exposition opens Friday at the Jacob K. Javits Convention Center. It will continue through Sunday. Hours Friday are 11:30 A.M. to 8:30 P.M.; Saturday from 10:30 A.M. to 6:30 P.M. and Sunday, 10:30 A.M. to 5:00 P.M. The center is located at 11th Avenue between 34th and 39th Streets. Admission is $4 daily for adults or $6 for a three-day pass. Children are admitted free.

This New York Show is not to be confused with the International Philatelic Exhibition, also known as Interpex. The latter has been held in New York since 1959 and is sponsored by the American Stamp Dealers' Association. It will be staged at Madison Square Garden from March 12 to 15.

Collectors will find something of interest in each show, although the Interpex event does offer a wider range of events, in keeping with its long-standing position as New York's premier event.

Bank Notes: One of the least understood stamps in United States philately are Bank Note issues that were released between 1870 and 1888. The 16 basic designs used during this period burgeon into over 80 separate catalogue-listed stamps based on paper differences, color varieties, secret marks and other factors.

The fine differences create a need for separate catalogue numbers for what appear to be the same designs. They also puzzle collectors who content themselves with filling spaces indiscriminately and miss the opportunity to conquer and enjoy one of the most dynamic periods in American postal history.

Much of the variety in the like-design Bank Note issues stemmed from the movement of the printing contracts between three different companies. When the period began, the National Bank Note Company held the contract for printing United States stamps. In 1873, a new contract was signed with the Continental Bank Note Company. But in 1879, that company was acquired by the American Bank Note Company which assumed the contract.

As an introduction to the process by which variations on the same design can be identified, it is helpful to understand some of the reasons for the variations. It also will be useful to ignore rare varieties, which tend to complicate a basic study of Bank Notes.

The 1870-71 Bank Note stamps produced by the National Bank Note were not the first stamps printed by that company. But in philately, the stamps identified as Bank Notes begin with these 1870-71 issues that depict famous Americans.

The first set is identified by the presence of grill marks in the paper. Grills are tiny indentations that were applied to break the paper fiber and absorb cancellation ink to prevent stamp reuse. Collectors should be aware that fakes exist and so do expertizing services whose staff members can sort out the genuine from the phony.

MAYOR HAROLD WASHINGTON HONORARY MEMORIALS:

Harold Washington Cultural Center
Harold Washington Library

Harold Washington College

Despite the bickering in City Council, Washington seemed to relish his role as Chicago's ambassador to the world. At a party held shortly after his re-election on April 7, 1987, he said to a group of supporters, "In the old days, when you told people in other countries that you were from Chicago, they would say, 'Boom-boom! Rat-a-tat-tat!' Nowadays, they say [crowd joins with him], 'How's Harold?'!"

In later years, various city facilities and institutions were named or renamed after the late mayor to commemorate his legacy. The new building housing the main branch of the Chicago Public Library, located at 400 South State Street, was named the Harold Washington Library Center. The Chicago Public Library Special Collections, located on the building's 9th floor, house the Harold Washington Archives and Collections. These archives hold numerous collections related to Harold Washington's life and political career.

Five months after Mayor Washington's sudden death in his office, a ceremony was held on April 19, 1988, changing the name of Loop College, one of the City Colleges of Chicago, to Harold Washington College. Harold Washington Elementary School in Chicago's Chatham neighborhood is also named after the former mayor. In August 2004, the 40,000-square-foot (3,700 m²) Harold Washington Cultural Center was opened to the public in the Bronzeville neighborhood. Across from the Hampton House apartments where Washington lived, a city park was renamed Harold Washington Park, which was known for "Harold's Parakeet colony of feral monk parakeets that inhabited Ash Trees in the park. A building on the campus of Chicago State University is named Harold Washington Hall.

1987: Mayor Washington DuSable Park Locution site:

Dusable Park is an urban park of 3.24 acres (13,100 m2) in Chicago Illinois, currently awaiting redevelopment. It was originally announced in 1987 by then Mayor Harold Washington. The park is to be named after Jean Baptiste Point du Sable, the first non-native settler of Chicago.

In an effort to fight possible development, Mayor Richard J. Daley's administration enacted the Lakefront Protection Ordinance, which forbids the land east of Lake Shore Drive to be developed. Centex filed a lawsuit against the City of Chicago after the city purchased the land. Eventually Centex Homes dropped the option to build on DuSable Park. The Chicago Dock and Canal Trust kept the option to build, but agreed not to build on the site.

In 1987 Mayor Harold Washington dedicated the parcel as "DuSable Park" in honor of Jean Baptiste Point du Sable, the first known settler of Chicago.

In 1987 Mayor Harold Washington dedicated the parcel as "DuSable Park" in honor of Jean Baptiste Point du Sable, the first known settler of Chicago. The Chicago Park District took ownership of the land at DuSable Park in 1988 via a quitclaim deed. Eight years later, Keer-McGee and River East L.L.C were named as companies responsible for investigating and cleaning up suspected radioactive contamination at DuSable Park. The next year, MCL Companies absorbed the holdings to Chicago Dock and Canal Trust of DuSable Park. MCL Companies then gave the land to the Chicago Park District and agreed to pay $600,000 toward its development.

In July 2000 the Chicago Park District announced it was planning to lease the land to another developer to build a parking lot on the site. Following public outcry and the formation of the DuSable Park Coalition, the Chicago Park District indefinitely postponed the parking lot plan. Since that time, two public requests for proposals were sent out on the topic of developing the property in 2001 and 2004. Each of those public invitations ended in stalemates. The Art Institute of Chicago tapped Martin Puryear to design a statue of Jean Baptiste Point du Sable to be erected at DuSable Harbor, directly across the river.

CHAPTER TWELVE

DuSable Legacy During the Leadership of Mayor Richard M. Daley in Collaboration with Friends of DuSable

*1989 - 2011 Richard Michael Daley
the 43rd Mayor of Chicago, Illinois*

The DuSable "Legacy" under Chicago's second Richard Daley as the Mayor, in collaboration with Friends of DuSable In 1989 Daley's son, Richard M. Daley, took office as mayor and placed even more emphasis on attracting corporate headquarters, trade, tourism, and the convention business. The influx of new residents to downtown, as well as growing Hispanic and other ethnic communities brought a halt to half a century of population decline, and Chicagoans numbered some 2.8 million by the early 21st century.

Richard Michael Daley (born April 24, 1942) is an American politician, who served as the 43rd Mayor of Chicago, Illinois from 1989 to 2011. Daley was elected mayor in 1989 and was re-elected five times until declining to run for a seventh term. At 22 years, he was the longest-serving Chicago mayor, surpassing the tenure of his father, Richard J. Daley.

As Mayor, Daley took over the Chicago Public Schools, developed tourism, oversaw the construction of Millennium Park, and increased environmental efforts and the rapid development of the city's central business district downtown and adjacent near North, near South and near West sides. He also expanded employee benefits to same-sex partners of city workers, and advocated for gun control. Daley was a national leader in privatization and the lease and sale of public assets to private corporations.

Daley received criticism when family, personal friends and political allies seemed to disproportionately benefit from city contracting. He took office in a city with regular annual budget surpluses and left the city with massive structural deficits. His budgets ran up the largest deficits in Chicago history. Prior to serving as mayor, Daley served in the Illinois Senate and then as the Cook County State's Attorney. He came under criticism for focusing city resources on the development of businesses downtown, the North, Near South, and Near West Sides, while neglecting neighborhoods in the other areas of the city; in particular the needs of low-income residents. According to *Chicago Tribune* columnist Steve Chapman, "Daley lasted 22 years in office partly because he resolved to ingratiate himself with black Chicagoans. He appointed blacks to high positions, stressed his commitment to provide services to all neighborhoods, tore down public housing projects, and pushed reform of the minority-dominated public schools." Daley focused on Chicago as a tourist destination as opposed to a manufacturing base, improved and expanded parkland, added flower planters along many primary streets, and oversaw the creation of Millennium Park on what had previously been an abandoned train yard. He spearheaded the conversion of Navy Pier into a popular tourist destination. The Daley immigration reform and green building initiatives for which he was presented with an Honor Award, from the National Building Museum in 2009, as a "visionary in sustainability." Chicago avoided some of the most severe economic contractions of other Midwest Rust Belt cities such as Detroit and Cleveland. He also supported immigration reform, and green building initiatives.

Chicago River DuSable Harbor

1999: The DuSable Harbor was opened. It is located just outside of the entrance to the Chicago River and Lake Michigan. The entrance to the harbor is accessed through the far east of Randolph Street and Lake Shore Drive along the Lake Shore walk way north of Monroe Harbor. The DuSable Harbor is located in the heart of downtown Chicago at the foot of Randolph Street. It is surrounded by a towering skyline and being the only harbor with ships close to the loop, it is a very popular mooring location. Hemmed in by the Columbia Yacht Club to the South, the Harbor was completed in 2000 by closing in part of Monroe Harbor, thus the entrance is through Monroe Harbor, headed north along the eastern breakwater. There are 420 slips at DuSable Harbor with accommodations for boats 30'-60'+in length

FRIENDS OF DU SABLE
1999 CORE OF INITIATIVES

OBJECTIVE FUTURE INITATIVES:
DuSable Day Commemoration Ordinance

By Haroon Rashid

An ordinance was drafted and submitted to the City of Chicago Commission on Human Relations, the ordinance was awaiting approval by the City Council's Human Relations Committee. The ordinance called for the City of Chicago to incorporate a citywide day of commemoration of Jean Baptiste Pointe DuSable on March 4th, the day Chicago was incorporated. The ordinance, introduced by former Alderman Leonard DeVille, had 19 aldermanic co-sponsors.

Chicago Dinners

During Unity Month this past September, the Human Relations Foundation in conjunction with the Commission on Human Relations and Friends of DuSable hosted two "Chicago Dinners". The Chicago Dinners were implemented a decade prior in order to promote dialogue about issues of race in the Chicago land area. The Unity Month Chicago Dinners, held at the DuSable Museum and the American Indian Center, brought together the African American and Native American communities. Both parties expressed an interest in continuing the dialogue, and presenting the issues discussed to the various cultures in Chicago.

Publication

The development of two Elementary level text books was underway. The "Big Book" would cater to children in Kindergarten through 2nd grade. A second publication would be written for children in the 3rd – 4th and 5th grades. These publications were distributed in museums and school systems throughout Chicago, the State of Illinois, the greater U.S., Haiti, and France.

Speakers Bureau

The Speakers Bureau was formed to continue our outreach to the greater Chicago area. Our primary focus was educational institutions, schools, museums and libraries. In order to maximize our efforts, we would build upon our relationships with Chicago Public Schools, Chicago Catholic Schools, Chicago Public Library, Chicago Historical Society, DuSable Museum, Bronzeville Children's Museum, and the American Indian Center.

Newsletter

Our newsletter, that was launched March 2004, served as a central resource for current information on all the DuSable oriented initiatives. The initiatives: DuSable Park Steering Committee, DuSable Park Coalition, DuSable High School Administration and Alumni Groups, The DuSable League, DuSable Museum, The African Scientific Research Group and more, all of which we had close relationships.

Consuls Generals

The French Consul, Haitian Consul and most recently the South African Consul endorsed the DuSable Initiative. We worked to incorporate it into the DuSable Commemoration celebrations. In the spirit of diversity, we planned to build relationships with all 43 foreign Consulates based in Chicago.

Research

Efforts were in place to secure funding to conduct further research on Jean Baptiste Pointe DuSable's history. We collaborated with the historic DuSable League, the African Scientific Group, the French and Haitian Consulates, the Catholic Church, as well as the Native American community, to trace DuSable's roots and identify his living descendants. DuSable's travels took him to Haiti, France, Canada, Louisiana, Missouri, Wisconsin, Michigan and Illinois. There was a wealth of information at the various Historical Societies, Libraries and Museums in the aforementioned regions

PUBLIC, PRIVATE DUSABLE ACTIVISM, AT THE BEGINNING OF THE MILLENNIUM:

2000 Chicago Commission on Human Relations African Advisory Council on African Affairs members with Mayor Richard M. Daley

Since the untold story of Jean Baptise Pointe DuSable is about the first human relation experience in Chicago, I, on behalf of the Friends of DuSable asked the Commission on Human Relations to help in this effort. The goal was to get the Commission on Human Relations African Advisory Council to make this a council agenda. I was in turned asked by the Chicago Commissioner of Human relations, Mr. Clarence Woods, to seek to become a member of the Commission on Human Relations Advisory Council on African Affairs. I did that and was voted in by the City council as a new member and approved by Mayor Richard M. Daley. I became a member in the year of 2000.

As a council member we pushed for the DuSable recognition agenda to the members and they unanimously agreed to make it a line item. We drafted an ordinance and sent it to the Commission on Human Relations board for a Vote to be approved. The commission then approved and made the draft a Commission on Human Relations ordinance. The ordinance was then sent to City Council for a vote to have a day to honor DuSable.

To our surprise, half of the alderman or council members, mainly African Americans and the Latino Hispanic members, voted for the ordinance; the remainder did not. The bill remained unfinished for six more years before going into effect.

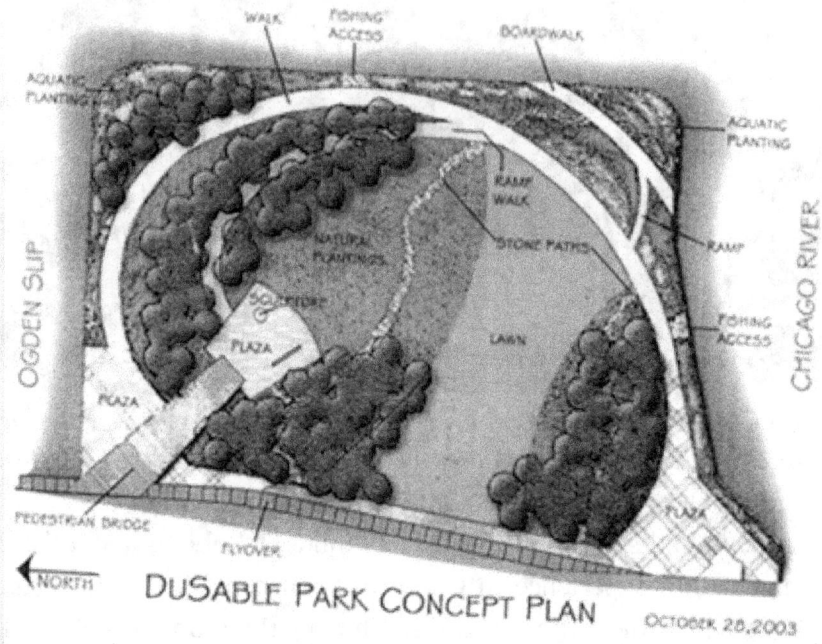

DuSable Park Schematic Conceptual Plan

In July 2000 the Chicago Park District announced it was planning to lease the land to another developer to build a parking lot on the site. Following public outcry and the formation of the DuSable Park Coalition, the Chicago Park District indefinitely postponed the parking lot plan. Since that time two public requests for proposals were sent out on the topic of developing the property in 2001 and 2004. Each of those public invitations ended in stalemates. The Art Institute of Chicago tapped Martin Puryear to design a statue of Jean Baptiste Point du Sable which will be erected at DuSable Harbor, directly across the river. January 25, 2001: Friends of Dusable Collaboration with the Potawatomi Indians Tribal Council

DuSable Legacy During the Leadership of Mayor Richard M. Daley in Collaboration with Friends of DuSable

POKAGON BAND OF POTAWATOMI INDIANS

TRIBAL COUNCIL
P.O. Box 180, 53237 Townhall Rd., Dowagiac, MI 49047

Telephone 616-782-6323 / FAX 616-782-9625

POKAGON BAND OF POTAWATOMI INDIANS
01-25-01-04

WHEREAS: The Pokagon Band of Potawatomi Indians of Indiana and Michigan is a Federally recognized tribe, as reaffirmed under P.L. 103-323, enacted September 21, 1994; and

WHEREAS: The Band and its members are eligible for all services and benefits provided by the Federal Government to Indians, as reaffirmed by P.L. 103-323, because of their status as Federally recognized Indians; and

WHEREAS: The interim governing body of the Band is authorized under P.L. 103-323, to conduct business on behalf of the Band members until such time as the new constitution and by-laws are duly adopted by the Band; and

NOW, THEREFORE BE IT RESOLVED: Tribal Council supports Mayor Richard M. Daley in support of Jean Baptist Pointe Dusable' Day. Dusable was the husband of a Potawatomi woman and the first Non-Native Antrepreneur in the City of Chicago.

CERTIFICATION: We do hereby certify that the foregoing resolution was presented and voted upon with a vote of **10** in favor, and **0** opposed, **0** absent, and **0** abstaining at the Board meeting held on the 25th day of January, 2001.

_____
John Miller
Tribal Council Chairman

_____
Marie Manley
Tribal Council Secretary

DUSABLE FOUNDERS DAY COMMEMORATION ESSAY COMPETITION

DuSable Commemoration Essay Winner Reading Her Essay

In 2001, the Friends of DuSable Commemoration Coalition promoted the writing of the famous, comprehensive "DuSable Essay Competition" for 3rd, 4th & 5th graders enrolled in Chicago area public and Catholic schools. That same year, we merged an ongoing partnership with the Chicago Department of Cultural Affairs, Mayor's Office of Special Events, City of Chicago Commission of Human

Relations: Advisory Council on African Affairs and the Chicago History Museum for the City of Chicago Annual Birthday Celebration/ DuSable Commemoration Day on March 4th. They then decided to celebrate Jean Baptiste Pointe DuSable the Man and his legacy without the ordinance and chose the City of Chicago's official Birthday as the day to do it. The way to do that was decided by having children's essays in Public and Catholic schools on how to celebrate DuSable, having programs in public Libraries and city colleges.

St. Frances De La Sale

The Friends of DuSable Second Annual Commemoration Celebration for Jean Baptiste Pointe DuSable: the DuSable Initiative and ensure that the legacy of Jean Baptiste Pointe DuSable is not forgotten.

We were working with the Mayor's Office of Special Events and a collaboration of organizations of like-vision organizations to continue an annual Jean Baptiste Pointe DuSable commemoration. This year was the first time the Mayor's Office of Special Events and Friends of DuSable partnered to sponsor the City of Chicago's birthday celebration and our event. Looking Back, March Fourth; The City of Chicago recognized this day as a way to honor Jean Baptiste Pointe

DuSable for his accomplishments. This celebration was an overwhelming success.

The Friends of DuSable continued to be a catalyst to bring people and communities together for a day of celebration in the spirit of diversity. With the commitment of supporters, we will all agree to advance toward our dream of making this event a major tourist attraction for the city of Chicago.

Musical Presentations: Aki Antonia, Jazz Pianist

The Friends of DuSable have said that they look forward to the continued support of the DuSable commemoration and are proud of the continuum of the DuSable Essay Contest as part of Chicago Public Schools/City's Chicago Birthday celebration. They encourage all citizens to support this initiative that will enlarge our public-private partnership and have a broader impact among Chicago youth by promoting education and reducing violence. The strong partners committed to supporting the work of Friends of Du Sable are; the city of Chicago Department Cultural Affairs Mayor's Office of Special Events, and Chicago Commission on Human Relation Advisory Council on African Affairs.

The American Indian Center Preformance

The American Indian Center, Bronzeville Children's Museum, Chicago History Museum, the United States Postal Service - the Chicago Office, The DuSable Museum, Chicago Public Library, Jean

Baptiste Pointe DuSable Hand in Hand School in Haiti, the Haitian American Historical Society/Community at large. DuSable Essay winners Friends of DuSable, the Chicago Commission on Human Relations, Chicago History Museum, the Bronzeville Children's Museum, Chicago Public Library, Chicago Public Schools and Chicago Catholic Archdiocese Schools introduced the DuSable Commemoration read, write and comprehension citywide essay competition in the 3rd 4th and 5th grades. The African Advisory Council made public that they are proud to partner in co-producing this stellar event. In these uncertain economic times we again are continually challenged as to how we were to put this event together. Our resolve was to press forward, knowing we not only owed it to our students, but to the entire city as well. It is equally important to stay committed to our focus, which remains single minded "To promote and maintain the legacy of the city's first non-native resident, Jean Baptiste Pointe DuSable.

THE "DU SABLE NOW" RALLY, IN PIONEER COURT

June 22, 2002 was the informase DuSable Now Information Rally in Pioneer Court; at the podium speaking is Dr. Margarett T. Burroughs Founder of the "DuSable Museum."

To bring awareness of this mission, the Friends of DuSable and the Commission on Human Relations held a rally, "DuSable Now", on June 22, 2002. the speakers included: Haroon Rashid, Founder of Friends of DuSable; Former Alderman Leonard Deville (21st Ward); Alderman Burt Natarus (2nd Ward); Commissioner Clarence Wood, Commission on Human Relations; Russell Lewis, Director of Collections and Research: for Chicago Historical Society; Bessie Neal, President, of the DuSable League; Commissioner Mary Dempsey, Chicago Public Library; Dr. Burroughs, Founder, of the DuSable Museum, and Commissioner of Chicago Park District; Antoinette Wright, DuSable Museum; Jesse White, Illinois Secretary of State/Jesse White Tumblers; Bishop Perry, Titular Bishop of Lead, Clausel Rosembert, Consul General, to the Haitian Consul; John Low, Former Attorney for the Potawatomi Indian Tribe; Arnold Romeo, Director of the African Council of the Commission on Human Relations. The Master of Ceremonies was John Davis of CBS 2; the featured performers were the American Indian Center Drum and Dance Group, Chicago Opera Theatre, Ben Sexton as "DuSable", Jesse White Tumblers, and Tamboula Haitian Drum and Dance Group.

A Chicago elementary school choir at the DuSable Now Rally

The event was purposely designed to show a broad multicultural inclusion, from the speakers to the entertainment as a way to convey the reality that the city of Chicago roots was centered in diversity from its Founding Father Jean Baptiste Pointe DuSable. Prior to the Friends of DuSable advocacy, that factor was the one thing that Chicago was not recognizing in its social and cultural history. The schools and, most importantly, the city of Chicago Commission of Human Relations: Advisory Council on African Affairs who I had just become a member of, whom we had a partnership with Friends of DuSable in the event because they wanted to be a part of the leadership in the discussion of Equal Human Rights, as the narrative for The Spirit of DuSable. That was the thinking in recruiting the elementary school that was of Native American and Catholic inclusion.

The Jessie White Tumblers

The Secretary of State Jesse White was a politician from the State of Illinois; he has served as the 37th Secretary of State of Illinois since 1999. History will record him as the longest-serving and the first African American to hold that position. Prior to his position as the Secretary of State, he served as the Cook County Recorder of Deeds for six years and he also served in the Illinois House of

Representatives for thirteen years earlier than that position. It is recoded that in 1959, He founded the Jesse White Tumbling Team to serve as a positive alternative for children residing in the Chicago area. Well over 10,700 young men and women have performed with the team. When we contacted him about our efforts to commemorate DuSable and to get the awareness of DuSable's legacy to the powers to be, Secretary White not only agreed to be a speaker but that he would bring his young Jessie White Tumblers to be a part of the entertainment. We conveyed to him that our goals were to put some visible presence of DuSable in the area of Chicago that DuSable resided in when he was alive: Pioneer Court near the Chicago Tribune building. *In the picture of the Tumblers that is the Secretary Jessie White holding the banner those young Tumblers were diving over.*

WRITTEN BY ANNAN BOODRAM NEW YORK TIMES: JULY 2002: IT'S TIME TO GIVE DU SABLE HIS DUE.

This is an example of the media coverage of the efforts and the events.

That's what supporters of Jean Baptiste Pointe du Sable said Saturday (June 22) as they rallied along the Chicago River near where the Haitian-born immigrant built a home and trading post after he became the first settler to arrive in what would become Chicago. Records do not agree on the precise spelling of his name and it may be found variously as Pointe de Sable, Au Sable, Point Sable, Sabre and Pointe deSaible. Du Sable, who appears to have been a man of good taste and refinement, was a husbandman, a carpenter, a cooper, a miller, and probably a distiller. In Du Sable's home, the first marriage in Chicago was performed, the first election was held, and the first court handed down justice. The religion of the first Chicagoan was Catholic and every contemporary report about Du Sable describes him as a man of substance, who started the story of Chicago, as well as the story of the African American in Chicago. Now the community leaders and history enthusiasts want Du Sable formally honored every March 4 as Chicago's founder's day when the city celebrates its birthday. Du Sable has history on his side; but until recent years at least, apparently lacked the support to leave his name as widely on Chicago's street map.

Just two tiny streets were named for du Sable--Jean Avenue, a two block long street on the West Side, and the oddly named De Saible Street, a private, block-long South Side street. Du Sable, though, did get a high school named in his honor, as well as the DuSable Museum, the nation's first African-American history museum, and Du Sable Harbor. A new park at the mouth of the Chicago River also bears his name, but the site is tainted with toxic waste that needs to be cleaned up before it can be used for recreation. A statue also is being planned in his honor. Du Sable was said to have been born a free Black in St. Marc, Saint Dominique (Haiti). He was the son of a French mariner and an African-born slave mother. His father took him to France to be educated. In about 1773 he made his way up the Mississippi to the Chicago area. He established a trading post on the North Bank of the Chicago River mouth, at what would later become Peoria. His business prospered and became the center of a permanent Chicago settlement. His trading post was the main supply station for White trappers, traders, les coureurs des bois and the natives. Du Sable made many trips to Canada to bring back furs and it was reported that he was very closely associated with the French in New France. His loyalty to the French and the Americans led to his arrest in 1779 by the British, who took him to Fort Mackinac. From 1780 to 1783 or 1784 he managed for his captors a trading post called the Pinery on the St. Clair River in present-day Michigan, after which he returned to the site of Chicago. By 1790 Du Sable's establishment there had become an important link in the region's fur and grain trade. In 1800 he sold out and moved to Missouri, where he continued as a farmer and trader until his death. His 20-year residence on the shores of Lake Michigan had established his title as Father of Chicago. But his admirers say du Sable remains underappreciated. "He is the founder and the reason we exist," said Antoinette Wright, president of the DuSable Museum of African American History. "He really put an imprint on it, but he wasn't recognized for it." For years, du Sable was overshadowed in the history books and in local honors--including streets and statues named and created in his honor- by late-arriving, white settlers whose names are still familiar in the city: Hubbard, Kinzie, and Wentworth. "It was the climate of the day," Wright said. It was only in 1999 that city officials formally recognized du Sable as Chicago's founder--almost 225 years after he and his family arrived at the unsettled, fertile land that would later become the city. Du Sable, who was married to a Potawatomi Indian woman by the name of Kittihawa (Catherine), presided over a frontier settlement that in some ways mirrored the diversity found in the sprawling city that exists today. His settlement welcomed American Indians, as well as Canadians, British, French and Americans. "There was an incredible fusion of cultures and languages," said Russell Lewis, director of collections at the Chicago Historical Society. Despite the existence of slavery in the United States, du Sable was the acknowledged leader of the settlement. "He came here, and he was a leader while others were enslaved," said Haroon Rashid, founder of Friends of du Sable, a community group.

Still, much remains a mystery about du Sable, including when he arrived in the Chicago area, as well as his reasons for selling his property around 1800 and moving away from the region. Even his birthday is unknown, although he is believed to have been born about 1745. "He's an enigma. There's a lot we don't know about him," Lewis said. "But that lack of knowledge, in some ways, adds to his appeal." Historians and history buffs are still trying to fill in the gaps about du Sable, which keeps alive interest in the city's founder. "I meet two or three people a year who have new theories about who he was," Lewis said, calling him "a very powerful symbol for who we are today." Community leaders, though, say there needs to be more official recognition of the role du Sable played. DuSable Museum founder Margaret Burroughs is calling for a 20-story arch to be built in his honor along the Chicago River, or even straddling the river near where du Sable once lived. Lewis thinks, at the very least, Pioneer Court along Michigan Avenue at the north bank of the Chicago River should be renamed in du Sable's honor, particularly because that spot is thought to be near where du Sable settled.

IN SEARCH OF DU SABLE SYMPOSIUM

Photo: Roberta Dupuis-Devlin

JIHAD MUHAMMAD THE AFRICAN SCIENTIFIC RESEARCH INSTITUTE SYMPOSIUM

2002: October 15-17 the African Scientific Research institute held an international symposium on the life and legacy of Jean Baptiste Pointe DuSable in anticipation of an archeological dig. The search for DuSable led to an empty grave at St Borromeo Catholic Cemetery in St Charles, Missouri. 10/27/04

Lisa Stodder

'One of our missions is to develop policy to protect these ancient African burial grounds all over the United States.'

Giving a face to the name Jean-Baptiste Point DuSable, early settler and founder of Chicago, has a plaque on Michigan Avenue, a park, a museum and a school named after him; his likeness appeared on a postage stamp. Nevertheless, much about his life is still unknown. So, begins, "In Search of DuSable," a Bill Kurtis-produced documentary about a project to exhume DuSable's remains. Jihad Muhammad set out to discover what DuSable actually looked like. "We have not found any drawings from that period of time. The only thing we can do is a reconstruction if we found his remains," says Muhammad, president of the African Scientific Research Institute, a nonprofit organization on campus that spearheaded the project. The institute, which specializes in archeological, anthropological and forensic reconstruction, is located in the College of Urban Planning and Public Affairs building. It is affiliated with the Institute for Research on Race and Public Policy.

IN SEARCH OF DUSABLE

Though some dispute the notion, it is usually claimed that DuSable was Haitian, born of African and French parentage. Most scholars agree he was a fur trader who came here roughly a half-century before Chicago was incorporated as a city. In 1779 he established a trading post on the banks of the Chicago River, where the Tribune Tower stands today. By 1800 business was thriving, but for unknown reasons he sold everything and moved to St. Charles, Mo., where he died destitute in 1818. According to records of the Catholic Archdiocese in St. Louis, Mo., DuSable is buried in the cemetery of the St. Charles Borromeo parish. The remains may have been moved and reburied twice, although a 4,000-pound granite slab marks the Missouri spot as DuSable's final resting place. Muhammad received permission in 1999 to exhume the remains. But when the marker was removed, investigators found only pig bones. Ground-penetrating radar failed to detect any disturbance. Muhammad acknowledges his disappointment but says he hasn't given up; he plans to investigate a second site in St. Charles.

Muhammad graduated from the department of bio-communication arts (now biomedical visualization) in medical illustration in 1972 and served as director of the College of Medicine's now-defunct Anatomy Museum for more than 20 years. The institute offers an internship program for students in computer technology and training for biomedical craniofacial art and forensic biological sciences. "We want to serve the underrepresented groups of students in the field of anthropological, archaeological research." Muhammad and others are looking at race, culture and public policy issues in historical and contemporary contexts. His collaborators include Ray Evenhouse, research assistant professor in biomedical and health information science. "We seek out first-generation Africans who came to the Americas as enslaved individuals for the purpose of identifying them," Muhammad says. The institute studied a slave burial ground in St. Louis uncovered during construction for a new police station. The specimens were brought back to UIC, where they were identified as former slaves from the 1740s. Since the skulls are fragile, researchers rely on digital models and a procedure called stereolithography for facial reconstruction. "One of our missions is to develop policy to protect these ancient African burial grounds all over the United States," Muhammad says. "These first generations of Africans are so important to the history of America. We felt that we had to try to do something to help instill pride back into the community."

Muhammad was raised by his grandparents in Sikeston, Mo. His grandfather, a follower of Marcus Garvey and a Muslim from the Sudan, owned a grocery store. His grandmother, also Muslim, was half-Blackfoot Indian. "When you're isolated in small communities, what's an artist? I couldn't define it. But I had an innate ability to draw." He did his first medical illustration in the window of his grandfather's store. "One day I took some crayons and began to draw what I thought was an anatomical image of a man. When we closed the store at night there'd be a light left on, so you could see the image on the glass at night. After that, people began to encourage me." He worked as a mortician's assistant at a local funeral parlor; at 18, he left home to attend Lincoln University. Biology was his major until he fell in with a different crowd. "I dated the daughter of Miles Davis and I began hanging around with musicians. One day they directed me to the art department." The department head took a liking to him and he began studying art. One summer, he was an assistant to muralist Thomas Hart Benton, who was restoring some of his paintings in the Missouri State Capitol.

"His specialty was egg tempera. My job was to crack the eggs."

After graduation, he received his draft notice. When he heard that deferments were possible for students in mortuary school, he enrolled in the Warsham College of Mortuary Science in Chicago, (formerly located in the Medical Center). He worked at Cook County Hospital preparing cadavers for the pathologists. One day he saw a body on the table and was inspired to draw it. "The chief of pathology came in. He put his arms behind his back and walked away. Two days later I got a message he wanted to see me in his office. I thought I was going to get fired. "Instead he asked me, 'Do you know what a medical illustrator is?' He walked me down to the school and told them he wanted to sponsor me to become a medical illustrator in their program."

A devout Muslim, Muhammad attends a mosque on the South Side. He has 13 grown children and seven grandchildren. His life is his work these days. "Generally, I'm in here seven days a week, from 7 a.m. until late at night." The institute recently identified three more sites of interest in Illinois and plans a statewide symposium highlighting the Underground Railroad and slavery. "We see great potential in what we're doing. Science is allowing us to go beyond the 1850s back to the early precolonial period of slavery and the university is allowing us to access this. "I try to put myself into that time and compare it to where I am now. It takes a very different kind of person to be a pioneer. I have great respect for anyone who can go out, not knowing what's beyond.

2003 FRIENDS OF THE PARK DUSABLE PARK COALITION TRIBUTE AWARDS

2003 The DuSable Park Coalition: Friends of the Parks 2003 Advocacy Award February 6, Left to right: Patricia Holloway, Bronzeville Children's Museum, Dr. Serge Pierre-Louis, Association of Haitian Physicians Abroad (presenter), Bessie Neal of the Chicago DuSable League, Bob O'Neill, Grant Park Advisory Council, Haroon Rashid Friends of DuSable, Susan Urbas, Chicago River Rowing & Paddling Center, Eleanor Roemer Friends of the Parks (presenter) and Rosalle Harris, Streeterville Organization for Active Residents.

In 2003 FOD was approached by other groups to help with their efforts to remember DuSable. One group was working to establish a public park that was designated to be called DuSable Park. This was done under the leadership of former Mayor Harold Washington. Friends of DuSable join in the efforts to complete the erection of the park.

HISTORY OF DUSABLE PARK

Timeline:

13,000 years ago – Glacial ice left the Chicago area

3,000 years ago - Chicago River and Lake Michigan shoreline formed

16th Century - Indian tribes, including the Potowatomi, Illinois, Chippewa, Ottawa, Miami, Wea, Ojibwe, Peoria, Sioux, traveled along the southern coast through the mouth of the river, now known as the Chicago River. In their canoes, they may have paddled over the area now known as DuSable Park

17th Century

The Potowatomie introduced Father Marquette and Joliet, French explorers, to the Chicago portage, which connected Lake Michigan to the Desplains River.

18th Century

1700 –1772 Portage closed to non-native traders.

1773 -The three-acre site was underwater when Jean Baptiste Pointe DuSable established a prosperous farm (with grist mill, smokehouse, poultry house, bake house, dairy, barn, and two stables with trading post) at what was then the mouth of the Chicago River – currently the site of Pioneer Court at the Tribune Towers

19th Century

1833 - Founding of Chicago

1857 - The Dock & Canal Company acquired 46 acres for industrial and commercial purposes.

1871 - Chicago fire

1893   Three-acre site filled in by U.S. Army Corps of Engineers to create   Ogden Slip

20th Century

The Dock & Canal Company continued to lease land for industrial and commercial purposes

1963 – Dock & Canal Trust prepares master plan for property, including parkland

1985 - Planned Development, including 3 ½ acre park site

1987 - Dedicated as DuSable Park by Mayor Harold Washington

1998 – Amended Planned Development, including DuSable Park

21st Century

2000 – Formation of DuSable Park Coalition

2001 – Coalition presents DuSable Park Exhibit and Symposium at the Chicago

Architectural Foundation

2002 - Park remains undeveloped, hidden in plain view

2002 – Coalition meets with public officials and Chicago Park District

2002 - Kerr-McGee commences thorium clean-up, under U.S. EPA

U.S. EPA continues to monitor environmental clean-up during park planning process

2002 – Meetings with Artist, Martin Puryear, DuSable Museum, and Chicago

Historical Society

March 19, 2003 – Chicago Park District Sponsors Community meeting to begin public process to design and develop DuSable Park

CITY COLLEGES OF CHICAGO:
GETTING TO KNOW DUSABLE SYMPOSIUM:

City Colleges of Chicago:
Getting To Know DuSable Symposium program

Friends Of DuSable planned and presented a major event with one of thier board members Miss Elsa Tullos, who was also an administrator for Chicago City Colleges. Through her guidance they were able to make plans to work with one of the City Colleges in the downtown districts of Chicago, the Harold Washington College, to create a symposium centered on the legacy of DuSable. Irony of that was that they were well aware that during the life of the former Mayor Harold Washington, who was the person that the new City College was dedicated to and named after, was that he had made attempts during his lifespan in city hall to bring national attention to the legacy of DuSable and it was because of his affiliation, It seemed fitting that the Friends of DuSable/DuSable Coalition, should be advocating building a bridge of relationships with the college in his namesake for that purpose.

PRESS RELEASE AND ADVERTISEMENT

HAROLD WASHINGTON COLLEGE HOSTS SPECIAL EVENT HONORING JEAN BAPTISTE POINTE DUSABLE

Chicago, IL (February 25, 2003) - On Tuesday March 4, 2003 from at 11 a.m. until 2 p.m., Harold Washington College (HWC) will be partnering with Friends of DuSable and the City of Chicago Commission on Human Relations, Advisory Council on African Affairs to host a commemoration on the life and achievements of Jean Baptiste Pointe DuSable. The commemoration is being presented as a symposium entitled "Getting to Know DuSable." HWC is located just blocks away from Pioneer Court, 401 N. Michigan, where DuSable founded the city. Also DuSable Park is just east of HWC, where the Chicago River meets the Lake. "This partnership provides a good opportunity for the HWC students and the community to understand that the important aspects of DuSable's legacy are right at their door step and this is just the beginning of the exploration" said Jada Goodlett, Director of Marketing for Friends of DuSable. Highlights of the event include music and dance presentations by the American Indian Center Drum and Dance Group and Tamboula Haitian Drum & Dance Groups. Special guest panelists will also engage in historical discussions with the attendees. HWC will serve as one of several sites celebrating the life of DuSable, an astute multicultural businessman who was instrumental in the development of Chicago.

CHICAGO PUBLIC LIBRARY, THE DUSABLE HISTORY LECTURE SERIES:

DuSable historian, Dr. Virginia Julian

In 2003, in partnership with the Chicago Public Library, the DuSable History Lecture Series featured notable DuSable historian, Dr. Virginia Julian During March 2003, the Chicago Public Library celebrated the life of Jean Baptiste Pointe DuSable. Throughout the month, the library featured a variety of programs that highlighted the heritage and contributions of the founder of Chicago.

HIGHLIGHTED EVENTS

Dr. Virginia Jullian leter to the Harold Washington Library; Department of Lectures to the Public:

HAROLD WASHINGTON PUBLIC LIBRARY
Chicago

Attention: DEPT OF LECTURES TO THE PUBLIC

Copyright 2003 by Sable City Productions

Page 1 of 3 pages:

    Several weeks ago, I received an invitation from the Library, relevant to a collaboration with the FRIENDS OF DU SABLE, a proposal to make a presentation on Jean Baptiste Point Du Sable early in 2004, as part of the plan of the HAROLD WASHINGTON LIBRARY to honor the Founder of Chicago.

This is to confirm that I shall be pleased to participate, provided FRIENDS OF DU SABLE are announced as PRESENTERS of a program entitled such as "THE MANY FACES OF DU SABLE" -- at which a panel of historians may each submit a fully documented theory of one of the popularly held origins of Du Sable, from a paper to be submitted a month prior to the concerted presentation at the Library, so that a resolution of consensus may be reached professionally, concerning the most plausible origin of Du Sable, in an effort to advance truth in history concerning the man who is recognized today as the Founder of Chicago.

Likewise, a second presentation might deal with his name, and the spelling of his name, as reported in the parish record books, by his contemporaries, and by the early historians, again, an effort to advance truth in history -- .

And a third presentation, dealing with the exciting published documents, long neglected, concerning the decisive impact of Du Sable's role in the Old Northwest through his command of Chicago -- the strategic connection between the Atlantic and the Gulf of Mexico, controlling trade and politics across this heartland of the world -- over the Mississippi River -- and western expansion over the Missouri River, and overland to the mouth of the Columbis River and the Pacific -- culminating in what Jefferson characterized as the rise of the "Empire of Liberty."

    I present my capability of directing such a panel, through my investigative efforts of the impact of DuSable at Chicago, presented in my MEd Thesis on the documents of DuSable produced at Northeastern Illinois U. at Chicago and Center for Inner City Studies, to qualify for my appointment as "Teacher of the Gifted in Inner City Schools", 1972 --
through my participation earlier, as a member of the CHICAGO EDUCATORS DU SABLE HERITAGE COMMITTEE which planned the marking of Du Sable's gravesite at St. Charles, Missouri, as a CELEBRATION EVENT OF THE OFFICIAL STATE OF ILLINOIS SESQICENTENNIAL CELEBRATION, in an impressive, HIGH MASS CEREMONIAL PROCESSIONAL

Copyright 2003 By Sable City Productions

from the St. Borromeo Cathlic Church to the St. Borromeo Cemetery, as a handsome, engraved stone was placed at DuSable's gravesite, and statesmen and citizens from the surrounding states stood alongside, photographed and shown at Chicago by Channel 7 TV, 1968-- (It was my pleasure to invite the Chicago Du Sable League to participate in that Sesquicentennial event, as community proponent for Chicago, under the direction of Alice J. Neal, who had founded the League in 1966, and had assisted Annie B. Oliver of Quinn Chapel, in the founding of the National Des Saible Memorial Society, in 1928, which had successfully placed a reproduction of the Du Sable home on the lakefront, IN THE CHICAGO CENTURY OF PROGRESS WORLDS FAIR, 1933, alongside the reproduction of Fort Dearborn built on the south side of the Chicago River in 1803, opposite the Du Sable establishment, cited as the most complete between Detroit -- one historian said Montreal -- and St. Louis, officially inventoried in 1800, as shown in records transferred from the Burton Historical Collection, transcribed from the French, and sent to Cook County Recorder, as noted by the Chicago Historical Society, in 1954, Document #16,000,000, and renumbered since that time --

Mrs. Neal was active in the movement to rename the new Wendell Phillips High School to honor Du Sable, and she was honored at the annual meeting of the Illinois State Historical Society at Belleville, in 1969, for her over forty years work in bringing history to her people)

and, through my work as a committee member of MAYOR RICHARD J. DALEY'S OFFICIAL CITYWIDE CHICAGO DU SABLE COMMITTEE TO SELECT THE PROPER MONUMENT FOR DU SABLE, 1969-1973,

when Mrs. Neal, also a member of the Mayor's Committee, won group consensus for a suggestion that the BURROUGHS' MUSEUM, TO BE PLACED IN WASHINGTON PARK AS THE DU SABLE MUSEUM, would be the city's monument to Du Sable, as other alternatives were also suggested including the marking of Du Sable's founding settlement along the north bank of the Chicago River from the official inventory of his realty holdings in 1800, Whistler's Blueprint of Fort Dearborn, and extant drawings by contemporaries, following the rejection of the CITYWIDE COMMITTEE RESOLUTION THAT A STATUE, A MUSEUM AND BANDSHELL ERECTED IN GRANT PARK IN HIS HONOR was the proper monument for Du Sable, citing a legal statute won by Montgomery Ward, prohibiting construction in Grant Park --

through my on-going research, when I won the NATIONAL HISTORIC LANDMARK DESIGNATION PLAQUE CURRENTLY INSTALLED ON PIONEER COURT AT 401 N. MICHIGAN AVENUE, with the inscription: "JEAN BAPTISTE POINT DU SABLE HOMESITE ...A NATIONAL HISTORIC LANDMARK...THIS SITE POSSESSES NATIONAL SIGNIFICANCE IN COMMEMORATING THE HISTORY OF THE UNITED STATES OF AMERICA" authorized by the Chicago DuSable League and southside Chicago Businesmen and in conjunction with the African-American Heritage Committee designated to select historic sites for designation across the nation, which was installed on the Plaza at that site, by officials of the Tribune and Equitable, which I photographed, as members of the League participated as invited guests, 1976-1977 --

Page 3   Copyright   2003   By Sable City Productions

and when, as historian for the League, after being honored at a dinner in the lower level of the Equitable Building, cited as "Du Sable's Dining Room" -- for my success in researching the role of Du Sable, -- with Reverend Reddick of PUSH, honored guest, 1972 -- I delivered lectures on Du Sable for some fifteen years, at the newly opened Du Sable Museum, at the League's annual commemorative programs, where printouts of my research were passed out, open free to the public --
and, as I prepared research presentations for speaking to classes at the Center for Inner City Studies -- and more recently, at the forums presented by FRIENDS OF THE PARKS and FRIENDS OF DU SABLE at the Architectural Center and Harold Washington College, (as the public movement for the development of the Du Sable Park site, heritage of Mayor Washington at the mouth of the Chicago River opposite Navy Pier, escalated) --
and, when I presented Mayor Washington's Proclamation of January 1, 1987, as DU SABLE DAY IN CHICAGO, on the Plaza, and the staff of the DU SABLE MUSEUM PLACED A WREATH OF FLOWERS ON THE PLAQUE, reviving an old tradition of the Memorial Society which placed a wreath on an old plaque citing 401 N. Michigan as the site of the "Kinzie Mansion, Home of Du Sable and Le Mai" -- who was described as a "Negre" living at Chicago in 1799, in a Catholic Parish record of the baptism of Du Sable's granddaughter at St. Louis --
when my documents on Du Sable, supported by eminent historians, moved the Chicago Historical Society to reprint postal cards describing the early founding settlement in honor of Kinzie, to the honor of Du Sable --
and as my research on the documents of Du Sable intensified, for articles published in the CONGRESSIONAL RECORD AT WASHINGTON -- in HISTORIC CITY CHICAGO, the Mayor's office -- and in THE ILLINOIS COMMUNICATOR at Springfield --
and in community media, THE CHICAGO READER, "WILL SOMEONE PLEASE STAND UP FOR THE REAL JEAN BAPTISTE POINT DU SABLE?" -- 'N DIGO, "MILLENIUM MAN"-- THE CHCAGO POST -- and GARY ICEBERG --
and in the program for the awards dinner of the community project for the construction of the old, historic Du Sable establishment on the lakefront south of McCormick Place, supported by Mayor Washington, THE CHECAGOU-DU SABLE-FT.DEARBORN PROJECT, 1986 --
my appointment to ILLINOIS STATE HISTORICAL SOCIETY LIBRARY COMMITTEE, under Ralph G. Newman --
and, as I prepared papers which I delivered at historical conferences, relevant to the historical period of Du Sable, held at LAVAL U. QUEBEC; UNIVERSITY COLLEGE, DUBLIN, IRELAND; GEORGE ROGERS CLARK NATIONAL MEMORIAL, VINCENNES,INDIANA; ILLINOIS STATE HISTORICAL SOCIETY, SPRINGFIELD; THE AFRICAN SCIENTIFIC RESEARCH INSTITUTE DU SABLE GRAVE SITE PROJECT SYMPOSIUM, FIELD MUSEUM, CHICAGO; and MES at COLUMBUS, OHIO -- only declining the invitation to present in southern France, spring 2003, due to current war politics --
****
V.W.JULIEN -- Copies: WTTW, CHICAGO DU SABLE LEAGUE, FRIENDS OF DU SABLE, FRIENDS OF DUSABLE PARK

DuSable Legacy During the Leadership of Mayor Richard M. Daley in Collaboration with Friends of DuSable

Dr, Virginia Jullian opening Lecture at the Harold Washington Library

BLACK PRINCE OF CHICAGO, FOUNDING FATHER
Jean Baptiste Point Du Sable

Copyright: August 27, 2004
by Virginia W. Julien

TODAY -- AS THE CHICAGO DU SABLE LEAGUE COMMEMORATES THE 204th ANNIVERSARY OF THE DEATH AND BURIAL OF JEAN BAPTISTE POINT DU SABLE, FOUNDER OF CHICAGO AND FOUNDING FATHER OF OUR COUNTRY, THE UNITED STATES OF AMERICA -- AUGUST 28-29,1800 -- AT ST. CHARLES, IN THE ST. BORROMEO CEMETERY, as recorded in the Parish record book, where his home on Second Street, became the residence of the first Governor of Missouri, and street signs, today, direct visitors to the lovely DU SABLE PARK, we offer --

A profile of Jean Baptiste Point Du Sable, Founder of Chicago, presenting for the first time, that the historical record supports in dramatic fashion, his role as decisive, AS A PRE-EMINENT FOUNDING FATHER OF HIS COUNTRY, THE UNITED STATES OF AMERICA, CARRYING GREAT IMPACT ON THE RISE OF OUR COUNTRY AS A RADICAL, DEMOCRATIC REPUBLIC.
****
Historians have long speculated about what forces brought this remarkable empire of liberty, this radical, unprecedented, democratic republic, the United States of America, into existence at a time when the very word "democracy" was reviled, hated and feared -- and what powerful forces have promoted its dramatic survival throughout world-wide political chaos, for more than two hundred years. Intensive study of the extant historical record, and the writings of early historians of the midwest, down to the present day, CULMINATING IN THE STRIKING RECORDS OF THE PUBLISHED CORRESPONDENCE OF LIEUT. GOVERNOR JOHN GRAVES SIMCOE, WITH ALLIED DOCUMENTS RELATING TO HIS ADMINISTRATION OF THE GOVERNMENT OF UPPER CANADA DURING THE CRITICAL PERIOD OF THE 1790S WHEN THE UNITED STATES COULD NOT ESTABLISH CONTROL OF THE HEARTLAND NORTH OF THE OHIO RIVER, CEDED IN THE TREATY OF 1783, AND THE BRITISH MADE DETERMINED EFFORT TO CONTROL CHICAGO AND BRING NORTH AMERICA BACK UNDER THE DOMINANCE OF THE BRITISH EMPIRE -- RECORDS COLLECTED AND EDITED BY BRIGADIER GENERAL E.A. CRUIKSHANK FOR THE ONTARIO HISTORICAL SOCIETY, FIVE VOLUMES, PUBLISHED IN 1923,--
IN WHICH LT GOV SIMCOE, OF THE HIGH BRITISH MILITARY COMMAND, WHO HAD BEEN CAPTURED WITH CORNWALLIS AT YORKTOWN BY GEN GEO WASHINGTON AND LAYFAYETTE, 1781, WAS TRANSFERRED TO UPPER CANADA IN 1791, AFTER THE TREATY OF 1783, HAD CEDED THIS OLD NORTHWEST, THE LAND LYING BETWEEN THE GREAT LAKES AND THE OHIO RIVER, BOUNDED ON THE WEST BY THE MISSISSIPPI, TO THE NEW AMERICAN REBEL GOVERNMENT -- AND TWO AMERICAN ARMIES, ATTEMPTING TO ESTABLISH AMERICAN CONTROL NORTH OF THE OHIO WERE DEFEATED IN 1790, AND 1791, IN THE MOST HORRENDOUS INDIAN WARFARE IN HISTORY -- BY THE FORMIDABLE NORTHERN

2) INDIAN CONFEDERACY,-- A REMARKABLE, RADICAL, DEMOCRATIC REPUBLIC! -- RED, BLACK AND WHITE -- INCLUDING WILLIAM WELLS, OF WELL STREET, CHICAGO, MARRIED TO THE DAUGHTER OF THE LEADER OF THE MIAMI INDIANS AGAINST THE AMERICANS -- CHIEF LITTLE TURTLE -- AT THE TIME DU SABLE, NOT REPORTED IN THAT CONFLICT -- CONTROLLED CHICAGO THROUGHOUT THE CRITICAL PERIOD, UNTIL --

THE BLACK CHIEF AT CHICAGO, AS POINT SABLE WAS KNOWN, IDENTIFIED AS POINT DU SABLE BY THE HISTORIAN PALMER -- WAS CHARGED BY SIMCOE, LT. GOV. OF UPPER CANADA, ANXIOUS TO SEND THE KING'S MEN THRU CHICAGO -- THAT DU SABLE HAD WEANED THE INDIANS FROM THE BRITISH INTEREST --

THAT DU SABLE HAD MOREOVER, BROKEN APART THE INDIAN HOSTIITY AGAINST THE AMERICANS AND THAT DU SABLE HAD THUS PERMITTED GENERAL WAYNE TO ADVANCE AND IN BATTLE WITH THE FEW REMAINING INDIANS AT FALLEN TIMBERS, WHERE WAYNE CONTRARY TO HIS REPORT, DID NOT SEE 50 INDIANS, ACCORDING TO A CREDITABLE BRITISH OBSERVER,

ENABLING WAYNE, WHEN BLUE JACKET, WHO HAD CHECKED OUT CHICAGO AT THE DIRECTIVE OF SIMCOE, REPORTED WITH A SMILE, HE WQAS GOING TO LIVE AT CHICAGO, BROUGHT IN THE FEW REMAINING RECALCITRANT CHIEFS TO GREENVILLE, 1795, WHERE WAYNE WON CESSION OF SIX MILES SQUARE AT THE MOUTH OF THE CHICAGO RIVER FOR THE AMERICAN

Fort Dearborn, marking the ascendance of the United States in the rising Empire of Liberty -- through Point Sable's incredible influence with the northern Indians, which recent academic investigation of the bonding of Africans and Indians on the frontier has cited Du Sable as the "Supreme reflection of the possibilities" OF THAT BONDING WHEN HE SETTLED AT CHICAGO WITH HIS POTAWATOMI WIFE AND WAS LATER CHARGED WITH INVOVLEMENT WITH THE AMERICAN REBELS WHEN CLARK INVADED ILLNOIS WITH THE DECLARATION OF INDPEENDANCE THAT ALL MEN ARE CREATED EQUAL AND WON PARTNERSHIP WITH THE NORTHERN INDIAN TRIRACIAL REPUBLIC, IN 1778 --

AN INFLUENCE DATING BACK TO 1763, WHEN HE WAS REPORTED EXHORTING SETTLERS AND INDIANS TO RESIST THE ANNOUNCED INCURSION OF THE BRITISH, VICTORIOUS OVER THE FRENCH AT QUEBEC, 1759 --

IN THE UPRISING OF PONTIAC'S WAR, CITED BY GLADWYN AT DETROIT, AS LED ON BY BLACK AND WHITE ALIKE -- WHICH MAY BE INTERPRETED QAS THE OPENING PHASE OF THE AMERICAN REVOLUTION --

Together with the astonishing Declaration of Independence citing that all men are created equal -- and the constitution to secure the rights of man against the rights of power -- THE DYNAMIC NORTHWEST ORDINANCE OF 1787 -- ASTONISHING THE WORLD WITH ITS FIRST NATIONAL EDICT OF EMANCIPATION -- JUST FOR THE NORTH -- TO PLEASE DU SABLE, WHO IS CITED AS COMMITTED TO THE FREEDOM OF HIS PEOPLE -- CREATING ILLINOIS AS A TERRITIORY GUARANTEED WITH STATEHOOD AND EQUAL RIGHTS AND POWERS TO EACH AND EVERY STATE IN THE UNION -- ILLINOIS WAS NEVER A COLONY -- AND THE STUNNING TREATY WITH THE INDIANS AT VINCENNES, 1792, ENABLING DU SABLE TO ACT WHEN THE U.S. GUARANTEED THE SOVEREIGNTY OF THE INDIANS ON THE LAND --

INCOMING INDENTURED EUROPEANS TO SUPPLY LABOR FOR RISING INDUSTRY SECURED THE AMERIAN DREAM, HUMAN RIGHTS, EDUCATION, HAPPINESS OF MANKIND WHEN THEY STOPPED MOVE TO OVERTHROW EMANCIPATION WITH:"NO! YOU RE-ENSLAVE THE AFRICANS -- AND WE'LL BE NEXT!!!! -----THOSE DOCUMENTS CREATED BY THE GENIUS OF THE FOUNDING FATHERS WHO SAW WHAT THEY HAD TO DO AND DID IT PRESERVE THE AMERICAN DREAM ---

2004: Friends of DuSable Founder DuSable Founder Commemoration Day

The city of Chicago In The Spirit of Du Sable

Letter of Support from the South African Counsulate General

SOUTH AFRICAN CONSULATE GENERAL
SUID-AFRIKAANSE KONSULAAT-GENERAAL
CHICAGO

Consulate General supports the Friends of Du Sable with regard to proposed visit of Archbishop Tutu.

The South African Consulate General in Chicago supports the efforts of the Friend's of Du Sable to invite Archbishop Desmond Tutu to Chicago to partake in the celebration around the Birthday of Chicago in March 2005.

The Friend's of Du Sable seeks to bring light to the life and numerous contribution of Jean Baptiste Pointe Du Sable, Chicago's undersung modern day founder. Chicago's first non-native settler is of African descent, whose life reconciled numerous divergent cultures and peoples.

The Friends of Du Sable has at the core of its mission the goal of sharing with the rest of Chicago and the world the unique qualities of our founder.

The spirit of Jean Baptiste Pointe Du Sable harkens to a way of life that truly reconciles the spirit and cultural diversity of all Chicagoans.

The Friends of Du Sable indicated their appreciation that Archbishop Tutu can inspire Chicago and convey the deeper meaning of Du Sable's life. We therefore support the efforts to have the Archbishop come to inspire Chicago on its hundred and sixty ninth birthday.

Mr. Machiel R. van Niekerk
Consul

08/18/2004

200 SOUTH MICHIGAN AVENUE, SUITE 600, CHICAGO, IL 60604
TEL: (312) 939-7929   FAX: (312) 939-2588 - ADMIN   FAX: (312) 939-0344 - LIAISON
EMAIL: sacongenchicago@worldnet.att.net

DuSable Legacy During the Leadership of Mayor Richard M. Daley in Collaboration with Friends of DuSable

CELEBRATING DUSABLE'S LEGACY ON CHICAGO's 167TH BIRTHDAY
MARCH 4, 2004

- Program -

Welcome Address: Russell Lewis, Chicago Historical Society

Ben Sexton as "DuSable"
Excerpt from "The Great Nitty Gritty" by Oscar Brown, Jr.

American Indian Center Drum and Dance Group

Essay Contest Winners

Voices of Praise Children's Choir
St. John DeLaSalle
Academy of Fine Arts

Keynote Address: Lerone Bennett, Jr.

In the Spirit of DuSable Award - The Pioneers
Dr. Margaret Burroughs,
The DuSable Museum of African American History
Virginia Julien, The DuSable League
Bessie Neal, The DuSable League

Tamboula Haitian Drum and Dance Group
Rafo International Combo De Chicago

Closing Remarks: Haroon Rashid – Founder and President
Friends of DuSable

DuSable Legacy During the Leadership of Mayor Richard M. Daley in Collaboration with Friends of DuSable

Chicago Public Library
DuSable Day Branch Programs

Brainerd Branch
1350 West 89th Street
Songwriting Contest
Starts Monday, March 1st - Ends Monday, April 5th
The Brainerd Branch is looking for songwriters to participate in their songwriting contest to honor Chicago's founder, Jean Baptiste Pointe DuSable.

Legler Branch
115 South Pulaski
Thursday, March 4th, 3:30 – 5 p.m.
Finding Library Resources about DuSable
The Legler Branch staff will take you on a tour of their library's resources about DuSable.

Northtown Library
6435 North California
March 3rd at 7 p.m.
French Cooking Demonstration, Encore!
In celebration of Jean Baptiste Pointe DuSable's French heritage, Chef Andrew Comens demonstrated the art of making mini quiches.

Woodson Regional Library
9525 South Halsted
March 4th at 7 p.m
In Search of DuSable
Uncovering the mystery of Jean Baptiste Pointe DuSable, Founder of Chicago, the film, "In Search of DuSable" will be shown in the Auditorium on the 1st floor.

> "I don't just share recipes. I write about traditions, history, cultures – stuff that's cool, even if you don't cook."
>
> Donna Pierce, Test Kitchen Director

OUR PASSION. YOUR PAPER.

Chicago Tribune

DuSable Legacy During the Leadership of Mayor Richard M. Daley in Collaboration with Friends of DuSable

DuSable Commemoration 2004

Master Class and Teachers Series
Chicago City Colleges

A panel of experts on Chicago history hosts the master class. The aim of this series is to generate discussions to introduce Jean Baptiste Pointe DuSable into the curriculum of the City's schools on every level.

Essay Competition
Chicago Public Schools and Catholic Schools

The Chicago Public and Catholic elementary schools, in conjunction with the Friends of DuSable and the Chicago Historical Society, hosted an essay competition as a part of the citywide DuSable Commemoration. The competition is open to all third and fifth grade public school students and fourth grade Catholic school students.
Essay theme: *"How to Celebrate DuSable."*

Contest winners participated in the City's Birthday Party hosted by The Mayor's Office of Special Events.
Winning essays are comprised in book commemorating the celebration.

Chicago Public Library

On Tuesday, March 2nd, the Harold Washington Library partnered with The Friends of DuSable and The DuSable League to host an evening of enlightenment and education as they explored the inimitable historical archives of the DuSable League.

For more information visit *www.dusableday.org*

The American Health & Beauty Aids Institute

Salutes

The Friends of DuSable in Your 2nd Annual

Commemoration of Jean Baptiste Pointe DuSable

Compliments of:
Luster Products, Inc.
Dr. Earles, LLC
Summit Laboratories

DuSable Legacy During the Leadership of Mayor Richard M. Daley in Collaboration with Friends of DuSable

Let's Keep Working Together for the Future DuSable Park and DuSable Founder's Trail

CHICAGO PUBLIC RADIO 91.5 FM

JOIN THE
FRIENDS OF DUSABLE
ON CHICAGO PUBLIC RADIO
IN MARCH AS WE CONTINUE
TO CELEBRATE THE LEGACY OF
JEAN BAPTISTE POINTE DUSABLE

2004 City of Chicago Birthday celebration & DuSable Essay WINNERS In this picture standing along with the DuSable essay winners: In the rear against the wall was CEO President of the Chicago History Museum Larry Johnson, on the stage was an Assistant to the Mayor, below the stage to the far right was Executive Director of the American Indian Center Joseph Podlasek, to his left is Founder and Executive Director of the Bronzeville Museum Peggy Montes, and in the front, was Mayor Richard M. Daley.

On March 4, 2004 during the City of Chicago Birthday celebration event that was held at the Chicago History Museum, the winners of the DuSable Commemoration Essay Competition the contestants were honored. The winners are 3rd 4th & 5th grade students from Chicago Public & Catholic Schools. Come and witness the students that will be selected to read their essays, along with their teachers, parents and guests in a private DuSable Commemoration display room as they are all recognized and receive awards for their accomplishments. There will be refreshments and photo ops for them and guests.

DuSable Legacy During the Leadership of Mayor Richard M. Daley in Collaboration with Friends of DuSable

2005 DUSABLE COMMEMORATION AND AWARD CEROMONY:

FEATUREING FIRST LADY MICHELLE OBAMA

Mayor Richard M. Daley Assistant Erika Summers on the right

The Mayors Office cosponserd the public welcoming along with Johnson Publishing Company Ebony Magazine, for the meet and greet entry at the DuSable Commemoration Welcome and information Station.

Keynote Speaker. Featuring First Lady Michelle Obama

On March 3rd 2005 Mrs. Michelle Obama, wife of newly elected Senator Barrack Obama. Mistress and Master of ceremonies were Ms. Allison Payne (WGN TV News) and Mr. Don Lemon (NBC TV News). There were artistic interpretations from all aspects of DuSable's background; including Haitian, French, Catholic, and Native American, and more.

Ms. Allison Payne (WGN TV News) and Mr. Don Lemon (NBC TV News)

In addition to the event series at the Chicago Cultural Society, the March 3rd 2005 citywide event series expanded from the core programs established in the first year. The City of Chicago shared our vision of a month long effort to celebrate diversity throughout the city of Chicago. Moving forward our programs targeted to bridge the many ethnic and cultural communities and institutions, not only throughout the week, but also for the entire month. The Mayor's Office of Special events joined with the Friends of DuSable, the Chicago Historical Society, Chicago Department of Cultural Affairs and all of the other 2005 co-sponsors to present a full week of activities throughout Chicago.

First Lady Michelle Obama, then the President of the University of Chicago Hospital Community Relations, and Lerone Bennett Jr.

In the Spirit of DuSable Awards: Recipients

This partnership was a promise to enhance the citywide recognition of DuSable and would help to forge new relationships throughout the city. The week began with a variety of activities throughout the city, including the Chicago Historical Society, Bronzeville Children's Museum, DuSable Museum and the American Indian Center, such as: Arts & Crafts Workshops, Lectures, and Films. Winners from the DuSable Essay Competition for grade school students from the Chicago Public Schools and Chicago's Catholic Schools 3rd 4th and 5th grade, which was co-sponsored by the Friends of DuSable and the Commission on Human Relation African Advisory Council, some of the winners read their winning essays as well as Cutting the Celebratory Cake with Mayor Richard M. Daley.

Dr. Lonnie Bunch President of the Chicago Historical Society

The week closed at the Chicago Historical Society with a special reception and performance entitled "Celebrating DuSable's Legacy" presented by the Friends of DuSable, also the second "Spirit of DuSable" awards ceremony, featuring keynote speaker: Friends of DuSable: March 4, 2005 DuSable Founders Day Commemoration & Award Ceremony and the City of Chicago's 168th. Birthday celebration at the Chicago History Museum keynote speaker, First Lady Michelle Obama, then President of Community Relations at The University of Chicago. Award recipient of the DuSable Leadership award was Chicago Mayor Richard M. Daley.

DUSABLE FOUNDERS WAY RIVER ESPLANADE ENACTMENT:

Alderman Burton Natarus, Haroon Rashid, Dr. Serge Pierre-Louis and Erma Tranter

2005: 42 Ward Alderman Burton Natarus and the DuSable Park Coalition: introduced and passed an ordinance designating the river esplanade between Pioneer Court and Michigan Ave. on the west end, to the proposed DuSable Park location on the east, as DuSable Founders Way.

The DuSable Park Coalition was represented by Haroon Rashid President and Founder of Friends of DuSable, Dr. Serge Pierre-Louis, President of the DuSable Heritage Association and Erma Tranter President of the Friends of the Park.

It was done in conjunction with the Mayor's Office of Special Events as the City of Chicago celebrates its annual birthday March 4th each year.

In time FOD established a Who's who list of supporters, of which without their support, none of the accomplishments would have been possible; Dr. Margaret Burroughs, Founder of the DuSable Museum, the City of Chicago Commission on Human Relations; City of Chicago Mayors Office of Special Events, the Chicago Historical Society, the United Way Metro Chicago, South African Consulate Chicago, Consulate General of Haiti, Consulate General of France, McCormick Tribune Foundation, Chicago Public Radio, Former Alderman Leonard DeVille, Alderman Burton Natarus, DuSable League, DuSable Museum, Friends of the Park, City Colleges of Chicago, Chicago Public Schools, Chicago Catholic Schools, Catholic Archdiocese of Chicago, Imam W. D. Mohammed - W.D. Mohammed Ministry, Chicago Public Library, Pokagon Band of Potowatomi Indians, Bronzeville Children's Museum, Chicago Tribune Newspaper, Chicago Defender Newspaper, American Indian Center, McGrath Lexus, Chicago Sheraton Hotel, Jessie L. Jackson Jr., U.S. Congress (dist. 2), State Senator Kwame Raoul 13 (dist.), Jessie White Secretary of State , Northwestern University Kellogg Law, Chicago Cultural Affairs Department, American Health & Beauty Aids Institute, Chicago From The Lake, Ltd., Sam's Wine & Liquor, Chicago Architectural and Historical Cruise, The University of Chicago Hospitals, Melanie Span Cooper - President WVON radio, Linda Rice Johnson - CEO Johnson Publishing Company, the Greater North Michigan Avenue Association, The Chicago Loop Alliances.

Honorary DuSable Founders Way Sign

2006: Former 42 Ward Alderman Burton Natarus and the DuSable Park Coalition: introduced and passed an ordinance designating the river esplanade between Pioneer Court and Michigan Ave. on the west end, to the proposed DuSable Park location on the east, as DuSable Founders Way.

Honorary DuSable Founders Way Chicago Riverwalk

When developers proposed a shopping center at the River East Center near the Chicago River, the city approved the project on the condition that the developers would leave an area along the Chicago River between DuSable Park and Pioneer Court on Michigan Avenue to the Chicago Park District.

In 1988 the Park District turned the area into a promenade, known as the River Esplanade, later renamed to DuSable Founder's Way, after Jean Baptiste Pointe du Sable who is known as the Founder of Chicago.

JEAN BAPTISTE POINTE DUSABLE FOUNDER COMMEMORATION ORDINANCE:

Mayor Richard M. Daley & the City of Chicago Commission of Human Relations, Advisory Council on African Affairs

2006: Friends of DuSable, the City of Chicago Commission of Human Relations, the Advisory Council on African Affairs and the Chicago City Council introduced, voted on and passed the Jean Baptiste Pointe DuSable Founder Commemoration Ordinance.

PROPOSAL

In acknowledging and recognizing the rich history of Chicago and the great accomplishments of Chicago's first citizen and founder, we are proposing that the City of Chicago introduce an ordinance that names March 4th as a day of celebration for Jean Baptiste Pointe DuSable Day. During the week of March 4th, a series of events will be hosted throughout the City of Chicago to honor DuSable and celebrate its beginning. The celebration series will be sponsored by Harold Washington College, the Chicago Historical Society, Chicago Public Schools, and various corporations. The implementation of a Jean

Baptiste Pointe DuSable Day will not only serve as a day to honor and recognize DuSable for his accomplishments, it will serve as a catalyst to bring the people and communities of Chicago together for a day of unified commemoration,

DuSable's House: Wood cabin 22 feet by 40 feet, 2 Barns, Horse Mill, 1 Bake House, 1 Poultry House, 1 Workshop, 1 Dairy, 1 Smokehouse, 2 Mules, 30 Cattle, 2 Calves, 28 Hogs, 44 Hens and Equipment: 8 sickles, 7 scythes, carts, saws, copper kettles, axes and other house tools.

Our proposal was ambitious yet comprehensive, which is why we called on all public and private agencies in Chicago to play a role. The DuSable Day project was an on-going collaborative effort with a 5-year projection plan in place to complete its goals which lead to state and national recognition.

DUSABLE FOUNDEERS DAY COMMEMORATION CITY ORDINACE:

ORDINANCE

WHEREAS, The City of Chicago is justifiably proud of its rich cultural and ethnic heritage; its rapid ascent from frontier trading post to major commercial, cultural and education center; and its place among the world's great cities; and

WHEREAS, Many aspects of Chicago's greatness were foreshadowed by the contributions of Jean Baptiste Pointe Du Sable; and

WHEREAS, Born a free black man in St. Marc, Haiti, in about 1745, Jean Baptiste Pointe Du Sable was the son of an African slave and a French mariner, and received his education in France; and

WHEREAS, After his schooling he returned to Haiti until about 1765, when he migrated to St. Louis, where he operated a fur trading post and became well known for his honesty and integrity in business dealings, including in transactions with the native peoples; and

WHEREAS, Du Sable was so trusted by the native peoples that in 1769 he was able to negotiate a peace treaty among the Illinois, Miami, Potawatomi and Ottawa nations; and

WHEREAS, Du Sable married Kiatihawa (called "Catherine"), a Potawatomi woman, in a native ceremony. They renewed their marital vows in a Catholic ceremony, the first recorded marriage in the outpost settlement of Chicago, in about 1788; and

WHEREAS, Du Sable exemplified human relations in early Chicago, as a man of African and French heritage dealing peaceably and honorably with the Potawatomi on the banks of the Chicago River; and

WHEREAS, Du Sable became the first permanent, non-native settler of Chicago when he built a cabin on the north bank of the Chicago River, at the current site of the Tribune Tower; and

WHEREAS, Du Sable became Chicago's first real estate developer and builder in about 1773, when he established a settlement for himself, his newly-arrived wife and about 100 other Potawatomi; built a trading post; established a dairy farm; and planted fruit orchards and fields of corn, hay and alfalfa; and

WHEREAS, Shortly after establishing the settlement, Du Sable established Chicago's character as a haven to immigrants, when 100 French Canadians arrived seeking refuge from the British and Spanish armies; and

WHEREAS, The Chicago settlement founded by Jean Baptiste Pointe Du Sable was characterized by racial, ethnic and cultural harmony and mutual respect among its divers inhabitants; and

WHEREAS, Du Sable's settlement was a premonition of Chicago's commercial success, as it expanded under his leadership to include barns, a bake house, a smoke house, a grist mill, stables, a workshop and other business concerns, all of which made the trading post thrive; and

WHEREAS, Anticipating Chicago's status as a transportation and hospitality center, Du Sable became Chicago's first hotelier when he built two guesthouses for travelers; and

WHEREAS, Du Sable opened Chicago as a regional and continental trading center by opening the Chicago portage to trade with Wisconsin, Detroit and Canada; and

WHEREAS, Chicago's reputation as a city of churches began in about 1778, when Jean Baptiste Pointe Du Sable built a Catholic church and mission school in the settlement and placed them under the direction of Father Gibault; and

WHEREAS, In 1796 the birth of Du Sable's granddaughter was the first birth recorded in Chicago; and

WHEREAS, On May 7, 1800, after setting Chicago on its course into history, Du Sable sold his extensive holdings, including his trading post, his home, his books, furnishings and art works and his farm, to Jean Le Lime, and then moved to Missouri where he farmed until his death on August 28, 1818; and

WHEREAS, In 1833 the Du Sable settlement, with 350 residents, was incorporated as the Town of Chicago; and

WHEREAS, On March 4, 1837, Du Sable's settlement had grown to 4,170 inhabitants and was reincorporated as the City of Chicago; and

WHEREAS, It is appropriate that the City of Chicago, in so many ways influenced by the activities, efforts and accomplishments of its first non-native settler, recognize and celebrate Jean Baptiste Pointe Du Sable as its founder; now, therefore,

BE IT ORDAINED BY THE CITY COUNCIL OF THE CITY OF CHICAGO:

SECTION 1. The recitations in the preamble of this ordinance are incorporated herein as the findings of the City Council.

SECTION 2. Chapter 1-8 of the Municipal Code of the City of Chicago is hereby amended by inserting a new Section 1-8-110, as follows:

1-8-110 Commemoration of City Founder.

In conjunction with annual celebrations of its date of incorporation, the City of Chicago shall commemorate and promote public awareness of the life and accomplishments of its founder, Jean Baptiste Pointe Du Sable.

SECTION 3. This ordinance shall be in full force and effect from and after its passage and approval.

STATE OF ILLINOIS)
)
COUNTY OF COOK)

I, EDMUND W. KANTOR, Deputy City Clerk of the City of Chicago, in the County of Cook and State of Illinois, DO HEREBY CERTIFY that the annexed and foregoing is a true and correct copy of that certain ordinance now on file in my office of an Amendment of Title 1, Chapter 8 of Municipal Code of Chicago by addition of New Section 110 entitled "Commemoration of City Founder"; which ordinance was passed by the City Council of the City of Chicago at its regular meeting held on the first (1st) day of March, 2006.

I, DO FURTHER CERTIFY that the original, of which the foregoing is a true and correct copy is on file in my office and that I am the lawful custodian of the same.

IN WITNESS WHEREOF, I have hereunto set my hand and affixed the corporate seal of the said City of Chicago aforesaid, at the said City, in the County and State aforesaid, this twenty-eighth (28th) day of March, 2006.

[signature]

EDMUND W. KANTOR, Deputy City Clerk

A CRUISE FOR DUSABLE!

Second Annual Unity Cruise & Fundraiser   "A Success"!!!

A friend of DuSable NFP is very pleased by the warm reception it received at the DuSable Unity Cruise and Fundraiser on October 11, 2007. FOD received such welcomed support in favor of the DuSable Welcome Center from all of the prestigious individuals who attended. Such support at the event compelled FOD President, Haroon Rashid to say:

"That the time for honoring Chicago's Founder in this way, has finally come". He goes on to say that, "honoring DuSable in such a way gives recognition to all those who came before and after the Founder of this great city."

FOD would like to thank all of the individuals who attended the cruise and ask for your continued support. FOD is aware that a project of this size will require the assistance of many, which essentially requires the need for funding. Our organization relies solely on your contributions.

Friends of DuSable NFP (FOD) *Second Unity Month Dinner Discussions Will Be an Evening Boat Cruise, Departing from the Chicago River on the Original Settlement Sight of Chicago's Founder, Jean Baptiste Pointe DuSable*

This year's networking will consist of a pre-event VIP Reception at a River Chicago Restaurant before departure, followed by a Gala Banquet Dinner on the Historical Wendella Boat Cruise line +36`; as well as a tour guide of Chicago waterways and culminating with an after Party at a popular Chicago Jazz Night Club. The theme of discussions is about Chicago's past and present as a City developed in diversity by immigrants and business pioneers like Chicago's Founder Jean Baptist Pointe DuSable. The DuSable Unity Day Cruise will be focusing on the Continuance of that unique Spirit in today's Chicago growing global community. The program includes elements supplied by FOD that recognize the role DuSable played in welcoming a very diverse group of settlers and traders to Chicago in the 1780's and 1790's.

The event will be taped and broadcast, on a tape-delay basis, by Columbia College School of Media and visual Arts and will be viewed on Chicago Public Television Cable Network channels in over 1.5 million homes. Chicago's most noted celebrities, as well as, political, business cultural and community leaders will be in attendance.

Sponsors and supporters will be recognized at all of the above events through program listings, announcements and appropriate signage. Event publicity including press releases will also include recognition of major sponsors.

There is a sponsorship and supporters' package under cover of this letter that details the levels of sponsorship available with corresponding benefits. I thank you in advance for your time and consideration.

"All Aboard"! Friends of DuSable Executive Board members Arnold Romeo, Andréa Knowles, Pat Patterson, Elsa Tullos, William Walley and Haroon Rashid

The brand new *Wendedlla MV* for the Second Annual Unity Cruise and Fundraiser, hosted by Friends of DuSable (FOD). This year's cruise featured the unveiling of a proposed new Welcome Center commemorating Chicago's Founder, Jean Baptiste Pointe DuSable.

The cruise departed at around 6, but prior to departure Aldermen Brendan Reilly (42nd) and Walter Burnett (27th) spoke great volumes in support of the proposed Welcome Center. The Aldermen both exited for other scheduled events and the cruise was blessed with prayer by Reverend Green of Pleasant Ridge M.B.C. Bill Walley/Treasurer & Haroon Rashid/President, both of FOD, spoke and introduced some of the distinguished guests that were on board. The first to speak on behalf of the DWC was Chicago History Museum President, Gary Johnson. Following Mr. Johnson was Phil Levin Planning Director/Greater North Michigan Avenue Association. He welcomed FOD and the DWC to the neighborhood and is looking forward to assisting in any way possible. Antoinette Wright of The DuSable Museum was in favor of the Welcome Center, as well. Bob O'Neill President of the Grant Park Conservancy was also in attendance and seemed to be the most inquisitive of the guests that evening. Ty Tabing, Executive Director/Chicago Loop Alliance said that the DWC is going to be a place that will be supported from his organization. After the guests gave their say, Jack Kelley and Greg Battoglio of McBride Kelley Baurer Architects, presented the drawings and conducted the presentation. As they spoke of the DWC the cruise headed eastward towards DuSable Park. The park is instrumental in the development of the DWC, as it will be the eastern-most point of the Riverwalk. Bill Walley discussed the significance of the park and how key the developmental process is. As the cruise toured downriver, there was a question and answer session that took place. Everyone had great questions pertaining to the development of the DWC.

Overall the cruise was a great success, and everyone onboard showed an unbelievable amount of support. Everyone who attended seemed to have an appreciation for the Welcome Center and wanted to assist in any way possible.

Others in attendance were Arnold Romeo, Advisory Council of African Affairs, Commission on Human Relations; Rob Rejman, Chicago Park District/Director Lakefront Construction, The Haitian Consul, Sarah Fleming/Planning Manager of the Greater North Michigan Avenue Association.

Presentation from the Chicago Park District and the Chicago Department of Transportation on a schematic plan: to build DuSable Park and the proposed DuSable Heritage corridor.

On this cruise there was a public private interest and discussions in the development of the proposed Du Sable Park and Heritage corridor.

The Chicago Park District, the Chicago Department of Transportation and the Chicago City Consul representatives were in partnership with community organizations to enact progressive changes of inclusion. The plan was for the State of Illinois and City of Chicago Departments of Tourism to highlight the legacy of Chicago's Founder and the "First People." Centering on the official location of early Chicago settlement, which was along the Chicago River and Lake Michigan shorelines.

Second Annual Unity Cruise & Fundraiser   "A Success"!!!

Friends of DuSable: was very pleased by the warm reception it received at the DuSable Unity Cruise and Fundraiser on October 11, 2007. FOD received such a welcomed support in favor the DuSable Welcome Center from all of the prestigious individuals who attended. Such support at the event compelled FOD President, Haroon Rashid to say: *FOD would like to thank all of the individuals who attended the cruise and offered their continued support. FOD was aware that a project of this size that we were committed to do would require the assistance of many, which essentially required the advocating for our DuSable legacy mission. That type of progressive outreaching was instrumental in eventually the lobby successes of the newly elected Alderman of the 42 Ward Brendan Reilly to continue the support of FOD missions.*

Haitian dignitaries on one table while South African representative is on another

The individuals who attended the cruise were a mixed multicultural body of guest and supporters. The guests were reminded of the need for their continued support. FOD was aware that a project of this size will require the assistance of many, which essentially requires the need for funding.

OFFICIAL OPENING OF THE DUSABLE HARBOR BOAT DOCK REST HOUSE

Mayor Richard M. Daley, the Chicago Park District and Friends of DuSable cut the ribbon to officially open the DuSable Harbor Dock and Rest House.

In 2008; Friends of DuSable was asked by the Mayor's Office of Special Events, to participate in the official Ribbon Cutting ceremony to represent the DuSable Park Coalition, the group of private public principles that was responsible for the enactment that lobbied for the continuum of the proposed DuSable Heritage Corridor development plan. The structural and demographical components of the targeted area included The DuSable Founders Way, the Chicago River Walk on the northeast side of the river from the Michigan Avenue DuSable Bridge to the designated DuSable Park area located just before Lake Michigan. Then on the south side of the Chicago River from the DuSable Bridge to the DuSable Harbor on the far southeast end of the Chicago River and Lakeshore Drive. This area was considered by members of the DuSable Park Coalition as a historical heritage landmark that should be honored as such.

DuSable Harbor Dock and Rest House

The DuSable Harbor Dock Rest House during the summer months houses a restaurant and gift store: that makes touring, and participating in recreational events more relaxing and entertaining when walking, bike riding or jogging along the Lakefront.

It also provides restrooms for the public and storage lockers for boat owners that are docked in the Harbor.

During the Fourth of July holiday, thousands of people are lined up along the Lakefront to watch the fireworks; and the DuSable Harbor Rest House is an extremely popular place for citizens and tourists to watch the fireworks. Because of the great location near the coast of the Chicago River and Lake Michigan, it is used as a great outdoor special events location.

CHAPTER THIRTEEN

The First Elected: African American President, of the United States of America, was from Chicago

FIRST AFRICAN AMERICAN PRESIDENT OF THE UNITED STATES OF AMERICA

2008 Presidential Campaign of Barack Obama

History has recorded that President Obama, having a Caucasian mother and Kenyan father of the Luo ethnic group, became the first African American as well as the first bi-racial president. Although he may have been the first black president to win an election, Obama was not the first African American to run for president. Shirley Chisolm, Jesse Jackson, Lenora Fulani, Carol Moseley Braun, Alan Keyes, and Al Sharpton, all at some point, were in the process for presidential nomination. The Obama-Biden ticket was also the first winning ticket in American history, on which neither candidate was a White Anglo-Saxon Protestant. Biden is Roman Catholic and is the first Roman Catholic to be elected Vice President; all other tickets with Catholic vice presidential candidates had been defeated (1964, 1972, 1984). Obama and Biden were the first President and Vice President elected from the Senate since 1960 (John F. Kennedy/Lyndon B. Johnson) (in the previous election cycle (2004) Democrats also nominated two sitting Senators, John Kerry of Massachusetts and John Edwards of North Carolina, but they lost to incumbents Bush and Cheney), Obama became the first Northern Democratic president since Kennedy, and the Obama-Biden ticket was the first winning Democratic ticket to feature two Northerners since 1940 (Franklin D. Roosevelt/Henry A. Wallace). Also, Obama became the first Democratic candidate to win a majority of the popular vote since Jimmy Carter in 1976, the first to win a majority of both votes and states since Lyndon Johnson in 1964, and the first Northern Democrat to win a majority of both votes and states since Franklin Roosevelt in 1944. This was the first presidential election since 1952, where neither of the major party candidates was either the incumbent President or Vice-President.

Swing by state. States are listed by (increasing) percentage of Democratic votes, showing how the share of the vote changed between 2004 and 2008. Excluding the candidates' home states, only five states trended more Republican: Arkansas, Louisiana, Oklahoma, Tennessee and West Virginia.

Prior to the election, commentators discussed whether Senator Obama would be able to redraw the electoral map by winning states that had been voting for Republican candidates in recent decades. In many ways, he was successful. He won every region of the country by double digits except the South, which John McCain won by nine percent. Obama won Delaware, the District of Columbia, Maryland, North Carolina, Florida, and Virginia in the South (region as defined by the US Census Bureau). McCain won most of the Deep South, where white voters have supported Republican candidates by large margins in the last few decades. Obama also defied political bellwethers, becoming the first person to win the presidency while losing Missouri since 1956 (as well as the first Democrat ever to do so) and while losing Kentucky and Tennessee since 1960. He was the first Democrat to win without Arkansas, since that state joined the Union in 1836 and the first Democrat to win the presidency without winning West Virginia since 1916. Because one West Virginia elector voted for the Democrat in 1916, Obama was the first Democrat to win without any electors from the state, since its founding in 1863. Indiana and Virginia voted for the Democratic nominee for the first time since 1964. Although Obama did not win other normally Republican states, such as Georgia and Montana (which were won by Bill Clinton in 1992), he nonetheless was competitive in both. He lost Montana by just fewer than 3% and Georgia by slightly more than 5%. Also, notably, Barack Obama won all of the 2004 swing states (states that either Kerry or Bush won by less than 5%) by a margin of 8.5 percent or more except for Ohio, which the Democrat carried by 4.5 percent.

Obama was the first presidential candidate to split the electoral votes from Nebraska. Together with Maine, which would not split its votes until 2016, Nebraska is one of two states that split their electoral votes, two going to the statewide popular vote winner and the rest going to the winner of each respective congressional district (Nebraska has three, and Maine has two). Obama won the electoral vote from Nebraska's 2nd congressional district, which contains the city of Omaha. Nebraska's other four electoral votes went to John McCain.

As of 2016, this election is the last time that Indiana and North Carolina voted Democratic.

This election exhibited the continuation of some of the polarization trends evident in the 2000 and 2004 elections. McCain won whites 55–43 percent, while Obama won blacks 95–4 percent, Hispanics 67–31 percent, and Asians 62–35 percent. Voters aged 18–29 voted for Obama by 66–32 percent while elderly voters backed McCain 53–45 percent. The 25-year age gap between McCain and Obama was the widest in U.S. presidential election history among the top two candidates.

Joe Biden and Barack Obama after the presentation of Biden as the vice-presidential running-mate in Springfield, Illinois

The 2008 presidential campaign of Barack Obama, then junior United States Senator from Illinois, was announced at an event on February 10, 2007 in Springfield, Illinois. After winning a majority of delegates in the Democratic primaries of 2008, on August 23, leading up to the convention, the campaign announced that Senator Joe Biden of Delaware would be the Vice Presidential nominee. At the 2008 Democratic National Convention on August 27, Barack Obama was formally selected as the Democratic Party nominee for President of the United States in 2008. He was the first African American in history to be nominated on a major party ticket.

On November 4, 2008, Obama defeated the Republican nominee, Senator John McCain of Arizona, making him the President-elect and the first African American elected President. He was the third sitting U.S. Senator, after Warren G. Harding and John F. Kennedy, to be elected President. Upon the vote of the Electoral College on December 15, 2008, and the subsequent certification thereof by a Joint Session of the United States Congress on January 8, 2009, Barack Obama was elected President of the United States and Joe Biden Vice President of the United States, with 365 of 538 electors.

Further information: Barack Obama presidential primary campaign, 2008

On June 3, 2008, after the Montana and South Dakota primaries, he secured enough delegates to clinch the nomination of the Democratic Party for President of the United States. His opponent in the general election, Republican John McCain, passed the delegate threshold to become the apparent nominee of his party on March 4. On June 7, Hillary Clinton, Obama's remaining opponent in the quest for the Democratic nomination, conceded defeat and urged her supporters to back Obama. After a June 26 dinner at which Obama encouraged his fundraisers to donate to Clinton's debt-saddled campaign, Obama and Clinton ran their first post-primary event together in Unity, New Hampshire, on June 27. Over the first two weeks of July, the campaign ran a heavier schedule of fundraising events, drawing from former donors to Clinton's campaign. Obama strategically had pictures made with financial experts Warren Buffett and Paul Volcker so the public would perceive him as having inside knowledge of Wall Street.

Barack Obama, Michelle Obama, Jill Biden and Joe Biden at the Vice President announcement on August 23, 2008 in Springfield, Illinois

Obama's vice-presidential running-mate had been a subject of speculation since the end of the primaries. As of August 2008, some of the most popular choices for VP included, but were not limited to, Clinton, Biden, Indiana Senator Evan Bayh, Kansas Governor Kathleen Sebelius, Virginia Governor Tim Kaine, retired General and former Secretary of State Colin Powell, New Mexico Governor Bill Richardson, and retired General Wesley Clark.

On August 21, 2008, Obama announced that he had made a selection for the VP spot, but would not reveal until August 23 who it was. Obama's campaign encouraged supporters to sign up for a text messaging system that would alert them the moment he announced his choice. On August 22, KMBC News of Kansas City spotted bumper stickers of an Obama/Bayh '08 ticket that were being printed in Lenexa, Kansas. Three sources close to a local printing plant reported that such material was being produced. The image of the bumper sticker circulated on the internet. However, NBC News later quoted sources stating that Bayh had been informed by Obama's campaign that he was not the pick. According to an Associated Press report that same evening, Joe Biden was selected as Obama's candidate. The Associated Press report was confirmed several hours later, on August 23, on his official campaign website and by a mass text message to supporters. Obama selected Biden to be vice president for three reasons: he could relate to blue-collar Americans (i.e. he is originally from Pennsylvania—arguably a blue-collar state); he has a multitude of connections on Capitol Hill; and he has more personal connections in foreign policy than Obama.

Middle Eastern and European tour:

In July 2008 Obama traveled to Kuwait, Afghanistan, Iraq, Jordan, the West Bank, Israel, Germany, France, and Britain. During the course of this trip he met with assorted international leaders, including President Hamid Karzai of Afghanistan, Prime Minister Nouri al-Maliki of Iraq, King Abdullah II of Jordan, Palestinian President Mahmoud Abbas, Prime Minister of Israel Ehud Olmert, Chancellor Angela Merkel of Germany, President Nicolas Sarkozy of France, and Prime Minister

Gordon Brown of the United Kingdom, as well as former British Prime Minister Tony Blair and Conservative opposition leader David Cameron.

On July 24, 2008 he gave a speech at the Victory Column in Berlin before a crowd of estimated 200,000 to 240,000 people.

PRESIDENTIAL DEBATES

Main article: United States presidential election debates, 2008

There were three presidential debates between Obama and McCain. No third-party candidates or Independent candidates were offered an invitation to join in any of the debates, as Obama and McCain were the only candidates on the ballot in all 50 states and the District of Columbia. The Commission on Presidential Debates proposed, and the candidates agreed, that two of three 90-minute debates would be in an informal, seated, talk show format, while the third would be in a town hall format that allowed both candidates to walk around.

Joint Town Hall Meeting with Senator Barack Obama and Senator John McCain

On June 4, John McCain proposed a series of ten joint town hall meetings with Obama, at which the two could engage each other. Obama first agreed in principle to the notion, but later rejected McCain's proposal, offering instead one town-hall event on the Independence Day holiday and four traditional debate-style joint appearances. Hank Paulson, President Bush's Treasury Secretary, said Obama's comprehension of the financial crisis compared to McCain's was as broad as "night and day". McCain's confidence vastly lowered when Obama questioned his ideas on the financial crisis in a meeting on September 25 at the White House with Bush and other congressmen. McCain did not have suggestions regarding what he would do to fix the economy, particularly Henry Paulson's $700 billion three-page bank recovery plan (TARP). Neither McCain nor Bush had read it. Obama's confidence escalated from that point. This was the turning point of the campaign.

Financial Crisis

On September 15, 2008 financial services firm Lehman Brothers filed for Chapter 11 bankruptcy protection, setting off a series of events leading to a 4.4% Dow Jones loss, at the time the largest drop by points in a single day since the days following the attacks on September 11, 2001. That stock market loss was subsequently exceeded by an even larger −7.0% plunge on September 29, 2008.

On September 24, 2008, after the onset of the 2008 financial crisis, McCain announced that he was suspending his campaign to return to Washington to help craft a $700 billion bailout package for the troubled financial industry, and he stated that he would not debate Obama until Congress passed the bailout bill. Despite this decision, McCain was portrayed as not playing a significant role in the negotiations for the first version of the bill, which fell short of passage in the House. He eventually decided to attend the first presidential debate on September 26, despite Congress' lack of immediate action on the bill. His ineffectiveness in the negotiations and his reversal in decision to attend the debates were seized upon to portray McCain as erratic in his response to the economy. Days later, a second version of the original bailout bill was passed by both the House and Senate, with Obama, his vice-presidential running mate Joe Biden and McCain all voting for the measure (Hillary Clinton would as well).

The Civil Forum on the Presidency was the venue of back-to-back interviews of U.S. presidential candidates John McCain and Barack Obama by Pastor Rick Warren on August 16, 2008, at Saddleback Church in Lake Forest, California.

Newly elected; Vice President Joe Biden, President Barack Obama, Sasha Obama, Jill Biden, Malaya Obama and First Lady Michelle Obama.

Victory speech

> "If there is anyone out there who still doubts that America is a place where all things are possible, who still wonders if the dream of our founders is alive in our time, who still questions the power of our democracy, tonight is your answer."

Following his victory, Obama gave his victory speech at Grant Park in his home city of Chicago on November 4, 2008, before an estimated crowd of 240,000. Viewed on television and the Internet by millions of people around the globe, Obama's speech focused on the major issues facing the United States and the world, all echoed through his campaign slogan of change. He also mentioned his grandmother, who had died two nights earlier.

The Obama campaign's fundraising broke previous records for presidential primary and general campaigns, and has changed expectations for future presidential elections. The campaign avoided using public campaign funds, raising all of its money privately from individual donors. By the general election the campaign committee raised more than $650 million for itself, and coordinated with both the Democratic National Committee (DNC) and at least 18 state-level Democratic committees to create a joint-fundraising committee to raise and split tens of millions of dollars more.

Post-election fundraising continued for the separate transition administration, called the Obama-Biden Transition Project, and also the separate inaugural ceremonies and celebrations committee.

According to reports filed with the Federal Election Commission, Obama's campaign raised more money in the first quarter of 2008 ($133,549,000) than it had risen in all of 2007 ($103,802,537). The campaign had a relatively small total of $21.9 million in May, but went on to raise $52 million in June, after Obama had secured the nomination.

On June 19, Obama was the first major-party presidential candidate to turn down public financing for a general election campaign since the system was created in the aftermath of Watergate. Obama was expected to raise $265 million between the time of the announcement and Election Day. By rejecting the funds in favor of private donations, the campaign was in a position to outspend John McCain prior to the election. Had he signed on to the plan, the campaign would only have been able to spend $84.1 million between the party convention in August and the general election in November.

Obama explained his decision to opt out of the public financing system, saying, "public" financing of presidential elections as it exists today is broken, and we face opponents who've become masters at gaming this broken system. Critics of the decision argued that the decision contradicted earlier statements that he would attempt to reach agreement with McCain to obtain public financing, and asserted that Obama's campaign was receiving as much support from unregulated 527 groups as McCain's.

On September 4, 2008, the Obama campaign announced they raised $10 million in the 24-hour period after Republican Vice-Presidential nominee Sarah Palin's acceptance speech. The RNC reported raising $1 million in the same period.

On October 19, 2008, Obama's campaign announced a record fundraising total of $150 million for September 2008. This exceeded the campaign's single-month record ($66 million) for August 2008.

The campaign raised much of its cash in small donations over the internet, with about half of its intake coming in increments of less than $200. Both major party campaigns screened regularly for patterns of abuse and returned or rejected donations in excess of legal limits, from overseas, from untraceable addresses, or from fraudulent names. After some criticism of the Obama campaign on conservative blogs, the Republican National Committee asked the Federal Election Commission to investigate the Obama campaign's screening practices.

Obama's campaign used the slogan "Change we can believe in" and the chant "Yes We Can". The latter slogan is shared with the United Farm Workers and associated with its founder César Chávez and is well-known amongst Latinos in its Spanish form Sí se puede. The "Change we can believe in" has been used in parodies both during and since the campaign. John McCain attempted to criticize Obama by enumerating various controversial policy positions he allegedly took and proclaiming "that's not change we can believe in" alongside a banner proclaiming McCain as "a leader we can believe in". Since the campaign it has been used to parody campaigns against incumbents as being "change you can't believe in" such as by British blog Left Foot Forward against David Cameron or by the Economist against the People's Democratic Party of Tajikistan.

Barack Obama "Hope" poster by the designer Shepard Fairey

The "hope" poster was an iconic image of Barack Obama designed by artist Shepard Fairey. It consisted of a stylized stencil portrait of Obama in solid red, white (actually beige) and (pastel and dark) blue. Either the words "progress", "hope", or "change" were under the image of Obama (in some versions other words were used). It was created and distributed widely—as a digital image, on posters and other paraphernalia—during the 2008 election season. Initially it was distributed independently but with the approval of the official Obama campaign. The image became one of the most widely recognized symbols of Obama's campaign message, spawning many variations and imitations, including some commissioned by the campaign itself. In January 2009, after Obama had won the election, Fairey's mixed-media stenciled portrait version of the image was acquired by the Smithsonian Institution for its National Portrait Gallery.

The signature campaign typeface was Gotham, typically using capital letters with occasional use of the script Snell Round hand. Gotham, was designed in 2000 by Jonathan Hoefler and Tobias Frere-Jones, originally for GQ' magazine. Prior to Gotham, the campaign used the typeface Gill Sans in upper case and lower case. Another Hoefler and Frere-Jones font, Requiem, was used for the campaign logo.

U2's "City of Blinding Lights" was often played in anticipation of Obama's speeches during campaign events. Bruce Springsteen's "The Rising" was also played heavily during his campaign rallies. Barack Obama personally asked Joss Stone in August to write and record his presidential campaign song, reportedly due to the fact that she appeals across racial boundaries. Ben Harper's "Better Way" was also played at a few events throughout the campaign. Furthermore, Obama's candidacy inspired artists to create more unsolicited music and music videos than any other candidate in American political history. Examples include "Yes We Can" by will.i.am, of the band The Black Eyed Peas; "Make it to the Sun" by Ruwanga Samath and Maxwell D; "Barack Obama" by JFC; and "Unite the Nation" by the Greek-American Hip Hop group Misa/Misa.

Obama was particularly noted for his use of the Internet to rally supporters and make his policies known. He is the first US president to have effectively used the internet and social media for successful political outcomes. His successful presidential campaign raised the bar and are, now presidential standards.

"The integration of technology into the process of field organizing is the success of the Obama campaign," says Sanford Dickert, who worked as John Kerry's chief technology officer for the 2004 campaign. "But the use of technology was not the end-all and be-all in this cycle. Technology has been a partner, an enabler for the Obama campaign, bringing the efficiencies of the internet into the real-world problems of organizing people in a distributed, trusted fashion."

Obama's campaign was further strengthened by his opponent John McCain's comparatively limited use of the Internet. McCain did not have the organization of Obama's campaign, nor did he spend a comparable amount of money on this portion of the campaign. Both opportune timing and usage of online campaigning gave Obama significant advantage over McCain.

Through forums and social websites such as MySpace and Facebook, Obama built relationships with his supporters, and would-be supporters. He developed an upfront, personable and face-to-face quality that gave his supporters a sense of security and trust, which inspired them to rally others in their local communities. The supporters of Obama themselves formed a nationwide community.

All of his policies were made available online, and updates were sent to the subscribers of his political party via email and text message, ultimately making him the most technologically savvy candidate to date, increasing his popularity among youth voters.

In early 2007, the Obama campaign launched a social-networking site called my.barackobama.com, or MyBO for short, and recruited 24-year old Facebook co-founder Chris Hughes to help develop the platform and their social networking strategy. MyBO became the hub of the campaign's online efforts to organize supporters.

The nationwide community provided useful and effective tools, such as the Neighbor-to-Neighbor tool, allowing supporters to reach a large number of people in a short time in their own community, which in turn led to campaign rallying for more Obama support. An unprecedented communication strategy was the "online call tool". Over one million calls were made from residential, personal laptops and desktops. Online communication led to Obama supporters engaging in social activities such as sign making and door-to-door petitioning for Obama support, as well as simply discussing their opinions about policies and issues they supported along with Obama. As described by campaign adviser Steve Spinner, the campaign grew "from zero to 700 employees in a year and raised $200 million. That's a super-high-growth, fast-charging operation."

In 2008, campaign staffers stationed in the long-shot battle ground state of Georgia, reinvented the tedious, messy process of reporting and aggregating nightly data and intelligence upward through the campaign apparatus—making the organizing work of vast Obama field infrastructure more immediately measurable. National Field became an internal social network within the field organization, used to monitor the daily activities of the sprawling grassroots effort. It allowed staff to share what they were working on and benchmark themselves against other staffers. Unlike a standard social graph, where all users have access to all information, National Field was based on a hierarchical social graph where the higher level you were in the organization, the broader your view of the information below you.

The platform closely reflected the team-building model of the Obama Campaign, often associated with organizer and Harvard professor Marshall Ganz in that it was an intensely structured social network.

After trailing Republicans for many election cycles in their use of micro-targeting, the 2008 Obama campaign was the first Democratic presidential campaign to benefit from the existence of a national voter file. In 2007, DNC chairman Howard Dean centralized data collection and management by hiring the Voter Activation Network and creating the database Votebuilder. Votebuilder created a web-based interface for the database and permitted the Obama campaign to give neighborhood-level volunteers access to the registered voter list for their area of responsibility.

In October 2008, Obama was voted Advertising Age magazine's "Marketer of the Year" by members of the Association of National Advertisers for the campaign, surpassing Apple and Zappos.com. In a post-election analysis of the campaign, the magazine lauded its "understanding of ground-level marketing strategies and tactics, everything from audience segmentation and database management to the creation and maintenance of online communities."

Online advertising

The Obama web campaign used consumer marketing to target individuals with customized information to their predicted interests. Political communication to viewers was based on data collected about them. This data was collected by volunteers, surveys on the website and records of consumption habits. Website surveys took a short amount of time to fill out and the company used A/B testing to determine which forms converted most effectively, led by the team's Director of Analytics Dan Siroker. More detailed surveys were requested and received through email. Records of consumption habits helped the campaign make predictions about people based on statistical models. People received messages tailored close to their beliefs. Marketing based on consumer data also enabled effective grassroots organizing through the website. Data gathered from the website indicated who the most dedicated constituents were; the website tracked how often a person visited and when. The campaign team then targeted and encouraged activists in contested, winnable areas, such as through the website program Neighbor-to-neighbor.

Television advertisements

Soon after becoming the presumptive nominee, Obama began a biographical commercial campaign emphasizing his patriotism. The advertisements ran in 18 states, including traditionally Republican Alaska and North Carolina. Between June 6 and July 26, Obama's campaign spent $27 million on advertisements, against McCain and Republican National Committee's combined total of $24.6 million.

In a September 15, 2008 interview with Good Morning America, Obama stated, "If we're going to ask questions about, you know, who has been promulgating negative ads that are completely unrelated to the issues at hand, I think I win that contest pretty handily." What he apparently meant was that McCain had put out more negative ads.

On October 29 at 8:00 pm EDT, the Obama campaign's 30-minute infomercial "American Stories, American Solutions" was simulcast on NBC, CBS, Fox, Univision, MSNBC, BET and TV One, focusing on a wide range of issues including health care and taxation. The infomercial then showed an Obama speech live from Florida. Fox asked for the second part of Game Five of the 2008 World Series to be delayed by 15 minutes in order to show the commercial, and that request was granted. ABC was the only major US network not to show the ad after being indecisive during the initial approach and the Obama campaign later declined the offer. The Obama ad got 30.1 million viewers across networks compared to ABC's Pushing Daisies which garnered 6.3 million viewers. Prior to this, the last presidential candidate to purchase a half-hour ad was H. Ross Perot, who ran as an independent candidate in 1992. The Obama campaign also bought a channel on Dish Network to screen Obama ads 24/7. Wyatt Andrews reported on a "Reality Check" on the *CBS Evening News* the next day with doubts over the factual accuracy of some of the promises Obama made in the advertisement, given the government's enormous financial deficit.

Israel for Obama

Originally started by American-Israelis in late May, the "Israel for Obama" campaign aimed to refute the allegations made against Obama concerning Israel and the Jewish community. This was done by gaining endorsements from Israel. When he took a Middle East trip from Afghanistan to Iraq, Jordan and finally to Israel, they organized a small "Israel for Obama" rally for him.

Ira Forman, executive director of the National Jewish Democratic Council stated that "The Democratic operation in the Jewish community was more extensive than I've seen in 35 years, The chairman of the campaign in Israel, Yeshiyah Amariel, and others such as the Jewish Alliance for Change and the Jewish Council for Education & Research used YouTube to release video endorsements from officials and normal people in Israel for Obama and his positions (such as "Israelis for Obama" and "right man for the job.") In the closing weeks of the election the campaign used support from Israelis to fight the smears spread online by bloggers. Its success caused the polls of Jewish support for Obama to increase so that by the time of the Nov 4 election, according to exit polls, 77% of the voting American Jewish community voted for Obama over the 23% that were for John McCain.

Main articles: Political positions of Barack Obama and Comparison of United States presidential candidates, 2008

Obama has taken positions on many national, political, economic and social issues, either through public comments or his senatorial voting record. Since announcing his presidential campaign in February 2007, Obama emphasized withdrawing American troops from Iraq, increasing energy independence (that includes New Energy For America plan), decreasing the influence of lobbyists, and promoting universal health care as top national priorities.

The day after Obama's acceptance speech at the Democratic National Convention, Obama's Republican opponent, Arizona Senator John McCain, announced his selection of Alaska Governor Sarah Palin as his running mate. Almost immediately, the Obama/Biden ticket plunged in the polls: in a Gallup poll of likely voters, the McCain/Palin ticket gained a 10-point lead. The erosion of support for the Obama/Biden ticket was especially pronounced among white women who had previously shown strong support for Hillary Clinton. However, Obama regained and maintained the national poll average after September 19.

A RealClearPolitics average of 14 national polls taken between October 29 and November 2 showed an average 7.3% lead for Obama over McCain. Obama's highest support in the polling average was 8.2% on October 14. Among individual polls tracked by RealClearPolitics, Obama's highest support was recorded in a *Newsweek* poll conducted between June 18 and June 19 and a Pew Research poll conducted between October 23 and October 26 showing a 15% lead.

Gallup conducted weekly polls of registered voters to measure support among the candidates. The final poll conducted between October 27 and November 2 showed 24% of pure Independents supporting

Obama, trailing the 32% who favored McCain. Obama's Independent support peaked at 33% the week of October 6–12.

A RealClearPolitics average of four national polls measuring favorable/unfavorable opinions taken between October 28 and November 2 showed an average 55.5% favorable rating and 39.8% unfavorable rating. Obama's highest ratings in the polling average were 61.2% favorable and 32.5% unfavorable on July 8.

As of November 3, 2008, one day before the election, the RealClearPolitics electoral map excluding toss up states showed 278 electoral votes for Obama/Biden, an electoral majority, and 132 electoral votes for opponents McCain/Palin. Including toss up states, the Obama/Biden ticket led with 338 votes.

*President Barack Husain Obama
and First Lady Michelle Robinson Obama*

On November 4, 2008, Barack Obama became the first African American to be elected President of the United States, sparking many celebrations in the United States and around the world. He gained almost 53% of the popular vote and 365 electoral votes. The popular vote percentage was the best showing for any presidential candidate since George H.W. Bush in 1988. His 365 electoral votes were the best showing since Bill Clinton had 379 in 1996. He won Colorado, Nevada, Virginia, Indiana, Florida, Ohio, and North Carolina, all states that were won by President George W. Bush in 2004. In addition, he became the first Democratic candidate to win one of Nebraska's electoral votes since the state decided to split their electoral votes. He was the first candidate to be elected President without winning Missouri since 1956. Obama also received more total votes than any Presidential candidate in history, totaling well over 69 million votes.

63% of Americans, who met the voting requirements, voted the highest percentage in fifty years. Obama won the moderate vote 60–39 and the independent vote 52–44. Joe Biden also made history by becoming the first Roman Catholic to be elected Vice President. In addition, he is the longest-serving Senator to become Vice President, having served in the United States Senate for the 36 years prior to the election. Biden also won reelection to the Senate, but served only briefly in the 111th Congress before resigning to take his place as vice president.

CHAPTER FOURTEEN

The DuSable Bronze Bust Instalment and DuSable Bridge Naming

Participants in the honorary DuSable Bust Ceremony: Lesley Conde' Consulate General of Haiti, Mr. Lesley Benodin, Ms. Aliette Marcelin, Mr. Harry Fouche, Haitian supporter and Haroon Rashid.

Haroon Rashid, founder and president of the Friends of DuSable (NFP) and a member of the Greater North Michigan Avenue Association, said that he was pleased that the language on the monument reflects the city's official acknowledgment of Pointe DuSable as the founder of Chicago. The Friends of DuSable partnered with the Chicago Commission on Human Relations African Advisory Council to co-author the city's DuSable Commemoration Ordinance.

Mr. Rashid further expressed gratitude for Alderman Brendan Reilly's (42nd Ward) support and demonstration of civic leadership in his bid to pass through City Council a resolution renaming the Michigan Avenue Bridge the "Jean Baptiste Pointe DuSable Bridge." Special gratitude is also extended to Mr. Harry Fouche of Chicago and Ms. Aliette Marcelin of Evanston, who provided much-needed logistical assistance with the monument.

Sculptor Mr. Erik Blome, and the Donor Mr. Lesley Benodin

The Jean Baptiste Pointe DuSable Bronze Sculpture was designed and installed by artist Mr. Erik Blome, in the location of Pioneer Court next to the DuSable Bridge.

The monument was given to the City of Chicago by Haitian-born, Mr. Lesley Benodin, to honor the legacy of its founder.

Legal advisor for the Friends of the Park Mrs. Eleanor Roemer: in the center with large crowd of Haitian American and many other enthusiastic Chicago citizens

What a great day for the Magnificent Mile! A bust of Jean Baptiste Pointe DuSable, the founder and first businessman of the city of Chicago: The monument also recognizes the vibrant presence of the Haitian American community in the city today. The bronze sculpture was received by the Department of Cultural Affairs on behalf of the city, and on Friday, October 16th, city officials, dignitaries, activists, and Chicagoans-at-large rejoiced in celebration of the historical dedication.

The crowd of participants in the crowd was a very diverse mixed audience of Haitian Americans, African Americans, Native Americans, European Americans, French, Haitian, South African & Camorra Consulates that were a part of the DuSable Commemoration coalition in attendance.

Chicago Consulate General of Haiti: Mr. Lesley Conde` on the left of the bust and Mr. Lesly Benodin the donor on the right.

Special gratitude is also extended to Mr. Harry Fouche of Chicago and Ms. Aliette Marcelin of Evanston, who provided much-needed logistical assistance with the monument.

The Jean Baptiste Pointe DuSable Bronze Sculpture was designed and installed by artist Mr. Erik Blome, in the location of Pioneer Court next to the DuSable Bridge. The monument was given to the City of Chicago by Haitian born, Mr. Lesley Benodin, to honor the legacy of its founder.

THE DUSABLE BRIDGE PROCLAMATION:

42 Ward Alderman Brendan Reilly

October 15, 2010: Friends of DuSable encouraged the city of Chicago Department of Transportation to post signs on the Michigan Avenue Bridge and street to rename it The DuSable Bridge in honor of Chicago's first permanent resident, Jean Baptiste Pointe DuSable. An ordinance was introduced by 42 Ward Alderman Brendan Reilly and passed by the Chicago City Council in 2009 for the DuSable Bridge dedication. The ordinance was the result of years of advocacy by the Friends of DuSable Coalition and the greater Chicago Haitian American leadership.

This is a copy of that enactment that went into law through the lobbying of the Chicago City Council that was introduced by BRENDAN REILLY, Alderman - 42nd Ward in the form of a City Ordinance.

Authority Granted to Rename Michigan Avenue Bridge: To "Jean Baptiste Pointe Du Sable Bridge".

WHEREAS, The City of Chicago is justifiably proud of its rich cultural and ethnic heritage; its rapid ascent from frontier trading post to major commercial, cultural and education center; and its place among the world's great cities; and

WHEREAS, Du Sable became the first permanent, non-native settler of Chicago when he built a cabin on the north bank of the Chicago River, at the current site of the Tribune Tower; and

WHEREAS, Du Sable became Chicago's first real estate developer and builder in about 1773, when he established a settlement for himself, his wife and about one hundred Potawatomi; built a trading post; established a dairy farm; and planted fruit orchards and fields of corn, hay and alfalfa; and

WHEREAS, shortly after establishing the settlement, Du Sable established Chicago's character as a haven to immigrants, when one hundred French Canadians arrived seeking refuge from the British and Spanish armies; and

WHEREAS, The Chicago settlement founded by Jean Baptiste Pointe Du Sable was characterized by racial, ethnic and cultural harmony and mutual respect among its diverse inhabitants; and

WHEREAS, in 1833, the Du Sable settlement, with three hundred fifty residents, was incorporated as the Town of Chicago; and

WHEREAS, On March 4, 1837, Du Sable's settlement had grown to four thousand one hundred seventy inhabitants and was reincorporated as the City of Chicago; and

WHEREAS, DuSable is such an important part of Chicago History that DuSable High School was dedicated in 1934 and the Du Sable Museum of African American History and DuSable Harbor are named in his honor; and

WHEREAS, the State of Illinois and City of Chicago declared DuSable the Founder of Chicago on October 26, 1968; and

WHEREAS, It is appropriate that the City of Chicago, in so many ways influenced by the activities, efforts and accomplishments of its first non-native settler, recognize and celebrate Jean Baptiste Pointe Du Sable as its founder; now, therefore,

Be It Resolved, That we, the Mayor and the members of the City Council of the City of Chicago, do hereby state that the name of the Michigan Avenue Bridge be changed to Jean Baptiste Pointe du Sable Bridge as a memento of the high esteem in which he is held.

"Honorary DuSable Bridge" Street Signs:

The Friends of DuSable partnered with the Chicago Commission on Human Relations African Advisory Council, The DuSable Coalition and the Chicago Department of Transportation to create, find funds and place signs on the upper and lower four corners of the Michigan Avenue DuSable Bridge.

The Michigan Avenue DuSable Bridge

Keynote Speaker Mrs. Bessie L. Neal President of the DuSable League

October 15, 2010
By Alejandra Cancino, Tribune reporter

Alice J. Neal devoted her life to having a street in downtown Chicago named after Jean Baptiste Pointe DuSable, a black man known as the city's first non-native settler. But she died before DuSable had citywide recognition.

On Friday, her daughter-in-law, Bessie Neal stood before politicians and leaders of various organizations at the ceremony to officially rename the Michigan Avenue Bridge as the DuSable Bridge. It isn't a street, but it is a Chicago landmark.

"Anything that is no trouble to you is no good to you," said Neal, who celebrated her 90th birthday in February. "You are going to have to have some ups and downs; I don't care what it is. And I believe that we had some ups and downs before we got this, but we are proud that we got it."

Historians debate DuSable's early years, but it has become widely accepted that he was a free, black man born in Haiti in the mid-1700s. He was the son of an African slave mother and French mariner.

In the late 1700s, DuSable moved to Chicago, a zone of trade for the Potawatomi, Ojibwe and Lakota tribes, said Joseph Podlasek, president of the American Indian Center. DuSable married a Potawatomi woman named Kittihawa and had two children, Susanne and Jean.

DuSable and his family settled near the Chicago River, where DuSable built a home, and later, a trading post, with a mill, a bake house and a barn, among other small buildings. Kittihawa was instrumental in DuSable's career as a businessman, Podlasek said.

On May 7, 1800, DuSable sold his properties in Chicago. Soon after, he moved to St. Charles, Mo., where he lived until he died in 1818.

Through the years, many fought to erase DuSable's tale from Chicago's official history, but it was never forgotten.

In the 1930s, Alice J. Neal helped form the National DuSable Memorial Society, which set up an exhibit at the 1933 Chicago World's Fair to educate people about him. As the years passed, the society began to fade. So, in 1966, Neal organized the Chicago DuSable League, through which she pushed for a street and a statue named after him. She died in 1981, before achieving those goals.

Through the years, a public high school, museum, harbor, marina and an undeveloped lakefront park have been named after DuSable in the city. Until Friday, a variety of more prominent proposals, from renaming City Hall to Lake Shore Drive after him, either failed or stalled in the City Council.

"Many times, we have introduced ordinances in the City Council, some of them have passed and some of them just sat on the table, but we've come a long way," said Alderman Walter Burnett at Friday's ceremony.

In 2000, Haroon Rashid formed Friends of DuSable and pushed for the renaming of the bridge. Bessie Neal, president of the DuSable League, was there to help him. Neal said she has spent many sleepless nights and a lot of money "to try to get this going."

"I can't tell you what this means to me," Neal said. "It means so much."

Alderman 24 Ward Walter Burnett & Chairman of the Aldermanic Black Caucus

Alderman Burnett giving a heartfelt speech, talking about the long-awaited ambitions of the Black Caucus to do something like the DuSable Bridge enactment that would be a permanent monumental visible sign of the pride of Chicagoans' city Founder Jean Baptiste Pointe DuSable, glorious roots and legacy.

Mr. Patrick Brutus videotaping Illinois: United State Senator Richard Durban

The DuSable bridge ceremony drew out the leadership of Chicago and the State of Illinois to partake in the historical enactment. State Senator Richard Durban was in attendance as an honorary speaker to give his support and acknowledgment for the historical renaming of the Michigan Avenue Bridge to the DuSable Bridge located in the heart of Chicago. In the background of the picture is Mr. Patrick Brutus who was then President of the Chicago Haitian American Association.

United States Illinois Congressman Danny Davis

Longtime supporter of "Friends of DuSable", whose efforts to preserve the legacy of DuSable, along with United States Illinois Congressman Danny Davis who was a key speaker on the efforts to commemorate DuSable in the State of Illinois.

Official Ribbon Cutting of the DuSable Bridge

United States Postal Services Honorary DuSable Bridge Envelope

October 15, 2010: Friends of DuSable: the DuSable Coalition and the United States Postal Services collaborated and partnered in the creation of an honorary DuSable Bridge envelope as a way of instituting a Federal level of importance to the DuSable Bridge dedication.

CHAPTER FIFTEEN

President Obama Second Presidential Election: In The Spirit of "From DuSable to Obama"

Logo design by Camille Enrique's

IN THE SPIRIT OF "FROM DUSABLE TO OBAMA"

The President Barack Obama voter campaign in Chicago that was called: in The Spirit of "From DuSable to Obama"

The United States presidential election of 2012 was the 57th quadrennial American presidential election. It was held on Tuesday, November 6, 2012. The Democratic nominee, incumbent President Barack Obama, and his running mate, Vice President Joe Biden, were elected to a second term, defeating the Republican nominee, former

Governor of Massachusetts Mitt Romney and his running mate, Representative and future House Speaker Paul Ryan of .

President Barack Obama Reelection Campaign

As the incumbent president, President Obama secured the Democratic nomination with no serious opposition. The Republican Party was more fractured; Mitt Romney was consistently competitive in the polls, but faced challenges from a number of more conservative contenders whose popularity each fluctuated, often besting Romney's. Romney effectively secured the nomination by early May as the economy improved, albeit at a persistently laggard rate. The campaign was marked by a sharp rise in fundraising, including from new nominally independent Super PACs. The campaigns focused heavily on domestic issues: debate centered largely on sound responses to the Great Recession in terms of economic recovery and job creation. Other issues included long-term federal budget issues, the future of , and the Affordable Care Act. Foreign policy was also discussed including the phase-out of the Iraq War, the size of and spending on the military, preventing Iran from obtaining nuclear weapons, and appropriate counteractions to terrorism.

Obama defeated Romney, winning both the popular vote and the Electoral College, with 332 electoral votes to Romney's 206. Obama carried all states and districts (among states that allocate electoral votes by district) that he had won in the 2008 presidential election except North Carolina, Indiana, and Nebraska's 2nd congressional district. As such, his margin of victory decreased from 2008. Consequently, Obama became the first incumbent since Franklin D. Roosevelt in 1944 to win reelection with fewer electoral votes and a lower popular vote percentage. Nonetheless, Obama also became the first two-term president since Ronald Reagan to win both his presidential bids with an absolute majority of the nationwide popular vote. Not since 1820 had three consecutive American presidents succeeded in securing two consecutive terms.

Candidates with considerable name recognition who entered the race for the Republican presidential nomination in the early stages of the primary campaign included Representative and former Libertarian nominee Ron Paul, former Minnesota Governor Tim Pawlenty, who co-chaired John McCain's campaign in 2008, former Massachusetts Governor Mitt Romney, the runner-up for the nomination in the 2008 cycle, and former Speaker of the House Newt Gingrich.

The first debate took place on May 5, 2011, in Greenville, South Carolina, with businessman Herman Cain, former New Mexico Governor Gary Johnson, Ron Paul, Tim Pawlenty, and former Pennsylvania Senator Rick Santorum participating. Another debate took place a month later, with Newt Gingrich, Mitt Romney, former Utah Governor Jon Huntsman, and Representative Michele Bachmann participating, and Gary Johnson excluded. A total of thirteen debates were held before the Iowa caucuses.

The first major event of the campaign was the Ames Straw Poll, which took place in Iowa on August 13, 2011. Michele Bachmann won the straw poll (this ultimately proved to be the acme of her campaign).

Pawlenty withdrew from the race after a poor showing in the straw poll, as did Thaddeus McCotter, the only candidate among those who qualified for the ballot who was refused entrance into the debate.

It became clear at around this point in the nomination process that while Romney was considered to be the likely nominee by the Republican establishment, a large segment of the conservative primary electorate found him to be too moderate for their political views. As a result, a number of potential "anti-Romney" candidates were put forward, including Donald Trump, Sarah Palin, Chris Christie, and Texas Governor Rick Perry, the last of whom decided to run in August 2011. Perry did poorly in the debates, however, and Herman Cain and then Newt Gingrich came into the fore in October and November.

Due to a number of scandals, Cain withdrew just before the end of the year, after having gotten on the ballot in several states. Around the same time, Johnson, who had been able to get into only one other debate, withdrew to seek the Libertarian Party nomination.

For the first time in modern Republican Party history, three different candidates won the first three state contests in January (the Iowa caucuses, the New Hampshire primary, and the South Carolina primary). Although Romney had been expected to win in at least Iowa and New Hampshire, Rick Santorum won the non-binding poll at caucus sites in Iowa by 34 votes, as near as can be determined from the incomplete tally, earning him a declaration as winner by state party leaders, although vote totals were missing from eight precincts.

The election of county delegates at the caucuses would eventually lead to Ron Paul earning 22 of the 28 Iowa delegates to the Republican National Convention. Newt Gingrich won South Carolina by a surprisingly large margin, and Romney won only in New Hampshire.

Those who understood the dynamics of the Iowa caucus process realized after the Iowa caucuses that Ron Paul could dominate the delegate selection process at the Iowa Republican Convention, but national media significantly underestimated Paul's delegate count during the first half of 2012. The New York Times and the Associated Press projected until the Iowa Republican convention in June that Paul would only get one Iowa delegate at the national convention.

An accurate delegate projection would have had Paul in the lead after the January 3 Iowa caucuses and after the January 10 New Hampshire primary, where Romney earned 8 delegates, Paul earned 3 delegates and Jon Huntsman earned 1 delegate.

A number of candidates dropped out at this point in the nomination process. Bachmann withdrew after finishing sixth in the Iowa caucuses, Huntsman withdrew after coming in third in New Hampshire, and Perry withdrew when polls showed him drawing low numbers in South Carolina.

Mitt Romney on the campaign trail

Santorum, who had previously run an essentially one-state campaign in Iowa, was able to organize a national campaign after his surprising victory there. He unexpectedly carried three states in a row on February 7 and overtook Romney in nationwide opinion polls, becoming the only candidate in the race to effectively challenge the notion that Romney was the inevitable nominee. However, Romney won all of the other contests between South Carolina and the Super Tuesday primaries, and regained his first-place status in nationwide opinion polls by the end of February.

The Super Tuesday primaries took place on March 6. Romney carried six states, Santorum carried three, and Gingrich won only in his home state of Georgia. Throughout the rest of March, 266 delegates were allocated in 12 events, including the territorial contests and the first local conventions that allocated delegates (Wyoming's county conventions). Santorum won Kansas and three Southern primaries, but he was unable to make any substantial gain on Romney, who became a formidable frontrunner after securing more than half of the delegates allocated in March.

On April 10, Santorum suspended his campaign due to a variety of reasons, such as a low delegate count, unfavorable polls in his home state of Pennsylvania, and his daughter's health, leaving Mitt Romney as the undisputed front-runner for the presidential nomination and allowing Gingrich to claim that he was "the last conservative standing" in the campaign for the nomination. After disappointing results in the April 24 primaries (finishing second in one state, third in three, and fourth in one), Gingrich dropped out on May 2 in a move that was seen as an effective end to the nomination contest. After Gingrich's spokesman announced his upcoming withdrawal, the Republican National Committee declared Romney the party's presumptive nominee. Ron Paul officially remained in the race, but he stopped campaigning on May 14 to focus on state conventions.

On May 29, after winning the Texas primary, Romney had received a sufficient number of delegates to clinch the party's nomination with the inclusion of unpledged delegates. After winning the June 5 primaries in California and several other states, Romney had received more than enough pledged delegates to clinch the nomination without counting unpledged delegates, making the June 26 Utah Primary, the last contest of the cycle, purely symbolic. CNN's final delegate estimate, released on July 27, 2012, put Romney at 1,462 pledged delegates and 62 unpledged delegates, for a total estimate of 1,524 delegates. No other candidate had unpledged delegates. The delegate estimates for the other candidates were Santorum at 261 delegates, Paul at 154, Gingrich at 142, Bachmann at 1, Huntsman at 1, and all others at 0.

August 28, 2012, delegates at the Republican National Convention officially named Romney the party's presidential nominee. Romney formally accepted the delegates' nomination on August 30, 2012.

Combined with the re-elections of Bill Clinton and George W. Bush, Obama's victory in the 2012 election marked only the second time in American history that three consecutive presidents were each elected to two or more full terms (the first time being the consecutive two-term presidencies of Thomas Jefferson, James Madison, and James Monroe). This was also the first election since 1944 in which neither of the major candidates had any military experience.

The 2012 election marked the first time since Franklin D. Roosevelt's last two re-elections in 1940 and 1944 that a Democratic presidential candidate won a majority of the popular vote in two consecutive elections. Obama was also the first president of either party to secure at least 51% of the popular vote in two elections since Dwight Eisenhower in 1952 and 1956. Obama is the third Democratic president to secure at least 51% of the vote twice, after Andrew Jackson and Franklin D. Roosevelt.

Romney lost his home state of Massachusetts, becoming the first major party presidential candidate to lose his home state since Democrat Al Gore lost his home state of Tennessee to Republican George W. Bush in the 2000 election. Romney lost his home state by more than 23%, the worst losing margin for a major party candidate since John Frémont in 1856. Even worse than Frémont, Romney failed to win a single county in his home state. In addition, since Obama carried Ryan's home state of Wisconsin, the Romney–Ryan ticket was the first major party ticket since the 1972 election to have both of its nominees lose their home states. Romney won the popular vote in every county of three states: Utah, Oklahoma, and West Virginia; Obama did so in four states: Vermont, Massachusetts, Rhode Island, and Hawaii.

Romney's loss prompted the Republican National Committee to try to appeal to the American Latino population by concentrating on different approaches to immigration. These were short-lived due to activity and anger from the Republican base and may have contributed to the selection of Donald Trump as their presidential candidate four years later. Gary Johnson's popular vote total set a Libertarian Party record, and his popular vote percentage was the second-best showing for a Libertarian in a presidential election, trailing only Ed Clark's in 1980. Johnson would go on to beat this record in the 2016 presidential election, winning the most votes for the Libertarian ticket in history. At the time, Green Party candidate Jill Stein's popular vote total made her the most successful female presidential candidate in a general election in United States history This was later surpassed by Hillary Clinton in the 2016 election.

2012: President Obama Second Presidential Election Victory Celebration

Obama's vote total was the second most votes received in the history of presidential elections and the most ever for a re-elected president. Obama owns the all-time record for votes in a single election, as well, in 2008. However, Obama also became the first president in American history to be re-elected to a second term by smaller margins in every way possible: Compared to his victory in 2008, he won fewer states (28 to 26), fewer electoral votes (365 to 332), fewer popular votes (69.5 million to 65.9 million), and a smaller percentage of the popular vote (52.9% to 51.1%).

The 57th Presidential Inaugural Weekend National Day of Service

The Presidential Inaugural Committee had its official launch today and named several co-chairs. They committee also announced a preliminary schedule. Actress Eva Longoria was named an inaugural co-chair along with many others. Information about the Inauguration, which was held on Monday, January 21, 2013, can be found at www.2013pic.org and on twitter@obamainaugural.

From the Inaugural Committee: Today the 2013 Presidential Inaugural Committee (PIC) announced its official launch, preliminary schedule of events and co-chairs for the second Inaugural of President Barack Obama and Vice President Joe Biden.

The 57th Presidential Inaugural weekend will kick off with a National Day of Service, a tradition started by the Obamas at the President's first Inauguration in 2009. President Obama will ask Americans across the country to organize and participate in service projects in their communities on Saturday, January 19th, to honor our shared values and celebrate the legacy of Dr. Martin Luther King, Jr. President Obama, First Lady Michelle Obama, Vice President Biden, Dr. Jill Biden and members of the President's Cabinet will participate in service projects in the Washington, DC area. In keeping with tradition for Inauguration Days that fall on a Sunday, the President will participate in a small private swearing-in ceremony on January 20. The President's public swearing-in, the parade and the official Inaugural balls will take place on Monday, January 21.

The PIC also announced the co-chairs and honorary co-chairs for the Inauguration. More details about official Inaugural events and the Presidential Inaugural Committee's theme for its events will be announced in the coming weeks.

"Vice President Biden and I are grateful to these distinguished women and men for agreeing to serve as co-chairs and honorary co-chairs, including Presidents from both sides of the aisle who have dedicated their lives to serving the American people," said President Obama. "This year's Inaugural will reflect our belief that working together, we can keep moving our country forward and fulfill the promise of the American Dream for all families."

The honorary co-chairs for the 2013 Presidential Inaugural Committee are: President Jimmy Carter 39th President of the United States, President George H.W. Bush, 41st President of the United States, President Bill Clinton 42nd President of the United State and President George W. Bush, 43rd President of the United States.

The co-chairs for the 2013 Presidential Inaugural Committee are: Ambassador Matthew Barzun, National Finance Chair of President Obama's reelection campaign and former Ambassador to Sweden Eva Longoria, Actress, Obama for America Campaign Co-Chair and Founder of the Eva Longoria Foundation Jane Stetson, National Finance Chair of the Democratic National Committee Frank White, former member of the National Advisory Council on Minority Business Enterprises *In addition, the PIC announced the following positions:* Jim Messina, Chair, Inaugural Parade Stephanie Cutter, Chair, PIC Board of Directors Jen O'Malley Dillon, Chair, National Day of Service Julianna Smoot, Chair, Inaugural Balls and Receptions Rufus Gifford, Chair, PIC Finance - Patrick Gaspard, Chair, National Mall

The staff for the 57th Presidential Inauguration will be led by Stephen J. Kerrigan, who will serve as Chief Executive Officer, and David J. Cusack, who will serve as Executive Director.

The Presidential Inaugural Committee will work closely with the Joint Congressional Committee on Inaugural Ceremonies (JCCIC) which oversees the ceremonial swearing-in on the west steps of the Capitol and other Inaugural activities that occur on the Capitol grounds, and the Joint Task Force National Capital Region (JTF-NCR) the military joint force command composed of all five branches of the United States armed services that oversees security for all official Inaugural-related events.

President Obama Sworn into his Second Inauguration as the President of the United States of America

CHAPTER SIXTEEN

I am Haroon a. Rashid; In The Spirit Of DuSable

"I WILL!"

DuSable Essay Winners Field Trip to Chicago City Hall Council Chambers

2014: From left to right rear: Friends of DuSable Board member Arnold Romeo, Alderman 42 Ward Alderman Brendan Reilly, FOD Board members Peggy Montes, Haroon Rashid & Hannah Bonecutter.

This is a picture I am in with Friends of DuSable Board members and a Chicago City official in the Chicago City Council Chamber, with the 2014 Chicago Public and Catholic Schools, citywide DuSable essay winners. These children were taken on a field trip and were given an official reception and tour of Chicago City Hall; they were greeted by the City Council person that represented the 42 Ward Downtown District of Chicago Brendon Reilly.

The winners were given permission to sit in their Alderman's seats in the chambers and imagine themselves as a city official while they were there.

Haroon A. Rashid "I Will"!

In this part of the book I have revealed to the best of my ability, a list of manifestations of my character that I know have been induced in me from my research, knowledge and understanding of the in-creditable role models and examples from the legacy of Jean Baptiste Pointe DuSable.

What has further inspired and motivated me to write this chapter in the book, is that, after researching the many great Chicago legends, metaphorically speaking, it makes me feel like I am in a relay race and that I must pass a baton" of leadership on, as to what I will do for the next generations.

I do this with a mindset of what would DuSable do, within the Chicago timeline from the seventeenth until the twenty-first century of Chicago history?

The best two examples for me of those life lessons can be described in one sentence and that is "From DuSable to Obama".

It started with one man's world ambitions to explore and govern unchartered places. Jean Baptise Pointe DuSable has been recorded in history as that one man who made something out of nothing, whenever he was given the chance.

The late great DuSable League Historian from Chicago, Dr. Virginia Jullian, in one of her many lectures at the Chicago Public Library, is quoted regarding the founder of Chicago. She had made references to DuSable as being the forbearer of his country in United States of America before Illinois was yet considered a State in the union.

I am convinced that his legacy has ingrained a "can do" and "I will" spirit, in many peoples that tend to live in the city of Chicago.

I believe that this unique spirit in Chicago is the key force that has made so many globally diverse people that have come from, or are from Chicago. I further believe that when they embrace "I will" spirit, they have a tendency to achieve monumental success in Chicago and possibly the world community.

The far most premiere example of this phenomenon is that of the first African American President and First Lady of the United States of America, Barack and Michelle Obama. I contend that both of these history makers' glorious roots of fame are rooted in the spirit of Chicago.

With this knowledge and understanding of these factors, I have been motivated in so many ways. I can clearly see, and I am motivated to self-describe my version of what "I Will" declare is a window view of my personal, social-political agendas.

Whenever the questions are asked of me what I Will do? I give to you some of my thoughts for my answers.

That being said, as you have the chance to read my listed thoughts, I challenge you, after reading my short table of contents, to consider the same thing, as it might relate to "what will you do?"

1. "I Will" make no small plans and live my life knowing that I can achieve anything that I put my heart, mind and soul into.
2. "I Will" start by positioning myself in the mindset that at any given time, I might be the only adult in a room of others; unless I will witness that I am not alone.
3. "I Will" be a willing negotiator of disputes, rather than an inhuman contributor of discourse suffering and shame towards anyone for any reason.

4. "I Will" first look for the common equal human value in others and identify with the common thread that binds all humans as one of the same and embrace the spirit of diversity.

5. "I Will" respect multicultural social inclusion and seek to advance my personal ability to heighten my academic enlightenments by having the discipline and patience to research and learn all knowledge that will advance my intelligence.

6. "I Will" not participate in the greed and thirst for power or might through organized cults or societies at the expenses of the least among me.

7. "I Will" live the life and do that I want to see others live and do in a civilized world that brings the best out of us as opposed to the worst.

8. "I Will" walk, talk dress and characterize myself in a manner that gives a message to the youth, that I will be their mentor for progressive human value.

9. "I Will" never put sport and playing as an equal to social and moral leadership in my dialog of values.

10. "I Will" as a man, love, honor and respect women, children, and the elders, as I would want to be treated.

11. "I Will" build bridges and end divides that will enable others to be enterprising and develop opportunities.

12. "I Will" explore this earth as much as God will allow me to and learn about this world and other cultures that I have been blessed to be in.

13. "I Will" put no spirit or feelings over the spirit of love and compassion… period.

14. "I Will" treat evil as it looks when spelled in reverse "live".

15. "I Will" not ignore the threat that it may do.

16. "I Will" recognize it as the work of the "d-evil"

17. "I Will" not allow "d-evil" to live in me.
18. "I Will" follow the path to right guidance, whenever I see a need for it regardless of religion, creed, color, sex, race, nationality, age or conceptual ideology.
19. "I Will" adapt to a given society that will enable harmony and respect among its citizens, and support a custom of civilized equal justice through the law and orders.
20. "I Will" document and distribute progressive information and narratives of value by "whatever means necessary" in order to make vital information available to the inquiring minds.
21. "I Will" fight for and serve my country to protect my Human Rights as a Sovereign citizen of the United States of America.
22. "I Will" treat businesses and enterprises as one of the most important aspects in any progressive society.
23. "I Will" seek to establish my own business and entrepreneurial enterprises.
24. "I Will" support the institutions of arts and culture, as it is an intricate part of a civilized society.
25. "I Will" support higher education and advance research especially in the area of law and science.
26. "I Will" treat the business of nutrition and health as a vital part of any society among its citizens.
27. "I Will" not embrace or condone the subculture of gangs and blatant violence.
28. "I Will" support the rights to assembly and organize as a union for fair and equal rights
29. "I Will" observe and support the business of print, visual, radio and digital media enterprises.
30. "I Will" support any religious movements and institutions that bring a community together to help them lift themselves up in peace and harmony

31. "I Will" encourage and inform citizens about the value of personal progressive cultural grooming and support the businesses that promote hair, beauty and fashions.

32. "I Will" always find ways to remember and, if possible, memorialize the legacy of the founder of Chicago and The First people.

33. "I Will" forever give thanks to the Almighty Creator, for blessing me to witness the first African American family in America's history in the Whitehouse: President Barack Obama, First Lady Michelle and First Daughters Malia and Sasha.

May the spirit of DuSable motivate and inspire each of you that will give respect to his honorable legacy and in my conclusion, I encourage you to live and share in the motto of Chicago "I Will"!

From DuSable to Obama there has been a spirit of multicultual global diversity in the city of Chicago, that has always been the root and driving force for a "Can do" and "I will" spirit for success.   -- Haroon Rashid

ABOUT THE AUTHOR

In1999 Haroon Rashid became the Founder and former President of Friends of DuSable, a not for profit organization dedicated to educating the public on the legacy of the founder of modern day Chicago, Jean Baptiste Pointe DuSable. In 2000 he became a member of the City of Chicago's Commission on Human Relations Advisory Council on African Affairs for 13 years.

In acknowledging the rich and diverse history of the City of Chicago, as well as the great accomplishments of its founder, (Friends of DuSable & Chicago Commission on Human Relationa) was responsible for establishing a citywide commemoration in Honor of Jean Baptiste Pointe DuSable.

The now implementations of the DuSable Commemoration not only serves as a day to honor DuSable, it is a vehicle to bring communities together for a day of unity in celebration on March 4th each year of the origin of the great city of Chicago that they all share.

Haroon declares that he is an advocate for human rights and dedicates his free time to political and social causes. His view of America and the world is one that respects Equal Human Rights as the only expectable narrative and advocacy for the 21st century and beyond and, in that spirit, he will often quote that: ***In the Spirit of Du Sable, I Will.***

www.ingramcontent.com/pod-product-compliance
Lightning Source LLC
Chambersburg PA
CBHW071552080526
44588CB00010B/882